Microprogrammed Control
and Reliable Design
of Small Computers

Microprogrammed Control and Reliable Design of Small Computers

GEORGE D. KRAFT
Illinois Institute of Technology

WING N. TOY
Bell Telephone Laboratories, Incorporated

PRENTICE-HALL, INC., Englewood Cliffs, New Jersey 07632

Library of Congress Cataloging in Publication Data

Kraft, George D (date)
   Microprogrammed control and reliable design of small computers.

   Includes bibliographies and index.
   1. Microprogramming.   2. Minicomputers—Design and construction.   3. Microcomputers—Design and construction. I. Toy, Wing N., (date) joint author. II. Title.
QA76.6.K7   001.64′2   80–36811
ISBN 0–13–581140–6

Editorial production and supervision by Maria McKinnon and Ellen De Filippis
Interior design by Ellen De Filippis
Cover design by Carol Zawislak
Manufacturing buyer: Joyce Levatino

Printed in the United States of America

10 9 8 7 6 5 4 3 2 1

PRENTICE-HALL INTERNATIONAL, INC., *London*
PRENTICE-HALL OF AUSTRALIA PTY. LIMITED, *Sydney*
PRENTICE-HALL OF CANADA, LTD., *Toronto*
PRENTICE-HALL OF INDIA PRIVATE LIMITED, *New Delhi*
PRENTICE-HALL OF JAPAN, INC., *Tokyo*
PRENTICE-HALL OF SOUTHEAST ASIA PTE. LTD., *Singapore*
WHITEHALL BOOKS LIMITED, WELLINGTON, *New Zealand*

To our families
  Peggy, Stephen, Mark, and Michael Kraft
  and Romayne, Liane, Arthur, and Sue-lin Toy

To our families
   Peggy, Stephen, Mark, and Michael Kraft
   and Romayne, Liane, Arthur, and Sue-lin Toy

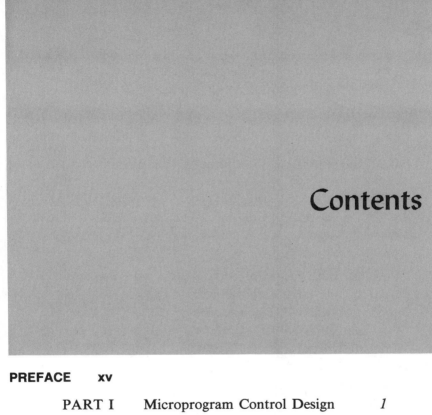

Contents

CHAPTER 3   MICROPROGRAM CONTROL OF MAIN STORAGE OPERATIONS   90

Preface

A subset of the material found in this book originally formed a portion of our first textbook on small computers.* Because of the significance of microprogram control techniques and fault-tolerant design to modern computing, this material was extracted and expanded to form a stand-alone volume.

This book is divided into two distinct parts: Part I is entitled *Microprogram Control Design,* while Part II is called *Fault-Tolerant Design.* These sections, while being distinct, are nonetheless interrelated since self-checking techniques used at the microcontrol level are discussed as one means of implementing a fault-tolerant processor. Specifically, we have attempted to outline how the concepts of modern microprogramming have been used to implement the Bell System 3A CC, a small computer designed to observe the high reliability requirements of the Bell System (i.e., two hours downtime in 40 years of operation).

* *Mini/Microcomputer Hardware Design,* George D. Kraft and Wing N. Toy, Prentice-Hall, Inc., Englewood Cliffs, N.J., 1979.

The text is a presentation of the design philosophies and techniques used by Bell Laboratories to implement the 3A CC; in several sections this text marks the first appearance of various design techniques as part of an overall practical design effort.   In particular, Chapters 7 and 8 may be considered as a definitive exposition on the various techniques used to detect faults and then diagnose them within the 3A CC.   These concepts can be extended quite readily to the design of special-purpose digital controllers, other types of small computers with architectures different from the 3A CC, and large-scale processors designed with high reliability features.   In each case, however, the control section of the processor *should* be implemented using microprogram control techniques.

The text has been written as a reference volume for the practicing electrical engineer or computer scientist who has a need to develop a fault-tolerant small computer.   The book could be used as a reference text in a college course taught at the junior, senior, or first-year graduate level.

Chapter 1 outlines the differences between the conventional control section of a computer and a control section implemented using microprogramming techniques.   The organization of a control store, the concept of emulation, and nanoprogramming are also discussed.

Chapter 2 considers the concepts of horizontal and vertical microprogramming, outlines several procedures for generating the address of the next microinstruction, specifies how a microprogram may be entered using the opcode of a macroinstruction, and considers how a microsubroutine may be implemented.   In addition, the transfer of control from a microinstruction sequence to a macroinstruction is discussed, including the development of the overall structure of the sequence of microinstructions into a microprogram.

Chapter 3 explains how main storage operations may be controlled using a control store.   Included in this discussion are techniques for controlling synchronous dedicated memory bus operations, synchronous multiparty memory bus operations using one or more DMA devices, and the asynchronous operation of both main storage and a multiparty memory bus.

Chapter 4 specifically addresses the area of performing input/output operations using microprogrammed control techniques.   In particular, two approaches which involve using either fixed timing signals or variable timing signals are discussed in some detail.

Chapter 5 begins the development of fault-tolerant design techniques by mathematically defining such concepts as reliability, mean-time-between-failures (MTBF), availability, and standby redundancy.   An example is given at the end of the chapter in which the reliability of a small computer system is predicted.

Chapter 6 outlines the considerations necessary to perform a practical maintenance design of a fault-tolerant system.   The term maintenance is used to describe the techniques used to achieve a high reliability computing environment (i.e., hardware redundancy; coding techniques, etc.).

Chapter 7 covers the area of fault detection in a digital system. Among the topics discussed in this chapter are error detection codes, fault detection (checking) techniques that can be used in evaluating the data transfer paths and the control logic paths, and error detection techniques for use in validating the sequencing of control from one microinstruction to another or for transfering control from a macroinstruction to the appropriate microprogram which will interpret the macroinstruction. In addition, checking procedures for use in arithmetic and logic operations are outlined. The concept of self-testing check circuits is developed, and several hardware detection methods used to expose bugs in program execution at either the microinstruction level or the macroinstruction level of a machine are discussed.

Chapter 8 introduces and expands the area of fault diagnosis. Included in this section are discussions on establishing the integrity of the basic hardware in a processor so that useful diagnostics may be run on the overall machine to validate its operation. This basic hardware is called the *processor hardcore*. Once the integrity of the processor hardcore has been established, diagnostics may be run on the processor in an ever-expanding circle of verification until all hardware associated with the processor has been successfully checked. In addition, the usage of microdiagnostics is explored, as well as the use of diagnostic observation points and microdiagnostics which are executed from *main storage*.

Chapter 9 gives a statement of how the Bell System has used these concepts in the design of their family of Electronic Switching Systems (ESS's). This discussion is comprehensive and covers such areas as maintenance design, diagnostic hardware and the techniques used by the various ESS processors to recover from a fault.

The appendix is included to provide a more detailed mathematical background for the calculation of mean-time-to-failure (MTTF) of systems which use either active redundancy or standby redundancy.

This manuscript was developed over a period of five years as part of the In-Hours Continuing Education Program (INCEP) at Bell Telephone Laboratories, Inc. Portions of this material were also developed in courses taught at the University of California at Berkeley and at the Illinois Institute of Technology in Chicago.

The authors would particularly like to acknowledge the assistance given them by the Bell Labs Education Center and Norman F. Foster, who assumed the partial support of writing this manuscript under the Bell Laboratories In-Hours Continuing Education Program (INCEP).

A special note of appreciation is extended to Professors E. S. Kuh and T. E. Everhart of the University of California at Berkeley who arranged for Wing N. Toy to spend the 1973–1974 academic year at Berkeley where portions of this text material were developed.

The encouragement, cooperation, and constructive criticism supplied by Professor Andre G. Vacroux, Chairman of the Department of Electrical Engineering of the Illinois Institute of Technology, was of particular help during the completion of the manuscript.

It is with a deep sense of appreciation that the authors acknowledge the assistance of Patrick Loprete, Jr., of the Bell Labs Indian Hill Technical Documentation Department. Mr. Loprete oversaw and coordinated all details involved in putting the final manuscript together.

Finally, without the full support of Bell Laboratories and the use of its associated facilities, this work could not have been produced in its present form.

George D. Kraft

Naperville, Illinois

Wing N. Toy

PART I

Microprogram
Control
Design

CHAPTER 1

Conventional and

Microprogram Control

1.1 INTRODUCTION

The *central processing unit* (CPU) of a modern digital computer can be represented as shown in Figure 1-1. Essentially, all information manipulation—
whether it is represented by movement of a data word from one machine

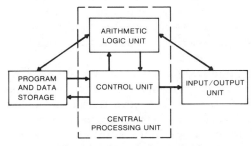

Figure 1-1 The Central Processing Unit of a Computer

3

register to another machine register or by the algorithmic operation of the CPU on the data word—is controlled by physical signals that are generated by the control unit and distributed to individual logic gates. The control unit, which is implemented in logic, also performs one or more elaborate control objectives according to the structure of its control sequencer. In general, each pattern of binary 1s and 0s stored in main memory (the machine instructions) is interpreted by the control sequencer as a sequence of control steps that are directed to the CPU. A machine instruction can direct the CPU to perform any one of the following operations:

1. Move a data word between two registers
2. Transform a data word using an algorithmic operation (i.e., passing the data word through the arithmetic logic unit [ALU])
3. Set select control points (flip-flops) associated with a specific machine operation
4. Identify the operand(s) to be used in the machine calculation
5. Fetch the required operand(s)
6. Select the next machine instruction to be executed and initiate the fetch of that instruction

In general, such machine operations are made up of a number of more fundamental control steps called *microoperations* or *microops.* The computing machines of the 1950s and early 1960s implemented such microoperations in *hardwired* or *random logic.* The implementation of such control structures proved to be quite complex and highly inflexible in terms of permitting design modifications to be introduced in the microoperation sequences. Since the control logic was hardwired, any modification required a redesign of the control unit, including a re-layout of one or more of the printed circuit boards associated with the hardware control unit. The modification procedure, which could be *expensive,* was prone to the introduction of additional errors being introduced into the hardware control logic because of the irregular pattern and inherent complexity of the hardwired control unit.

Microprogramming is used to simplify the design and maintenance of the control section of a computer by placing sequences of these microoperations in a random-access memory called a *control store* or *control memory.* An elementary machine operation implemented in this fashion is also called a *control primitive* or a *microorder.*

The control primitives (signals) that are to be generated at a specific time are designated by the contents of the microinstruction currently being executed. A microinstruction is fetched from control storage in a manner that is directly analogous to the fetch of an instruction from main memory. To distinguish between the levels of control a machine may be functioning in, the following terms will be useful:

1. A *macroinstruction* is a string of binary 1s and 0s that reside in the *main memory* of a machine; the actual interpretation of a macroinstruction is performed by a sequence of *microinstructions* that reside in *control memory* and are executed by the control sequencer.
2. A *microinstruction,* similarly, is a string of binary 1s and 0s that reside in control storage. Each microinstruction contains sufficient information, either explicitly or implicitly, to specify the location of the next microinstruction to be executed.

In direct analogy to the macroinstruction facility of a processor, a sequence of microinstructions is called a *microprogram,* whereas a sequence of macroinstructions (assembly language instructions) is called a *macroprogram* or, simply, a *main program.* Figure 1-2 illustrates the basic structure of a microprogrammed machine. Using this arrangement, much of the complex control circuitry that has traditionally been implemented using random logic has been replaced by the regular structure of a random access memory that can easily be manufactured using *large-scale integration* (LSI) techniques. Microprogram control units are inherently more flexible than their random logic equivalents since a modification to the control sequence can be obtained by simply replacing the current control memory with another control memory containing a different microinstruction sequence. The speed of the microprogram control sequencer is slower than that of its hardwired equivalent since a memory access must be performed to fetch each microinstruction. However, the availability of high-speed, low-cost random-access memories manufactured using LSI techniques has greatly reduced this speed penalty and has made microprogram control an attractive procedure for implementing the control section of a computer.

Aside from reducing the complexity and associated inflexibility of a control unit implemented using hardwired logic, the primary motivation for

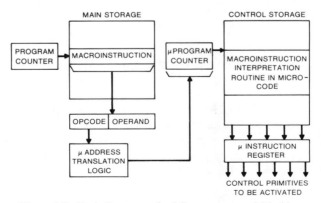

Figure 1-2 Basic Structure of a Microprogrammed Machine

using microprogram control is to maintain compatibility of operation between machines supplied by the same manufacture. Such machines represent a "family of computers" that allows a user to increase the capability of a system by moving up to a more powerful machine in the same computer family. This expansion may be done without having to rewrite any software or modify any original system design assumptions.

> One of the prime concepts that has emerged from the evolution of computing structures during the late 1960's and early 1970's has been the realization that a computer system should continue to have a useful life even in the presence of accelerated technological change. A newer model should at least support the software developed for an older model originally marketed by the same manufacturer. This is the concept of software compatibility. . . .
>
> The advantages of preserving an established software base and using mature, familiar peripheral devices that are well understood by maintenance personnel are obvious. The large mainframe manufacturers such as IBM recognized this in the early 1960's when they introduced the concept of a *computer family,* or line of successively more sophisticated machines. A computer family is characterized by each family member using the same basic instruction repertoire, fundamental I/O operations, and data formats (such as the 8-bit byte). Also, each member supports the same basic system software package. . . .
>
> The family concept is an easily accepted idea since the user of a computer structure does not have to pay a severe penalty for moving up to a more sophisticated model as application requirements become more mature. Consequently, many of the commercial minicomputer manufacturers . . . have adopted the computer family concept. In addition, the family concept has been observed at the microprocessor levels. . . .*

1.2 WILKES' ORIGINAL MICROPROGRAM SCHEME

Microprogramming was first suggested by M. V. Wilkes and J. B. Stringer in the early 1950s. Their original scheme is shown in Figure 1-3. It consists of a decoder, a clock signal, two registers, matrix C, and matrix S. The binary number stored in register A is decoded to select one of the horizontal lines that thread through both matrix C and matrix S. The clock signal is applied to the decoder to determine when the next access of the two matrices is made. The two matrices plus their access logic can be regarded as a control memory in which the vertical lines correspond to bits in the microin-

---

* George D. Kraft and Wing N. Toy, *Mini/Microcomputer Hardware Design* (Englewood Cliffs, N.J.: Prentice-Hall, 1979), pp. 164–65.

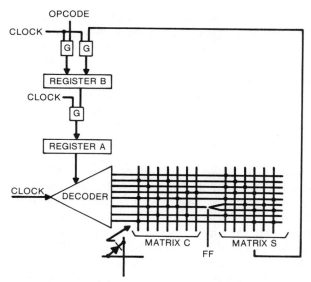

Figure 1-3 Wilkes' Microprogram Scheme

struction specified by the contents of register A.   Each matrix contains an array of diode crosspoints.   At each intersection, a dot indicates the presence of a diode.   If a particular microinstruction is selected and a diode is present at the intersection of the vertical line corresponding to the selected microinstruction and the kth vertical line, then a signal is allowed to appear on the kth vertical line if the kth bit in the microinstruction is a 1.   The vertical outputs of matrix C control the individual gates that form the basic microoperations or control primitives of Wilkes' machine.   In Wilkes' original scheme, each bit b_i of the matrix C is associated with a specific control line c_i. Thus, when $b_i = 1$ in the currently active microinstruction, c_i is activated or placed in the 1s state; otherwise, c_i is left inactive or in the 0s state. The selection of a horizontal line or microinstruction then causes a predetermined set of microoperations to be enabled.

The selected microinstruction passes through both the control matrix (C) and the sequencing matrix (S).   For each microinstruction, the bits in the matrix S field specify the address of the next microinstruction to be executed by the control unit.   Wilkes envisioned each microinstruction as containing the address of the succeeding microinstruction within the matrix S field.   This address is temporarily stored in register B until the microcontrol logic determines it is time to obtain the address of the next microinstruction. Just before the next clock pulse is to be applied to the decoder, the address of the next microinstruction is transferred from register B to register A. Wilkes visualized the next address in the microinstruction sequence as coming from either the matrix S or from an external register such as the opcode field of a new macroinstruction fetched from main storage.

Wilkes recognized the need for providing the capability to perform conditional branching in the microcontrol sequence. This requires that an alternate control sequence be transferred to depending on specified conditions which may arise in the system during the normal execution sequence of microinstructions. An alternate branching capability is shown in Figure 1-3. This capability is provided through the use of a conditional flip-flop whose state depends on the outcome of the previous microoperation. The conditional flip-flop can be initialized through the execution of an earlier microinstruction. The conditional flip-flop is used to select between one of two possible addresses in control memory. The selected address points to the next microinstruction to be executed. The decision logic that makes this selection is inserted between the control matrix C and the sequencing matrix S, using Wilkes' approach. Other implementations of conditional branching are possible using this basic arrangement. For instance, the decision logic could be inserted between the decoder and the control matrix (C), or it could be inserted between the sequencing matrix (S) and the A register. The objective, in each case, is to provide a conditional branching facility at the microinstruction level. This facility will redirect the microexecution sequence, depending on the outcome of a microoperation. Such a microoperation could involve an arithmetic calculation or the evaluation of a logical expression.

The two matrices can be viewed as a single matrix that is *functionally* divided into two parts: a *control field* and a *next address field.* In general, the conditional branching logic is made part of the overall logic that controls accessing of the control memory. The resulting combination is often packaged as a *read-only memory* (ROM) but may equally well be a writable random access memory. The functional diagram of a microprogram control structure that employs a ROM is shown in Figure 1-4. It is basically the same package envisioned by Wilkes, except that the control memory is implemented as an LSI ROM package. An output register provides the temporary storage for the current microinstruction that includes a field for the address

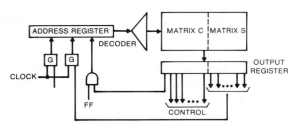

Figure 1-4   Microprogram Scheme Using ROM

of the next microinstruction.   An address register points to the location of the current microinstruction, and the address register may be loaded either from an external register or from the next address field of the current microinstruction.   The decision logic for conditional branching is conveniently placed between the two registers.   Typically, the condition flip-flop will control one bit of the next address field.   If a conditional branch is to be performed, that bit will normally be placed in the 0s state in the next address field. If the condition flip-flop is *not* set by the current microinstruction, the contents of the next address field are transferred unmodified into the address register. However, if the condition flip-flop is set, the bit it controls in the next address field will be set to the 1s state when the contents of the next address field are moved into the address register.   This will cause control to branch to a different microsequence.   If more than one conditional flip-flop is used, more than one bit in the next address field may be modified by the results of executing the current microinstruction.   Typically, there will be one bit in the next address field that will be uniquely assigned to each conditional flip-flop.   The bit(s) to be modified will all be placed in the zero state in the next address field of the current microinstruction.   Depending on what conditions are satisfied at the completion of execution of the current microinstruction, the microcontrol sequence will branch to *one* of several possible alternate microsequences.

1.3   COMPARISON BETWEEN CONVENTIONAL AND MICROPROGRAM CONTROL

Both the conventional implementation of the control section of a computer using random logic and a microprogram implementation are intended to perform the same functions: They generate the necessary microoperations or control signals to execute each microinstruction, and they provide the sequencing logic that permits execution to step from one microinstruction to another.   Although the purpose behind the implementation of conventional control logic and microprogram control logic is the same, the methods of achieving that purpose differ radically between the two implementations. The conventional control section consists of four distinct functional parts, as shown in Figure 1-5: the operation-code decoder, the timing and sequencing logic, the logic associated with the execution of the current macroinstruction, and the logic that combines the individual microoperations or control primitives generated by all the macroinstructions.   Each macroinstruction is realized on a computer through the activation of a subset of these control primitives.   Conventional control uses random logic to activate the appropriate control primitives in a prescribed sequence so that the current macroinstruction is interpreted on the host computer hardware.   Microprogram control uses a sequence of microinstructions to specify the individual control primi-

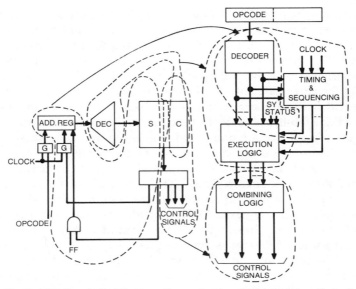

Figure 1-5 Comparison Between Conventional and Microprogram Control

tives that must occur. Each microinstruction defines one or more control primitives that must be activated when the microinstruction is executed. A macroinstruction fetched from main memory would be interpreted by a linked list of microinstructions fetched from control memory.

The sequencing of control primitives, which is handled by a hardwired sequencer using a random logic implementation, is administered by the addressing logic associated with the control memory. The opcode of the current macroinstruction points to a starting address in control memory which corresponds to the first microinstruction in a microprogram. This microprogram interprets the macroinstruction by executing a sequence of microinstructions. Various techniques may be used to point to the location of the next microinstruction to be executed. However, the most straightforward approach has been to store the address of the *next* microinstruction to be executed in a separate field of the *current* microinstruction. As each microinstruction is executed, its successor is automatically fetched from control memory and placed in the *microinstruction register* (**MIR**) to be executed next.

The counterpart of the logic in the microprogram control implementation that determines the address of the next microinstruction in control memory is the sequencing logic found in the conventional control arrangement that generates the timing signals associated with each control primitive. The number of machine cycles that are allocated for interpreting each macroinstruction depends on the number of control primitives required by the macroinstruction and the *precise* sequence in which these control primitives should be activated. The *execution logic* found in the conventional control implementation is directly analogous to the execution of a sequence of microinstructions. The execution logic defines the time sequence in which the control primitives are activated. The outputs of the opcode decoder, in conjunction with the timing and sequencing logic, are intimately combined with the execution logic using a random logic implementation. This means that the sequencing between control primitives is not as autonomous as it is for an equivalent implementation using microprogram control. (The details of this observation will be discussed further in Chapter 2.)

The combinational logic found in the conventional control arrangement tends to be highly irregular in terms of its interconnections. Typically, in this section, those outputs that perform the same elementary control operations (control primitives) are logically ORed together so that one control signal is activated no matter what macroinstruction has generated the control primitive. This complex interconnection introduces irregularities in a control structure realized with random logic. Microprogram control stores each control primitive as a part of the current microinstruction fetched from control memory. Even though the address of the next microinstruction may also be stored as a part of the current microinstruction, the sequencing information is separated from the control primitives—thus providing a highly regular pattern for the control logic implementation. They are not embedded together as they would be if a conventional implementation of the control section were used. Figure 1-5 attempts to show the corresponding functions of the two control section implementations. Note that the following associations may be made:

1. The combining logic section is equivalent to the control section of the control memory (i.e., the selection of the control primitives to be activated as specified by each microinstruction).
2. The timing and sequencing logic, together with the macroinstruction opcode decoder, is equivalent to the addressing logic associated with the control memory.
3. The execution logic section is equivalent to the access circuitry of the control memory (i.e., the circuitry that selects the current microinstruction as a location in the control store).

A comparison of the hardware costs for each of the two methods used to implement the control section of a computer is shown in Figure 1-6. In the case of microprogram control, the control memory has been designed so as to use fixed-sized ROM modules (e.g., modules consisting of 1024, 2048, or 4096 [and so on] memory locations). A disadvantage of this design approach is that even if the control memory requires only a few locations a minimum control memory configuration still requires that a full ROM module must be provided. Another disadvantage of the microprogram con-

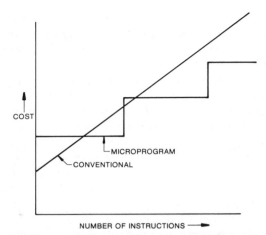

Figure 1-6 Cost Comparison Between Conventional and Microprogram Control

trol approach is that the control store address register, control store data register, and all the gating paths associated with the various control primitives must be implemented even if the control microprogram consists of a small number of microinstructions. Disadvantages such as these are sometimes referred to as "cost-overhead" in the design of a digital circuit. Analogous cost-overhead for conventionally implemented control circuitry is not as great. The cost of much of the control circuitry built from random logic grows linearly as the number of macroinstructions in the macroinstruction set of the processor increases. This situation is illustrated in Figure 1-6. The equivalent implementation of a control section using microprogram control requires that the control circuitry grow incrementally, in steps, according to the cost of each additional control memory module. The size of each step shown in Figure 1-6 (i.e., the incremental increase in cost of each expansion in microprogram control) depends on the size of each memory module. It is in the best interests of the designer to keep the step size or incremental cost as small as economically feasible.

The overhead circuitry associated with a microprogram implementation can be easily designed initially and incorporated into the overall logic of the processor. The overhead circuitry is built from logic elements that are structurally well defined (i.e., the control store address register, the control store data register, etc.). The sequence of microinstructions that interpret the individual commands in the macroinstruction set need not be specified at the same time as the microprogram control section, nor does the individual doing the design of the microprogram control section have to concurrently be involved in the development of the microprogram control sequences. In fact, the entire task of generating the microprogram control sequences for the system does not have to be considered until much later in the design process. It is possible to have another experienced logic designer work on developing the necessary microprogram sequences after the preliminary stage of early design has been completed. The development of these microprogram sequences can be done concurrently with the refinement of the hardware design details. Furthermore, the processor design can be carried out without a firm decision being made on the details of the macroinstruction set. The primary guideline to be observed in this situation is that the logic designer must be careful to provide for all possible microorders or control primitives that might be required to interpret any reasonable macroinstruction.

For a control section designed using conventional logic design techniques, the macroinstruction set must be firmly established prior to the initiation of the design process, and, in general, the hardware designer must have also participated in the planning of the command elements in the macroinstruction set. In addition, because of the complexity and irregular nature of a control section implemented using conventional logic techniques, it is very difficult to partition the hardware design cleanly into blocks that do not have a number of interconnecting leads between them and the rest of the system.

Perhaps the most important difference between conventional and microprogram control is the ease with which maintenance concepts may be implemented in a microprogram control section. The regular structure of the control store and its sequencing logic allows fault detection logic to be integrated into the control hardware, where individual errors may be detected at the microstep level. Since a microinstruction typically specifies one or more microsteps, faults may be localized more accurately than in a conventional control implementation. The difficulty with introducing fault diagnosis techniques in a conventional control realization is that sequencing and timing information are embedded in the control logic in an essentially random fashion. There is no systematic arrangement to the logic of a conventional control structure that would lend itself to any reasonable error detection schemes; a unified scheme of checking the total conventional control implementation is quite difficult and in many cases may be impossible. In such cases, error checking can only be done at the macroinstruction level (i.e., verifying that data has been correctly gated from one register to another and/or operated on properly by the ALU during the data transfer). A macroinstruction checking scheme, in many instances, is totally inadequate for any effective fault diagnosis and fault correction philosophy.

1.4 THE ORGANIZATION OF CONTROL STORE

The execution of a machine language program that is made up of a sequence of macroinstructions is performed at the microcontrol level by having each macroinstruction interpreted on the host machine hardware through a microprogram. Each microprogram, in turn, is comprised of a sequence of microinstructions that activate the control primitives of the host machine. The microprogram is kept in a high-speed, random-access storage unit that is called a *control store* or *control memory.* Control storage is normally found implemented as a ROM. However, control storage may also exist as a dynamically alternable memory known as *writable control store* (WCS). A read-only control memory cannot be modified by any executing microprogram. The contents of the control ROM are unalterable and provide a fixed, interpretation sequence for a given macroinstruction set. The contents of WCS can be modified by an executing microprogram. This is equivalent to allowing the architecture of the host machine to be redefined under microprogram control since a different microcode module may be loaded in WCS under control of the executing user program. A processor having this capability is also called a *flexible-architecture machine.*

A microprogrammed machine may often use a combination of writable control storage and read-only memory for its control memory. Typically, a computer manufacturer will supply the interpretive microprogram routines for its macromachine in ROM. These routines define the characteristics of the host machine the user believes exist. The manufacturer normally offers little encouragement to the user in terms of stimulating interest on the part of the user for supplementing the basic control ROM with WCS. If the user is unsophisticated, an attempt to introduce microcode not approved by the manufacturer can play havoc with the way the host machine appears to function to the user, since the user-oriented microprograms placed in WCS can interact with the basic control ROM microsequences. In general, WCS is used to introduce additional features to the application hardware. These features are normally closely coordinated with the manufacturer as they are placed in microcode, so that the user minimizes the possibility of compromising the operation of the basic machine.

In general, control storage may be represented as an ordinary memory array, as shown in Figure 1-7. The *microprogram counter* (μPC) contains the address of the next microinstruction located in the control store. Typically, it is an increment-by-1 forward binary counter, and program sequencing is done by adding 1 to the current contents of the μPC. The MIR contains the current microinstruction being executed by the host machine. For a read-only control store, the MIR would not provide input leads for data to be written into the control memory—it would only receive data from the control store. However, since many microprogrammed machines use a combination of read-only storage and writable storage, another register must be provided to supply data to be written into writable control memory. This register can be called the *control store data register* (CSDR). Since, in general, the microcode to be loaded dynamically into WCS will not be written into the same location as that of the next microinstruction, a fourth register needs

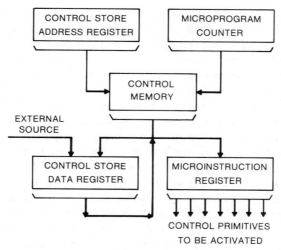

Figure 1-7 The Arrangement of Control Store

to be provided. This register, called the *control store address register* (CSAR), points to the location in WCS where the data word in microcode is to be stored. It is possible to combine the functions of the μPC and the CSAR as well as the functions of the MIR and the CSDR. In general, these four registers will be kept separated, with the CSAR and CSDR forming a register pair that references WCS and functions independently of the register pair formed by the μPC and the MIR. The μPC and the MIR, in turn, reference read-only control storage in terms of microprogram execution. Thus, a block of microcode could be loaded from a system peripheral, such as a floppy disk, into WCS using the CSAR and CSDR. If a portion of that microcode were to be executed as a microprogram, the μPC and MIR would be used to direct the associated microcontrol sequence. In particular situations, data, or blocks of binary words, stored in main memory may be copied over into WCS for usage by a specific microprogram. Similarly, data from either WCS or control ROM could be copied by control memory over into main storage. The precise reason(s) for performing these operations would be dictated by the requirements of the user.

1.5 MACHINE EMULATION AND THE UNIVERSAL HOST

A digital machine may be regarded as an interpreter of the macroinstruction set associated with it and seen by the user. In particular, microprogram control permits the interpretation sequences to be placed in control store and changed simply by having the user replace the current control store boards with a set of modified control store boards. This simple replacement operation permits a single machine to interpret *different* macroinstruction sets. If control store is not totally read-only, then the new microcode may be rolled into the writable portion of control memory from a peripheral device. Microprogram execution may then be directed to begin in the newly loaded portion of writable control store. In this manner, segments of microcode may be executed that are particularly relevant for a current application requirement. However, the microcode segment does not have to be incorporated as a permanent part of read-only control storage.

It is possible, through the use of microprogramming techniques, to cause one machine to simulate the behavior of another machine (insofar as all appearances are concerned for the user). The mechanism of employing microprogramming to create an image of a conceptual machine on an existing machine is called *emulation.* The physical processor on which the emulation is performed is called the *host machine;* the processor being emulated is called the *target machine.* The terms *target processor* and *virtual processor* have been used interchangeably in the area of emulation.

A primary advantage of emulation is that a host machine can employ a control memory arrangement in which the machine instructions of an earlier computer are interpreted on the host hardware. The programs written for the target processor can be executed directly on the host computer *without* modification. Thus, a user can acquire a new and more powerful processor that will still run the programs (software) associated with the older machine. No reprogramming effort is required to convert the software for the older (target) machine to machine code that will execute on the newer (host) machine. This feature can represent a substantial cost savings to the user.

An excellent example of machine emulation is the IBM System 360 series of computers. All members of the System 360 family appear to the programmer to have common architectural features. The System 360 architecture may be regarded as the *target* machine that is emulated by each of the models in the System 360 product line through the use of different microcode packages that run on separate *host* processors. The capabilities of these individual host processors are what determines the performance characteristics of each of the individual models in the System 360 product line.

The term *microprogrammable* is now used to describe machines in which a large portion of the control memory is electronically alterable. A microprogrammable machine thus provides the capability for the user to actively engage in *general-purpose microprogram development.* Digital machines that are regarded as *fully* microprogrammable often exclusively employ writable control stores; their architectures have been designed to be *highly flexible* so that a variety of target machines may be emulated on the host computer. It is possible to visualize a fully microprogrammable machine that does not possess a specific machine language—in the large-scale sense—but rather has its macrofeatures defined by the current microprogram that is controlling the processor. In a sense, each microinstruction can define a potential new architecture. A machine with the capability to easily modify its basic architecture can function as a *universal host* (i.e., a machine that may emulate any other target machine). No such universal host has ever been developed because of the real-world complexities involved in achieving efficient target machine emulation. However, several processor chip sets such as the AMD 2900 family do provide the processor designer with definite emulation capabilities for a selection of reasonably complex machines.

If writable control storage is available, different blocks of microcode may be rolled into the WCS. Thus, microcode images may be swapped in and out of WCS. This allows the host machine to appear to the user as a variety of target machines—the current microcode load in WCS determines which virtual machine is presently active on the host machine hardware. This capability, also called *dynamic microprogramming,* can, theoretically, provide the most efficient mechanism for executing an application program. For instance, if a FORTRAN program is to be run on the host machine, a microcode version of a highly efficient FORTRAN processor may be rolled into WCS and used to interpret the individual FORTRAN machine statements. Thus, different microcode images of separate language processors may be used on a host machine to optimize the execution of different programs written in these languages. In general, a microprogram executive must oversee the administration of WCS and protect resident microprograms from mutilation by a microprogram that is not executing properly. The administration and protection of WCS in a *multimicroprogramming environment* is extremely complex and is an aspect of dynamic microprogramming that is still not thoroughly understood.

1.6 NANOPROGRAM CONTROL CONCEPTS

A microprogrammed machine allows the individual microoperations or control primitives to be selected by a microinstruction. The control primitives, however, are fixed in the sense that the actual hardware interconnections (which implement each microoperation) to the gate are *not* changeable by a microprogram. In special instances, the period of the processor clock may either be extended or shortened by a microinstruction. But, in general, the microlevel architecture of the machine remains fixed even though different control store loads may be used to interpret different macroinstruction sets on the same *host* machine.

The concept of a flexible architecture machine (i.e., a machine whose macrolevel characteristics may be varied under microprogram control to emulate a variety of target machines) may be extended to the actual microstructure of the host machine itself.   In this case, it is possible to talk about a *flexible-microarchitecture machine* in which the actual logic signals that define the control primitives of the host machine may be physically reassigned and an entirely new set of microoperations created for the host machine.   Such a capability may be achieved by treating control storage as a two-level control structure.

1.   The first level of control memory is the microprogram memory.   The characteristics of this level of control are as follows:

    a. The interpretation of the target macroinstruction set is done by the microinstruction sequences placed in microcontrol store.

    b. The user application programs made up of command sequences from the target macroinstruction set reside in main program memory.

    c. The contents of microcontrol store also define the emulation of a target machine on the host machine's microlevel architecture.

2.   A second level of control may be introduced in that the control primitives associated with each microinstruction may be defined by programs that reside in a *nanocontrol store.*   Conceptually, a *nanoprogrammed machine* references the hardwired, gating level of the host machine.   Theoretically, a nanoprogrammed machine does *not* have to directly reference the hardwired machine level.   One or more levels of control storage could follow nanocontrol storage before the hardwired machine is reached.   In practice, the usage of a two-level control storage arrangement is referred to as *nanoprogramming,* and the contents of a location in nanocontrol store is called a *nanoinstruction.*   Figure 1-8 illustrates the nanoprogramming control concept.

    a. A macroinstruction is fetched from main storge and placed in the instruction register (IR).

    b. The macroinstruction opcode is used to point to a location in microcontrol store.   This location is the starting address of a microprogram that interprets the macroinstruction on the hardware of the host machine.

    c. Each microinstruction is read from microcontrol store and placed in the MIR.   The contents of the MIR activate certain control primitives and/or point to a location in nanocontrol store that controls the interconnection primitives of each microorder.   These interconnection primitives are also referred to as *architectural configuration primitives* and define the microorders that may be activated by each microinstruction.

Two commercial machines that have employed the nanoprogramming concept extensively are the Burroughs B1700 and the Nanodata QM-1 processor.   Figure 1-9 illustrates how a nanoinstruction might be decoded. The microinstruction provides a field, such as a microop code, which may be translated into an address in nanocontrol storage.   This is the address of the starting nanoinstruction in the nanoprogram sequence that either augments or interprets the macroinstruction fetched from microprogram memory.

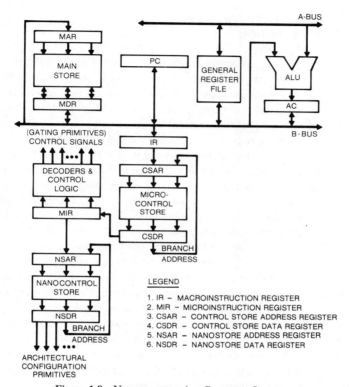

Figure 1-8 Nanoprogramming Computer Structure

LEGEND

1. IR – MACROINSTRUCTION REGISTER
2. MIR – MICROINSTRUCTION REGISTER
3. CSAR – CONTROL STORE ADDRESS REGISTER
4. CSDR – CONTROL STORE DATA REGISTER
5. NSAR – NANOSTORE ADDRESS REGISTER
6. NSDR – NANOSTORE DATA REGISTER

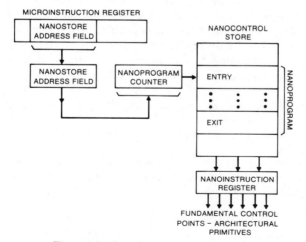

Figure 1-9 Decoding of a Nanoinstruction

1.7 HARDWARE, SOFTWARE, FIRMWARE: A MATTER OF DEFINITION

The characteristic of a control section implemented using random logic is that there is an obvious distinction that can be made between hardware and software: *Software* is composed of program modules that reside in main storage and execute on the physical *hardware* of the host machine. The introduction of a microprogram control section complicates the previous distinction. Since a microprogram is made up of a sequence of microinstructions, microprograms have many of the same characteristics as software except that a microprogram module is placed in control storage. The macrolevel machine is the machine that the applications programmer sees; the microlevel machine is manipulated by the microprogrammer. The macrolevel programmer never sees the microlevel (host) machine. Both programmers, however, write command sequences to compose source programs. If the microcode is supplied in a read-only control memory, then the macrolevel programmer regards the contents of the control store and its associated control logic as merely an extension of the processor hardware. If the control store is electronically alterable, the macrolevel programmer still perceives the microcode as an aspect of the host hardware. It is this dual perception of the characteristic of the contents of control store that has caused a problem in defining what is hardware and what is software. The term *firmware* has come to be identified with microprograms that reside in control store (either read-only or electronically alterable) and determine the behavior of a host machine at the microoperation (control primitive) level.

Control storage simply replaces the random interconnections of hardwired logic with the regular pattern of a memory matrix and its associated control circuitry. In point of fact, it is possible to replace most hardwired logic implementations by an equivalent realization in memory. If memory is used as the determining factor in these definitions, then the following observations may be made:

1. The contents of a read-only memory (ROM) may be regarded as part of the processor's *hardware.*
2. The contents of an electronically alterable (writable) memory may be regarded as *software.*
3. If the contents of the memory determines the behavior of the host machine by activating selected control primitives, then the memory contents may be regarded as *firmware.*

The dual nature of microcode has not been removed by these observations, but the term firmware is now associated closely with the utilization of control primitives provided by the host machine.

A typical small computer manufacturer, however, associates the term *firmware* with the ROM modules supplied with the manufacturer's host machine to interpret or extend the macroinstruction set of the host machine.

1.8 SUMMARY

Microprogram control is a technique used to implement the control section of a computer in which the control sequences are stored in a random-access memory called a *control store.* The primary advantages of a microprogram control unit over an equivalent unit implemented using conventional random logic is that the microprogram design provides greater flexibility and is considerably less complex. The control steps of microorders associated with the fundamental gating signals of a processor are specified by the contents of each location in control storage. A specific word found in control storage is called a *microinstruction;* a sequence of microinstructions forms a microprogram which is executed from control storage.

A microprogrammed processor uses the contents of its control store to interpret the macroinstructions that form its macroorder code. The collection of microprograms that interprets a specific macroinstruction set is also called an *emulator* of that macroinstruction set. In general, it is possible for one machine (the host processor) to emulate the characteristics of a second machine (the target processor). The target machine is the machine the macrolevel user visualizes as the user writes application programs.

Control storage does not have to be implemented as a single level of memory. Control storage can be realized by two or more levels of memory; the final level is the one that interfaces directly to the microlevel hardware of the host machine. Typically, two levels of control memory have been considered in some detail by commercial manufacturers of microprogrammable processors. The second level of control memory is called a nanocontrol store and provides a mechanism for interpreting the individual microinstructions associated with the host machine.

It is fairly common now to encounter microprogrammable machines that use a combination of *read-only memory* (ROM) and *electronically alterable memory* (RAM) for control storage. The electronically alterable control memory forms a *writable control store* (WCS), which allows a user to employ dynamic microprogramming techniques (i.e., microcode modules may be swapped between a bulk storage peripheral such as a floppy disk and WCS). The efficient usage of dynamic microprogramming is still not well understood and is not commonly supplied by the manufacturers of commercial microprogrammed machines.

It is not the intent of this book to explore the variety of ways microprogramming has been used. Rather, it is the intent of the authors to examine how the concepts of modern microprogramming have been implemented on a specific small computer that is designed with *high-reliability requirements* in mind. This small machine is the Bell System 3A CC, and the following chapters explore microprogram design considerations that lead to a fault-tolerant small computer implementation.

1.9   REFERENCES

1. A. K. AGRAWALA and T. G. RAUSCHER, *Foundations of Mircoprogramming: Architecture, Software, and Applications* (New York: Academic Press, 1976).

2. A. K. AGRAWALA and T. G. RAUSCHER, "Microprogramming: Prospective and Status," *IEEE Trans. Comput., C-23*, No. 8 (Aug. 1974), 817–837.

3. L. D. AMDAHL, "Microprogramming and Stored Logic," *Datamation, 10* (Feb. 1964), 24–26.

4. *The AM2900 Family Data Book* (Sunnyvale, Calif.: Advanced Micro Devices, Inc., 1976).

5. R. W. COOK and M. J. FLYNN, "System Design of a Dynamic Microprocessor," *IEEE Trans. Comput., C-19*, No. 3 (March 1970), 213–222.

6. M. J. FLYNN and R. F. ROSIN, "Microprogramming: An Introduction and a Viewpoint," *IEEE Trans. Comput., C-20* (July 1971), 727–731.

7. G. B. Gerace, "Microprogram Control for Computing Systems," *IRE Trans. Electron. Comput., EC-12* (Dec. 1963), 733–747.

8. J. P. HAYES, *Computer Architecture and Organization* (New York: McGraw-Hill, 1978).

9. G. D. KRAFT and W. N. TOY, *Mini/Microcomputer Hardware Design* (Englewood Cliffs, N.J.: Prentice-Hall, 1979).

10. R. J. MERCER, "Microprogramming," *J. ACM, 4* (April 1957), 157–171.

11. *QM-1 Hardware Level User's Manual,* 2nd ed. (Williamsville, N.Y.: Nanodata Corp., 1972).

12. R. F. ROSIN, "Contemporary Concepts of Microprogramming and Emulation," *Comput. Surv., 1* (Dec. 1969), 197–212.

13. M. V. WILKES, "The Best Way to Design an Automatic Calculating Machine," report of the Manchester University Computer Inaugural Conference (Manchester, England: 1951), 16–18.

14. M. V. WILKES, "Microprogramming," *Proc. EJCC* (Dec. 1958), 18–20.

15. M. V. WILKES, W. RENWICK, and D. J. WHEELER, "The Design of the Control Unit of an Electronic Digital Computer," *Proc. IEEE, 105* (March 1958), 121–128.

16. M. V. WILKES and J. B. STRINGER, "Microprogramming and the Design of the Control Circuits in an Electronic Digital Computer," *Proc. Cambridge Philos. Soc., 49,* Part 2 (1953), 230–238.

17. W. T. WILNER, "Design of the Burroughs B1700," in *1972 Fall Joint Computer Conference Proceedings* (Montevale, N.J.: AFIPS Press, 1972), 489–497.

18. W. T. WILNER, "Microprogramming Environment on the Burroughs B1700," in *COMPCON 72 Digest of Papers* (New York: IEEE, 1972), 103–106.

CHAPTER 2

Internal Processor

Control

2.1 ELEMENTARY CONTROL

The control section of the *read-only memory* (ROM), as envisioned by Wilkes, provides direct control of the elementary operations of the computer (such as the individual register gating paths). The control lines emanating from the ROM do not need to be decoded; instead, they are directly mapped into the system's control gates on a one-to-one basis. This means a system with several hundred control points would have the same number of control bits. All control points can be active simultaneously to carry out the designated operation. However, a control operation is usually limited to the usage of a small subset of the total number of possible control points in the machine and seldom involves a large number of simultaneously active controls. A practical design technique is to arrange for as many as possible related, but independent, data processing operations to occur simultaneously at a well-defined timing point within a given machine cycle. This approach will tend to maximize the execution rate of each individual microinstruction.

These operations may involve the usage of several registers or various groups of bits, including the arithmetic unit, to fully implement the available data processing capability of the machine. In other words, the actions to be carried out in one microcycle will match those of a conventional wired logic design, not including the overhead of sequencing the microprogram store. This technique is commonly used for a high-performance machine and is referred to as *direct* or *horizontal control.*

When many operations are carried out in one microcycle, the total number of microsteps is reduced for a given function. This approach influences the dimension of the microprogram store by using fewer microinstruction words for each control sequence. Each word will contain a larger number of bits than an alternative approach that does not employ horizontal control. The implication of such a wide store is that the cost of the support hardware associated with handling the outputs is increased. The outputs are normally buffered in flip-flop registers or gated by timing signals to allow proper sequencing operations (see Figure 1-4). In addition, using the direct control approach, bit utilization of the microprogram store will be somewhat inefficient since a machine operation tends to be directly concerned with only a small part of the total number of control points. What is gained, however, is that the additional hardware (in terms of an increased microinstruction word length) allows for a faster execution rate of the individual microinstructions.

2.1.1 Encoded Control for Speed

When performance is an important factor in a computer system (such as increased throughput) the processor is normally designed to allow parallel operation of independent functions. This implies the concurrent usage of multiple, independent data paths. However, in certain operations, such as addressing main storage, there may be many data paths from which the memory address can be obtained. The memory address, in general, is taken from one data path associated with a specific source register. This source register will usually be selected from a group of several registers, any one of which could supply the desired address. Because only one register may be used as the source at any given time, the data paths cannot be operated concurrently. Consequently, the microcontrol of the individual data paths is mutually exclusive, and a totally horizontal control approach will *not* be the best design approach for this case. Similarly, inputs to all logic and arithmetic functions are mutually exclusive.

Regardless of the number of sources that can be directed as inputs to a specific arithmetic or logic operation, only one can be selected. Only those inputs associated with a specific arithmetic operation can be enabled during any microcycle or the *inclusive-OR* of the other inputs will be provided to the *arithmetic logic unit* (ALU).   For example, in binary addition, the ALU may employ a three-bus structure: one bus for the addend, one bus for the augend, and the third bus for the sum.   Assume that N possible registers can be used as addend or augend inputs to the ALU and the result of the ALU operation can be directed to one of the N registers acting as a destination (Figure 2-1).   Since no more than one control signal can be enabled for each of the three buses, all the control signals associated with each bus can be grouped and encoded into a compact binary number, which may be placed in the microinstruction word.   Instead of having $3N$ control bits, one for each control point associated with the three buses in the microprogram memory, a binary number field may be decoded as opposed to having an individual bit for each register gating operation on each bus.   This method requires $3X$ bits, where $N = 2^x$.   If $N = 16$, then X is equal to 4.   This means, if there are 16 general registers, that the content of any two registers can be added and the result directed to any third register of the 16.   This procedure requires 12 control bits (4 for each of the buses), as opposed to the 48 needed for the direct control scheme, which requires one bit for each control point.

   This encoded method requires a unique decoder for each of the three control fields.   The decoded outputs will set up the desired data paths (one for each bus) by selecting the appropriate control signal from each group of 1-out-of-16 signals associated with each bus field.   In comparing the *strict horizontal control* approach with the *encoded field* method, the basic trade-

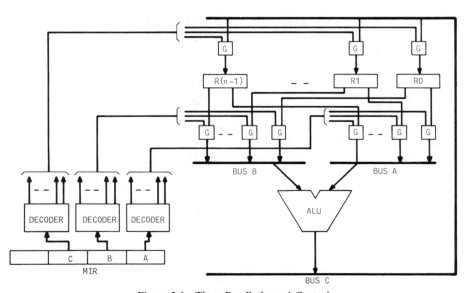

Figure 2-1   Three-Bus Paths and Control

off is the decoder hardware required by the encoded technique versus the larger word size and the associated hardware required by the direct control method. The total number of microinstruction words required by a specific microprogram will remain the same. The increased size of the microprogram memory for the horizontal control approach may be obtained by multiplying the additional bits in each microinstruction word by the number of words in the required microstore. The cost of this memory may be compared to the cost of a system using the encoded control technique which requires a smaller-sized microprogram memory. If the cost of the additional decoders associated with the encoded control method is less than the additional hardware cost for the direct control approach, then it is more economical to encode the individual control signals.

Since the control signals within the same field are mutually exclusive (no two control signals may be simultaneously enabled), there is no time penalty paid by the processor in executing such microinstructions except for the additional logic delay introduced by the added decoder circuitry. If each control signal in every encoded field were mutually exclusive with every other control signal in that field, the number of active controls per microinstruction would be the same for both the direct control approach and the encoded control approach. Consequently, the number of microinstructions per processor control function would be the same for both arrangements, and the execution time of a microprogram control sequence would be the same for both methods.

For both direct control and encoded control when no control signals are to be enabled by a given set of bits, the bits are all placed in the 0 state. For the encoded case, a unique binary code must be assigned to this condition since it represents a legitimate control pattern for a control field. Typically, this all-0s bit pattern is used to represent a microcycle *no-operation* (NOP). When the all-0s bit pattern is decoded, no action is generated by that field during that microcycle. The number of NOPs inserted as fillers in the microinstructions associated with a particular microprogram gives a measure of how inefficiently each of the control fields is used for all the microinstructions in the microprogram.

Since the control fields are encoded as binary numbers, the inefficiency is not as great as it is for the direct control scheme where a bit is *dedicated* in the microinstruction word to *each* individual control operation. The direct control approach normally requires that *each* microinstruction word provide for the specification of the *maximum* number of control operations that could take place in a microcycle. Since not all microinstructions require anywhere near the maximum number of control signals for executing, a substantial *inefficiency* in the usage of the bits in a microinstruction formulated for the direct control approach occurs. This bit inefficiency (i.e., the nonusage of bits in an individual microinstruction) is the penalty that is paid by the machine designer for providing a full set of potentially concurrently active control signals for each microinstruction. The compensating advantage is the faster execution rate for each microinstruction. This, in turn, yields a higher-performing machine with increased processor throughput.

The number of bits required by the ROM associated with a direct-control-oriented microprogram machine can be reduced by a factor of one-third to one-fourth by properly grouping the control signals into mutually exclusive groups that are associated with each microinstruction word. Each control signal within a group is then encoded as a unique binary number. This is done at no sacrifice in the speed of execution of the individual microprograms.

2.1.2 Encoded Control for Equipment Efficiency

To optimize the use of microprogram memory, the design of the control and the rest of the system must be considered at the same time. NOPs can be eliminated if the microorder fields are fully utilized in each microinstruction. This can be realized by having a single encoded field generate only one control function over each microinstruction. Consequently, the internal operation will be completely serial in nature. The system organization, in turn, must be structured to be compatible with this type of control. For example, a data transfer between two registers over a common data bus must be done in two steps. As shown in Figure 2-2, the first control operation transfers the contents of register A onto the data bus. The information must be temporarily stored in a bus register that acts as a buffer. The

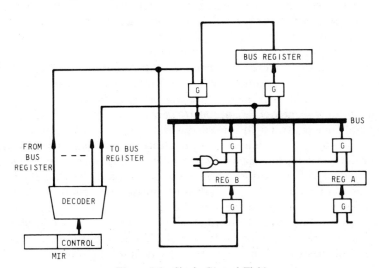

Figure 2-2 Single Control Field

second microorder transfers the data from the bus register back over the bus and into destination register B. The serial nature of this control sequence necessitates the inclusion of the additional bus register since a data word cannot be simultaneously gated on the bus and off it into a target register using this approach. Every microinstruction activates one and only one control point; hence, an NOP is not required to fill an unused control field.

The use of a single control field for microsequencing severely limits the performance of the system. If a majority of the operations involves data transfers that require two control signals, subdividing the microinstruction into two steps will not reduce the total number of control bits in the microprogram memory. In fact, this subdivision of the microinstruction may *increase* the number of bits required by the microinstruction if the address of the next microinstruction is included as part of the current microinstruction. The single encoded field has not been used in commercially available small machines because of its inherent low performance; the serial nature of this microcontrol technique requires additional real time when executing even simple control sequences. If two control fields are provided in the microinstruction and if both fields may specify microcontrol operations that can occur concurrently, a greater flexibility is achieved in controlling the data flow within the machine. Any data transfer over a common data bus can be done with a single microinstruction. One field controls the gating of a data word onto the bus; the second field controls the transfer of the data word from the bus into the destination register. This usage of two control fields, in general, increases the *utility* and *real-time efficiency* of each microinstruction. The control sequence associated with binary addition requires the usage of two control steps; one control step presents the addend to the ALU, and the other control step presents the augend. A third control step is required to transfer the result of the ALU operation into the destination register. If such complex control sequences (i.e., microinstructions that require more than two independent control fields) comprise a relatively small percentage of the total number of microinstructions, the use of only two control fields in each microinstruction can prove to be very efficient in the amount of control memory required by each microprogram. In some instances, only one control field is needed within a microinstruction to perform an elementary operation, such as setting or clearing individual bits in a register. If one of the two fields is assigned for these elementary operations, the second control field of the microinstruction must be encoded with an NOP. As was discussed previously, the NOP performs *no* useful function and represents an inefficient usage of bits in the second control field. Figure 2-3 illustrates a decoding arrangement in which either one control signal or two simultaneous control signals may be generated from a single microinstruction.

Each of the two control fields in this example contains six bits. Each control field is decoded into one unique control signal out of a possible set

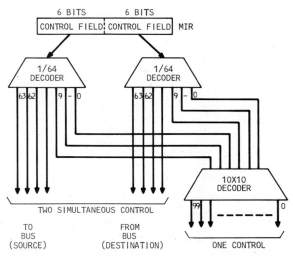

Figure 2-3   Two Control Fields

of 64 control signals.   One output from each decoder can be active simultaneously to effect such operations as data transfer from one register to another
or data transfer from a register to the ALU.   Ten outputs from each of
the two decoders are used as inputs into a 10-by-10 decoder matrix to derive
100 single control signals (only *one* of which can be active at any given
time).   Each of these individual control signals can be used to activate simple
control operations such as clearing a specific register to all 0s; they can
also be used to activate a more complex control function such as the initiation
of an *input/output* (I/O) operation in which the control unit for a specific
I/O device actually presides over each individual I/O transfer (i.e., channel-
type I/O operations).

   This arrangement allows either two control signals or one control signal
to be generated per microinstruction, thereby utilizing code space in control
store more efficiently.   The efficiency is realized by the control store's smaller
width: Only 20 decoded outputs are required to generate 100 outputs.

   The basic scheme shown in Figure 2-3 can be extended to more than
two simultaneous control signals: Figure 2-4 shows such an arrangement
for one, two, or three control fields per microinstruction.   It is assumed
the controls are distinct and not duplicated.   A more flexible scheme would
be to assign a separate opcode for each group of concurrent control operations.
The number of simultaneous controls can then be identified by the microinstruction format, as shown in Figure 2-5.   This type of encoding is referred
to as *indirect encoding*.   The opcode field defines the function of each of
the other fields.   Depending on the value of the opcode, the other fields
(X_1, X_2, X_3) are interpreted differently.   This arrangement provides consider-

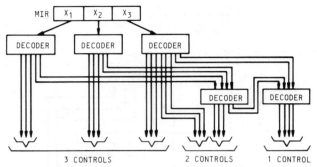

Figure 2-4   Variable Control Fields

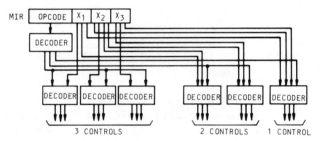

Figure 2-5   Indirect Encoded Control

able flexibility in the use of the bits associated with each microinstruction word.

2.1.3   Maximum and Minimum Encoding

The horizontal control and encoding techniques previously described (i.e., the usage of individual bits in the microinstruction to specify simultaneous control operations and the employment of encoding techniques to reduce the number of bits in the microinstruction) dictate the organization of the internal structure of the *central processing unit* (CPU).   Horizontal control is designed to permit as many parallel (concurrent) control operations as possible to be specified by a microinstruction: The number of required individual control signals dictates the number of bits in the microinstruction; the length of a microinstruction word determines the number of bits that form the width of the microprogram memory.   The horizontal control structure is termed *minimum encoding* or *no encoding*.   The objective of the minimum encoded control arrangement is processor performance (i.e., how rapidly will the processor execute a macroinstruction?).   Consequently, most larger machines are designed with microinstructions that have many control fields. The usage of many encoded control fields permits one microinstruction to direct a potentially large number of concurrent control operations. Increased processor speed is obtained at the expense of a wider microprogram memory and associated decoding hardware.

If a single control field is used by each microinstruction, the sequential execution of many individual microinstructions by the processor may be required to carry out a complex control operation. Such a technique is sometimes called *maximum encoding* of the microinstruction. Since each individual microinstruction may specify only one control operation that can take place, such completely encoded microinstructions tend to use hardware more efficiently; additional decoders are *not* required, but the equivalent processor control operations require a longer period of time to be implemented by the processor since several microinstructions will normally have to be executed. With the cost of hardware continuously decreasing, the limitations of the maximally encoded microinstruction have become of considerable less concern to the microcontrol unit designer.

In the modern small computer, the control format for the microinstructions lies somewhere between these two encoding limits. For some of the more frequently used machine operations such as memory access, direct control signals are used to allow independence from other control operations. A balance between processor performance and microprogram control efficiency is usually the design objective for smaller machines. Another important design consideration is the ease with which other designers can modify and add features. Maintenance considerations are also very important in choosing the number of fields and the method of encoding and decoding the microinstruction. A serial structure with little usage of parallel control operations would enhance the task of fault detection and diagnosis since it is much easier to determine where in the execution sequence of the microprogram a fault occurred.

Two viewpoints may be adopted in considering what format(s) should be used for the control fields of a microinstruction. The first viewpoint is derived from the philosophy of directly replacing the wired logic control circuits with a microprogram. This is a strictly *hardware approach* in which the number of control signals that may be activated at the microlevel of the machine are individually associated with specific bits in a microinstruction word. In this case, there is a one-to-one relationship between a control bit in the microinstruction word and a specific microlevel control signal. The design objective using this approach is to optimize the generation of these control signals and achieve the performance of the wired logic control circuitry. The emphasis, therefore, is on the direct control of data paths and signals that are required to implement a specific macroinstruction. The second viewpoint is a *software approach,* which attempts to specify a set of flexible microinstructions for controlling the elementary operations or microlevel control signals of a processor in a manner similar to that done for a conventional macroinstruction set associated with a small computer. This approach is concerned with the algorithmic structure of the microinstruction set which would permit the efficient implementation of a macroinstruction with a sequence of microinstructions. Such an approach results in a relatively simple set of microinstructions; each microinstruction contains several encoded control fields. This technique results in the microprogram memory being more efficiently coded than the direct encoding scheme, but the execution time of a macroinstruction, typically, is correspondingly longer.

2.1.4 Example of Integer Multiplication Using Direct and Encoded Control Techniques

Binary integer multiplication can be used to illustrate the variations of the two different microcontrol implementations. Assume that only positive fixed-point integers are used to represent both the multiplicand and multiplier. The most frequently encountered form of the multiplication algorithm is a procedure that forms the resultant product by the successive addition of the multiplicand to the cumulative sum. The exact number of additions is determined by the value of the multiplier. Before proceeding, consider the basic scheme. As shown in Figure 2-6, the hardware consists of four registers, R1 through R4. The multiplicand will be stored in R2, the multiplier in R1, and the product in R3 and R4. Since the fixed-point multiplication of two binary numbers that are n bits wide may result in a $2n$-bit product, two registers are required to hold the full product, with the most-significant bits stored in R4. The contents of these registers can be directed to the ALU to be added or shifted or simply directed to the data bus to be transferred from one register to another. Within the ALU, the binary adder can add two numbers, one from the right (R1 or R2) and the other from the left (R3 or R4). The adder output can be shifted or rotated by one bit position, with the result placed directly on the data bus. The end bit that is shifted out is stored in a 1-bit register; the link (L) bit, the bit at the opposite end of the data word, is loaded with a 0. If a rotation operation is performed, the control sequence is the same except that the L bit is gated into the bit at the opposite end of the data word. This operation is basically a *circular shift* with the link bit connecting the two ends. It is necessary to count the number of bits of the multiplier which have been processed at any given stage of the calculation to determine when the multiplication operation is complete. This is done by a hardware counter designated by the label CTN in Figure 2-6. At the beginning of the multiplication routine, the counter CTN is initialized to a number $n - 1$ which represents n successive additions of the multiplicand to the contents of the product register (R3). Each iteration decrements the counter (CTN) by 1. When the count reaches 0, the multiplication process terminates.

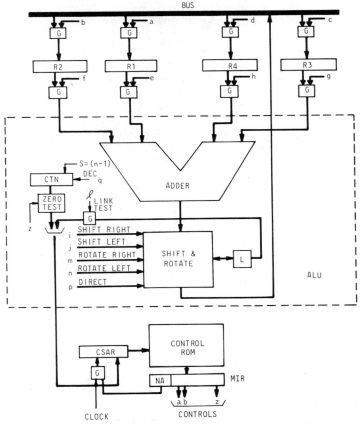

Figure 2-6 Functional Diagram of Arithmetic Hardware Using Direct Control

A flow diagram of the multiplication routine is shown in Figure 2-7. It is assumed that the multiplier and the multiplicand have already been loaded in R1 and R2, respectively. At the start of the sequence, registers R3 and R4 are cleared, and the counter (CTN) is loaded with the count of $n - 1$. The first control operation shifts the least-significant bit of the multiplier into L. If the bit is a 1, the multiplicand in R2 is added to the partial product in R4. If the bit is a 0, no addition will take place. Register R3 and register R4 are treated as a single, concatenated register; the contents of this double-length register are shifted right one position to develop the proper partial product. The shift operation is performed in two steps. First the contents of R4 are shifted right one bit position; then, second, R3 is rotated right by one bit position so that the end bit of R4 is propagated to the most-significant bit of R3. The formation of this partial product

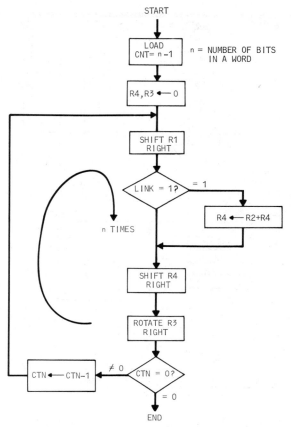

Figure 2-7   Flow Diagram of Multiplication Routine

term is repeated *n* times, corresponding to the number of bits in the multiplier. Each iteration results in the new partial product term shifted right by one additional bit position in register R3 and register R4. The last iteration results in a final product term that has twice as many bits as the initial operands found separately in R1 and R3.

In the normal process of multiplication, the multiplicand term is shifted left before each addition operation. This arrangement requires a double word length adder that requires additional hardware. To avoid this difficulty, the scheme shown in Figure 2-7 provides the required facility for addition *without* using double word length gating paths. Each bit of the multiplier is inspected prior to the addition operation being performed; the resultant sum (product term) is shifted right one bit position. Figure 2-8 shows this

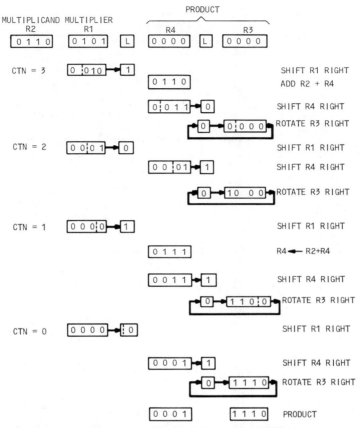

Figure 2-8 Multiplication by Successive Addition

multiplication process for two 4-bit operands. The dashed line in R3 indicates
the movement of the least-significant bit of the final product.

The implementation of the multiplication algorithm using the technique
of direct encoded microcontrol words is shown in Figure 2-9. For each
control point shown, there is one bit dedicated in each microinstruction word
for that function. As a microinstruction is read out of the control memory,
a 1 in a given bit position activates the associated control point. By simultaneously enabling the proper set of control points, data can be moved from
one register to another or processed by the ALU. A coordinated sequence
of microinstructions would then perform the multiplication algorithm.
Figure 2-9 shows the contents of the control memory that implements the
multiplication algorithm; the sequence of microinstructions represents the

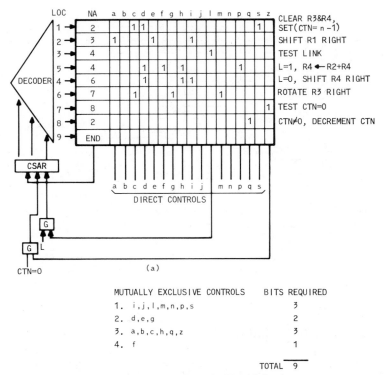

Figure 2-9   Direct Control of Multiplication

physical realization of the flow diagram shown in Figure 2-7. A detailed description of the control sequences follows. Figures 2-6 and 2-9 may be used as a step-by-step guide in the discussion that follows:

  1. The first microinstruction initializes registers R3 and R4 and the counter (CTN). This is done by enabling the gating paths between the BUS and R3 and R4 with control points *c* and *d*. Since none of the control points are enabled from the shift and rotate circuit, the BUS would contain all 0s. This action gates all 0s into both register R3 and register R4. The microcontrol sequence sets the counter (CTN) to a value of $n - 1$; *n* represents the number of bits in the multiplier.

  2. The multiplier that has previously been placed in register R1 is shifted right one bit position with the least-significant bit of R1 stored in the link bit (L). Control point *e* directs register R1 into the ALU; control point *i* shifts the output to the right by one position (onto the BUS). Control point *a* gates the shifted data from the BUS and back into register R1. This completes the shifting operation for this iteration. Since all control operations occur simultaneously, with the final data directed back into register R1, a race condition will exist unless the gating of the BUS back into register R1 is delayed. This difficulty can be eliminated by having

registers R1 through R4 constructed from edge-triggered D flip-flops. The transfer of data from the BUS is done using the trailing edge of the associated control signal.

3. The link bit (L) corresponding to the least-significant bit of the multiplier is tested to determine whether or not the multiplicand should be added to the partial product. This microinstruction is a conditional type of operation. If L is a 0, the microprogram sequence proceeds to the next microinstruction specified by the next address field (next address = 4 as shown in Figure 2-9). The value of the next address field is chosen so that the least-significant bit of the CSAR is initially 0. This is done so that if L is found to be a 1 during testing, the least-significant bit of the CSAR will then be changed to a 1. This allows the microprogram sequence to go to either location 4 or 5, depending on the state of the link bit (L). If the multiplier bit is a 0, the control sequence goes directly to location 4 and skips the addition done in step 5. If the multiplier bit is a 1, the control sequence performs the addition indicated in step 5, and the control sequence is then directed to step 4.

4. R4, which contains the partial product, is shifted right one bit position. The associated microinstruction directs the data in R4 to the ALU; this data is then shifted right, with the result returned to R4. The rightmost bit in R4 is shifted into the link bit (L); it represents the final bit in the partial product. It must be concatenated with the contents of R3, shifted one bit position right, and the result placed back in R3 (see the control sequence in step 6).

5. This step of addition is required if the L bit is a 1. The microinstruction directs the data in register R2 and register R4 to the two inputs of the adder, and the resulting sum is returned to R4. (For simplicity of description, it is assumed that no carry is generated beyond the most significant bit of R4.)

6. The least-significant bits of the product are accumulated one bit at a time in R3. Each successive bit, as it is generated, accomplishes this operation; microcontrol signals (points) are provided to rotate the data so that the L bit is inserted in the most-significant bit position of R3.

7. Steps 2 through 5 are repeated for each multiplier bit. The control sequence must determine the end of the multiplication process. The counter (CTN) is provided for this purpose. At the end of each iteration, the counter (CTN) is tested for a 0 count. If the count is 0, the control sequence terminates by setting the least-significant bit of the microprogram address to a 1. As a result, the next address is the end of the routine. If the count is not 0, the microprogram control sequence continues at step 8.

8. The counter (CTN) is decremented by 1, and the addition operation is repeated for the next multiplier bit. A total of eight microinstructions are used to implement the multiplication algorithm as a microroutine. The few bit positions that contain 1s in the microprogram memory indicate the inefficient use of the code space provided by the bits in a microinstruction word. By examining the memory content, it can be seen that certain bits or control functions are mutually exclusive. For example, the SHIFT RIGHT and SHIFT LEFT control operations would never occur simultaneously; neither would the ROTATE RIGHT, ROTATE LEFT, or NO ROTATE control operations. This means that only one of the five control signals (i, j, m, n, or p) need to be active in any given microinstruction. A similar situation exists for control signals l and s. They are also mutually exclusive; therefore, these seven control signals (i, j, m, n, p, l, and s) can be encoded using a more

compact 3-bit binary code. Only one control signal in this group will ever be active at any given time. An NOP must be used when none of these seven control signals are required for a specific microinstruction. Other control bits may be grouped in a similar fashion, as indicated in Figure 2-10. The 17 bits required by a directly encoded microinstruction word may be compressed into a microinstruction consisting of four encoded control fields. These four fields, in turn, are made up of 3 bits, 2 bits, 3 bits, and 1 bit, respectively, as shown in Figure 2-10. When the microinstruction is decoded, a maximum of four control signals will be produced concurrently (one from each field). Since each field represents a grouping of mutually exclusive control signals, the full complement of 17 independent control signals will be produced, but only 9 bits will be required in each microinstruction word to specify the desired control signals. This is identical to the direct control scheme. The only difference is that the outputs from the microinstruction register must be decoded, resulting in an additional stage delay in the execution of the microinstruction. This delay corresponds to the propagation time through the decoders that monitor the outputs of the microinstruction register. This logic delay must be taken into consideration in the sequence associated with the execution of a microinstruction.

The grouping of the control signals into fields is based upon the requirement that each group will only have outputs that are mutually exclusive. A substantial reduction in memory size, from 17 bits to 9 bits, is realized using this approach, even though the total number of words required by the microcontrol sequence remains the same. As shown in Figure 2-10, only one of the eight microinstructions has a control signal active from each of the four encoded fields; this is also true for the direct control technique.

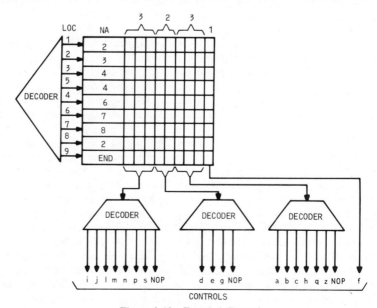

Figure 2-10 Encoded Control

Consider the other extreme in which only one fully encoded control field per microinstruction is provided. This scheme will reduce the microinstruction word length still further, but more microinstructions will be required to carry out the same control sequence. The control operation will appear as a serial execution sequence of individual control steps as opposed to a parallel control operation composed of several concurrent control primitives enabled simultaneously.

The 17 control signals described previously can be encoded using five bits, with only one control signal active at any given time. To accommodate a single control operation per microinstruction, the internal bus structure and the ALU must be provided with additional hardware registers to buffer the data at each control step. Figure 2-11 shows three registers (A, B,

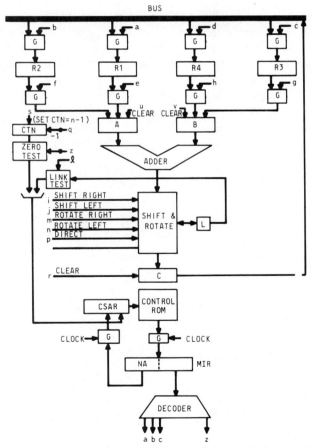

Figure 2-11 Functional Diagram of Arithmetic Hardware Using Single Control Field

and C) and the controls (*r, u,* and *v*) necessary to clear these registers. The bus is connected directly to register C. Whenever any one of the four control signals (*a, b, c,* or *d*) is enabled, the content of register C is gated directly either to R1 (*a* is enabled), R2 (*b* is enabled), R3 (*c* is enabled), or R4 (*d* is enabled), respectively. Similarly, when the contents of R1, R2, R3, or R4 are directed to the adder, the data is buffered by register A and/ or register B. The result is that the data can either be shifted or rotated and then gated into register C, or the data can be directly gated into register C without modification. When only a single microcontrol signal may be specified per microinstruction, more microinstructions are required to perform an individual operation such as rotation. The sequence of microinstructions for the multiplication algorithm is shown in Figure 2-12. Note that each microinstruction specifies one microcontrol function (e.g., the contents of register C are moved into register R3). As indicated, the initialization procedure that involves the counter (CTN) and registers C, R3 and R4 is done in four control steps rather than one. Register C, which is connected directly to the bus, must be cleared prior to clearing R3 and R4. Eighteen microinstructions are required to perform the same multiplication function discussed earlier that needed only 8 microinstructions in each of the other two schemes.

Table 2-1 summarizes the memory usage of each of the microcontrol

STEP	CONTROL	OPERATION	REMARKS	
0	s,	CTN←n−1	LOAD COUNTER=n−1	
1	r,	C←0	CLEAR C	INITIAL-
2	c,	R3←C	CLEAR R3	IZATION
3	d,	R4←C	CLEAR R4	
4	e,	A←R1	LOAD A FROM R1	CHECK
5	i,	C←A	SHIFT RIGHT A INTO C	MULTIPLIER
6	l,	L: 1,(=,≠)→(7,11)	L=1 BRANCH TO 7 / L=0 BRANCH TO 11	BIT
7	f,	A←R2	LOAD A FROM R2	
8	h,	B←R4	LOAD B FROM R4	SUM PARTIAL
9	p,	C←ADDER	LOAD C FROM ADDER	PRODUCT
10	d,	R4←C	LOAD R4 FROM C	
11	u,	A←0	CLEAR A	
12	h,	B←R4	LOAD B FROM R4	SHIFT
13	i,	C←B	SHIFT RIGHT B INTO C	PARTIAL
14	d,	R4←C	LOAD R4 FROM C	PRODUCT
15	g,	B←R3	LOAD B FROM R3	RIGHT
16	m,	C←B	ROTATE B INTO C	
17	c,	R3←C	LOAD R3 FROM C	
18	z,	CTN: 0,(≠,=)→(19,20)	COUNTER=0,BRANCH TO 20 / COUNTER≠0,BRANCH TO 19	CHECK COUNTER
19	q,	CTN ←CTN−1,→4	DECREMENT COUNTER AND BRANCH TO 4	AND REPEAT
20	END			

Figure 2-12   Control Sequence of Multiplication

TABLE 2-1 **Memory Usage for Three Encoding Schemes**

ENCODING SCHEME	NO. OF WORDS	NO. OF BITS PER WORD	TOTAL BITS
DIRECT	8	17	136
MULTIPLE ENCODED FIELDS	8	9	72
SINGLE ENCODED FIELD	20	5	100

realizations that implemented the multiplication algorithm. Note that each encoding scheme requires a different number of bits per microinstruction word and a different number of microinstructions to implement the identical control sequence. Table 2-1 is a limited example of the implementation of one particular function using different encoding schemes for a microinstruction. It illustrates the possibility of going too far in one direction, resulting in more bits being required by the overall microprogram with a loss of performance at the same time since more microinstructions must be executed to complete the microprogram. In a large- or medium-sized machine, there may be several hundred direct control bits. If these control signals were to be divided into mutually exclusive fields, the number of bits required by the individual microprograms would probably be reduced by one-third, keeping the number of words the same. On the other hand, if the individual control signals were divided functionally and separate fields assigned to those control signals that occurred the most frequently, then most of the fields would be fully utilized by the microinstructions. The few microinstructions requiring more control signals in a single word than can be provided by this approach could be subdivided into several independent microinstructions and executed serially. As discussed thus far, each microcontrol signal may be represented either by the state of a single bit in a microinstruction or *one* output from a decoder attached to the microinstruction register. It may be advantageous to have one bit or decoded output select several control points rather than using additional microinstructions or control fields within a microinstruction to accomplish the same operation. The previous example has shown that several control signals frequently must occur simultaneously to perform an overall microcontrol function. This characteristic tends to tailor the microinstruction design to a specific application. When done excessively, however, this approach tends to lose the flexibility to combine system control primitives to realize future overall control functions efficiently.

On the other hand, if this technique is carried out properly, it can enhance the execution speed of the individual microprograms and reduce the size of the microprogram store. Again, the trade-off is in terms of the additional logic circuitry needed to provide the fan-out and fan-in requirements required to combine selected microcontrol signals.

In general, Figure 2-13 gives a comparison between the usage of direct control and encoded control in terms of memory size and execution time. The direct control approach provides the maximum number of permissible concurrent microcontrol operations. A system using the direct control approach is structured for high-speed microcontrol operation; it allows *parallel* control of all functional blocks wherever possible. This type of control organization is called *horizontal control*. Since many microcontrol functions can be realized with a single microinstruction, a smaller number of microinstructions are needed to implement a specific microprogram. If the design approach is to use heavily encoded microinstructions, only a few control signals will be generated per microinstruction. Hence, the overall microcontrol oper-

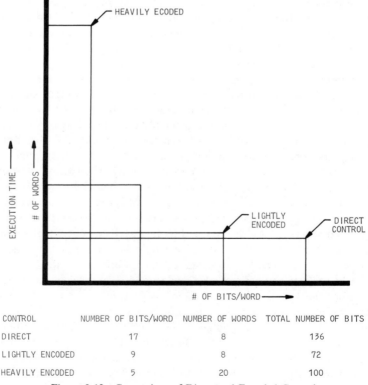

CONTROL	NUMBER OF BITS/WORD	NUMBER OF WORDS	TOTAL NUMBER OF BITS
DIRECT	17	8	136
LIGHTLY ENCODED	9	8	72
HEAVILY ENCODED	5	20	100

Figure 2-13 Comparison of Direct and Encoded Control

ation will be done by the sequential execution of many small microinstructions. This approach is often referred to as *vertical control.* Less hardware is required to implement the heavily encoded microcontrol approach. For small machines, the optimum encoding technique usually falls between the two limits dictated by lightly and heavily encoded control. Essentially, these considerations allow a small machine to realize the economies of a smaller microprogram memory while still permitting the execution of a microprogram control sequence at reasonable speed. There is no clear-cut solution for the choice of an optimum encoding technique for many engineering problems. As usual, there are many factors and constraints in the design of a microinstruction set that may make each problem that is encountered a unique one. Factors such as performance (speed of execution), flexibility, and cost (of the control memory and associated logic) play an important role in the choice of alternative encoding schemes. In some instances, a combination of several alternatives may provide the best solution. The direct control technique may be best applied to a few control signals that occur frequently throughout the entire microinstruction set; other control signals may be grouped into several independent fields and encoded separately within the individual fields.

2.2 MICROPROGRAM STORE ADDRESSING

The word length of a microinstruction is the major factor influencing how the contents of the microcontrol store are addressed. Wilkes divided the microprogram store into two parts: a *control* portion and a *sequencing* portion. The sequencing portion contains the full address of the next microinstruction. This permits the next microinstruction in the microcontrol sequence to be identified by the microinstruction currently being executed. The use of a full address allows the next microinstruction to be chosen from anywhere within the control memory. This addressing flexibility eliminates the need for a conventional unconditional branch capability since the use of a next address field provides an unconditional branch capability for each microinstruction in addition to the normal control operation(s) specified by the microinstruction. Figure 2-14 shows a next address field stored in each microinstruction word that is capable of specifying any address in the full address

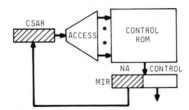

Figure 2-14   Random—Full Range Next Address Field

range of the control ROM. This field is used to select the next microinstruction. For a 1K ROM, a 10-bit next address field is required, and this increases the microinstruction word size by 10 bits.

2.2.1 Limited Range Next Address Field

To reduce the number of bits per microinstruction word in the microprogram store, the next address field can be made smaller. This means the range of addresses in which the next microinstruction can be found is limited to a block of addresses determined by the size of the next address field. If the number of microinstructions in a microprogram sequence is considerably smaller than this block size, the limited addressing capability provided by this technique does not seriously penalize any microinstructions that reference a successor microinstruction(s) that is located within the fixed boundary of this block.

Figure 2-15 illustrates the usage of a next address field in which only the low-order bits are changed from one microinstruction to the next. For example, the use of a 5-bit next address field would allow a group of 32 contiguous address locations to be referenced. To reference microinstruction(s) located beyond this fixed block of 32 control store locations, two possible approaches may be used:

1. A separate branch instruction may be employed in which the control field is used in conjunction with the next address field to specify an address that may reference any location in the control store.
2. If the microinstruction word is too short to provide an address that will reference any location in the control memory, the target address of the branch microinstruction may be stored in a separate hardware register in the normal branch type of instruction.

Alternatively, a special register called the FILL buffer, shown in Figure 2-15, could be used to derive an address that will cover the full range of

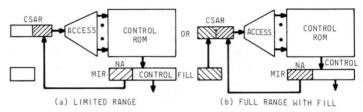

Figure 2-15   Random—Limited Range Next Address Field

addresses for the control store. Instead of changing only the low-order bits of the memory address register (MAR), the high-order bits of the MAR are also altered. A composite address is formed by concatenating the next address field (the low-order bits of the address) with the FILL register (the higher-order bits of the address) to produce the full address word. The exact mechanism for filling the FILL register will be discussed in later sections. For the present, assume the FILL register contains the high-order bits of the address of the next microinstruction. The control section of the microinstruction contains a field (not shown in Figure 2-15) that directs the selection of either the partial next address, as shown in Figure 2-15(a), or the composite full address, as shown in Figure 2-15(b), as the address for the next microinstruction.

2.2.2 Sequential Addressing

The simplest addressing mechanism for locating the address of the next microinstruction is the sequential addressing technique. This technique implies that the next microinstruction will normally be contiguous to the current microinstruction and will be stored in the next sequential location in the microprogram memory. If the microprogram sequence is to deviate from a normal straight-line execution sequence, a separate microinstruction is required to designate that a branching operation is to be performed. Figure 2-16(a) shows the sequential addressing arrangement for referencing a control

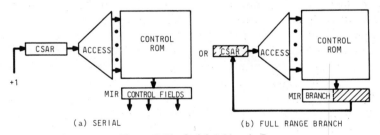

(a) SERIAL   (b) FULL RANGE BRANCH

Figure 2-16 Serial Addressing

memory. Since a next address field is *not* used by a microinstruction, the word size of the microinstruction can be made much smaller than a microinstruction that employs a next address field. This is the memory referencing technique that has been commonly used by many microprogrammable small computers. In such machines, whenever a branch operation is required in the microprogram sequence, a separate branch instruction is used to perform the operation; see Figure 2-16(b).

2.3 MICROPROGRAM MEMORY ALLOCATION FOR MICROINSTRUCTION SEQUENCING

Each microprogram is made up of a sequence of independent microinstructions. The mechanism of assigning locations in control memory to store these microcontrol sequences is much simpler than the mechanism used to assign storage locations to a program executing in main memory. In main memory, space is allocated dynamically by the operating system to fill the requirements of individual programs that are active on the system. Often a complicated algorithm is used by the operating system to allocate main storage; the algorithm is used to provide flexibility in handling diverse memory requirements that may arise in a multiprogramming environment. When a microprogram memory is used, the memory assignment scheme is static; that is, once the memory assignment is made, it is implemented in hardware that remains fixed for all systems. Therefore, the memory assignment scheme for a microprogram store must be both efficient in its usage of storage space and optimize the execution time of the associated microprograms.

2.3.1 Allocation by the Use of Branch Vector Table

The opcode of a macroinstruction found in the *instruction register* (IR) is normally used as an entry point into the microprogram store. Figure 2-17 shows how the opcode (usually three to eight bits wide) goes directly into the *control store address register* (CSAR) to start the microprogram sequence that implements the macroinstruction. The high-order bits of the CSAR, as shown in the figure, are set to all 0s. The zeroing of these most-significant bits maps the entry point for the associated microprogram sequence at the beginning of the microcontrol store. In effect, a block of words is reserved in the lowest address range associated with the control memory to function

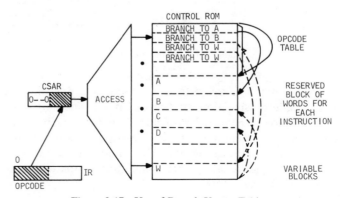

Figure 2-17 Use of Branch Vector Table

as entry points for each microprogram associated with a macroinstruction opcode. The block size is determined by the number of bits in the opcode. This fixed block can be shifted to a different section of the store by setting the high-order bits of the CSAR to a non-0 value instead of using all 0s.

Since the block of entry point addresses associated with the macroinstruction opcodes is reserved, the first microinstruction *must* be a branch instruction. This branch instruction directs the microcontrol sequence to a preassigned block of microinstructions that interpret the specified macroinstruction opcode. The size of these blocks varies directly with the number of microinstructions that are required to interpret the desired macroinstruction. For example, as shown in Figure 2-17, the first microinstruction in the opcode table, or *branch vector table*, branches to location A, and the second microinstruction branches to location B. The number of microcontrol words between A and B represents the storage allocation for the macroinstruction with an all-0s opcode. It is good practice to assign a few spare microstore locations in the storage allocation for each microprogram for any future design changes. This allows additional microcode to be assigned to a specific microprogram module without disturbing the contents of the entire microprogram store.

To reduce the number of microstore locations that may be needed for a microprogram module, several macroinstruction opcodes may share a common microroutine either at the beginning or at the end of the microprogram sequence. (The case of sharing a microroutine in the middle of the microprogram sequence will be covered later.) Sharing a common routine among several microprograms can be done as shown in Figure 2-17. The third and fourth words in the opcode table cause the microcontrol sequence to branch to the same location (location W) in the microprogram memory. Location W is the entry point of the microprogram sequence which is shared by microroutines C or D. The shared microroutine executes the associated microcontrol sequence and then examines the opcode in the IR to determine whether the microcontrol sequence is to branch to microroutine C or microroutine D. If the common routine is called at the end of a microprogram sequence, the microcontrol sequence branches directly to the shared routine without any concern for how control should return to a particular microinstruction sequence.

The opcode table provides a means of branching to a specific microroutine which is unique to a given macroinstruction. The execution of each branching microinstruction in the opcode table is simply the overhead required to implement this technique. The usage of an opcode table requires additional memory and increases the execution time of each microprogram sequence which interprets a macroinstruction opcode since the additional branching microinstructions are required in the opcode table. Therefore, it would be desirable to remove the usage of an opcode table in the microcontrol store.

2.3.2   Allocation by the Use of Offset Addressing

One scheme for eliminating the need for an opcode table is to offset or shift the opcode a predetermined number of bit positions left when the opcode is gated into the CSAR to initiate the beginning of the microprogram sequence (see Figure 2-18).   In this case, the number of bit positions in the offset represents the block size allocated for each microprogram sequence; it is arranged to be the same size for each microprogram sequence that interprets a macroinstruction opcode.   The offset must be large enough for the most complex sequence of microinstructions.   As a result, for many simpler microinstruction sequences, the number of unused locations in microcontrol memory can be rather excessive and wasteful.   Although this scheme eliminates the use of an opcode table and the related overhead of having to use

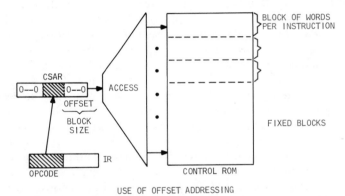

USE OF OFFSET ADDRESSING

Figure 2-18   Sequential Addressing and Memory Allocation by Software

one branch microinstruction per entry in the opcode table, the use of a fixed block size in allocating microcontrol memory results in inefficient usage of the available storage in microprogram memory.   Consequently, this technique is not commonly used by itself but, instead, is used in combination with the other methods of microstore addressing to provide a more graceful means of allocating storage.

2.3.3   Allocation by the Use of Hardware Mapper

The drawbacks of the previous memory allocation schemes can be eliminated through the use of a hardware microinstruction address mapper.   The *hardware mapper* is used to translate the macroinstruction opcode directly to an address in the microprogram memory (see Figure 2-19).   The mapper serves the same function as the opcode table except that the overhead of a branch microinstruction per entry in the opcode table is eliminated.   By

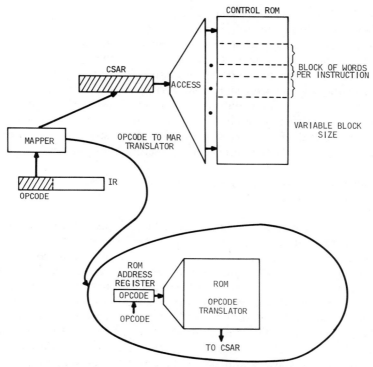

Figure 2-19   Sequential Addressing and Memory Allocation by Hardware

appropriately assigning the associated starting address in microstore for each macroinstruction opcode, blocks of different memory size can be allocated to interpret each macroinstruction.   The mapper is a relatively simple combinational logic design.   It can be a binary decoder that coverts the macroinstruction binary opcode to a logic signal in which only one output is active out of n possible outputs; n represents the number of possible binary combinations of the bits in the opcode.   The decoder outputs can then be combined to form a new binary number that is gated into the CSAR.   Alternatively, the mapper can be implemented by using a second small ROM.   The macroinstruction opcode is used as a data address in the small ROM.   The contents of the location selected in the small ROM represent the starting address of the associated microprogram sequence in the microcontrol store.   The use of a hardware mapper, particularly a ROM type of structure, offers (1) flexibility in the reassignment of the entry address for each microcontrol sequence and (2) an enhanced speed of microprogram execution since the branching operations required by the sequential address scheme for microprogram sequencing are eliminated.   Mappers of both types (combinational logic translator and ROM decoder) have been employed in commercial small computers to facilitate the addressing and memory allocation of the microprogram store.

A common microprogram sequence may be shared by a group of microprograms in the same manner as was discussed for the opcode branch table. The mapper can translate two or more macroinstruction opcodes to the same address in the microcontrol store that corresponds to the first location in the common microprogram routine. Within this routine, the return address for each macroinstruction can be derived directly from the associated opcode so that at the end of the common microprogram sequence execution can branch to the appropriate microprogram interpretation sequence.

2.3.4 Allocation Scheme Using a Limited Random Address Field

The memory allocation scheme in which a limited next address field is used offers more flexibility than the sequential addressing method. Since the contents of the next address field may be a random address in control store, this technique is also called the *limited random-access method*. Figure 2-20 illustrates this memory allocation technique. A two-step process is used to direct control to the appropriate microcontrol sequence. The macroinstruction opcode is *first* offset (shifted left) one bit position and then gated into the control store address register (CSAR) with the higher-order bits of the CSAR reset to all 0s. A structure similar to a branch table is then used to derive the starting address of the desired microprogram sequence. Each entry in this structure may reference any location in the microcontrol store. The offset opcode uses two words to set up the appropriate branch address to the target microprogram. The precise way of setting up the branch address is a function of the microstore addressing scheme associated with the limited range next address technique.

Figure 2-20 illustrates how a full branch address is set up. The process requires the execution of two consecutive microinstructions that are associated with the macroinstruction opcode. The macroinstruction opcode defines the address in control store of the first microinstruction of an address pair that is uniquely assigned to that opcode. The entry address is formed by offsetting the opcode and bit position left and gating the result into the CSAR. The least-significant bit of this address is always set to 0. Consequently, the first microinstruction of this address couplet always falls on an even address. The FILL buffer register is used in conjunction with the offset opcode address to permit the formation of a control store address that may point to any location in control memory. To do this, the FILL buffer register must be loaded with the high-order bits of the control store address. This is accomplished by having the first microinstruction treat its next address field as address data. This address data is placed in the FILL register as shown

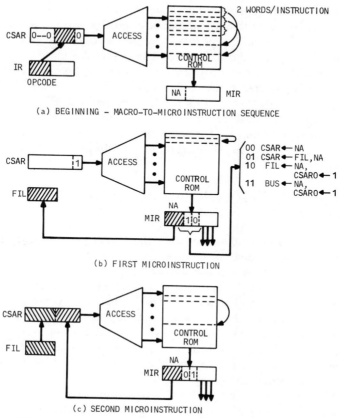

Figure 2-20 Sequential Addressing and Memory Allocation for the Limited Random Address Range

in Figure 2-20(b). It is assumed that the size of the next address field is equal to or larger than the size of the FILL register. Since the next address field is used for this purpose, the address of the next microinstruction can be generated by setting the least-significant bit of the CSAR to 1. As shown in Figure 2-20(b), a 2-bit field in the first microinstruction is used to define precisely what quantity will be loaded into the CSAR. The normal state (00) of this field permits the address of the next microinstruction to be gated from the next address field (NA) directly into the CSAR. The 10 state directs that the contents of the next address field be gated into the FILL register. The address of the next microinstruction is formed by setting the least-significant bit of the CSAR to a 1. The 01 state specifies that the full address of the next microinstruction be formed by gating the contents of the next address field and the FILL register into the CSAR. The fourth state (11) can be used to specify a data source for other microcontrol functions; the address of the next microinstruction is formed by setting the least-significant bit of the CSAR to 1. In this case, the next address field is treated as data and gated onto the data bus. The actual destination of the data can be specified by other control fields not shown in Figure 2-20(b). This technique will be covered in more detail in a later discussion. When the first microinstruction of an address pair is executed, the FILL buffer is set up. The second microinstruction forms the composite address of the next microinstruction and branches the microcontrol sequence directly to the area in control store allocated for the interpretation of the associated microinstruction opcode.

2.4 MICROINSTRUCTION-TO-MACROINSTRUCTION ADDRESS SEQUENCING

The usage of a macroinstruction opcode, either directly or indirectly, to derive the starting address of a microprogram sequence which interprets the macroinstruction is referred to as a *macroinstruction-to-microinstruction address sequencing operation*. At the end of the current microprogram sequence, it is necessary to begin another microcontrol sequence that will interpret the next macroinstruction. The transition of control back to evaluating a macroinstruction opcode is referred to as a *microinstruction-to-macroinstruction sequencing operation*. Whenever this type of control transition is to take place, a special microinstruction is used. If the next microinstruction is specified using sequential addressing as shown in Figure 2-21(a), the last microinstruction of the current microprogram sequence may combine several control steps into a single operation. One of these control operations tests to determine if the next macroinstruction opcode is ready to be processed or if the opcode must still be delivered to the IR before the opcode can be transferred into the CSAR. It is assumed that the fetch of the next macroinstruction will result in the macroinstruction being routed to the IR. The *branch-to-opcode* (BTO) *microinstruction* shown in Figure 2-21(a) contains a next address field of all 0s. Location 0 in the control store also contains the same BTO microinstruction. Consequently, so long as the macroinstruction opcode has not been gated into the CSAR, the microcontrol sequence continuously executes the BTO microinstruction found at location 0. The repeated execution of the BTO microinstruction represents a *microcontrol wait loop*. The BTO microinstruction also enables the data path from the IR (which contains the microinstruction opcode) to the CSAR if the condition (DATA READY) has occurred. This condition indicates that the macroinstruction word from main storage has been successfully gated into the IR. When both data paths are enabled, the data transfer logic is arranged to simultaneously "OR in" the macroinstruction opcode and the all-0s address

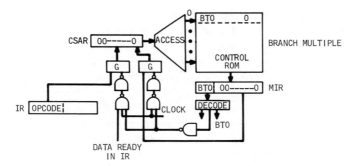

(a) SEQUENTIAL ACCESS

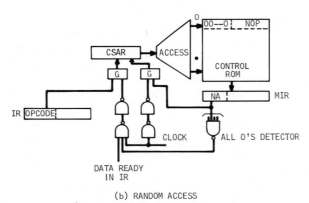

(b) RANDOM ACCESS

Figure 2-21 Micro-to-Macro Address Sequencing

word from the **MIR** into the **CSAR**. The resulting microstore address is then simply the value of the opcode found in the **IR**. The **DATA READY** signal must be synchronized so as not to occur during the clock interval in which the transfer of the opcode takes place. Otherwise, an incorrect opcode may be gated into the **CSAR**. This conditional transfer of the macroinstruction opcode into the **CSAR** allows the microcontrol memory to run asynchronously with the main program memory. The microprogram sequence is, therefore, loosely coupled to the main memory access time (i.e., it is initiated when the macroinstruction word has been moved from main storage into the **IR**). The microcontrol interpretation sequence can interface directly with different main memory modules each with different access times within the same machine. The microcontrol sequence handles this situation by automatically increasing or decreasing the wait interval generated by repeatedly executing the **BTO** microinstruction.

When the next opcode is available in the **IR**, the **BTO** microinstruction represents an overhead in terms of execution time for obtaining the next macroinstruction opcode.   For a microinstruction format that employs a next address field, it is not necessary to provide a special microinstruction for the microinstruction-to-macroinstruction transfer operation.   The next address field, normally, provides an addressing range that will allow any microinstruction to branch to any location in the control memory.   To make a distinction between a standard microinstruction in a microprogram and the last microinstruction in the microprogram sequence, a unique address such as one using all 0s can be chosen for the last microinstruction.   This situation is shown in Figure 2-21(b).   A logic gate would be used to detect the all-0s state.   If the DATA READY signal is active, the data path from the opcode portion of the IR into the CSAR is enabled.   This transfers the opcode into the CSAR in a manner similar to that used with the BTO microinstruction.   If the memory data is not ready in the IR upon execution of the last microinstruction, control will branch to the all-0s location in the microprogram memory.   At the all-0s location, the microinstruction contains an NOP, with the next address field again assigned the all-0s location. The microcontrol sequence will stay in this all-0s loop, repeating the NOP microinstruction, until the DATA READY lead signifies that the next macroinstruction has been placed in the IR.

If either a BTO microinstruction or a next address field of all 0s is used, the operation of transferring control from the last microinstruction to the next macroinstruction is similar.   If the sequential addressing method is used, a special microinstruction (BTO) is required.   This adds one additional microinstruction to each microprogram interpretation sequence. If a next address field of all 0s is used, the full use of the last microinstruction is allowed as part of the microcontrol sequence.   If the next address field is limited in terms of the number of locations that may be referenced by the microinstruction, either technique can be used to transfer control to the next macroinstruction opcode.

2.5   CONDITIONAL BRANCH MICROINSTRUCTION

In any control operation, provision must be made for *conditional* execution of a control sequence.   This behavior requires that the execution sequence make a choice between several possible control responses.   Such choices are made constantly by the control logic in the course of processing involving arithmetic or logic operations.   Such decisions are made at all levels of control, based upon both external and internal conditions.   In many instances, the results of several previous control operations determine the course of action taken by the execution sequence.

In conventional logic design, a typical circuit (see Figure 2-22) may

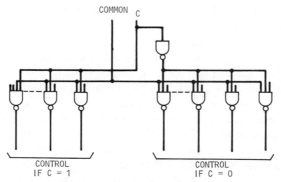

Figure 2-22   Conventional Control Logic

consist of two groups of logic gates; each group represents two sets of possible control actions.   The action to be taken depends on condition C shown in Figure 2-22.   If C is in the 1 state, the left group of gates is selected; if C is in the 0 state, the right group is selected.   This control decision is incorporated in hardware as part of the logic elements.   Because of this, the hardwired control logic is very irregular since every conditional decision is usually unique.   In microprogramming, the control action is stored in memory as a sequence of microinstructions.   If C represents a conditional decision point in the control sequence, a means must be provided for the executing sequence to branch to one or more independent microcontrol sequences, depending on the value (0 or 1) assumed by the variable C.

A *branch-on condition* (BC) command is usually included as a member of the microinstruction set.   The branch address may be part of the microinstruction, as shown in Figure 2-23.   As shown in the figure, the control field specifying the BC microoperation is decoded and then combined logically with a condition control signal.   The resulting logic signal is used to transfer the branch address into the CSAR.   If the indicated condition is not satisfied, one is added to the contents of the CSAR to generate the address of the

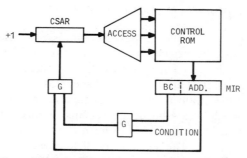

Figure 2-23   Conditional Branch—Sequential Address

next microinstruction. This is the normal sequential addressing procedure used with a control memory.

For the random address scheme in which a full-range next address field is employed in the microinstruction, the conditional branch is easily implemented by changing one bit in the address of the next microinstruction, as shown in Figure 2-24. Instead of using a special microinstruction (i.e., BC) with an associated address field, a binary code located in one of the control fields can be used to designate a conditional testing operation that will be performed at the microlevel. Normally, the next address field is arranged to contain an even binary number as the next address. If the condition under which branching is to occur is *not* met, the least-significant bit of the CSAR is left at 0 (this specifies an even address). However, if the condition under which branching is to occur *is* met, the least-significant bit of the CSAR is set to a 1. Several tests may be performed by the same

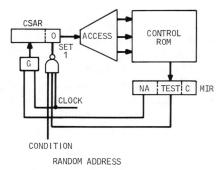

Figure 2-24   Conditional Branch—Random Address

microinstruction with the result of each test associated with one of the low-order bits in the CSAR. For example, two test fields can change the two low-order bits of the CSAR and, thereby, specify one of four possible addresses that could be used as the address of the next microinstruction.

2.6   FUNCTIONAL BRANCH MICROINSTRUCTION

The ability to select one of several possible addresses as the next address in a microprogram sequence provides the flexibility to execute a variety of micro-control functions more efficiently and easily. In the case of a conditional branch operation, a dedicated function field specified by the microinstruction can direct a microexecution sequence to a number of successor addresses. As shown in Figure 2-25, a 4-bit field associated with the macroinstruction register (IR) is gated into the CSAR to form the low-order bits of the next microinstruction address. The next address field of the current microinstruction is arranged such that the four least-significant bits of that field contains

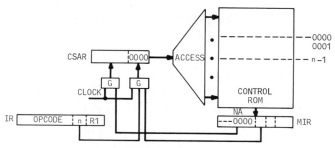

Figure 2-25   Functional Branch

all 0s. The 4-bit binary number *n* is loaded into the CSAR by performing the inclusive-OR of *n* with the four least-significant bits of the next address field. This implementation has two advantages: (1) speed and (2) the simplicity of the required hardware.

Alternatively, *n* can be treated as an index quantity and arithmetically added to the contents of the next address field in the microinstruction to form the *effective address* of the *next* microinstruction. This approach does *not* require that the low-order bits of the next address field contain all 0s. The end result is a more flexible addressing procedure that is used to reference microprogram memory. However, an adder is required to perform the index operation. And, more importantly, the addition operation will delay the microexecution sequence by one or more microcycles. The procedure of forming the *inclusive-OR* of an *n* bit number and an all-0s number is effectively the same as forming the arithmetic sum of the two numbers. The difference between the two operations is that the inclusive-OR procedure involves the simple step of simultaneously gating the two numbers into the CSAR. The functional branch field *n* can come from many different sources (i.e., the macroinstruction register [IR], etc.), with the choice specified by the microinstruction. Although Figure 2-25 shows only one functional branch field, several alternative functional branch fields may be used, with each functional field having a separate gating path to the CSAR. The selection of the specific functional field to be used in forming the address of the next microinstruction will be done by the current microinstruction.

To illustrate the usefulness of the functional branch in the implementation of a variety of control functions, consider a relatively simple example. Assume that a hardware accumulator (AC) is provided as a working register for microprogramming and is transparent to the main program. It can be rotated either right or left with a special link bit (L) included in the rotation (see Figure 2-26). For simplicity, other arithmetic and logical operations are not shown. The macroinstruction set is assumed to deal directly with a set of general hardware registers (R*n*) rather than a single accumulator. Given the microcontrol arrangement shown in Figure 2-26, many macroin-

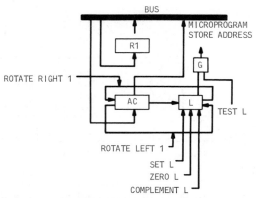

Figure 2-26   Common Accumulator for Microprogram Operations

structions that involve the manipulation of a single bit in one of the general registers can be processed easily when the functional branch capability is used at the microinstruction level.   Instructions for zeroing, setting, complementing, or testing a specified bit of a general register can all be carried out by a combination of microinstructions.   These microinstructions move the content of the general register into the accumulator, rotate the specified bit into the link, perform the indicated bit operation, restore the bit to its original position, and then move the result back to the specified general register.   By using primitive microorders, no special hardware is required to decode and identify the prescribed bit associated with the macroinstruction. The problem of rotating the accumulator by the proper number of positions so that the selected bit will always end up in the L bit can be done by a table structure, as shown in Figure 2-27.   For this example, assume that the following macroinstruction is to be implemented:

$$Zn\,\text{R}1 \qquad \text{\# zero bit } n \text{ of general register R}1^{*}$$

Also, assume that R1 has already been moved into the accumulator; consider the procedure for rotating the accumulator $n + 1$ bit positions to the right so that the nth bit will be rotated into the L bit.   If R1 is a 16-bit register, a table of 16 words will be needed for rotating the accumulator from 1 to 16 bit positions to the right.   For this example, the values n may assume will range from 0 to 15.   If a functional branch field is used, the current microinstructions will *point* the address of the next microinstruction to the starting address of a *rotation table* stored in control memory.   The parameter n will be used as an index into the rotation table.   For instance, a shift of n bit positions will direct the microcontrol sequence to enter the rotation table n microstore locations from the starting address of the rotation table.

---

* The notation "#" will be used to represent a comment and *not* a string of characters associated with a microinstruction.

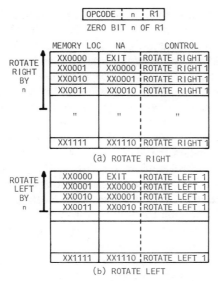

ZERO BIT n OF R1

(a) ROTATE RIGHT

(b) ROTATE LEFT

Figure 2-27 Rotation Table

The index is generated by gating the value *n* into the CSAR concurrently with the next address field. The next address field in each succeeding microinstruction will advance execution to the next consecutive location in the rotation table; each new microinstruction will rotate the AC one additional bit position to the right. When the last microinstruction has been executed, the *n*th bit of the AC will have been moved into the link bit (L); the link bit will then be cleared by a separate microinstruction. To restore the data in the AC back to its original bit configuration, a second table can be used to perform the ROTATE LEFT operation on the accumulator. The table is entered using a functional branch microinstruction. The second table is identical to the right rotation table except that each microinstruction rotates the AC one bit position to the left rather than to the right. The data is restored to its original bit positions in the AC with the selected bit cleared to the 0 state.

This example illustrates mainly how a functional branch microinstruction can be used to index into a special function table. By simple inspection of either rotation table it appears that many microinstructions are required to replace a relatively simple decoder that can perform the same operation.

2.7 MICROSUBROUTINE

The number of microinstruction words used in interpreting one macroinstruction may not be a good trade-off for the elimination of a relatively small amount of hardware. This was illustrated in the previous discussion covering the usage of a table of microinstructions used to rotate the AC. However, if there are several macroinstructions that can be implemented by sharing the same microinstruction tables, the cost of each of the shared tables may be spread over several macroinstructions rather than having one macroinstruction bear the total hardware cost. For example, other macroinstructions such as setting, complementing, or testing bit n of a general register can use the previously discussed rotation tables to move a specified bit into the link bit. Any microinstruction in the microinterpretation sequence of one of these macroinstructions can enter the rotation table directly by a branch operation. However, when the microprogram sequence in the rotation table has been concluded, control must be directed to the proper microinstruction sequence to implement any operations unique to the macroinstruction being interpreted. In particular, such operations as clearing the link bit for one operation and complementing the link bit for another each need to be implemented by separate microinstructions. For example, Figure 2-28 shows three macroinstructions (A, B, and C) sharing a common microprogram sequence (T). At the completion of microroutine T, the microcontrol sequence must return to the correct macroinstruction since each macroinstruction contains a unique microcontrol sequence. The problem in sharing a common microroutine between two or more microprogram sequences is how control is returned to the original microsequence.

An additional hardware register is normally used to temporarily store

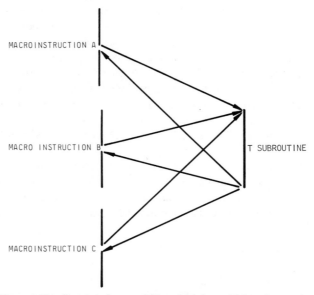

MACROINSTRUCTION A

MACRO INSTRUCTION B   T SUBROUTINE

MACROINSTRUCTION C

Figure 2-28   Common Sequence Shared by Several Macroinstructions

the next microprogram address prior to microcontrol being directed to branch to the common microsequence. Figure 2-29 illustrates the usage of a 2-bit address mode field in conjunction with the current microinstruction that controls the sequencing of addresses in the CSAR. There are four possible combinations of the two bits that form this field. The 00 state dictates normal address sequencing in which the next address field of the current microinstruction is gated into the CSAR as the address of the next microinstruction. The 10 state indicates that the same function as that performed in the 00 state is to be executed and, in addition, that the return address in the original or "calling" microprogram is to be saved in a hardware register specifically *reserved* for this type of microcontrol operation—the *return address register* (RAR). The assembly language programmer has no means of access to the RAR—it is transparent to any machine language instruction. This return address is normally chosen to be the next sequential address in the calling microprogram sequence. For ease of implementation, the address prior to the common routine is an even address. The return address is generated in a very simple manner; the address of the current microinstruction is gated from the CSAR into the RAR, and the least-significant bit in the RAR is set to the 1s state. This is an addressing technique, which is similar to the approach used to handle the generation of the address for the next microinstruction when the current microinstruction represents a conditional branch operation. The microcontrol sequence returns from the microsubroutine by branching to the address saved in the RAR. One of the four addressing modes specified by the 2-bit address mode field in the microinstruction can be used for this purpose. As indicated in Figure 2-30, the 01 state provides the control signal to gate the RAR into the CSAR as the next microprogram address. Since the next address field is not used for sequencing, a unique bit pattern such as the all-1s code can be used to specify that the microcontrol sequence is to be a return to a calling microprogram from a microinstruction subroutine. This approach may be taken instead of using one of the bit combinations in an address mode field of the microinstruction. In this case,

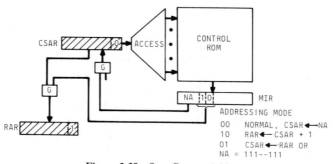

Figure 2-29 Save Return Address

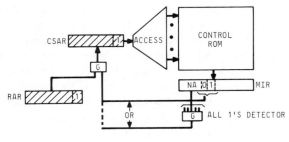

RETURN FROM SUBROUTINE
Figure 2-30   Microsubroutine

a hardware decision element, called an all-1s detector, is needed to recognize the special code in the next address field.   When the all-1s code is detected, a logic signal is generated which gates the contents of the RAR into the CSAR.   The choice of which implementation to use depends on whether the microcontrol designer feels that the bits in a microinstruction dedicated to an address mode field could be better used for one or more other microcontrol operations.

This simple one-level subroutine capability used at the microprogram level has been discussed mainly for the purpose of illustrating how a common microinstruction routine may be shared among several control sequences. The purpose of using a microinstruction routine is to save microprogram instruction words.   If a pushdown stack is provided instead of the RAR, microinstruction subroutines can be *nested,* as is done at the main program level of control.

2.8   ALTERNATE INDIRECT CONTROL

The opcode of a macroinstruction sometimes indicates that a variety of macro-level machine operations is to be performed.   The exact mechanism of how the macroinstruction is to be implemented in terms of microcode is specified by the contents of the operand fields.   A macroinstruction opcode may be assigned to cover many simple control functions such as clearing, setting, or complementing the link bit, disabling and enabling interrupts, etc.   To implement specific individual macrocontrol functions, several techniques can be employed.   One technique, the functional branch microinstruction, is performed by having the microcontrol gate the operand field directly into a microprogram store address register as part of the next address (a variation of this technique was discussed in the previous section).   This approach is quite satisfactory when the number of bits in the operand field is relatively small and the microorders to perform the functions already exist at the microinstruction level.   However, if the operand field is large, a considerable number of microinstruction words may have to be executed merely to perform a single macrocontrol operation. In this situation, it may be advantageous to use a separate decoder, as shown in Figure 2-31. The use of a separate decoder assists in keeping the microprogram store within a reasonable size. A microorder from one of the control fields enables the separate decoder so that the macrocontrol operation specified by the operand field in the main instruction sequence may be executed.

When the operand field specifies control functions that have already been incorporated as microorders within a microinstruction, a portion of the macroinstruction decoder replicates part of the decoder associated with the decoding of the microinstruction. This situation is illustrated in Figure 2-31. If this is the case, two signals, one from each decoder, either fan out separately to the same control point or are combined logically before a single signal lead is connected to the appropriate control point. This particular implementation requires additional logic circuitry, which makes the control interconnections more complex. An alternate solution would be to have the macroinstruction operand field and the microinstruction share the same decoder. This is done by using *multiplexers* (MPXs) to select one of the three possible input sources for decoding (see Figure 2-32). Instead of the

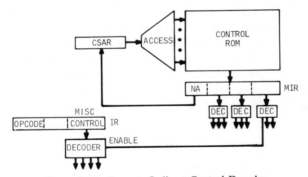

Figure 2-31   Separate Indirect Control Decoder

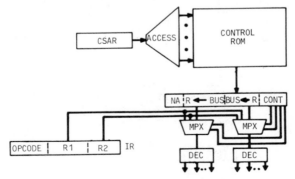

Figure 2-32   Share Common Decoders

control logic enabling a separate decoder associated with the macroinstruction register (IR), a *control field* (CONT) directs the operand to the appropriate decoder.

2.9 EMIT (DATA) FIELD

The primary function of the microprogram store is to provide control and sequencing information; the use of a data field as part of a microinstruction facilitates the implementation of these operations. A variety of control actions specified at the macroinstruction level requires data to be stored in the micro-program memory. For instance, information may be needed to direct address-ing of the main memory, or interrupt masking information may be needed to prevent low-priority interrupts from interfering with higher-priority inter-rupts. In addition, arithmetic and logical operations can be specified through the use of a function field and the control information routed to the ALU to select a particular ALU function. This function field can also be treated as a data field of the current microinstruction.

The microinstruction data field can vary in size according to the format-ting convention used with the microinstruction. As shown in Figure 2-33, the data field can be placed in one of several different bit groupings within the microinstruction. If a data word is relatively small and used quite fre-quently by a microinstruction sequence, a separate field within the microin-struction may be allocated specifically for interpretation as a data element with no microcontrol actions associated with the contents of the field. This approach increases the size of the microinstruction word since any microcon-

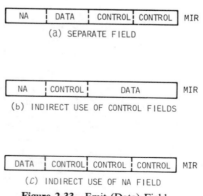

USE – TO DEFINE FUNCTIONS IN ALU AS CONSTANTS
FOR MASK, ADDRESS, & DATA

| NA | DATA | CONTROL | CONTROL | MIR |

(a) SEPARATE FIELD

| NA | CONTROL | DATA | MIR |

(b) INDIRECT USE OF CONTROL FIELDS

| DATA | CONTROL | CONTROL | CONTROL | MIR |

(*C*) INDIRECT USE OF NA FIELD

Figure 2-33   Emit (Data) Field

trol information must be placed in a separate field. Consequently, if the data field and the control field can share the same bit group in the microinstruction, the size of the microinstruction can be reduced. When such bits are used as data, the control functions associated with them are disabled or ignored. When the bit group is used to specify control functions, the data aspects of the bits are ignored. A separate bit in the microinstruction can be assigned to specify whether the common bit group is to be used as control information or as data. Using this arrangement, the bit group is optimally utilized. Similarly, if the microinstruction contains a next address field, the next address field can also serve as a data source for a variety of microoperations. Again, some means must be provided to specify whether the next address field is to be gated into the CSAR as addressing information or whether it is to be directed somewhere else as data. If it is to be used as data, the address of the next microinstruction must be the next control store location in the current microprogram sequence.

In the ALU, standard MSI circuits that are quite flexible in implementing both arithmetic and logic operations involving two variables may be used. To provide a static control signal for the ALU, a function register within the ALU is provided to store the function specified in the current microinstruction. The contents of the function register are decoded to generate the appropriate control signal for the ALU (i.e., SHIFT, ROTATE, AND, . . .). Figure 2-34 shows the use of the next address field as data for the function register in the ALU. A special direct control bit can be assigned

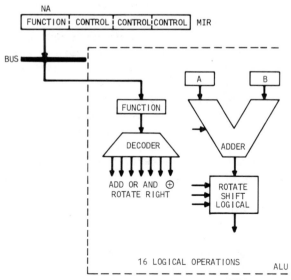

Figure 2-34 Use of Emit Field to Load Function Register in ALU

in the current microinstruction, which will cause the microcontrol logic to increment the next microprogram address by setting the least-significant bit to 1 if the current address is chosen to be an even number.   The remaining control fields of the microinstruction that remain unchanged can be used to direct the contents of the next address field onto the data bus and then gate the resulting data word into the ALU function register.

2.10   MICROPROGRAM ACCESS
BY INTERRUPT

In general, interrupt facilities are provided in a digital machine to handle I/O requests and other internally or externally initiated events that require the immediate attention of the processor.   By convention, the handling of an interrupt requires the processor to stop the current main program sequence and service the interrupt request.   For the interrupt to be transparent to the interrupt program (that is, have no effect on the main program executing in the processor prior to the occurrence of the interrupt), the current machine state must be stored in memory.   Upon completion of the interrupt service routine, the former state of the processor must be restored so that the interrupted program can continue execution from the point of interruption.

To the executing program, it appears that a short period of time has been taken away from its execution sequence while the interrupt is in service. It is critical to the effective execution of a program that an interrupt be allowed to intrude in the normal program sequence at times that make the transfer of control from the interrupted program to the interrupt service routine as graceful as possible.   The timing of the recognition of an interrupt request is particularly sensitive when a microprogrammed control arrangement is employed.   The remainder of this section will deal with the techniques for accessing the control store where an interrupt request has been recognized by the processor.   Each macroinstruction is basically interpreted by an independent microprogram sequence.   There is no data at the microprogram level that must be passed from one macroinstruction interpretation sequence to another interpretation sequence.   The most appropriate time to handle an interrupt would be at the *end* of a macroinstruction interpretation sequence. Figure 2-35 shows an interrupt structure and a mechanism for accessing the microprogram store to handle an interrupt request.   The states of the request lines from the interrupt sources are temporarily stored in a special register called the *request interrupt* (RI) *register.* Interrupt requests may be made to the processor at different priority levels.   For each priority request level that is represented by a dedicated bit in the RI register, a corresponding bit in the *mask interrupt* (MI) *register* is provided to enable or disable the individual interrupt requests from interrupting the current main program execution sequence.   By appropriately setting the bits in the MI register, a

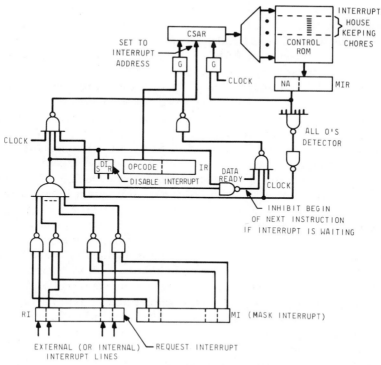

Figure 2-35 Interrupt Begin Sequence

structure to handle priority interrupt requests can be established. For example, interrupt requests that are of a lower priority than the current request being serviced are disabled by setting the corresponding bit in the **MI** register while higher-priority requests are left enabled. This procedure, which is called *nesting,* permits higher-priority interrupts to be serviced so that the more important tasks associated with the system can be done on a preassigned priority arrangement. For each interrupt level there is a unique mask that can be stored as data in the microprogram store. As shown in Figure 2-35, the interrupt request bits are logically ANDed with the corresponding mask bits. If an interrupt request is generated and the corresponding mask bit is not set, a signal is generated to indicate that an interrupt is pending (waiting to be serviced). Since many of the control operations associated with the servicing of an interrupt request are the same for all interrupts, a single microprogram sequence may be used to perform the initial servicing of *all* interrupt requests.

Consequently, when the last microinstruction in the current microprogram sequence is executed, the next address field will contain all 0s. If an interrupt request is pending, the normal sequence of gating the opcode of the new macroinstruction into the CSAR to begin a new microprogram interpretation sequence will be suspended. Instead, the all-0s detector gate shown in Figure 2-35 will cause the CSAR to be set to a unique address in control storage. This is the starting address of the microprogram routine that handles interrupt identification and servicing. It is possible that several interrupt requests at different priority levels may be waiting to be serviced concurrently. Since the processor can only service the highest-priority device which requested an interrupt at any time, the microprogram interrupt service routine will examine the contents of the MI and IR registers to determine the highest-priority interrupting device. Upon identifying this device, the microprogram service routine will branch to another microprogram which handles the specific device. The primary function of the microprogram interrupt service routine is to save the state of the processor after an interrupt request has been recognized so that control may be returned to the interrupt macroinstruction program at the conclusion of the interrupt service program. In particular, the *disable interrupt* (DI) *flip-flop* shown in Figure 2-35 must be set to prevent further interrupt requests from interfering with the processor until the initial interrupt housekeeping chores have been completed.

The amount of circuitry involved in gaining access to the microprogram store on the recognition of an interrupt request by the processor is small. Microcontrol is directed to a predetermined location in control store between macroinstruction interpretation sequences. A single entry point into a common microprogram interrupt service module may be satisfactory for many applications that have identical interrupt servicing requirements. In some instances, several different entry points into the microprogram store may be necessary for a multiple-priority interrupt environment in which the interrupt servicing requirements are different at each priority level. As an example, consider how the function of *direct memory access* (DMA) is handled when a microprogram sequence is used to control the operation of transferring data directly between memory and an I/O device. In the DMA operation, none of the processor hardware is used; therefore, the sequence of saving the internal state of the machine is not necessary. A DMA interrupt may be used to direct the microcontrol sequence to the appropriate microprogram for handling the individual data transfers.

When there is more than one address entry point into the microprogram store, additional hardware logic is required to determine which interrupt should be given priority in gaining access to the control store when two or more interrupt requests occur simultaneously. In Figure 2-36, the interrupt corresponding to the DMA operation is set apart from the other interrupts and assigned a higher priority. Consequently, should multiple interrupt requests occur at the same time, the interrupt associated with the DMA operation will be selected. Although Figure 2-36 shows only two priority levels

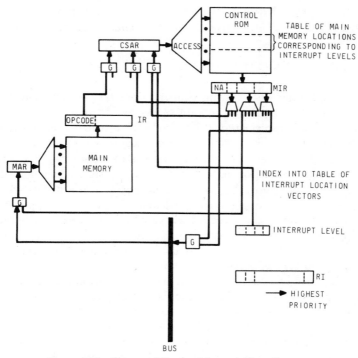

Figure 2-38 Interrupt Micro-to-Macro Address Sequence

stored in main memory, then, prior to completion of the common interrupt service microprogram, the microcontrol sequence must derive the starting address of the interrupt service program in main storage. By convention, the last microinstruction in the common interrupt service microprogram has the entry address of the device-related interrupt service program stored in the next address field of the microinstruction as data. This data may then be moved into the program counter associated with main storage and a macroinstruction service program executed from that point. It is also possible that the interrupt service routine may be entirely implemented as a microprogrammed sequence without transferring control to a macroinstruction execution sequence. A practical example of this approach might be the use of a processor control panel to allow a person-to-machine interface by means of manual switches on the control panel. In addition, a group of display lamps on the control panel could be used to exhibit the actual state of the processor. The selection of a control panel switch would cause a processor interrupt; the common interrupt service microprogram would then interrogate the switch settings to determine which specific operation was requested from the control panel. The entire operation of recognizing the interrupt, identifying which switch was depressed on the control panel, and performing the associated processor function may be done by a single microprogram sequence.

2.11   REPETITIVE MICROINSTRUCTION

In certain applications, several microinstructions frequently occur together, as a group, in the same microprogram sequence.   If these microinstructions are combined and implemented as a single microinstruction, not only are microprogram store words saved, but the execution time of the processor is enhanced.   One such example would be a microprogram sequence for finding the rightmost 1, or rightmost 0, in a register.   The microcontrol sequence could, then, save the associated bit position in a dedicated storage location.   This type of operation is used quite frequently in applications in which a large number of devices are allocated and released continuously to a common resource pool for system use.   In a telephone switching office there are many interconnecting lines (trunks) that run between local switching exchanges called *central offices*. It is often necessary to interconnect subscribers' lines between two central offices by having the switching exchange select a trunk that is not in use.   In a modern electronic switching facility, a central processor keeps track of all trunks; the information as to their usage (busy, idle, etc.) is recorded in main memory.   Each trunk is assigned a unique bit position in a specific word in main storage.   This bit defines the status of the trunk.   When a trunk is needed, the call processing program examines the trunk status words and selects a trunk that is in the idle condition (that is, a trunk that is not being used by any active call).   An idle trunk

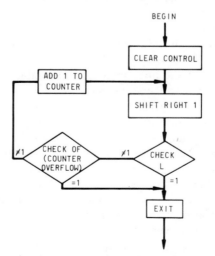

Figure 2-39   Flow Diagram First "1" Detection

circuit is uniquely identified by the address of the status word in main storage that contains the first idle trunk. The idle state can be chosen to be either a logical 1 or a logical 0. For example, let us assume that a 1s state indicates that a trunk is in the idle condition and that a 0s state indicates that the trunk is either in use or busy. A microprogram that examines each trunk status word on a bit-by-bit basis can be quite time-consuming. Each bit must be rotated right into the least-significant bit position of a register (such as an accumulator), and this least-significant bit must be tested until a 1 is found. For each rotation, a count is kept of the bit position being examined. If all the bits in the trunk status words have been examined and a 1 could not be found, the microsequence must be terminated. The operation remains in a microprogram loop until all trunk status words have been tested, as shown in Figure 2-39. This same sequence is similar to determining the highest-priority interrupt that has requested service.

The hardware implementation of the microcontrol sequence shown in Figure 2-40 can best be done by placing the entire sequence into a single microinstruction. The microinstruction will be executed repeatedly until either the first idle trunk is located or all trunk status words have been examined. Figure 2-40 shows the microcontrol logic that performs the closed-loop repetitive execution of the microinstruction. For simplicity, only those

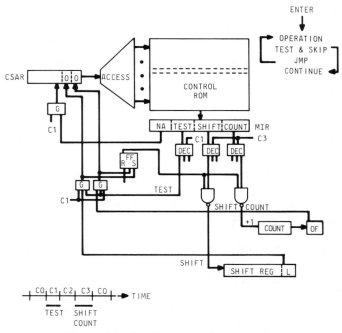

Figure 2-40 Close Loop Repetitive Operation

parts directly involved with the microinstruction implementation are shown. The microinstruction consists of three control fields. The first field specifies that the counter (COUNT) is to be incremented by 1. The second field specifies that the data word in the shift register is to be rotated right one bit position. The third field directs the microcontrol logic to test the counter (COUNT) overflow (OF) bit and the least-significant bit of the shift register. Assume that the microexecution cycle is divided into four clock intervals (shown as C0 through C3 in Figure 2-40). At the beginning of each new execution of the microinstruction, the two bits (OF and L) are gated as part of the next address into the CSAR. The next address field contains the address of the current microinstruction. This address has been arranged to have zeros in its two least-significant bit positions. The counter (COUNT) contains the binary representation of the bit position of the bit moved into the L bit. If either the OF bit or the L bit is a 0, the current microinstruction is executed again. If one of these two bits is a 1, the microcontrol sequence would end the repeated execution of the current microinstruction. The microexecution sequence would branch to one of two locations in the control store, depending on whether bit 0 or bit 1 of the CSAR is set to a 1. If the OF bit was a 1, bit 0 of the CSAR will be set; if the L bit was a 1, bit 1 of the CSAR will be set. Both the OF bit and the L bit *cannot* both be 1 at the same time. The counting and rotation functions are inhibited to preserve the information about which bit has been selected. The microcontrol logic may then change the state of the selected bit to a 0, to indicate that its associated trunk has been placed in the busy state. The bit may then be rotated back to its original bit position in the trunk status word to update the status information in that word. If an idle trunk is not found, the microcontrol sequence does *not* need to restore the original word since all 0s remain in the trunk status word. The amount of logic required to implement the repetitive execution of this microinstruction is quite small, and the gain in machine performance is considerable.

2.12 MICROPROGRAM SEQUENCE STRUCTURE

The following basic control functions must be performed for each macroinstruction that is interpreted by a microprogram sequence:

1. Fetch the macroinstruction from main storage
2. Decode the macroinstruction
3. Fetch the operand(s) identified in the macroinstruction from main storage
4. Execute the macroinstruction

Thus far, this discussion has been mainly concerned with implementing the more elementary control operations of the processor (such as microorder formats, branching operations at the microinstruction level, etc.). It has been assumed that by using the macroinstruction opcode as the starting address of a sequence of microinstructions, a microprogram can be accessed in control store which carries out the function(s) specified by the macroinstruction. By implication, the macrocontrol sequence has included fetching the next macroinstruction. This means that the four basic control operations must be performed within the interpretation sequence associated with each macroinstruction. Some microcontrol operations, such as address modification and fetching an operand from main storage, are common among several microprogram sequences. It is advantageous to share these common microinstruction sequences so that the common microcode is *not* replicated in each microprogram. This procedure tends to keep the microprogram memory as small as possible. This sharing can be done by means of a subroutine facility implemented at the microinstruction level. There are other techniques of implementation that also accomplish the same result, and they will be the topic of the following discussion.

Figure 2-41 shows the general flow of microcontrol operations required to sequence from one microinstruction to another. There is one microprogram sequence that is common to the control of all macroinstructions, and that is the operation for fetching the next macroinstruction from main storage. In conventional logic design, a special control flip-flop, called the *end-of-instruction* (EOI) *bit,* is set during the last cycle of the currently executing macroinstruction. The output of the EOI flip-flop is combined with the appropriate clock signals to generate the control operations associated with

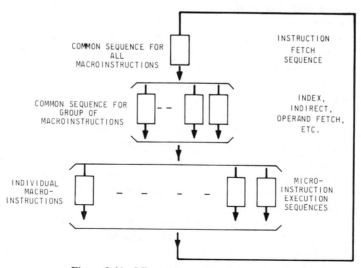

Figure 2-41   Microprogram Sequence Structure

fetching the next macroinstruction from main storage. These control operations are as follows:

1. The contents of the *program counter* (PC) are used to reference main storage.
2. The data in the referenced location is placed in the *memory data register* (MDR).
3. The MDR contents are then gated into the macroinstruction register (IR), where the microinstruction is to be decoded.
4. The PC is incremented by 1 to point to the next macroinstruction in the main program sequence.

A microprogram is required to perform the same sequence of control operations when a new microinstruction is fetched from control store. It is wasteful not to use the same sequence for all instructions.

In the execution of the various macroinstructions associated with a given machine, there are certain general classes of macroinstructions (i.e., register-to-register, register-to-storage, storage-to-register, storage-to-storage, etc.) which have common microcontrol sequences. These microcontrol sequences may be shared among the microprograms that interpret the various macroinstruction classes. Typically, address calculations may be placed in a common microroutine. In addition, special combinations of addressing modes may be placed in common microinstruction sequences. These address mode combinations can include indexing, indirection, and base register addressing.

The individual interpretation sequence for each macroinstruction forms the major portion of the macroinstruction sequence. The microprograms that implement the macroinstruction set consist of several levels of microinstruction sequences. Figure 2-41 illustrates such a microcontrol structure. The first microcontrol level consists of a common microinstruction routine that fetches the next macroinstruction; the second level consists of microinstruction routines that are common to *groups* of macroinstructions; the last level is made up of separate microroutines that are each associated *solely* with an individual macroinstruction.

The organization of a microprogram structure into several levels of microroutines requires that a procedure be established for microcontrol to exit from a microroutine at one level and gracefully enter a microroutine at the next level. The mechanism or technique of transferring from one sequence to another depends very much on the system structure. For instance, not all macroinstruction interpretation routines must use a common sequence from the second level of microcontrol. The implementation may employ either hardwired logic or firmware to perform the transfer from one microinstruction sequence to another. The exact design choice is intimately tied in with the addressing scheme of the microprogram control and the microorder structure.

2.12.1 Microprogram Sequence Transfer by Hardware

The transition from one sequence of microinstructions to another requires that the control logic make a choice of one microroutine from several possible alternatives. The decision mechanism for branching at the microinstruction level can be implemented in several different ways. One implementation, which is shown in Figure 2-42, uses a phase counter and a special control bit located in the microprogram memory. The phase counter is only two bits wide. It indicates the level on which the current microprogram sequence is being executed. At the end of a microcontrol sequence, a special control signal called the *end-of-sequence* (EOS) *signal* is generated as part of the last microinstruction. The EOS signal signifies that a particular control sequence is completed. The EOS signal, in combination with the state of the phase counter, determines the next level of the microprogram sequence that will be entered by the microcontrol logic. In effect, the phase counter acts as a 2-bit execution sequence pointer that selects the current level of

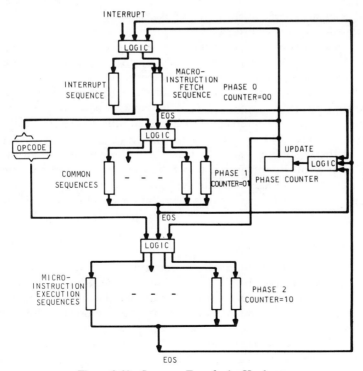

Figure 2-42 Sequence Transfer by Hardware

microcontrol. The EOS signal is used to advance the execution sequence to the next level and to update the phase counter by adding 1 to its contents.

2.12.2 First Level

When control is transferred from one level of microcontrol to another, an address must be generated in the current microprogram. This address corresponds to the entry address of the next microroutine. At the first level of microcontrol, the instruction fetch sequence is common for the execution of *all* macroinstructions. The instruction fetch sequence is entered from the level 3 microcontrol sequence (phase counter = 10). The occurrence of the EOS signal while microcontrol is executing in the level 3 instruction sequence causes the entry address of the microroutine for the instruction fetch sequence to be jam-set into the microinstruction counter (μIC). It is possible during the execution of any macroinstruction that an interrupt request may be made to the processor. Since a macroinstruction is being interpreted by a microinstruction routine, the best time for the processor to handle the interrupt request is after the execution of the current macroinstruction is completed. The microroutine that implements the macroinstruction fetch sequence may also perform the function of checking for an interrupt request. If an interrupt request is present, a branch to the microroutine that handles interrupt identification and servicing will be generated. The actual branch decision logic may be performed entirely by the hardware. In this case, the hardware automatically generates the entry address of a microroutine that corresponds to either the macroinstruction fetch control sequence *or* the interrupt service sequence. The actual control store address generated depends on whether an interrupt is pending (waiting to be serviced) by the processor. Figure 2-42 shows the interrupt decision logic as occurring at the top of the execution sequence structure. The presence of an interrupt inhibits microcontrol from being transferred to the macroinstruction fetch microroutine and initiates the interrupt service microprogram. The next macroinstruction will be fetched into the IR at the conclusion of the interrupt service microroutine.

2.12.3 Second Level

Once the macroinstruction fetch microroutine has been completed, the macroinstruction is available for processing and execution. The entry into the second-level microcontrol sequence may also be initiated by the EOS microorder from the last microinstruction in the macroinstruction fetch microroutine. The phase counter directs the present EOS signal to initiate the second-level microcontrol sequence. At this point, a decision must be made as to exactly what procedure should be used to derive the entry address into the second-level control sequence. Two possible methods may be employed: either the microcontrol sequence will algorithmically generate the entry address, or the hardware will automatically resolve the entry address into the appropriate sequence using the high-order bits of the macroinstruction opcode and one, or more, of the mode bits specified in the macroinstruction.

In the first case, the microprogram sequence examines the macroinstruction and branches to the proper routine. A simple example involving either index addressing or address indirection used in conjunction with the current macroinstruction is illustrated in Figure 2-43(a). In this case the EOS signal and the state of the phase counter (00) cause the hardware to generate a unique entry address in control store which corresponds to the beginning of the second-level microprogram sequence. The microcontrol sequence proceeds to examine the index bit of the macroinstruction. If indexing is indicated, the microcontrol sequence performs a branch to the microsubroutine that performs the index operation in an effective address calculation for main

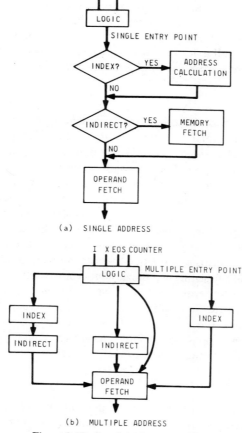

(a) SINGLE ADDRESS

(b) MULTIPLE ADDRESS

Figure 2-43 Level Address Generation

storage. If the index bit is not set, the microcontrol sequence next examines the indirect bit in the macroinstruction and takes the appropriate action. This microcontrol process is done entirely as a *serial* operation in which individual bits in the macroinstruction are interrogated one at a time. The associated set of machine functions is executed sequentially. Because each option bit (mode bit) must be sequentially interrogated by the control microprogram, a separate *test-and-branch* microinstruction must be executed. Such test-and-branch microinstructions can increase the execution time of a microprogram sequence significantly.

The sequence of testing individually each option bit appearing in the microinstruction by a microprogram represents a *real-time overhead* (i.e., it degrades the execution time of a macroinstruction because of the additional microinstructions that must be executed). This overhead can be eliminated by using control logic implemented as a pure hardware structure. The control logic explicitly decodes four distinct operand addressing sequences, as shown in Figure 2-43(b). A separate entry address into control store is used for each addressing sequence. The states of the option bits (I and X) are used to generate the appropriate entry address. In transferring control from level 0 to level 1 in the overall macroinstruction sequence, the specific microcontrol sequence is completely specified by the hardware.

2.12.4   Third Level

The third level contains those execution sequences that are *unique* to the interpretation of individual macroinstructions. Since there can be a large number of macroinstructions in the instruction set of a small computer, it can be quite time-consuming to use firmware to decipher the different possible macroinstruction execution sequences. A hardware mapper is often used to select the proper entry point into a specific microinstruction interpretation sequence. The hardware address mapper translates the macroinstruction opcode into a binary address located in control store. The mapper can be implemented either by using combinational logic or through the use of a small ROM that performs the opcode-to-entry address translation. At the end of every execution sequence, the last microinstruction in the sequence contains the EOS microorder that terminates the current microcontrol sequence and initiates the next phase of the macroinstruction execution sequence. In this case, the microcontrol sequence always cycles back to the macroinstruction fetch phase. The entire process is then repeated to provide a continuous stream of macroinstructions.

2.12.5   Second-Level Bypass

There are always some exceptions to the general flow of the microprogram sequences that were previously outlined. Such exceptions are dictated by the particular macroinstruction being interpreted. This is particularly true of the second level of execution, where various microroutines are shared by groups of macroinstructions. In certain cases, several of the macroinstructions may have *no* control features in common. In these cases, it is usually best for these macroinstruction execution sequences to bypass the second control level, which makes use of common microroutines. For example, the register-to-register class of macroinstructions does not need to perform any address modification to locate the necessary operand. The implementation of the microcontrol sequence for such macroinstructions is facilitated by designing the microprogram to skip the second control level, as shown in Figure 2-44. The hardware generates a signal that enables the address mapper associated with the macroinstruction opcode instead of the normal path through the second level. The phase counter must be updated to the count of 10 instead of using the normal count of 01.

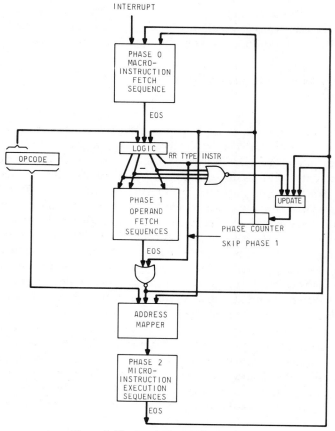

Figure 2-44 Level Skip Implementation

2.12.6 Replacement of Phase Counter by Microorders

The phase counter identifies the level in the execution sequence in which the EOS signal occurs. This permits the appropriate entry address in control store to be generated when the macroinstruction execution sequence transfers from one control level to another. The same result may be realized by assigning a unique EOS microorder for each level, such as EOS0 for the EOS signal occurring in level 0, EOS1 for the EOS signal occuring in level 1, etc. The occurrence of a particular EOS microorder indicates that the associated microprogram has ended and designates the control level within the microprogram at which the microorder was given. For example, EOS1 automatically enables the opcode mapper; EOS2 automatically enables either the macroinstruction fetch sequence or the interrupt service sequence. The trade-off to be considered in using a single EOS signal versus multiple EOS microorders is the additonal number of microorders that must be placed in control store versus the generation of a single EOS signal by the hardware. The speed of operation is essentially the same for both methods.

2.12.7 Microprogram Sequence Transfer by Firmware

The previous microprogram sequence that transfers control from one execution level to another can also be implemented entirely in firmware. Several approaches have been adopted which use the macroinstruction opcode to specify the entry address in control store to a microcontrol sequence that performs the functions indicated by the macroinstruction. The sequence transfer from one execution level to another can be done as a series of individual control operations (each executed one after the other); the sequence transfer can be done entirely as a parallel control operation in which *all* elementary control functions are performed concurrently. Alternatively, some combination of serial and parallel transfer of control may be used. The format of the macroinstruction, the procedure for referencing the next microinstruction in control memory, and the structure of the microprogram itself determine the *parallelism* of operation of the macroinstruction interpretation routine. This influences the cost of the hardware in terms of microprogram memory size and associated logic. As in any operation, the serial technique tends to be more time-consuming, but it requires less hardware. Which approach is used must be determined from a total system viewpoint. In the following discussion, the various techniques of transfering control from one microprogram sequence to another, using special firmware routines, will be considered.

2.12.8 Serial Transfer

As the microprogram sequence enters into the macroinstruction fetch phase, the sequence examines the interrupt status of the processor to determine if an interrupt has requested service. If an interrupt is pending, the microcontrol sequence will branch to an interrupt service routine located in control store; otherwise, the microcontrol sequence will proceed to fetch the next macroinstruction. Figure 2-45 illustrates the general arrangement of the microcontrol sequencing through a macroinstruction interpretation without the use of any additional control hardware (other than that associated with the control store). Although the macroinstruction interpretation sequence is functionally divided into three phases (phase 0, phase 1, and phase 2) or levels, the interpretation sequence is basically one continuous loop, with the microcode making all the control decisions.

Once the macroinstruction has been fetched from the main memory, the interpretation sequence begins its interpretation of the macroinstruction on a step-by-step basis. Each control operation is performed sequentially,

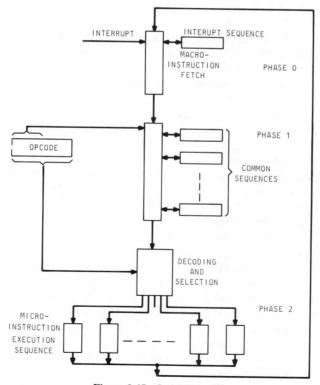

Figure 2-45   Serial Transfer

using a library of common microroutines. The interpretation sequence uses the bits of the opcode field in conjunction with the addressing mode bits to direct the serial execution of the required microcontrol operations.

A microinstruction branch operation is normally used to direct the interpretation sequence into the next execution level or microprogram sequence. When the transfer of control was performed entirely by hardware, the macroinstruction opcode was mapped into a unique entry address in control store for each macroinstruction. For the case shown in Figure 2-45, in which the decision as to which microsequence is to be branched to is determined by a sequence of individual elementary decisions, the address mapping is done by special firmware in control store. The firmware examines the contents of the opcode field and translates the contents into an entry address in control store which corresponds to the appropriate microcontrol sequence for interpreting the macroinstruction at that phase or level. When a macroinstruction opcode and the associated addressing mode bits are decoded as a serial sequence of individual elementary control decisions, a fair amount of real time can be consumed. An alternative approach which can reduce the use of real time considerably is the use of a branch table in control store. This branch table is entered as a function of the opcode of the macroinstruction and the addressing mode bits which are set. For even relatively small processors, the transfer of microcontrol based on the *serial* examination of each control bit in the macroinstruction is not a good practice in view of rapid advances in LSI technology.

2.12.9 Multilevel Sequence Transfer by Functional Branch

Any decision making operations that are performed by firmware usually require additional real time when compared with the same operations performed entirely by pure hardware. A functional branch operation permits the interpretation sequence to transfer from one execution level to another without employing a sequence of elementary decisions. Figure 2-46 illustrates the use of a functional branch facility to accomplish the selection of the appropriate microroutine for the next execution level.

The high-order bits of the macroinstruction opcode are used to form the least-significant portion of the entry address in control store. This, effectively, provides a hardware mechanism for branching the microcontrol sequence to the appropriate microprogram at that particular execution level or phase. To facilitate this hardware branching technique, the high-order bits of the opcode are organized to define groups of macroinstructions that use common microroutines. Such control sequences are concerned mainly with the calculation of the effective address for an operand named in the macroinstruction. Typically, three or four bits of the opcode are used; this

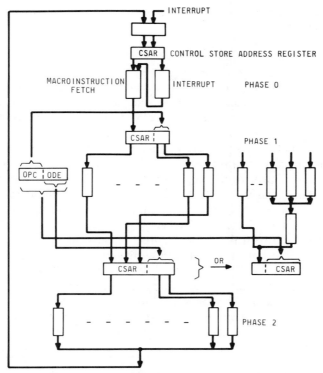

Figure 2-46   Direct Transfer by Functional Branch

provides a maximum of 16 possible entry points into control store for micro-control sequences that are common to a preassigned group of macroinstructions. The microcontrol overhead in performing this type of microcontrol sequence transfer is kept to a minimum.

When a functional branch approach is used, the transfer of microcontrol from one microroutine to another is done in a manner identical to the previous technique except that the remaining bits of the macroinstruction opcode are also used.   If the opcode is eight bits wide, there are a maximum of 256 possible macroinstructions that may be used and a corresponding 256 interpretation routines that may be placed in control store.   Assume that the four most-significant bits of the opcode are used to specify one of the 16 possible microcontrol sequences that may be shared among the macroinstruction interpretation sequences.   The four least-significant bits of the opcode are used to select one of the 256 possible macroinstruction control sequences in control store.   This requires that the entry address into control store from the second level of control *must* be unique for each of the 16 common microcontrol sequences.

2.12.10 Single-Level Sequence Transfer by Functional Branch

The microprogram control structures described, up to this point, have been functionally organized into three execution phases or levels for the purpose of sharing common microroutines between macroinstruction interpretation sequences. These sequential execution phases can be combined (as shown in Figure 2-47) into an arrangement of completely parallel microinstruction sequences. The full microinstruction opcode is used as an address pointer to a unique entry address in control store. Each individual macroinstruction has a unique microprogram assigned in control store. The opcode is used to vector microcontrol to the appropriate microinterpretation sequence for the current macroinstruction. In this arrangement, the common microcontrol sequences are *either* replicated in each macroinstruction interpretation routine, or the common microcontrol sequences are accessed by use of subroutine facilities associated with the control store. *No* attempt is made to separate the common microcontrol sequences into different execution phases. If the microcontrol sequence does not use a large number of microinstructions, and if only a few macroinstruction interpretation sequences employ it, replication of the microcode is the most straightforward implementation. If a large number of microinstructions are required, the shared microcontrol sequence should be implemented as a subroutine in control store.

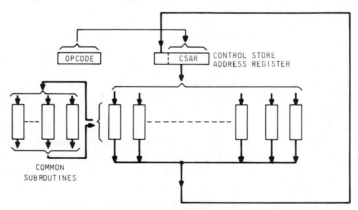

Figure 2-47 Complete Parallel Instruction Sequences

2.12.11 Factors Influencing the Type of Structure

Several types of microprogram sequencing structures have been described which make use of features of the macroinstruction set and allow the microcontrol sequences that interpret separate macroinstructions to share common microroutines. The technique used to derive the entry address in control store for each microcontrol sequence and the order structure of the individual microinstructions play an important part in determining the overall plan of implementing the sequencing structure. These considerations influence the size and cost of the microprogram memory and hence the cost and performance of the processor itself. A majority of microprogrammed small machines employ a microprogrammed counter to generate the address of the next microinstruction in control store. This approach, which generates microinstruction addresses sequentially, requires less bits in control store than the technique of using a next address field in each microinstruction. The reduction of the number of bits required for control storage reduces the cost of control storage and, consequently, the cost of the processor. Every decision is made by firmware, and the sequential nature of the microprogram structure is organized to keep the microprogram memory as small as possible.

The use of hardware logic to translate the system condition into a direct microprogram memory address eliminates the overhead of the firmware to perform the address translation. This is a compromise which provides a small amount of hardware to achieve a higher performance for macroinstruction interpretation and execution.

2.13 SUMMARY

The precise method of implementing the activation of the internal control points of a microprogrammed machine was discussed in this chapter. Such internal control points represent *enabling signals* at the hardware level of the processor. These signals permit data to be transferred from one register to another over preselected gating paths. In addition, the data may be modified arithmetically or logically as it is moved from one register to another. There may be several hundred of these internal control points in a typical processor. By appropriately controlling these points in a prescribed manner through the use of a microprogram, a particular machine operation may be realized. The microinstruction format and the encoding of control information in the microinstruction determine how many of the individual control points are activated at one time and how rapidly the microcontrol sequence is executed. The organization of the microinstruction may be largely *horizontal* (multiple control points may be activated in parallel) or largely *vertical* (one control point at a time is activated; a *new* microinstruction must be executed for each new control point that is activated). In most modern microprogrammed machines, a composite of these two formats is observed which produces a machine structure called a *diagonal* microarchitecture.

The second aspect of microprogram implementation discussed in this chapter is the technique that is employed to specify the address of the next microinstruction. Because of the low cost of control storage and the large number of bits that may be assigned to an individual microinstruction, it is economically feasible to have the current microinstruction carry the address of the next microinstruction along with it in control store. This allows each microinstruction to function as a potential branch operation, in addition to activating specific control points within the processor. Alternatively, control store addressing can make use of a microprogram counter in which the address of the next microinstruction is generated by adding 1 to the contents of the microprogram counter.

It is implicit in the usage of control storage that a microprogram sequence will be stored in *consecutive* control memory locations. When the microprogram deviates from its normal sequential execution sequence, a separate branch microinstruction *must* be executed to perform the JUMP operation in control storage. A *partial* next address field may be carried along with each microinstruction to obtain the advantage of a *short* JUMP (i.e., a branch relative to the location of the current microinstruction). The advantage of this procedure is that a full next address field does not have to be assigned to each microinstruction.

2.14 REFERENCES

1. A. K. AGRAWALA and T. G. RAUSCHER, *Foundations of Microprogramming: Architecture, Software, and Applications* (New York: Academic Press, 1975).

2. A. K. AGRAWALA and T. G. RAUSCHER, "Microprogramming: Perspective and Status," *IEEE Trans. Comput.,* C-23, No. 8 (Aug. 1974), 817–837.

3. L. D. AMDAHL, "Microprogram and Stored Logic," *Datamation, 10* (Feb. 1964), 24–26.

4. F. F. COURY, "Microprogramming and Writable Control Store," *Hewlett-Packard J.* (July 1972), 16–20.

5. P. M. DAVIS, "Readings in Microprogramming," *IBM Syst. J., 11,* No. 1 (1972), 16–40.

6. M. J. FLYNN, "Microprogramming Revisted," *Proc. Natl. Conf. ACM, 22* (Aug. 1967), 457–464.

7. S. H. FULLER, V. R. LESSER, C. G. BELL, and C. H. KAMAN, "The Effects of Emerging Technology and Emulation Requirements on Microprogramming," *IEEE Trans. Comput., C-25,* No. 10 (Oct. 1976), 1000–1009.

8. G. B. GERACE, "Microprogram Control for Computing Systems," *IRE Trans., EC-12* (1963), 733–747.

9. H. T. GLANTZ, "A Note on Microprogramming," *J. ACM,* No. 2 (March 1956), 77–84.

10. M. E. HOFF, JR., "Designing Central Processors with Bipolar Microcomputer Components," *AFIPS Conf. Proc., 44* (1975), 55–62.

11. S. S. HUSSON, *Microprogramming—Principles and Practices* (Englewood Cliffs, N.J.: Prentice-Hall, 1970).

12. L. H. JONES, "Instruction Sequencing in Microprogrammed Computers," *AFIPS Conf. Proc.,* *44* (1975), 91–98.

13. L. H. JONES, and R. E. MERWIN, "Trends in Microprogramming: A Second Reading," *IEEE Trans. Comput., C-23* (Aug. 1974), 754–759.

14. T. W. KEMPE, "The Design of a General-Purpose Microprogram-Controlled Computer with Elementary Structure," *IRETEC-9, 6* (June 1960), 208–213.

15. R. L. KLEIR and C. V. RAMAMOORTHY, "Optimization Strategies for Microprograms," *IEEE Trans. Comput., C-20* (July 1971), 783–791.

16. H. W. LAWSON, JR., and B. K. SMITH, "Functional Characteristics of a Multilingual Processor," *IEEE Trans. Comput., C-20,* No. 7 (July 1971), 732–742.

17. W. G. MATHESON, "User Microprogrammability in the HP-21M Minicomputer," *ACM Micro-7* (Aug. 1974), 168–177.

18. R. J. MERCER, "Microprogramming," *J. ACM, 4* (April 1957), 157–171.

19. *Microprogramming with the Eclipse Computer WCS Feature* (Westboro, Mass.: Data General Corporation, 1974).

20. J. A. OBERZEIR, "Writable Control Store Saves Microprogramming Time and Expense," *Electronics* (June 21, 1971), 121–125.

21. S. R. REDFIELD, "A Study in Microprogrammed Processors; A Medium Sized Microprogrammed Processor," *IEEE Trans., C-20* (1971), 743–750.

22. E. W. REIGEL, U. FABER, and D. A. FISHER, "The Interpreter—A Microprogrammable Building Block System," *AFIPS Conf. Proc., 40* (1972), 705–723.

23. R. F. ROSIN, "Contemporary Concepts of Microprogram and Emulation," *Comput. Surv., 1,* No. 4 (Dec. 1969), 197–202.

24. A. B. SALISBURY, *Microprogrammable Computer* (New York, Amsterdam: Elsevier, 1976).

25. N. SONDAK and E. MALLACH, *Microprogramming* (Artech House, Inc., 1977).

26. S. G. TUCKER, "Microprogram Control for System/360," *IBM Syst. J., 6,* No. 4 (1967), 222–241.

27. *2100 Computer—Microprogramming Guide* (Cupertino, Calif.: Hewlett-Packard, 1972).

28. M. V. WILKES, "The Best Way to Design an Automatic Calculating Machine," in *Report of the Manchester University Computer Inaugural Conference, July 1951* (Manchester, England, 1951), pp. 16–18.

29. M. V. WILKES, "Microprogramming," *Proc. EJCC* (Dec. 1958), 18–20.

30. M. V. WILKES, W. RENWICK, and D. J. WHEELER, "The Design of the Control Unit of an Electronic Digital Computer," *Proc. IEEE, 105* (1958), 121–128.

31. M. V. WILKES and J. B. STRINGER, "Microprogramming and the Design of the Control Circuits in an Electronic Digital Computer," *Proc. Cambridge Philos. Soc., 49* (1953), 230–238.

CHAPTER 3

Microprogram Control

of Main Storage

Operations

3.1 MAIN STORAGE CONTROL OPERATIONS

The throughput* of a computing system depends on a variety of factors. Among these are (1) the frequency of the processor clock, (2) the logic delays encountered by the CPU in executing various instructions, and (3) the technology used to implement main storage (i.e., whether core memories or semiconductor memories or both are employed to configure main storage). A factor that significantly influences processor performance is the maximum data transfer rate which can take place between main memory and the *central processing unit* (CPU). The data transfer rate is normally measured in words per second or megabits per second and is often referred to as the *bandwidth* of the memory bus. Because of the different technologies used to implement the CPU and its associated main storage unit, a substantial difference can exist between the cycle time of main storage and the response time of a series of

* *Throughput* is usually defined as *millions of instructions per second* (MIPS).

90

interconnected logic gates in the CPU. In many instances, the CPU must pause in its execution sequence and wait until an item has been fetched from main memory. This halt in execution affects the average rate at which instructions are executed and, consequently, the throughput of the system.

3.1.1 Core Memory Technology

Core memory technology has steadily improved throughout the 1960s and early 1970s in terms of decreasing cost and increasing performance. Core memory cycle times of less than 500 nanoseconds (ns) became a reality. However, the macroinstruction execution speed of the processor remained considerably *faster* than the cycle time of main memory. One means of enhancing the performance of systems using core memories was to supply a computing system with a *memory interleaving* capability. In memory interleaving, consecutive addresses are not assigned to sequential locations in the same memory module. Instead, consecutive addresses are distributed among the physical modules that make up main storage. For instance, two-way memory interleaving would assign odd addresses to one module and even addresses to the other module. Four-way interleaving would distribute the binary addresses as follows:

Module 0	Module 1	Module 2	Module 3
0000	0001	0010	0011
0100	0101	0110	0111
1000	1001	1010	1011
1100	1101	1110	1111

An approach such as memory interleaving attempts to optimize the information flow between the processor and main storage by maximizing the number of operations that may be performed concurrently while the processor is executing a macroinstruction. This allows the next macroinstruction and its successor to be fetched by the processor while the current macroinstruction is being executed.

3.1.2 Semiconductor Memories

The rapid evolution of LSI technology led to rapid advances in the implementation of semiconductor memories. A semiconductor memory offers a speed enhancement of from one-half to one-quarter the cycle time of a core memory. A semiconductor memory is more densely packaged and offers a higher system bandwidth for programs executed from such main memory modules. One type of semiconductor memory is the dynamic *random-access memory* (RAM) in which the information stored in the memory must be *periodically refreshed* to retain the data. When a memory operation is requested at the time of the refresh cycle, the request is put off until the refresh cycle has been completed. For a dynamic RAM, the memory response time will vary; it depends on when the CPU issued a request to perform a memory operation and the time relationship of that request to the refresh cycle of the memory. In general, to accommodate the wide variation in possible memory response times, the communication mechanism between the processor and main storage is designed to be an *asynchronous, handshaking operation.* Every signal sent by the processor to the memory controller requires that an acknowledgment signal be sent to the processor before another control step may be executed by the processor.

3.1.3 Memory Communication

A contention problem can arise between the CPU and a peripheral device that wishes to transfer a data word between a location in main storage and the peripheral without the CPU participating in the I/O transaction. Both the CPU and the peripheral device issue requests to a memory bus arbitrator for use of the memory bus during the next main memory cycle. In the event of a tie between the two bus requests, the peripheral device is normally given the bus. (It has the highest priority for an access of main storage.) Thus, the CPU halts for a memory cycle, and the peripheral engages in an I/O transaction with the main storage unit without the participation of the CPU. The peripheral appears to "steal" a memory cycle from the CPU, and for that reason such an I/O transaction is sometimes called a *cycle-stealing operation* or a *direct memory access* (DMA) *operation.* The arbitration process is repeated for the usage of the next memory cycle if the peripheral device has another DMA transaction to be performed.

Because the DMA operation normally shares the main store bus with the CPU, the DMA must be considered a major factor in establishing the control sequence between an I/O device and main storage. The communication between an I/O device or the CPU and main storage can take place either *synchronously* (i.e., the processor clock coordinates each control step in the transaction) or *asynchronously* (i.e., a request-response convention is observed by the control logic such that for every signal sent by the device controlling the memory bus, a reply must be returned by the unit with which the dialogue has been established). In the asynchronous case, no further control signals will be generated until the source controller has received the acknowledgment from the target device.

Communication takes place between main storage and the CPU or a DMA device via the memory bus. This communication makes use of three types of signal leads found in the memory bus: control leads, address leads, and data leads. The control leads are used to direct the specific operation to be performed by the main storage unit, such as a **READ** from main storage or a **WRITE** into main storage. The address leads specify the location in main memory that is to be referenced by the **CPU** or **DMA** device. The data leads act as a bidirectional pathway for data words to be read from or written into the location in main memory pointed to by the address leads.

3.2   SYNCHRONOUS DEDICATED MEMORY BUS

The most straightforward communication link that can be employed between main storage and the processor is a dedicated busing structure that uses a *synchronous* timing arrangement. The control and timing logic of the bus are simplified since they are placed under direct control of the processor. In the conventional logic design of a digital computer, the cycle time of main storage is used as the basic time interval of a machine execution cycle. Typically, the machine cycle is divided into a number of clock phases of equal width. These clock pulses are used by the control logic to generate whatever timing signals are needed by the processor. Figure 3-1 illustrates a typical timing sequence of main storage operations in which the processor cycle time has been taken to be equivalent to the cycle time of main storage. T0 through T4 are clock phases generated from the basic computer clock. These five clock phases occur sequentially within a memory cycle. The **READ** and **WRITE** operations associated with main storage always occur during the same clock phases. For example, a **READ** or a **WRITE** operation is always done during clock phases T1 through T3. The T4 interval is allocated for the memory circuits to recover fully before another memory

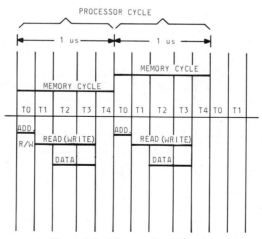

Figure 3-1   Memory Cycle Timing

operation can be initiated.   This synchronous timing relationship tightly couples the processor to main storage.   Because each timing pulse is clearly defined and each control signal is activated by these clock phases, the actual control logic will be much simpler than a design that incorporates an *asynchronous* timing arrangement.

3.2.1 Microprogram Timing

The synchronous timing scheme shown in Figure 3-1 can be extended to a microprogram control implementation of a main storage access.   The time intervals, T0 through T4, are no longer considered clock pulses but intervals during which a microinstruction is to be executed.   Each interval, T0 through T4, is further subdivided into several basic timing pulses that can be associated with the execution of a microinstruction.   Figure 3-2 shows a memory of 1 microsecond (μs) divided into five intervals of 200 ns each.   The 200-ns interval may be regarded as the basic machine cycle for this microprogram control implementation rather than the 1-μs interval used in the conventionally designed control unit.   The timing for a main storage operation is derived from the basic processor clock source; the necessary control signals are arranged to occur at the same 200-ns intervals as the conventionally designed control unit.   As in the case of conventional logic design, the READ and WRITE operations associated with main storage always occur during the intervals T1 through T3.   The address of the location to be referenced in main storage is presented to the memory control unit during T0; any additional control information required by the memory control unit such as the designation that a READ or WRITE operation is to be performed is also made

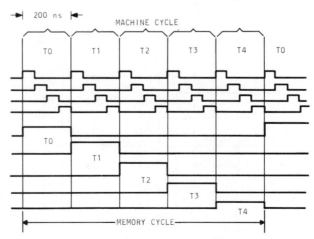

Figure 3-2   Microprogram Cycle Timing

available to the memory control unit during T0. On a memory READ operation, the contents of the location referenced in main storage is assumed to be available at the output of the memory control unit starting with interval T3. If a microinstruction specifying a READ of main storage is executed during T0, the microcontrol sequence may do one of two possible things:

1. The microcontrol sequence may execute a microinstruction during T1 and T2 that does not directly relate to the main storage read operation initiated during T0, or
2. The microcontrol sequence may execute a *no-operation* (NOP) microinstruction during T1 and T2 and wait during these time intervals for the output from main storage to become available at the start of T3.

3.2.2 Fixed Memory Timing Cycle

In processing a microinstruction, a set of clock pulses that occur every 200 ns are used. These timing pulses define the intervals T0 through T4 as shown in Figure 3-2. The timing associated with main storage operations synchronizes the generation of the 200-ns-wide pulses that represent the intervals T0, T1, T2, T3, and T4 to the fixed cycle time of main memory. This causes the microinstruction execution sequence to be kept in step with the timing of main storage. As an example, consider a microprogram in which a microinstruction that specifies a READ of main storage is to be executed during interval T2. The fixed timing sequence of a main memory access requires that the execution of the READ microinstruction be delayed until the start of interval T0. The microinstruction execution sequence must be arranged to pause during T3 and T4 so that a main memory operation begins during T0 as required by the fixed timing of the memory control unit. The equivalent of executing a pause in a sequence of microinstructions that involve accessing main storage may be achieved as follows:

1. The generation of the address for the next microinstruction is inhibited during T3 and T4.
2. The READ microinstruction is inhibited from being executed until the appearance of the T0 timing pulse.

This has the effect of repeating the disabled microinstruction until it is synchronized with the timing associated with a main storage access. Once the microinstruction sequence is in step with the timing of main memory, it can be kept in step if a READ or WRITE microinstruction is executed as a multiple of five 200-ns machine cycles.

If the microinstructions that initiate main memory operations do not occur during the T0 timing interval, the microprogram sequence will attempt to synchronize these microinstructions with the fixed timing of main storage access. The results of this situation are shown in Figure 3-3. It is possible

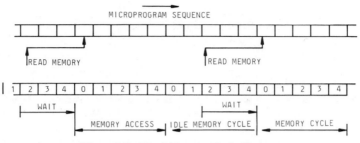

Figure 3-3   Fixed Memory Cycle Timing

for this lack of synchronization to result in idle main memory cycles and a longer execution time for the sequence of microinstructions. In most instances, the sequence of microinstructions which involve accesses of main storage can be arranged to coincide with the timing of a memory cycle. This permits the *maximum rate* of microinstruction executions to be closely approximated, but it requires that the microprogrammer be completely familiar with the timing requirements of main storage and the detailed functioning of each microinstruction.

3.2.3   Nonfixed Memory Timing Cycle

Figure 3-4 illustrates a scheme in which the access of main storage is not fixed to a set sequence of processor clock pulses. The execution of a READ or WRITE microinstruction automatically begins the timing sequence of a main memory operation. The execution of these microinstructions does not have to be deferred until timing interval T0 has occurred. In other words, the memory timing pulses, T0 through T4, are initiated with the execution of the READ or WRITE microinstructions. These timing intervals do *not* recur after the end of the current access of main storage until another READ (WRITE) microinstruction is executed. Consequently, a memory reference operation may be initiated by any microinstruction; the READ (WRITE) microinstruction does not have to be deferred until the T0 timing pulse has been generated. The basic restriction on this scheme is that two consecutive

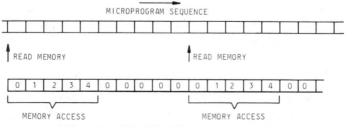

Figure 3-4   Non-Fixed Memory Cycle Timing

main storage operations cannot occur closer in time than the execution time required by five microinstructions or 1 μs since the first main storage operation must continue to completion before the second can be initiated. The nonfixed timing scheme will permit two consecutive READ (WRITE) microinstructions to be executed one right after the other with no time delay between the two memory reference operations. In the fixed memory timing scheme, the microcontrol logic automatically delays the execution of the second READ (WRITE) microinstruction until the occurrence of the next T0 timing interval. This synchronizes the microinstruction execution sequence for two consecutive READ (WRITE) microinstructions to the timing requirements of two consecutive accesses of main storage.

3.2.4 The Timing of a Main Memory Read Operation

Figure 3-5(a) illustrates the basic timing of a main storage operation. It is assumed that the data read from main memory is settled in the *memory*

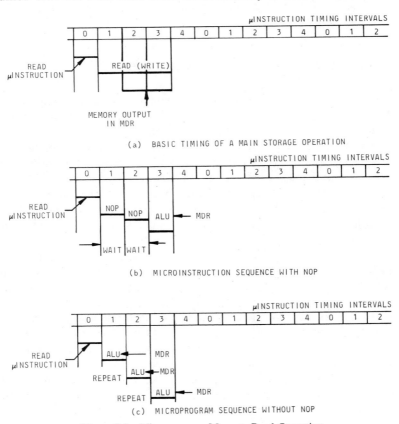

(a) BASIC TIMING OF A MAIN STORAGE OPERATION

(b) MICROINSTRUCTION SEQUENCE WITH NOP

(c) MICROPROGRAM SEQUENCE WITHOUT NOP

Figure 3-5 Microprogram Memory Read Operation

data register (MDR) *after* timing interval T2.   If no useful processing can be performed during time intervals T1 and T2 without the data requested from main storage, NOP microinstructions must be inserted to cause the microcontrol sequence to execute a pause until the data word is available in the MDR.

An alternate approach would be to make the execution of the microinstruction which transfers data from the MDR to the ALU a conditional operation to occur only if time interval T3 has been entered.   If the ALU ← MDR microinstruction occurs at T1, its execution will be delayed, or, as discussed in Section 3.2.3, the microinstruction will be executed thrice, once during T1, once during T2, and again during interval T3.   This procedure is illustrated in Figure 3-5(c).   Note, however, that the microinstruction executed during T1 and T2 transfers no useful information into the ALU. The operation shown in Figure 3-5(c) is performed by having the next address generation logic inhibited during T1 and T2 so that the same microinstruction is executed again during T2 and T3.   Using this technique, the NOP microinstruction shown in Figure 3-5(b) is eliminated at the expense of some additional control logic.

3.3 SYNCHRONOUS MULTIPARTY MEMORY BUS

When *only* the CPU is connected to the main storage bus, communication can take place between the CPU and main storage with *no* arbitration of the memory bus required to determine which device will act as the bus master for the next cycle of main memory.   In this restricted configuration, the processor has full control of a main storage access; the memory bus functions as a dedicated communication pathway.   This busing arrangement permits a very simple arbitration scheme to determine the bus master (i.e., the CPU is *always* in control).   In many applications, it is essential to allow devices other than the CPU direct access to main storage in order to satisfy the real-time requirements of the application.   Since only one unit can get access to main storage at any given time, the memory bus must be time-shared by the processor and the DMA devices.   The usage of a time-shared bus reduces the number of signal leads and logic circuitry that would be required if separate dedicated buses were used from main storage to each DMA device.   In addition, it provides flexibility for the user so that other DMA devices may be easily added to the system.   However, a contention problem occurs when more than one unit attached to the memory bus wants to gain access to the bus.   A priority structure must then be arranged between the DMA devices attached to the memory bus to designate which device will be the bus master for the next memory cycle and thus avoid any conflicts between devices that want to concurrently use the memory bus.

3.3.1 Priority Structure with One DMA Device

In a synchronous memory system with fixed cycle timing, synchronization of the microinstruction stream is done by holding the memory operation until interval T0 is generated to begin the next cycle of main storage. If a DMA device is attached to the main memory bus, it is normally assigned a higher bus request priority than the CPU. The most direct priority scheme requires that the DMA device set a bus request flag prior to T0 whenever the DMA device wants to access main memory. Since the main memory operation is *tightly coordinated* with the processor clock, the next memory cycle beginning with T0 is reserved for a DMA transaction. Figure 3-6 shows the timing relationship between the DMA transaction (which is given the next cycle of main storage) and the microprogram-controlled access of main storage by the CPU (which is deferred to the cycle following the DMA transaction). The microinstruction that initiates a main storage operation can occur at any time in the microprogram sequence. If the microinstruction occurs at a timing interval other than T0, its execution will be delayed until the T0 of the following main storage cycle. If a DMA request is issued by a device other than the CPU at T4 and the DMA request flag is allowed to extend beyond T0, the DMA flag can be used to inhibit the execution of the next microinstruction until T0 of the following memory cycle. During this period, the peripheral device that raised the DMA request flag performs a cycle-stealing data transfer with main storage.

The main storage timing signals (T0 through T4) that are generated by the processor may also be used to perform a READ or WRITE operation of a DMA device. A READ of a DMA device corresponds to a WRITE of main memory; similarly, a WRITE of a DMA device corresponds to a READ from main memory. In each operation, a memory cycle is stolen from the CPU and given to the highest-priority peripheral device that has issued a DMA request. The DMA device then exchanges a data word with a specified location in main storage *without the participation of the CPU.* Figure 3-7 illustrates the control and timing leads that must exist between

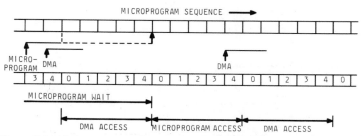

Figure 3-6 Timing Relationship Between DMA and Microprogram Memory Access

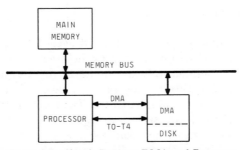

Figure 3-7　Signals Between DMA and Processor

the processor and the DMA device so that a cycle-stealing data transfer may be performed. The lead designated as "DMA" is the request signal sent to the processor to reserve the next cycle of main storage for a cycle-stealing operation. The DMA request signal functions as an inhibit signal to delay the execution of the main memory **READ** or **WRITE** microinstruction.

3.3.2　Bus Priority Structure with Multiple DMA Devices

Figure 3-8 illustrates a hardware configuration in which multiple DMA devices or channels share the memory data bus with the processor. The highest-priority DMA device is the device farthest to the right of the processor (DMA device 0). The DMA request leads are physically interconnected through each DMA device starting with the request lead from the highest-priority device. The DMA request leads form a daisy chain that proceeds from right to left. A DMA request from a device on the extreme right automatically claims the next cycle of main memory when the DMA device issues a DMA request. The presence of the DMA request signal disables all lower-priority units in the daisy chain from issuing DMA requests.

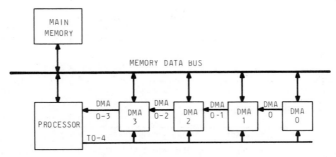

Figure 3-8　Multiple DMA Channels

Each succeeding unit repeats the DMA requests of the higher-priority units to its right.   A DMA request is allowed to continue onto the processor only if a higher-priority unit has not issued a request.   The priority request logic permits only one DMA unit to gain access to the memory bus and reference main storage.   The DMA inhibit signal occurs early enough from the highest-priority device requesting a DMA operation that the inhibit signal blocks all lower-priority DMA units *and* the processor from executing a main storage operation.

3.4   ASYNCHRONOUS MAIN STORAGE OPERATION

Asynchronous communication techniques are more compatible with the usage of semiconductor memories in modern computing systems.   Asynchronous control allows a computer system to mix memories of different technologies and varying cycle times.   For instance, a single large main store could be organized into different memory blocks in which the more frequently used programs and data words could be placed in an expensive, very fast semiconductor memory, while less frequently used programs and data could be stored in a less costly, slower semiconductor or core memory.   The different memories would appear transparent to the system in an asynchronous, handshaking control environment since each control signal must wait for a response from the memory control unit before the next step in the communication control sequence is initiated.   For future improvement in system performance, the slower, older technology memory modules can be replaced by faster memory modules that incorporate the latest technology.   This replacement operation normally will require few hardware changes in memory control logic.   The asynchronous control operation is based upon a "handshaking" or request-response procedure in which, for every action, there is a reaction; the response time of the memory unit can vary without affecting the proper operation of the computing system.

3.4.1   Bus Signals

Figure 3-9 shows a typical set of signals between main memory and the processor.   The address leads for selecting a word from memory are always directed in one direction—from the processor toward the memory.   The data leads are used by either a READ or WRITE operation; they act as a bidirectional bus for data.   The bidirectional use of the data leads reduces the total number of leads between the processor and main storage.   The processor initiates the memory operation by transmitting a READ or WRITE control signal to the memory control logic.   This control signal must be sent at a time when the memory control logic is ready to accept the order.

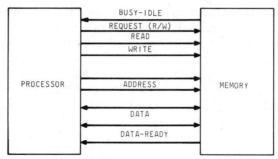

Figure 3-9   Typical Signals Between Memory and Processor

Typically, a status bit in the memory control logic may be examined by the processor to determine if the memory is BUSY or if it is IDLE. If the memory is in the IDLE state, the processor can initiate a memory READ or WRITE. The usage of a memory status bit prevents starting a new memory operation before the current operation is completed. The processor must also possess a mechanism for determining when the data word fetched from main storage has settled in the MDR and is ready for processing. The actual settling time of the data word may vary from one memory reference to another. As an example, a memory reference during the refresh period will take more time than during a nonrefresh period. Consequently, the processor must wait until the memory control logic indicates that the data word has been placed in the MDR and is available for processing.

3.4.2   Bus Timing Relationship Using Microprogram Control

Figure 3-10 illustrates the timing relationship for an access of main storage which was initiated by a microprogram sequence. Each individual block in the microprogram sequence represents a processor timing interval during which a microinstruction can be executed. The processor control signals are generated by fundamental timing pulses initiated by a READ or WRITE microinstruction. The control signals generated by the memory unit occur *asynchronously* with respect to the processor timing signals. Prior to any memory operation, the status bit of the memory control logic must be tested by the processor to determine if the memory is currently completing an operation. If the memory is in the BUSY state, the READ or WRITE microinstruction will be deferred until the memory status flip-flop is placed in the IDLE state. When the IDLE state is detected by the processor, the READ or WRITE microinstruction will be executed and initiate the main storage operation.

Certain timing relationships are assumed to exist so that a FETCH

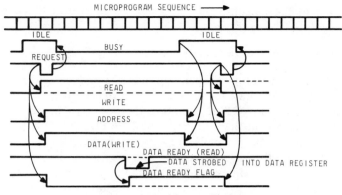

Figure 3-10 Memory Timing

of a data word from main storage may be done correctly. For example, the address of the selected data word must be settled in the *memory address register* (MAR) before the memory control unit can start a READ or WRITE operation of main storage. If this settling time is not accounted for by the control logic, the wrong word may be referenced. As indicated in Figure 3-10, a REQUEST pulse is sent to the memory control unit that initiates the main storage operation. During the execution interval of the microinstruction that generated the REQUEST signal, it is assumed the address of the desired data will become stable in the MAR. The memory operation of a READ or WRITE is specified during this execution interval. The memory control unit can then proceed with the specified READ or WRITE operation on the trailing edge of the request.

For a WRITE operation, the data is normally moved into the MDR by the previous microinstruction. In response to the memory REQUEST signal, the memory STATUS flip-flop is set to the BUSY state. The STATUS flip-flop will stay in the BUSY state until the memory control unit completes the current memory reference operation. At that time, the STATUS flip-flop will again be placed in the IDLE state.

For a READ operation, the processor waits for a response signal from the memory control unit indicating that the selected data word has been placed in the MDR and that the data word is available for use by the processor. This condition is indicated by the state of the DATA-READY line which sets the DATA-READY flag in the memory control unit. The DATA-READY flag is checked by a conditional branch microinstruction. If the DATA-READY flag is *not* set, the microinstruction enters a microexecution WAIT loop. The duration of the WAIT loop is a direct function of the cycle time of main storage. The WAIT loop is terminated when the conditional branch microinstruction detects that the DATA-READY flag has been set by the memory control unit. The WAIT loop automatically handles any variation in the response time of main storage through the usage of the DATA-READY flag.

3.4.3 Static or Dynamic Data Signals

During a WRITE operation of main storage, the address and data signals must remain in a stable state for the duration of the complete memory cycle. This means that for a WRITE operation the address and data signals to main memory remain unchanged until the STATUS flip-flop is placed in the IDLE state. If these signals are kept in a static state throughout a main storage access, the memory control unit may use them without storing the information in an address buffer register and a data buffer register. However, if buffer registers are provided in the memory control unit, the address and data signals can be strobed into these registers with the REQUEST signal. In this case, the processor no longer needs to interrogate the STATUS flip-flop to determine when the contents of the address register and data register may be changed.

A common address and data register located in the processor requires less hardware control logic; however, no information may change during a cycle of main storage. This design may or may not increase the execution time of macroinstructions which involve a memory reference to fetch an operand(s). The actual response of the memory control unit is a function of the microinstruction sequence that is used to access main storage. The discussion that follows assumes that a common address and data register exists in the processor so that the address and data signals supplied to the memory control unit will be stable during an entire cycle of main memory.

3.4.4 Memory Bus Control

Figure 3-11 illustrates the hardware implementation of a dedicated communication interface between main storage and the processor. The READ and WRITE *pulse* signals are generated by the execution of a microinstruction and are buffered in the RW flip-flop. For instance, a READ pulse will set the RW flip-flop, while a WRITE pulse will reset it. The RW flip-flop controls the direction of the data transferred between main memory and the processor. For a READ operation, the RD gates are enabled to allow the data word fetched from main storage to be gated into the MDR. For a WRITE operation, the WD gates are enabled to allow data previously placed in the MDR by the processor to be directed to the memory for storage. The direction of the data transfer is then determined by the state of the RW flip-flop. The READ control pulse also clears the MDR and the DR flip-flop so that data can flow directly into the MDR. A conditional branch microinstruction interrogates the DR flip-flop; when the DR flip-flop is set by the DATA-READY signal, the memory data is assumed to be settled

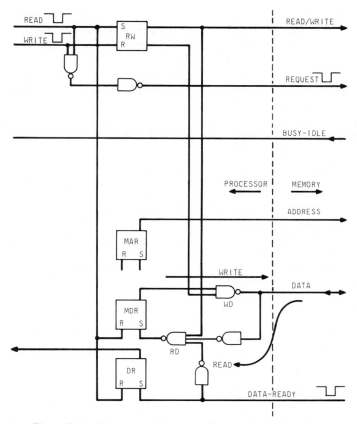

Figure 3-11 Memory and Processor Communication Interface

in the MDR. The microinstruction sequence can then proceed to process the data word fetched from main storage.

The *same* microinstruction may be used to load the address of the location to be referenced in main storage into the MAR *and* to generate the READ or WRITE order. Consequently, any decoding associated with the contents of the MAR must be delayed until the information in the MAR has settled. If the contents of the MAR are settled by the end of the READ pulse, the trailing edge of the REQUEST signal can be used to begin decoding the address of the target word in main storage.

3.4.5 Microprogram-Controlled Main Memory READ Operation

To initiate a memory READ operation, the microinstruction sequence must check the BUSY-IDLE lead to ensure that the previous cycle of a main storage operation has been completed. If not, the microcontrol sequence enters a WAIT loop and pauses until the memory control unit indicates via the BUSY-IDLE lead that the memory is in the IDLE state. Similarly, the microcontrol sequence must also check to see if the data word fetched from main storage is available (i.e., the DR flip-flop has been set by the DATA-READY signal) since the actual response time can vary a number of microexecution cycles. Figure 3-12 shows the flow diagram of a micropro-gram-controlled memory READ operation. As shown in Fig. 3-12, the memory READ operation requires the sequential execution of the following four microinstructions:

1. TEST $\overline{\text{BI}}$: Test the BUSY-IDLE lead. If it is not in the 1s state (IDLE condition), repeat the current microinstruction. If the BUSY-IDLE lead is in the 1s state, execute the next microinstruction.
2. Gate the *address* of the target location in main storage into the MAR and initiate a memory READ operation.
3. TEST $\overline{\text{DR}}$: Test the DATA-READY lead. If it is not in the 1s state (data is ready), repeat the current microinstruction. If the DATA-READY lead is in the 1s state, execute the next microinstruction.
4. Gate the data word from the MDR to the specified general register (destination).

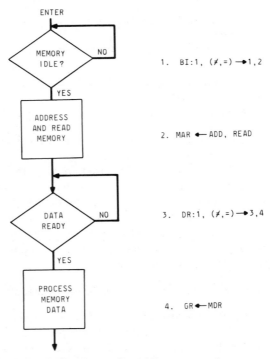

Figure 3-12 Memory Read Microprogram Sequence

The necessity to check both the BUSY-IDLE lead and the DATA-READY lead represents *overhead* in terms of execution time and additional locations that must be used to store the microinstructions in control store. Main storage accesses occur frequently in many microprograms to obtain operands for processing. These frequent main storage accesses can cause this overhead to become severe. Therefore, it is desirable to eliminate this overhead by combining these two separate microinstructions into a single microinstruction. This approach uses hardware instead of firmware to provide more concurrent operations by executing several microorders simultaneously.

3.4.6 Conditional Microorders

The implementation of conditional microorders can be realized without much added circuitry if a microinstruction format such as the format shown in Figure 3-13 is used. Five fields within the microinstruction are shown. They are as follows:

1. The *next address* (NA) *field* provides the address in control store of the next microinstruction to be executed.
2. The *SOURCE* and *DESTINATION fields* specify a data transfer from one register (SOURCE) to another register (DESTINATION) within the processor.

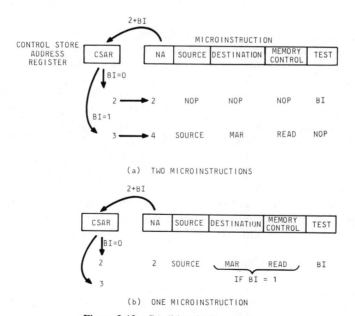

Figure 3-13 Conditional Micro-Orders

3. The *MEMORY CONTROL field* initiates a READ or WRITE operation of main storage.
4. The *TEST field* provides a conditional branching capability at the microinstruction level; it permits the specified bit to be tested to be gated into the *least-significant bit* of the CSAR when the address of the next microinstruction is formed.

Figure 3-13(a) gives the sequence of two microinstructions required to test the *BUSY-IDLE* (BI) flip-flop of the memory control unit. The first microinstruction will be repeatedly executed as long as the BI bit is in the 0 state. When the BI bit is placed in the 1 state (this indicates the main store is in the IDLE state), the least-significant bit of the CSAR is set to the 1 state. In Figure 3-13(a), the NA field is shown as containing the value 2. Consequently, setting the least-significant bit of the CSAR to the 1 state makes the address of the next microinstruction 3 rather than 2. This takes the microcontrol sequence out of the loop which repeatedly executes the microinstruction at location 2. The microinstruction at location 3 gates the address in main storage from the register specified in the SOURCE field into the MAR. The same microinstruction also supplies a READ signal to the memory control unit.

The first microinstruction contains three NOPs; this coding represents a very *inefficient* use of the control fields. The two microinstructions can be collapsed into a single microinstruction without any overlap of the control fields. This is shown in Figure 3-13(b), where all the NOPs have been eliminated and every field is fully utilized.

The logic required to combine the two microinstructions makes use of the state of the BI bit. If the BI bit is in the 0 state, the address of the target location in main storage is *not* gated into the MAR, and the memory READ operation is *not* initiated. Both control steps are performed *only* when the BI bit is in the 1 state. This procedure is necessary so that the contents of the MAR are not disturbed while the memory is still in the process of completing the previous memory cycle. Effectively, the DESTINATION and MEMORY CONTROL fields are treated as NOPs when the BI bit is in the 0 state. When this combined microinstruction attempts to set up the main storage address and initiate a memory operation, it first checks the BI bit. If the BI bit is in the 1s state, the microinstruction will be successfully executed, and the microcontrol sequence will step to the next microinstruction; otherwise, the microcontrol sequence will repeat the combined microinstruction until the BI bit is placed in the 1s state.

3.4.7 Implementation of Conditional Microorders

The decoding logic shown in Figure 3-14 implements the interpretation of a microinstruction that observes the format described in Sec. 3.4.5. The DESTINATION decoder output controls when information is gated from

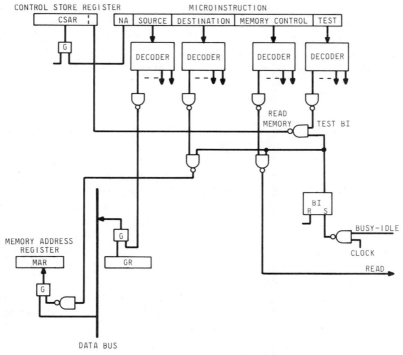

Figure 3-14 Implementation of Conditional Micro-Orders

the DATA BUS into the MAR. This decoder output is enabled only if the BI flip-flop is in the 1s state. Similarly, the READ control signal to the memory control unit of main storage and the conditional setting of the least-significant bit in the CSAR are enabled only if the BI flip-flop is in the 1s state. The BI signal is generated by the memory control unit synchronously with respect to the timing of the processor operations. The BI flip-flop is used as a single-bit buffer register that synchronizes the main storage operation with the microinstruction execution sequence in the processor.

Both the control step that tests the state of the *DATA-READY* (DR) flip-flop and the control step that gates the content of the MDR into the specified destination register can be combined into a single microinstruction without any additional changes to the processor hardware. A conditional branch microinstruction would be used in this case. The conditional microinstruction would be virtually identical to the microinstruction used to test the BI flip-flop and gate information from the DATA BUS into the MAR. The only differences are (1) the DR flip-flop would be tested instead of the BI flip-flop, and (2) information would be gated from the MDR onto the DATA BUS and then into the target internal processor register. The data transfer from the MDR to the specified register can be repeated until the

DATA-READY signal has been received from the memory control unit. When this condition is detected by the processor, the conditional branch microinstruction will set the least-significant bit of the CSAR to the 1s state and direct the microcontrol sequence to execute the next sequential microinstruction. This causes the repeated execution of the current microinstruction.

3.4.8   Instruction FETCH Wait

A basic consideration in referencing main storage is the amount of time the microcontrol unit may have to wait before an IDLE condition is sent to the processor by the main storage control unit so that the next main memory operation may be initiated. In general, it is a good design procedure to have the microsequence organized to avoid any pause or WAIT loop. If a WAIT loop cannot be avoided, then the microcontrol sequence is arranged to limit the duration of the wait interval. This arrangement uses the designer's prior knowledge about the cycle time of main storage so that other microinstructions are allowed to execute while the main memory is completing its current operation. It may be quite difficult, however, for the designer to plan the *exact* number of microinstructions that may be used to fill the WAIT interval required by main storage. For instance, the microcontrol sequence may execute a sufficient number of microinstructions so that main memory becomes idle before the microcontrol sequence completes. This can cause main storage to remain idle for a period considerably beyond its associated WAIT interval. Since the access time of main storage is typically a major factor in limiting the processing capability of the processor, it is desirable to keep the main memory busy whenever possible. Rather than the microprogram sequence being required to wait for main storage to be in the IDLE state, it is possible to buffer the request for a main memory access using additional hardware. This would allow the microcontrol sequence to proceed with other control functions. As soon as the main memory completes its current operation, the additional hardware can initiate a new main storage operation, provided the microinstruction sequence permits the initiation of a new main memory access.

The technique of using a hardware buffer arrangement to initiate a main memory operation lends itself to the macroinstruction FETCH mechanism. The address of the next macroinstruction to be interpreted is normally stored in a distinct hardware register called the *program counter* (PC). The PC is automatically incremented by 1 after each macroinstruction is fetched from main storage. One of the microorders specified by the MEMORY CONTROL field of a microinstruction can be assigned to initiate a FETCH of the next macroinstruction. When such a microorder is issued, it is temporarily stored in a flip-flop and executed by the microcontrol sequence only if main memory is in the idle state. This situation is illustrated in

Figure 3-15 in which the BI flip-flop *must* be in the IDLE state for an instruction FETCH to be initiated by the hardware. The microorder to perform an access of main memory merely sets the *instruction fetch* (IF) flip-flop; the microcontrol sequence continues execution with *no* WAIT loop being executed. Assuming that the IF flip-flop has been set, a group of microcontrol signals will be generated when the main memory is placed in the IDLE state. One of these microcontrol signals gates the content of the PC into the MAR; a second signal updates the PC by adding 1 to it so that the PC points to the address of the next macroinstruction; and a third signal transmits a READ REQUEST to the main storage control unit. At the end of the READ operation (i.e., when the BI flip-flop is placed in the IDLE state), the IF flip-flop is toggled to the RESET state so that the microorder is not repeatedly executed.

For a conditional branch macroinstruction, the address of the next macroinstruction to be executed will not sequentially follow the address of the current macroinstruction (i.e., the address of the next macroinstruction may not be generated by simply adding 1 to the content of the PC). Instead, an entirely new address must be generated and then gated into the PC. This procedure may also be implemented using the hardware buffering scheme previously described. Figure 3-16 shows the layout of a microinstruction that is used to FETCH the next macroinstruction, based upon the fact that the current macroinstruction is a conditional branch command. The MEM-ORY CONTROL field specifies that a *FETCH instruction* (FI) operation is to be performed. The SOURCE and DESTINATION fields identify that a data transfer operation is to take place at the microcontrol level between a specified *general register* (GR) and the PC. The content of the GR is the address to be used if the conditional macroinstruction is successfully executed. When the microinstruction of Figure 3-16 is executed, the PC

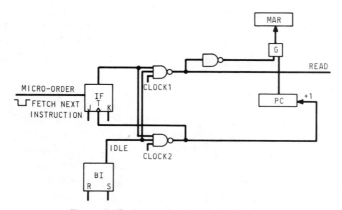

Figure 3-15   Instruction Fetch by Hardware

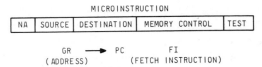

Figure 3-16   Branch Instruction Fetch Format

is loaded with the branch address found in the GR, and the IF flip-flop is set to initiate a memory FETCH operation as soon as the main storage control unit is placed in the IDLE state. Conditional testing of the BI flip-flop no longer has to be done by a microinstruction WAIT loop since the hardware automatically provides any delay required by the main memory.

3.4.9   Data (Operand) FETCH Wait

The control of a data FETCH operation is somewhat different. In this case, the address of the operand cannot be buffered in the PC since the PC contains the address of the next macroinstruction to be executed. Instead, the address of the operand must be gated directly into the MAR after the operand address has been generated by the processor. This information transfer can be performed *only* if the main memory is in the IDLE state; otherwise, the content of the MAR *must* be left unchanged. A buffer register that temporarily stores the address of the operand in main storage until the current memory operation is completed can be provided. This approach allows the microinstruction execution sequence to proceed without having to wait until the memory operation is done. In this case, the hardware will initiate the required operand FETCH when the memory becomes IDLE. Since an operand FETCH is a portion of the overall execution of a *memory reference macroinstruction,* no real advantage is gained in using additional hardware to buffer the operand address while the current main storage operation is completed. In general, for a data FETCH operation, it is an entirely *adequate design procedure* to have the microinstruction that initiates the operand FETCH loop on itself until the memory is in the IDLE state. This looping mechanism has been previously described in Sec. 3.4.7 and 3.4.8.

3.4.10   Instruction PreFETCH

A significant advantage in having a specific memory control field assigned in a microinstruction is that an explicit memory FETCH for data may be specified as well as an explicit FETCH of the next macroinstruction. To use this microinstruction format effectively, a microprogrammer must have an intimate knowledge of the complete hardware control structure for the machine. It is quite advantageous if the microprogrammer participated in specifying the microorder structure of the machine since it allows the microprogrammer additional insight in writing microcontrol sequences of microinstructions.

A macroinstruction involving a data FETCH operation often requires an address calculation (indexing, indirection, etc.) to determine the effective address of the operand. These calculations must be implemented in microcontrol steps. Depending on the extent of the microinstruction repertoire, several microinstructions are normally needed to perform an address modification. While these calculations are being performed, no data FETCH operation may be performed since the effective address of the operand has not been determined. This means that the main memory must remain in the IDLE state for several microinstruction cycles. It would be attractive to use this idle time of main storage to initiate a FETCH of the next macroinstruction to be executed. To preFETCH the next macroinstruction, a separate *data buffer* (DB) register is required to hold the data until the current macroinstruction has been completed. Figure 3-17 illustrates the usage of two buffer registers to implement a macroinstruction preFETCH operation: the *instruction buffer* (IB) register buffers the next macroinstruction to be executed, while the DB register buffers the operand required by the current macroinstruction. The MEMORY CONTROL field of the microinstruction must specify two different memory READ microorders: One microorder directs the data word from main storage to the IB, while the other microorder directs the data word to the DB. The state of the *instruction data* (ID) flip-flop determines whether the output from main storage is to be gated either to the IB or the DB. The use of these two buffer registers permits the microcontrol sequence to initiate a FETCH of the next macroinstruction

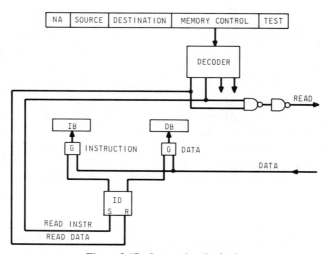

Figure 3-17 Instruction Prefetch

while the effective address of the operand to be used by the current macroinstruction is being calculated. If this approach is not taken, the FETCH of the next macroinstruction must be performed at—or near—the end of the execution of the current macroinstruction.

3.5   ASYNCHRONOUS MULTIPARTY MEMORY BUS

The previous discussion of memory operations assumes that a dedicated communication pathway (bus) exists between main storage and the processor. It is possible that several peripheral units may share the memory bus with the processor. Consequently, conflicts may arise when more than one unit in the system wants access to main storage simultaneously. A protocol must be established to resolve such conflicts to ensure proper operation of the main memory.

In an asynchronous multiparity memory bus, the bus is time-shared among several units attached to the bus. Only the selected unit is allowed to use the bus to communicate with main storage. The other peripheral units are disabled in the sense that they are completely inhibited from using the memory bus. In the dedicated communication structure shown in Figure 3-9, the address signals from the processor come directly from the address register. A main storage operation requires that the signals on the address leads remain stable for the duration of the access interval. When the memory is in the IDLE state, the signals on the address leads act as "don't care" conditions to main storage. In the time-shared communication structure, the memory bus is assigned to the selected unit *only* during the access interval associated with the main storage; hence, all signals to the bus from the selected device must be disabled at the end of the current main storage operation since another peripheral may be requesting usage of the memory bus.

A significant difference between the dedicated memory bus structure and the time-shared memory bus occurs when a request to access main storage is generated and serviced. For a dedicated memory bus structure, the request is always honored since there is *no* competition among the devices attached to the bus for an access of main storage. This is not true for an asynchronously controlled time-shared memory bus in which multiple peripheral devices may be attached to the bus and each device can have a DMA capability. The problem of arbitrating simultaneous bus requests from two or more devices attached to the bus must be handled by the hardware in a manner such that the highest-priority device issuing a bus request will be given access to main storage.

3.5.1   Bus Arbitration

Figure 3-18(a) illustrates a memory bus arrangement in which the processor and a DMA device share a common main storage bus. Either the processor or the DMA device can access the memory independently. However, an

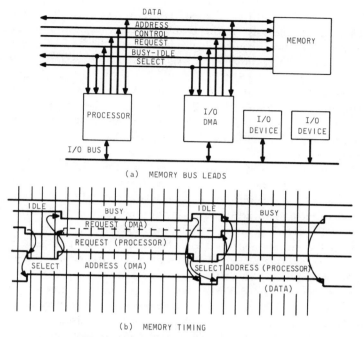

Figure 3-18 Memory Request and Select

additional control signal from the memory control unit is required to resolve bus request conflicts and assign the memory to the appropriate unit. This additional control signal, designated as the **SELECT** lead, selects the unit (i.e., the processor or the DMA device) to be connected to the memory bus. Figure 3-18(b) shows the timing diagram of this approach. The timing is similar to the microprogram control scheme shown in Figure 3-10 except that a signal on the **REQUEST** lead does not guarantee that an access to main storage may be performed by the requesting device since both the processor and the DMA device may request the memory simultaneously when the memory becomes **IDLE**. Only one memory request can be handled at a time by the memory control unit. The **REQUEST** signal must be held in the active state until the arbitration logic selects the unit that is to use main storage.

As shown in Figure 3-18(b), it is assumed that the **REQUEST** signal from either the processor or the **DMA** device becomes *active* during the time in which the memory control unit is in the **IDLE** state. It is possible for both units to simultaneously issue request signals to the memory control unit. In this case, only one unit is selected to have use of the memory bus to communicate with main storage. The **REQUEST** signal from the other unit is ignored until the first device has completed its memory reference. In response to the **REQUEST** signal, the memory control unit generates a

SELECT signal. The SELECT signal is first directed to the DMA device and then to the processor. If the DMA device is requesting access to the memory bus, the DMA control logic will accept the SELECT signal and proceed to put the necessary control signals and address information onto the bus. At the end of the SELECT signal it is assumed that all information on the memory bus has stabilized. At this time, the main storage operation can be initiated. The trailing edge of the SELECT pulse updates the memory control unit to the BUSY state and removes the REQUEST signal from the DMA device. This indicates that the DMA request to use main storage has been processed.

While the DMA transaction is in progress, the REQUEST lead is held in the active state by the processor. The processor is also attempting to request usage of the memory bus. As a result, the REQUEST signal does not appear to have changed its state during this period. When the BI lead is placed in the IDLE state, a main storage operation has been completed. All data on the bus is then disabled. Since the REQUEST lead is still in the active state, another access of main storage is initiated when the memory control unit generates a new SELECT pulse. The select pulse passes through the DMA device since the DMA device is no longer requesting usage of the memory bus and is received by the processor. The processor accepts the SELECT signal and observes the protocol just discussed; this action sets up the memory address and performs the required main storage operation.

The SELECT signal is generated by the memory control unit only when the REQUEST lead is in the active state and main storage is IDLE. While the processor or the DMA device can generate a REQUEST pulse at any time, a REQUEST signal will be processed *only* when the memory is in the IDLE state. The BI signal is used to remove information from the memory bus. The transition of the BI signal from the BUSY state to the IDLE state indicates to the selected unit that the data on the bus is no longer needed and must be removed to allow a new memory operation to be initiated. Instead of the BI signal, a completion pulse occurring at the end of the main storage operation may be used to terminate the information on the memory bus.

3.5.2 Time-Shared Memory Bus Operation

The SELECT signal is transmitted by the memory control unit and is daisy-chained* through the DMA device and the processor. Figure 3-19 illustrates this daisy-chain structure. Since the DMA device is the first unit in the daisy chain, it is the highest-priority unit. If the DMA device has placed

---

* George D. Kraft and Wing N. Toy, *Mini/Microcomputer Hardware Design* (Englewood Cliffs, N.J.: Prentice-Hall, 1979), pp. 389, 391, and 400.

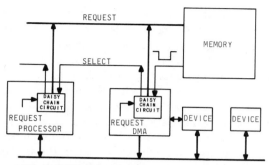

Figure 3-19   Selection by Daisy-Chain Structure

its REQUEST lead in the active state, the SELECT signal will be inhibited by the DMA device from propagating farther down the daisy chain to the processor; the DMA device will be granted usage of the memory bus. Otherwise, the SELECT signal is passed on to the processor. When both units simultaneously place their respective REQUEST leads in the active state, the first unit in the daisy chain automatically receives priority access in the use of the memory bus. Any REQUEST signal that occurs during the active interval of the SELECT signal is ignored by the memory control unit in order to avoid a situation in which both units attempt to perform a main memory reference simultaneously.

Figure 3-20(a) gives the logic circuitry that is required to process the SELECT signal and pass the SELECT signal to the next unit in the daisy chain if the current unit has not placed its REQUEST in the active state. The following control steps are performed by the logic:

1. If a REQUEST is pending in the current unit (i.e., the REQUEST lead of the current unit is in the active state), the SELECT signal is directed by the STEER flip-flop (Q = 1) to setting the SEL flip-flop. The STEER flip-flop inhibits the SELECT signal from propagating to the next unit in the daisy chain.

2. The setting of the SEL flip-flop enables the current unit to control all signals to and from the bus. The REQ flip-flop is cleared on the trailing edge of the SELECT pulse (output of G5), indicating that the REQUEST from the current device has been accepted.

3. If a REQUEST signal is not pending in the current unit, the SELECT signal is directed by the STEER flip-flop (Q = 0) to the next unit in the daisy chain.

4. Any REQUEST signal that occurs during the interval in which the SELECT signal is being propagated to the next unit in the daisy chain is automatically ignored. The REQ flip-flop in the device(s) that has issued a REQUEST pulse is set by the logic which generates the REQUEST pulse. The REQ flip-flop remains set until the unit has been selected.

Whenever an access of main storage is required, a REQUEST signal is generated.   The REQUEST signal is derived from the MEMORY CONTROL field of the current microinstruction.   The REQUEST signal is temporarily buffered in the REQ flip-flop and provides a constant signal to the memory control unit until the unit is selected.   The REQUEST signal also allows the STEER flip-flop to be set.   When the memory control unit responds with the SELECT signal *and* the STEER flip-flop is in the 1s state, the SEL flip-flop will be set.   The REQ flip-flop is toggled to the 0s state with the trailing edge of the SELECT pulse.   When the memory operation has been completed, the transition of the BI signal in the bus from the BUSY state to the IDLE state toggles the SEL flip-flop to its normal cleared state.

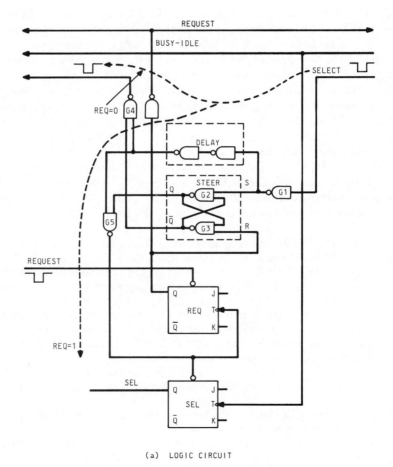

(a) LOGIC CIRCUIT

Figure 3-20   Request and Select Circuit

3.5.3 Detailed Description of Bus Control

The timing diagram of the REQUEST and SELECT logic is shown in Figure 3-20(b). It is assumed that the SELECT signal is generated in response to a REQUEST pulse. Since the SELECT signal is daisy-chained through the units connected to the memory bus, a variable delay may be experienced by the unit issuing the REQUEST. This delay is a direct function of where main storage is in its current operation and how much additional time must elapse before the memory operation is completed. Prior to the occurrence of the SELECT signal, the STEER flip-flop in the highest-priority unit issuing a REQUEST is set to the 1s state. If the REQ flip-flop has not been set, the STEER flip-flop is held with both the Q and $\overline{Q}$ outputs in the high voltage level, which enables the SELECT signal to be steered to the next unit in the daisy chain via gate G4. The two-gate delay element inserted at the output of G1, as shown in Figure 3-20(a), provides sufficient time for the STEER flip-flop to become stable in the Os state before gate G5 is enabled. This ensures that *only one* of the two gates processes the SELECT signal; otherwise, both of the logic gates would be enabled and an indeterminate logic condition would arise in the SELECT logic.

In the unit with the REQ flip-flop SET, the STEER flip-flop is set with the output of G2 kept in the high state and the output of G3 kept in

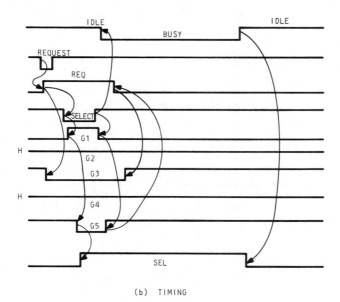

(b) TIMING

Figure 3-20 (*cont.*)

the low state. When the SELECT signal becomes active, it is directed toward G5 so that the SEL flip-flop of the current device may be set. The *action* of setting the STEER flip-flop prevents the SELECT signal from being passed on to lower-priority devices in the daisy chain. The action of setting the SEL flip-flop connects the memory bus to the current unit (since it is the highest-priority device issuing a REQUEST). It is assumed that when the SEL flip-flop is set, the address, data, and control signals are ready to be gated onto the bus. Figure 3-21 illustrates how the SEL flip-flop is used to control all signals that go *to* or *from* the memory bus by the selected unit. It is critically important that when several units time-share the bus, only one unit is connected to the bus. Otherwise, the signals appearing on the bus would be formed by the inclusive-OR of all similar signals gated onto the bus from the multiply active units.

The data portion of the memory bus is a bidirectional communication path. The direction of data transfer on the data bus is determined by the type of memory operation to be performed: a READ from main storage or a WRITE into main storage. A *read-write* (RW) flip-flop in the selected unit provides the control information to the memory control unit as to the direction of data flow: (1) *from* the selected device *to* main storage for a memory WRITE and (2) *to* the selected device *from* main storage for a memory READ. For a READ operation, the data path from main storage is enabled so as to allow the data to be directed into the MDR. For a WRITE operation, the outputs from the MDR are gated onto the same bus lines. The address signals are used directly from the MAR; they must

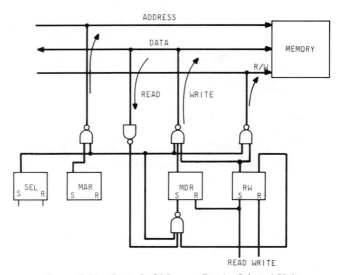

Figure 3-21 Control of Memory Bus by Selected Unit

not be allowed to change until the memory reference operation has completed *and* the SEL flip-flop has restored to the 0 state.

3.5.4 Processing of the Memory Microorder

The same microinstruction format can be used to access main storage as the format discussed in Sec. 3.4.5. The format is independent of the number of units connected to the memory bus. However, some slight variations in the hardware implementation are required. The BI bit does not have to be in the IDLE state before the main storage address contained in the MAR can be changed.

A separate bit indicating whether the processor is in the midst of a memory cycle is needed. This bit can be the processor SEL flip-flop since it is set *only* during the memory cycle in which the processor is accessing main storage. The logic associated with a microinstruction that initiates a READ of main storage is shown in Figure 3-22. This microinstruction

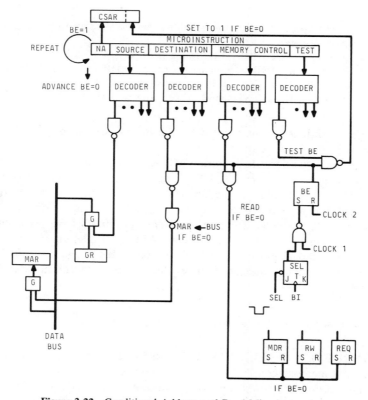

Figure 3-22 Conditional Address and Read Microinstruction

functions as a conditional branch command; it is repeatedly executed until the current memory operation is completed. The conditional branch operation is inhibited until the IDLE signal returned by the memory control logic puts the *bus-enabled* (BE) flip-flop in the 0 state. This permits the least-significant bit of the CSAR to be set to the 1s state. The address of the next microinstruction is changed to one more than the address of the microinstruction that has been repeatedly executed. The SEL flip-flop in the processor is reset at the end of the current memory cycle.

To execute a main storage reference properly, the SEL signal is used to synchronize the presentation of control information to the memory control unit with the execution timing of a microinstruction. The BE flip-flop is used in this synchronization process; it is the BE flip-flop that the current microinstruction checks to determine if the address of the *next* microinstruction should remain unchanged for another memory cycle. The execution of a microinstruction that specifies a READ of main storage performs the following control operations:

1. It sets up the MAR with the address of the location to be referenced in main storage.
2. It specifies that a READ operation is to be performed.
3. It clears the MDR in anticipation of the MDR acting as the destination of the data word fetched from main storage.
4. It issues a REQUEST signal to the memory control unit.

All these operations are performed by the microinstruction *only* if the BE flip-flop is in the inactive or 0s state.

The memory reference operation will be initiated only when the memory control unit responds to the REQUEST signal from the processor by sending the SELECT signal back to the processor. When the data word fetched from main storage is put onto the bus, the DR from the memory control unit indicates to the processor that the memory outputs have been buffered in the MDR and are ready for processing. At the completion of the memory cycle, the BI lead is placed in the IDLE state; this triggers the SEL flip-flop in the processor to indicate that another memory operation can be initiated.

3.5.5   Centralized Memory Control

The REQUEST and SELECT signals provide a communication protocol between the memory control unit and the devices connected to the memory bus. This protocol ensures that only *one* unit is in possession of the bus at any given time and may access main storage. Each unit functions autonomously in that the timing and control signals required to reference memory are independent of all other devices connected to the memory bus. The daisy-chained SELECT logic is distributed throughout all these devices. It is possible to centralize all memory timing and control logic so that the logic resides exclusively in the processor. In this arrangement, the REQUEST signal from a DMA device is sent to the processor and treated as a special interrupt signal instead of being sent to the memory control unit. Figure 3-23 illustrates this approach in which a memory request is made by using the processor as an intermediary. At the end of the execution of the current macroinstruction, the memory control unit is either in the IDLE state or about to go into the IDLE state. The interrupt from the DMA device would cause the processor to enter a state in which all processor activity would be suspended. All data would remain undisturbed while the microcontrol sequence handles the details of the DMA transfer. Other control functions associated with the DMA operation can be incorporated as part of the microprogram control sequence for the DMA → main storage data transfer.

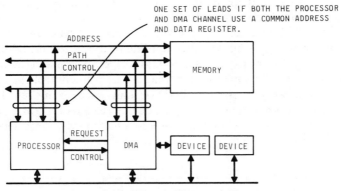

Figure 3-23   Memory Request via Processor

Since the processor is halted, there is no competition from the processor for the usage of main storage. The microprogram in the processor provides the control signals to implement a main memory operation by either the DMA device or the processor. When the memory control unit is in the IDLE state, the microcontrol sequence can initiate a READ or WRITE operation without having to use the SELECT signal. If both the processor and the DMA unit share common address and data registers, a single group of leads may be used to connect onto the memory bus. The use of the bus is under the complete control of the microprogram(s) that reside(s) in the processor.

3.5.6 Dedicated DMA Microorders

The next problem that must be considered is the structure of the microinstruction to handle the control of a DMA operation. Part of the control fields of the microinstruction must be specifically assigned to control the circuitry in the DMA unit. Figure 3-24 shows the microcontrol arrangement in which several control signals from each field in the microinstruction are assigned to direct the DMA operation. The number of control signals assigned to each field depends on the precise way the DMA operation is implemented in hardware. It is desirable to keep the number of control points to a minimum since they are used only for a DMA operation and do not perform any internal control operations in the processor which are not associated with DMA control. If the DMA-related control points were specified as a separate set of bits in the microinstruction (more than one of these control points may have to be activated concurrently), an increase in the number of bits in the microinstruction would be necessary to accommodate the additional control points. This structure can result in inefficient utilization of the bits in the control store since the DMA control points would be used much more infrequently than the other bits in a microinstruction which relates to internal processor functions.

Figure 3-25 illustrates the case when a second DMA unit is attached to the memory bus. A separate interrupt line from the second DMA device is used to notify the processor that a DMA operation has been requested by the second unit. The microorders that are used to control the operation of DMA unit 1 can be shared with DMA unit 2; the same set of control points specified by a microinstruction can be used to direct a DMA operation in either unit. The interrupt logic selects which DMA unit accepts the DMA microorders supplied by the processor.

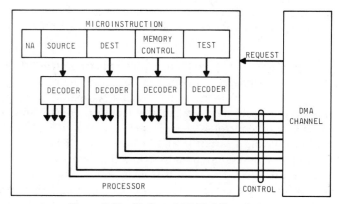

Figure 3-24 Dedicated DMA Micro-Orders

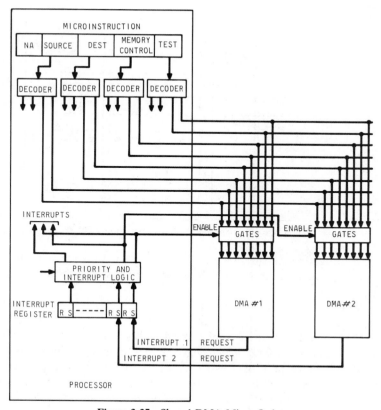

Figure 3-25 Shared DMA Micro-Orders

3.5.7 Bit Steering of Microinstruction Control Fields

When a large number of individual control points are needed to direct the DMA units, a better microinstruction format is to make use of the *bit-steering technique*. Using this approach, a separate bit in the microinstruction is assigned to direct the contents of the microinstruction to either a buffer register in the processor or to a separate buffer register located in the selected DMA unit. For multiple units, enough additional bits in the microinstruction are required so that all units on the memory bus may be uniquely addressed.

Figure 3-26 illustrates the case of two DMA units (both attached to the memory bus) that are controlled by a common sequence of microinstructions. Each microinstruction contains an additional field which specifies the address of the unit (processor, DMA 1, DMA 2) to which the current microinstruction is to be gated. Its interpretation can be a function of the application the DMA device is being used in. The complete flexibility to interpret the control bits at each DMA device in a unique manner provides

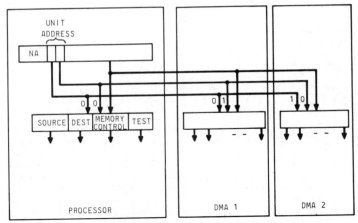

Figure 3-26   Bit Steering of Microprogram Control

maximum utilization of the bits in the microinstruction gated to the unit without a large increase in the width of the control store word.

3.5.8   Interrupt Steering of Microinstruction Control Fields

Figure 3-27 illustrates the case of one DMA unit sharing the use of microinstructions in control store.   Whenever a DMA data transfer needs to be performed, an interrupt is generated by the DMA logic and passed onto the processor.   The interrupt signal sets the REQ flip-flop in the processor. At the end of the sequence of microinstructions that interprets the current macroinstruction, and *prior* to the start of execution of the next macroinstruction, the interrupt is recognized by the microcontrol logic.   The CSAR is set to the starting address in control store of the microprogram that handles an interrupt.   At the same time, the interrupt timing logic sets the *interrupt enable* (IE) flip-flop in the processor.   The IE flip-flop directs the microinstruction to the microcontrol logic in the DMA unit instead of the microcontrol logic in the processor.   The setting of the IE flip-flop is synchronized by the processor microcontrol logic to provide a smooth transition from the execution of a microinstruction by the processor to the execution of a microinstruction by the DMA unit.   At the end of the DMA microcontrol sequence, the last microinstruction in the sequence contains all 0s in the next address field.   This all-0 code defines the end of the microcontrol sequence.   If the REQ flip-flop is *not* set, the contents of the opcode field of the next macroinstruction will be gated to the CSAR to initiate the interpretive microroutine for the next macroinstruction.   The IE flip-flop is cleared at the time the next microinstruction is gated into the MIR from the microprogram memory.   This switches the microcontrol sequence back to the processor and ends the interrupt-initiated microcode-controlled DMA operation.

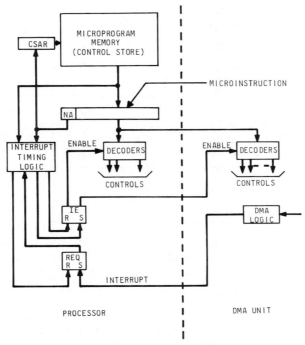

Figure 3-27 Interrupt Steering of Microprogram Control Fields

However, if the REQ flip-flop is again set by an interrupt request from the DMA unit, the starting address of the interrupt service microroutine will be set into the CSAR instead of the opcode of the next macroinstruction being gated into the CSAR. The IE flip-flop will *not* be cleared until this second interrupt request is serviced. If the interrupt requests are issued at a sufficient rate by the DMA unit, the processor will be prevented from executing another macroinstruction until *all* the words in the DMA operation have been completely transferred.

Several other DMA units can similarly share the use of the microcontrol logic. The general arrangement is shown in Figure 3-28. Each DMA unit makes use of a separate interrupt request line into the processor; the use of these separate request leads provides quick identification of the requesting unit. The interrupt logic is more complex than the logic used when only one DMA device is connected to the memory bus. The interrupt logic must handle conflict situations in which simultaneous interrupt requests from multiple units must be detected and control (service) directed to the highest-priority device requesting an interrupt. A single sequence of microinstructions can be used to control either DMA unit. The individual interrupt lines provide the information necessary to the processor for it to determine the highest-priority DMA device and direct the microinstruction stream to it.

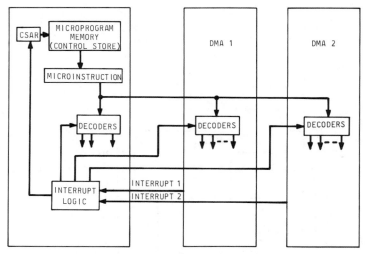

Figure 3-28 Expansion of Interrupt Steering

3.5.9 Effect of Sharing the Microprogram Control Sequence

When multiple units share the microcontrol logic, the processor is forced to *pause* in its macroinstruction interpretation sequence whenever a DMA unit issues an interrupt request to initiate a DMA operation. The microcontrol sequence is then directed over to the appropriate DMA device. This means the performance of the processor will be degraded. On the other hand, if the DMA units and the processor are sharing a memory with a relatively long cycle time, the memory will be the bottleneck. Whenever a DMA unit is accessing the memory, the processor must pause before it can execute the next macroinstruction. In this situation, since the processor cannot perform any useful work, it might as well share its microprogram control logic with the DMA devices. The performance of the processor would not suffer appreciably if the microprogram control logic were used by a DMA device mostly during the processor WAIT period. At worst, the system performance will be degraded by the amount of time the processor is halted when it is sharing its microprogram control logic.

3.6 DAISY-CHAINED MEMORY BUS

Certain control signals associated with a bus structure are sometimes daisy-chained from unit to unit for the purpose of allowing individual units to examine the data on the bus and either accept the data or pass it on to the next unit. For instance, the SELECT signal discussed in Section 3.5 is daisy-chained from unit to unit while the other bus leads fan out directly to all units. When data is placed on the bus, it will fan out to all units. It is up to each individual unit to accept or ignore this data. In the daisy-chained arrangement, however, the data can be relayed or left unaltered, inhibited from further transmission or modified as the data flows from one unit to another.

Figure 3-29(a) gives a functional diagram of the memory bus, daisy-chained from the DMA to the processor. The direction of data flow is bidirectional: Data is directed from the memory to the DMA unit or processor on a READ and in the reverse direction for a WRITE. To keep the number of leads to a minimum, the signal paths are used to transmit data in both directions, as indicated by the arrows in Figure 3-29(a). The address leads are always directed toward the memory control unit, while the individual control signals can be directed in either direction.

Figure 3-29(b) shows the unidirectional and bidirectional signals of the daisy-chained memory bus. For the unidirectional leads, each signal goes through two stages of logic gates. The two logic stages provide a double inversion which is necessary to preserve the polarity of each signal. It is also good design practice to assign ground as the *active* level of each signal. Any unconnected leads in the bus would then appear to be *inactive* signals. In some equipment the unused leads in the daisy-chained bus are not terminated with a load resistor. It is desirable *not* to be required to make any

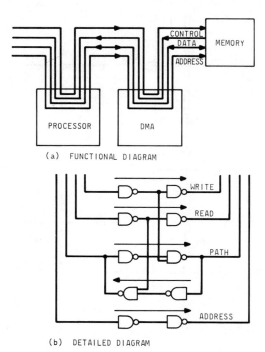

(a) FUNCTIONAL DIAGRAM

(b) DETAILED DIAGRAM

Figure 3-29 Daisy-Chained Memory Bus

special connections to these unterminated leads since this represents additional work for the service personnel. For signals appearing on the bidirectional leads, the direction of signal flow is determined by the READ or WRITE control signals. A separate set of gates is required to direct the data flow in each direction. In a READ operation, the READ control enables the path from the memory to the unit (DMA device or processor) and disables the path in the reverse direction. For a WRITE operation, control of the data flow is in the direction opposite to that for a READ. Obviously, a READ operation and a WRITE operation cannot occur simultaneously. The bidirectional leads, therefore, are time-shared, with the direction of signal flow determined by the memory operation.

3.6.1 Memory Bus Data Transfer

The insertion of data onto the daisy-chained bus can be done as shown in Figure 3-30. Any information from the left unit to be sent to main storage

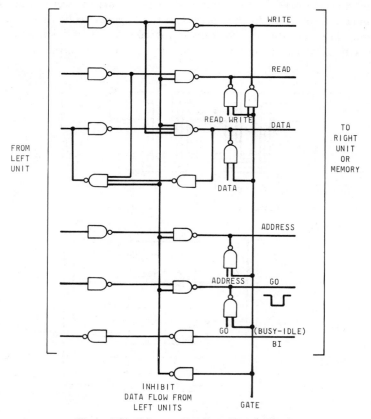

Figure 3-30 Memory Bus Data Transfer Logic

on a READ must not be present when a WRITE operation is to be performed. Consequently, data flow from the left signal leads is inhibited on a WRITE. The DMA unit physically nearest the memory has priority in the use of the memory bus in the event of simultaneous bus requests since the SELECT signal is daisy-chained through all units. Each unit examines the state of the BI lead; if it is in the IDLE state, the unit initiates a memory operation by gating data onto the bus, *but* the signals from the lower-priority units to its left are disabled by the same control signal that gates the data onto the bus from the current highest-priority unit.

To synchronize the memory operation with the DMA device, a GO pulse is transmitted to the memory control unit indicating that a memory request is being serviced. In response to the GO pulse, the memory control unit changes the state of the BI lead to BUSY. This action is done sufficiently rapidly by the memory control unit to prevent another unit attached to the bus from attempting to seize the memory at the same time. At the termination of the GO pulse, all signals on the bus are assumed to be stable; this includes the state of the BI lead that was changed to BUSY. The memory control unit is triggered by the trailing edge of the GO signal to start the memory operation.

3.6.2 Memory Bus Control

Since the state of the BI lead cannot be instantaneously changed from IDLE to BUSY (due to logic and propagation delays), there is a possibility of two units attempting to seize the memory bus. If a higher-priority unit requests the memory at the same time as a lower-priority unit, the BI lead will remain in the IDLE state for a short period of time. Refer to Figure 3-31 for the following discussion. With the BI lead in the IDLE state *and* the appearance of a request signal, the GO and GATE flip-flops are set. The output of the GO flip-flop is the starting signal to the memory control unit of a new main storage operation. The GATE output enables the address leads, data leads, and control signals to the memory bus and, simultaneously, inhibits all information from being placed on the memory bus by lower-priority devices. If two simultaneous requests have been issued, a similar action occurs in the lower-priority unit which issued the request. The REQ, GO, and GATE flip-flops in this unit are also all set. The circuitry of the lower-priority device goes through the motion of accessing the memory in the same manner as the higher-priority unit. However, no signals from the lower-priority device are propagated to the bus since they are inhibited by the control logic of the daisy chain.

At the completion of either a READ or WRITE operation, the memory control unit sends a COMPLETE pulse to the unit currently in control of the bus. This pulse toggles the GATE and REQ flip-flops to their *inactive* (CLEAR) states. The toggling operation is achieved using the trailing edge

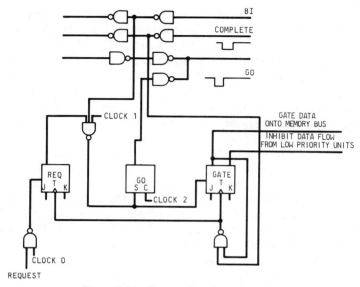

Figure 3-31   Memory Bus Control Logic

of the COMPLETE pulse.   This action completes the main storage operation controlled by the higher-priority DMA unit.   The REQ and GATE flip-flops are still set in the lower-priority unit which has issued a concurrent memory request.   However, the GO flip-flop in this unit has been cleared by a clock timing pulse.   When the higher-priority unit releases the INHIBIT on the bus, the memory control unit will restore the BI lead to the IDLE state.   When the BI lead again becomes IDLE, the GO flip-flop in the lower-priority device will be set to initiate the main storage operation for this unit.

Assume for a moment that the GO signal is propagated through the DMA unit and onto the memory control unit.   Before the memory control unit responds by changing the BI lead to the BUSY state, the DMA unit will again request access to main storage.   If both the GO and the GATE flip-flops are set in the unit, all signals to the memory bus from lower-priority units are inhibited, and the highest-priority DMA unit still making a RE-QUEST will gain control of the memory bus.   Figure 3-32 gives the timing diagram of the GO signals, with the GO signal from the processor being the first signal to reach the memory control unit.   When the GO signal is generated from the DMA unit, it is ORed onto the memory bus until the INHIBIT signal from the DMA logic is generated.   The resultant signal to the memory control unit begins with the GO signal from the processor and ends when the GO signal from the DMA unit ends.

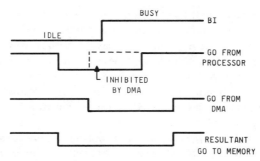

Figure 3-32 Timing of GO Signal

3.6.3 Factors Concerning Daisy-Chained Memory Buses

The main features of the daisy-chained memory bus are as follows:

1. Its ability to permit a considerable number of I/O devices to be concatenated on the bus
2. Its ability to use a SELECT pulse to *isolate* the lower-priority devices in the chain from affecting the current memory operation

The first feature is obtained through the use of repeaters or logic signal amplifiers that regenerate the individual daisy chain control signals from unit to unit. Since repeaters are used, there is *no* fan-out problem when a large number of devices are connected in a daisy-chain arrangement. Also, the physical distance of each device from the memory bus can be extended to any distance so long as the signals returned by the device are not degraded beyond the electrical tolerances of the cable receivers in the bus. The capability of isolating the lower-priority units in the daisy chain permits *fault diagnosis of bus failures* and isolation of these faults to a specific unit. This is done by successively isolating and testing individual units in the daisy chain to identify the faulty unit. This type of checking can be done automatically by software in conjunction with a small amount of hardware.

The advantages just discussed are obtained at the expense of additional gates that are used to repeat control signals in the daisy chain from unit to unit. Because these signals are amplified through two additional logic gates per lead per unit, an additional delay in transmitting signals over the daisy chain bus will be experienced. This factor *must* be considered if timing is a critical consideration and a daisy-chain memory bus is being considered.

3.7 SUMMARY

The mechanisms for controlling the access of main storage by either the processor or DMA devices that share the memory bus were discussed in this chapter. Two approaches to clocking the control steps in an access of main storage were described: synchronous and asynchronous. In the synchronous case, the macroinstruction execution is synchronized with the memory FETCH operation. In the asynchronous case, a request-response handshaking protocol is required by the control logic; no new control signal may be activated until a response has been received by the control logic to the currently active control signal. The characteristics of a daisy-chained memory bus were outlined, including the procedure for allowing an interrupt to initiate the DMA transfer of individual data words. It was pointed out that the microprogram control sequence for main storage operations can often be shared between multiple DMA devices attached to the memory bus. In general, the use of microprogram control to direct memory operations between main storage and the processor or DMA devices which share the memory bus requires that the microprogrammer have a detailed knowledge of the timing involved in all types of main storage operations. However, the DMA microcontrol becomes an extension of the microcontrol concepts used in the processor.

3.8 REFERENCES

1. ASHOK K. AGRAWALA and T. G. RANSCHER, *Foundations of Microprogramming Architecture, Software and Applications* (New York: Academic Press, 1976).

2. R. P. CAPECE, "Memories," *Electronics* (Oct. 26, 1978), 126–137.

3. R. P. CAPECE, "The Race Heats up in Fast Static RAM," *Electronics* (April 26, 1979), 125–135.

4. H. Y. CHANG, R. C. DORR and D. J. SENESE, "The Design of a Microprogrammed Self-Checking Processor of an Electronic Switching System," in *IEEE Trans. on Comput.*, C-22, No. 5 (May 1973), 489–500.

5. YAOHAN CHU, *Computer Organization and Microprogramming* (Englewood Cliffs, N.J.: Prentice-Hall, 1972).

6. S. J. DURHAM, "Fast LSI Arbiters Supervise Priorities for Bus-Access in Multiprocessor Systems," *Electron. Des.*, 27 (May 24, 1979), 128–133.

7. D. C. FORD, "Semiconductor Memories: Speed-Power Products Still Dropping," *Electron. Prod.* (June 1979), 51–54.

8. S. H. FULLER, V. C. LESSER, C. G. BELL, and C. H. KAMAN, "The Effects of Emerging Technology and Emulation Requirements on Microprogramming," *IEEE Trans. Comput.*, C-25, No. 10 (Oct. 1976), 1000–1009.

9. R. N. GOSSEN, JR., "The 64-Kbit RAM: A Prelude to VLSI," *Spectrum, 16* (March 1979), 42–44.

10. E. R. HNATEK, "Current Semiconductor Memories," *Comput. Des.*, 26 (April 1978), 115–128.

11. D. A. HODGES, *Semiconductor Memories* (New York: IEEE Press, 1972).

12. S. S. HUSSON, *Microprogramming—Principles and Practices* (Englewood Cliffs, N.J.: Prentice-Hall, 1970).

13. G. LUECKE, J. P. MIZE, and W. N. CARR, *Semiconductor Memory Design,* Texas Instrument Electronics Series (New York: McGraw-Hill, 1973).

14. *Meta 4 Computer System Microprogramming Reference Manual* (Publication 7043MO) (San Diego, Calif.: Digital Scientific, 1972).

15. *Microprogramming Handbook* (Irvine, Calif.: Microdata Corp., 1971).

16. *Microprogramming the 2IMX Computers* Manual 02108–90008 (Cupertino, Calif.: Hewlett-Packard, 1972).

17. *Model 80 Micro-Instruction Reference Manual* (Oceanport, N.J.: Interdata, 1973).

18. *Model 4 Micro-Programming Reference Manual* (Oceanport, N.J.: Interdata, 1968).

19. *Module 70 User's Manual* (Oceanport, N.J.: Interdata, 1971).

20. R. L. MORRIS and J. R. MILLER, *Designing with TTL Integrated Circuits,* Texas Instrument Electronics Series (New York: McGraw-Hill, 1971).

21. A. B. SALISBURY, *Microprogrammable Computer* (New York, Amsterdam: Elsevier, 1976).

22. T. F. STOREY, "Design of a Microprogram Control for a Processor in an Electronic Switching System," *Bell Syst. Tech. J., 55,* No. 2 (Feb. 1976), 183–232.

23. *2100 Computer Microprogramming Guide* (Cupertino, Calif.: Hewlett-Packard, 1972).

24. ANDREW VOLK, "Dynamic RAM Controller Performance/Cost Tradeoffs," *Comput. Des., 27* (March 1979), 127–140.

CHAPTER 4

Microprogram Control

of Input/Output

Operations

4.1 PROGRAMMED I/O

An *input/output* (I/O) transaction between a peripheral device and the *central processing unit* (CPU) in which the CPU executes I/O macroinstructions fetched from main storage is called a *program-controlled data transfer operation.* The state of a peripheral device may be characterized by the contents of its status word register. In its simplest form, a status word can be a single bit which specifies whether the peripheral is busy (i.e., already engaged in an I/O operation) or whether it is available to participate in an I/O transaction.* A processor initiates a programmed data transfer operation by requesting the status word of the target peripheral device. The processor examines the status word to determine if the peripheral is in the ready state (i.e., if it is available for use in an I/O operation). If the peripheral is

* George D. Kraft and Wing N. Toy, *Mini/Microcomputer Hardware Design* (Englewood Cliffs, N.J.: Prentice-Hall, 1979), Chap. 8.

ready (not in the BUSY state), the processor jumps to the program sequence in main storage to carry out the desired I/O transaction.

In a typical small computer system, a variety of peripheral devices may be connected to the processor via an I/O bus (a parallel busing path that a processor uses to pass data and control signals to and from its peripheral environment under the direction of a program placed in main storage). Each of these I/O devices may have a different *response time* (i.e., the time it takes an I/O device to respond with its status word to the processor after the processor has executed an I/O macroinstruction which queries the device about its current status). These response times can *vary* from a few microseconds to hundreds of milliseconds. In an attempt to accommodate this wide variation in the response times of peripheral devices, a programmed data transfer operation may be subdivided into several control steps. This subdivision process allows a standard software interface to be established between the processor and each I/O device.

The basic control steps associated with a programmed data transfer operation are shown in the flow diagram of Figure 4-1. A process called *polling* is used to determine the status of an I/O device attached to the processor. This procedure simply involves the processor requesting the status word of the target peripheral device to determine if the device is available to participate in an I/O transaction with the processor. The processor executes an I/O macroinstruction to request the status word from the peripheral and waits to receive a response from the target device. The first step in this program-controlled data transfer operation is for the processor to select the specific I/O device with which it wishes to dialogue. Typically, it does this by *either* broadcasting an address on the I/O bus which is recognized by the target device *or* by transmitting a selection pulse on a hardwired, dedicated control lead. The processor examines the status word supplied by the target peripheral to see if the processor should proceed with the I/O transaction. The flow diagram of Figure 4-1 shows the processor program control sequence continuously fetching and testing the status word of the target peripheral. This control loop is only broken when the status word indicates the peripheral is available to engage in a program-controlled data transfer operation.

When data is transmitted *from* the processor *to* the selected peripheral device (a *data output operation*), the examination of the status word by the processor ensures that the current I/O transaction is complete before another programmed I/O operation that also references the currently selected device is initiated.* Typically, a data output transaction will take the form of a

---

* Similarly, a *data input operation* corresponds to a data word transmitted *from* the peripheral device *to* the processor. In either case, the actions of the processor define whether the I/O transaction is an *input* operation or an *output* operation.

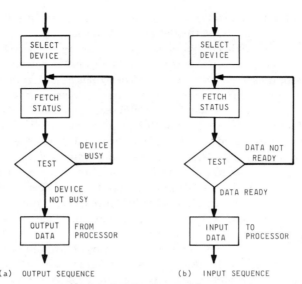

Figure 4-1 I/O Programmed Sequence

data word supplied by the processor to the peripheral. This data word may represent a command to the device controller associated with the target peripheral; the command would represent an operation to be performed by the peripheral such as reading the binary word stored in the peripheral at a location specified by the contents of the peripheral's internal address register. A simpler command might tell the peripheral to halt its current operation. Alternately, the data word could be a binary word to be stored within the peripheral at a location specified by the peripheral's internal address register. The general structure of an I/O bus and a typical device controller are shown in Figure 4-2. It is quite common to find separate buffer registers used by a device controller; one buffer register is dedicated to storing command information sent by the processor to the peripheral, another is dedicated to status information associated with the peripheral, and a third register functions as a two-way buffer for pure data words which are exchanged between the processor and the peripheral.

Typically, four basic commands are employed by the processor to control an I/O transaction which has been established by the processor:

1. *Output data (OD) command:* The data word in the processor's I/O buffer register is gated into the target peripheral's data register.
2. *Output a command (OC):* A data word that is interpreted as a control word is sent to the device controller of the target peripheral.
3. *Input data (ID) command:* The contents of the target peripheral's data register are gated into the processor's I/O buffer register.

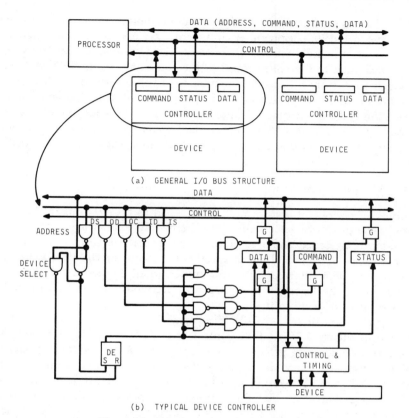

Figure 4-2 Processor-to-Device Data Transfer

4. *Input status (IS) command:* The contents of the target peripheral's status register are gated into the processor's I/O buffer register.

The preceding commands can be generated as the logical 1 outputs of four dedicated flip-flops with the same names located in the processor. Consequently, the sequence of fundamental I/O operations shown in Figure 4-1 can be implemented using the proper combination of the four basic commands. Microprogram control of programmed I/O operations implements the OD, OC, ID, and IS commands in microcode in addition to controlling the selection of the target peripheral device that is to respond to these commands.

4.2 GENERAL I/O DATA TRANSFER STRUCTURE

The basic information flow between the processor and a peripheral involves both data words and control signals. The I/O bus structure shown in Figure 4-2(a) is used as the communication facility over which this information flows. The I/O bus functions as a bidirectional communication link between the processor and its peripheral environment. I/O operations that originate at the processor include the address of the selected peripheral, the data word to be transmitted to the peripheral, and the command words (OD, OC, ID, IS) which specify that a specific function is to be performed by the device controller of the target peripheral. The peripheral, in turn, transmits status information and data words to the processor over the I/O bus in the opposite direction. A separate set of bus leads are dedicated to controlling the direction and timing of the data that flows over the I/O bus. They are not explicitly shown in Figure 4-2(a).

4.2.1   I/O Device Selection

A variety of peripheral devices may be attached to the I/O bus of the processor. The processor selects the target peripheral with which it wishes to communicate by broadcasting an address out over the I/O bus. It concurrently activates a control lead to specify the nature of the data word on the I/O bus. This information is transmitted to all devices attached to the I/O bus, but only the target peripheral will decode the control information and attempt to respond to it.

A functional diagram of the select logic in a typical device controller is shown in Figure 4-2(b). Five control leads (DS, OD, OC, ID, and IS) are shown as a separate group in the figure. The *device select* (DS) *lead* is used to select the target device controller. The other four control leads (OD, OC, ID, and IS) were defined in Sec. 4.1. The DS lead indicates to all the device controllers that the information appearing on the I/O bus is to be used to select which peripheral is the target device. The target device will decode its I/O bus address and, in conjunction with the activation of the DS lead, will set the *device enable* (DE) *flip-flop* of the target device. All other DE flip-flops will have been reset by the decoding process. Therefore, all subsequent data transfers will be with the selected device. Each peripheral device is assigned a unique address. The DEVICE SELECT gate, in combination with the DS lead, is used to set the DE flip-flop when the bit pattern on the I/O bus corresponds to the unique address of the target peripheral. Note that the DEVICE SELECT gate is used to clear the DE flip-flop of all unselected peripherals. This permits only one peripheral to be connected to the I/O bus at any given time.

4.2.2   I/O Data Transfer

For each I/O transaction between a peripheral device and the processor, a unique control signal is activated to direct the disposition of the data on the I/O bus. The control signals OD and OC are used by the processor to direct a data word from the I/O bus to the DATA or COMMAND buffer registers of the target device. The ID and IS signals are used to direct the contents of either the DATA buffer register or the STATUS buffer register onto the I/O bus.

The actual communication of control information between the processor and a peripheral device is done through the buffer registers provided in each device controller. The control logic associated with each controller is tailored to the characteristics of each peripheral. This means the commands will be interpreted by the control logic to perform operations that are peculiar to the target device. The device status information will typically be different for each new target device. It is up to the processor to interpret the information supplied by the target device accordingly.

4.3 I/O DATA TRANSFER CYCLE

A timing relationship must exist when data is transferred over the I/O bus from a buffer register in the processor to a buffer register in the target device controller. The timing requirements are normally incorporated in the sequence of control signals that are used to direct the I/O transaction. Typically, an I/O data transfer requires a longer interval to complete its operation than the execution of a simple machine macroinstruction that manipulates data internal to the processor. The physical separation of the target device controller from the processor may be sufficiently large to require an extended time interval for the device and the processor to complete their communication cycle. In addition, the cable drivers and cable receivers associated with the I/O bus require a longer time interval to operate properly.

In the design of a microprogram-controlled processor, the microprogram cycle is geared to the time to transfer a parallel data word between two registers that communicate with the same *internal* bus. Typically, this time, which can last 100 ns, can be used to define the duration of the elementary control operations or control primitives which are activated by a microinstruction. In contrast, an *external* I/O data transfer operation can require several microseconds. In terms of the microcycle time of a microprogrammed machine, an I/O data transfer operation may require in excess of 10 microcycles for successful completion. The longer I/O cycle time can be accomplished by executing a sequence of microinstructions which may include a series of micro *no-operations* (NOPs) that extend the microcontrol sequence for an I/O macroinstruction. An alternative approach is to have the processor clock enter an *extended internal cycle* when an I/O macroinstruction is initiated. A microcontrol signal would be used to extend the period of the clock. Both of these techniques will be covered in subsequent sections.

4.4 FULLY MICROPROGRAMMED CONTROL WITH FIXED TIMING SIGNALS

In an I/O transaction, the operation must be a coordinated effort between the processor and the target device controller. For an I/O transaction that uses a synchronous timing method, all control and timing information is furnished by the processor. The processor is responsible for placing the data and control information on the I/O *bus* and maintaining the state of the I/O bus for as many microcycles as are necessary to complete the I/O transaction. In addition, the processor must provide a strobe signal to the target device controller so that the data on the bus can be gated to the appropriate buffer register during the time interval in which the bus is stable. The generation of these control signals can be done fully under microprogram control.

Figure 4-3(a) illustrates the timing diagram and the relationship between the various control signals required to implement a transfer of data from the processor to a buffer register in a peripheral device. Each interval in the figure represents a microcycle or the time required to execute one microinstruction in the processor. Since the activation and duration of the I/O control signals are under microprogram control, their widths and spacings in time must be multiples of the basic microcycle associated with the processor. As shown in Figure 4-3(a), two consecutive data transfer operations are associated with an output transaction. The first data transfer provides the address that selects the target device controller; the second transfers the data word from the processor to the DATA buffer register in the device controller. It is assumed that the previous microinstruction has loaded the DATA buffer register in the processor with the device code.

4.4.1 Generation of Control Signals

To generate control signals that must remain active over several microcycles, microinstructions can be used to set and reset dedicated flip-flops. The outputs from these flip-flops can then be used to control the duration of I/O command pulses. Figures 4-3(a) and 4-3(b) illustrate a microprogram for performing an output data transfer. To select the target device controller, a microinstruction first sets the DATA flip-flop in the processor. The output of the DATA flip-flop gates the contents of the DATA register of the processor out onto the I/O bus. The next microinstruction sets the DS flip-flop in the processor, which, in turn, enables the DEVICE SELECT gate in the target device controller. This action sets the DE flip-flop in the device controller. As shown in Figure 4-3(a), the DS strobe pulse is arranged to be of sufficient width to ensure that it can set the DE flip-flop. This width adjustment takes into consideration the pulse propagation time from the processor

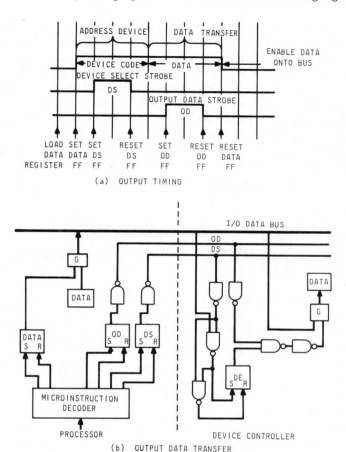

Figure 4-3 I/O Data Output Operation

to the device controller and the associated chain of logic gates through which the DS pulse must pass. Two microcycles are shown as allocated for the duration of the DS strobe pulse. In some cases, it may be necessary to make the next microinstruction an NOP to allow the DS pulse to extend for a second microcycle. The fourth microinstruction from the start of the output operation resets the DS flip-flop in the processor to terminate the DS control signal.

4.4.2 I/O Data Output Operation

Figure 4-3(a) shows an OD command immediately following the selection of the I/O device. Since the DATA flip-flop in the processor is already set, it is only necessary to update the information in the processor DATA register.   The present contents of the DATA register are the address of the target device selector engaged in the I/O transaction with the processor. The data word to be sent to the I/O device is taken from an internal register of the processor and moved into the DATA register with the execution of the next microinstruction.   To direct the data to the appropriate buffer register in the target device controller (i.e., the COMMAND buffer register or the DATA buffer register), the following microinstruction sets either the OC flip-flop or the OD flip-flop.   The OC or OD control signal, in conjunction with the output from the DE flip-flop in the target device controller, permits the data word on the I/O bus to be strobed into the appropriate register. The control signal (OC or OD) may be extended for a second microcycle by either of two methods:

1. An NOP microinstruction may be executed during the second microcycle, or
2. The next microinstruction may be used to activate other control primitives not used by the OC or OD control signals.

The OC or OD flip-flop is reset by a microinstruction to terminate the data transfer operation.   The last microinstruction in the output control sequence resets the DATA flip-flop in the processor.   This action removes the data word from the I/O bus and completes the output I/O transaction.

4.4.3   I/O Data Input Operation

The control of an I/O input operation is similar to the control of an output data transfer with the exception that the ID pulse can be generated by a single microinstruction rather than a sequence of microinstructions that can span several microcycles.   The reason for this simple control implementation is that the ID control signal can be well established within the processor. Figure 4-4 illustrates the timing and control logic associated with an input data transfer controlled by a sequence of microinstructions.   The two control signals (ID and DS) are generated by the processor and are used by the target device controller to gate data from either its DATA register or its STATUS register onto the I/O bus.   In general, these control signals can be several microcycles in duration; the actual pulse width is determined by the time sequence of the two microinstructions used to form the ID or IS signals, that is, the time relationship of the microinstruction used to set the ID or IS control flip-flop and the microinstruction used to clear the control flip-flop.

The microprogram control of the pulse width (duration) of various I/O control signals allows a wide variety of peripheral devices to be interfaced to the processor in a very straightforward manner.   If a different pulse width

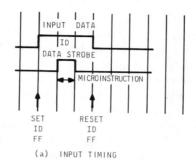

(a) INPUT TIMING

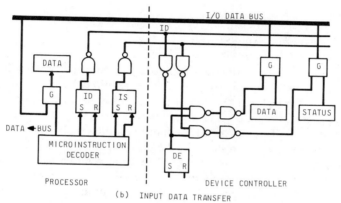

(b) INPUT DATA TRANSFER

Figure 4-4 I/O Data Input Operation

is required for a given control signal, it can be easily obtained by changing the associated sequence of microinstructions.

4.5 FULLY MICROPROGRAMMED CONTROL WITH VARIABLE TIMING SIGNALS

A microprogrammed control section that uses fixed timing signals is normally associated with a synchronous I/O operation. In a synchronous operation, the processor supplies the clock signals. For each control function (i.e., OD, OC, ID, and IS) the pulse width is fixed to ensure that the specified I/O operation will be completed even under the worst-case operating conditions (i.e., worst-case gate delays, length of logic chains, etc.). The same control signal is broadcast to all peripheral devices. If there are variations in the timing of these control signals between the peripheral devices, the control logic must account for these variations.

An alternative I/O communication technique is to use an asynchronous request-response data transfer operation. Each control signal transmitted to the target device controller is held in the active state until a completion signal (acknowledgment) is received from the target device. This type of operation is also called an *asynchronous, handshaking data transfer.* The time to perform the transfer of a single data word between the processor and its peripheral environment may vary from device to device. The determining factor in the timing of a data transfer is how rapidly the target peripheral generates an acknowledgment signal once it has recognized a control signal transmitted by the processor. The actual timing relationships of the control signals can be adapted to the requirements of each individual device in the peripheral environment using separate sequences of microinstructions in which each sequence could handle the I/O control signals for a specific peripheral.

4.5.1 Generation of Control Signals

Using a request-response timing relationship, a control signal will still be held active for as many microcycles as are required by the data transfer control logic. Typically, a flip-flop in the processor will be used to generate the desired control signal. The flip-flop will be set by the data transfer control logic and will stay in the SET condition until a reply signal is returned from the target device controller. In the previous fixed timing arrangement, the control flip-flop was reset at a fixed interval relative to when the flip-flop was set. The reset function was performed by a microinstruction after the microcontrol had determined that the appropriate timing interval had passed. In an asynchronous request-response data transfer, the reply from the device controller is used to reset the control flip-flop in the processor. For the asynchronous case, the response from a device controller may be received by the processor at a variable time interval from when the I/O command was transmitted by the processor. Hence, this type of I/O is also called a *variable control operation.*

Figure 4-5 illustrates the timing relationship of the control signals and the logic circuitry required to implement the DEVICE SELECT function. The control technique shown in the figure allows a control signal to be extended over several microcycles. This technique is based upon the repetitive execution of the same microinstruction until a predetermined condition occurs in the hardware. In this case, the condition is the reception of the response signal generated by the device controller. As shown in the figure, the decoded microinstruction controls when the contents of the processor DATA register are gated onto the I/O bus. The data transfer control logic must allow sufficient time for the data to settle on the I/O bus before the DEVICE SELECT (DS) flip-flop is set in the processor. The output of the DS flip-flop enables the addressed DEVICE SELECT gate in the device controller.

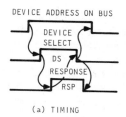

(a) TIMING

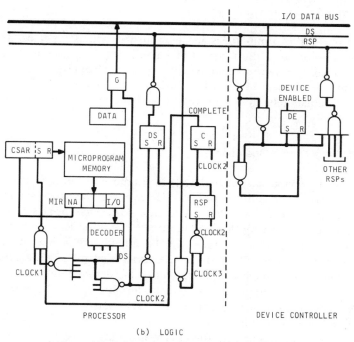

(b) LOGIC

Figure 4-5   Microprogram Device Select Operation

This action permits the **DEVICE ENABLE (DE)** flip-flop in the device controller to be set.   The device controller uses the reception of the DS control
signal to generate a **RESPONSE (RSP)** signal which is returned to the processor.   The RSP signal indicates to the processor that the **DEVICE SELECT**
function has been accomplished.   The RSP signal is coordinated with the
execution of the microinstruction sequence such that the leading edge of
the RSP pulse resets the DS flip-flop and sets the **COMPLETE (C)** flip-
flop in the processor.

The following technique is used by the logic circuit shown in Figure
4-5 to loop on a specific microinstruction:

1. The address of the current microinstruction is assumed to be an even address in which the least-significant bit in the CSAR is in the 0 state.
2. The address of the next microinstruction is formed by setting the least-significant bit of the CSAR to the 1s state.
3. When the C flip-flop is set, the least-significant bit in the CSAR is set to the 1s state; otherwise, the contents of the CSAR are left unchanged, and the current microinstruction is again executed.
4. The repetitive execution of the current microinstruction is terminated only *after* the C flip-flop has been set and the microcontrol sequence is permitted to proceed to the next sequential address.

The number of times the same microinstruction is repeated depends on the response time of the target device controller (i.e., how long it takes for the processor to receive an acknowledgment signal from the device controller). In the case shown in Figure 4-5, the response from the device controller is received immediately by the processor, and the current microinstruction is executed only once.

4.5.2 I/O Data Output Operation

As mentioned previously, the first step in establishing an I/O transaction between the processor and a peripheral device is for the processor to select the appropriate device controller. After the device has been selected, the microprogram must specify that a data output operation is to be performed. The data word from the processor will be directed to either the DATA register or the COMMAND register in the device controller. For simplicity, only the logic to implement a data transfer to the device controller's DATA register is shown in Figure 4-6. A separate flip-flop called the *output Data* (OD) *flip-flop* is dedicated to providing the OD control signal. The output of the OD flip-flop is used in combination with the output from the DEVICE ENABLE (DE) flip-flop to gate the data word transmitted by the processor from the I/O bus into the DATA register of the device controller. The RSP signal returned by the device controller resets the other I/O timing control flip-flops in the processor. The RSP signal also resets the OD flip-flop and the C flip-flop. The last action completes the execution of the current microinstruction. The timing for this operation is the same as the timing for the DEVICE SELECT operation discussed in Section 4.5.1.

4.5.3 I/O Data Input Operation

The timing relationship of the microprogram control signals used for an input data operation is somewhat different from the timing used for an output data operation. The basic concern in this case is that the data placed on

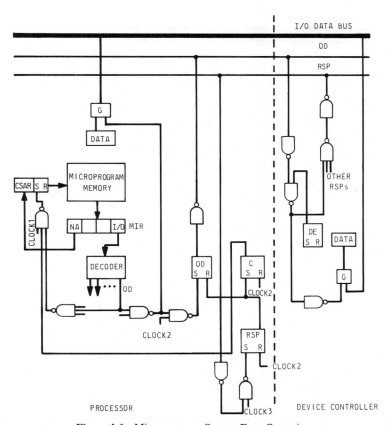

Figure 4-6 Microprogram Output Data Operation

the I/O bus by the device controller is gated into the DATA register of the processor. This gating operation must be performed after the data has settled on the bus. The correct design procedure to ensure that the information has stabilized on the bus is to first gate the data word from the buffer register of the device controller onto the bus, then apply the gate-in pulse to strobe the data from the bus, and finally remove the data word from the bus *after* the strobe pulse has been removed. In the logic implementation, the data word *must* be stable on the I/O bus during the entire time interval in which the strobe pulse is applied. Other logic arrangements such as a design that utilizes JK or D flip-flops may require the data to be stable on the bus only during the leading edge or trailing edge of the I/O control signals.

Figure 4-7 shows the logic involved in transferring a data word from a device controller to the processor. The ID flip-flop is set by the microin-

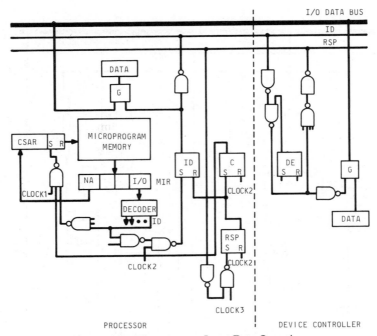

Figure 4-7 Microprogram Input Data Operation

struction that directs the target device selector to gate the contents of its DATA register onto the I/O bus. Once the ID flip-flop is set, it enables the input gates to the processor DATA register so that the data on the bus may be gated directly into the processor data register. Upon receipt of the ID command signal from the processor, the device controller returns the RSP signal to the processor, indicating that the desired data is available on the bus. The reception of the RSP signal from the device controller sets the C flip-flop in the processor to conclude the execution of the current microinstruction.

This logic design also allows the microcontrol sequence to repetitively execute the current microinstruction until the C flip-flop is set. The procedure is identical to that outlined in Sec. 4.5.1. To fetch I/O STATUS information, the same logic arrangement is used as that shown in Figure 4-7. The only difference between a data input operation and a fetch STATUS operation is that an IS command is used to select the contents of the STATUS register in the device controller as opposed to the contents of the DATA register.

The repetitive execution of the current microinstruction provides a variable delay in the completion of an I/O data transfer operation. This means that the same microinstruction may be executed a varying number of times, depending on the response time of the selected device controller.

4.6 I/O HARDWARE CYCLE TIMING

In many I/O transactions, the I/O command sequence must extend over several microcycles. The ability to provide an extended period of operation must be included in the way the I/O commands *interact* with the microinstruction sequence. This interaction does *not* require an external clock to generate the control signals whose durations may be multiples of the basic microexecution cycle. If external timing signals are provided, the I/O operation is arranged to work synchronously with the system timing signals associated with the microprogram control unit. The timing relationships used to implement an I/O transaction may be broken up into a major cycle that is composed of a series of minor cycles. A *major cycle* is determined by the time required by the processor to perform an I/O operation. A *minor cycle* is the period of time required to execute a single microinstruction.

As an example, Figure 4-8 shows a fixed cycle timing relationship in which a major cycle is made up of four minor cycles. A common clock

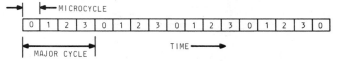

Figure 4-8 Fixed Cycle Timing

produces the timing signals that are used to FETCH and EXECUTE a microinstruction every microcyle; another set of timing signals is derived from this common clock. This other set is associated with each major cycle and is used to control the time sequencing of the I/O operation. These same two sets of timing signals may also be used to control an access of main storage by the processor. (This procedure minimizes the number of clock pulses that must be generated.)

4.7 PARTIAL MICROPROGRAMMED CONTROL WITH FIXED CYCLE TIMING

In an I/O transaction that is fully determined by a microprogram, the control flip-flops that generate the I/O command signals are set and reset by microinstructions that are executed at appropriate times determined by the I/O hardware. When a set of timing pulses which extend over several microcycles is provided by the microprogram control unit, the control flip-flops can be automatically reset by the appropriate extended clock pulses. This capability allows a single microinstruction to initiate the I/O transaction, but no further action would be required by the microprogram sequence. The I/O control logic would use the necessary timing pulses to continue the I/O transaction to completion. Additional hardware can be provided to facilitate the control

151

of the I/O operation.   Typically, such additional hardware is used to increase
the execution speed of the I/O transaction by allowing several control steps
to occur concurrently.   For instance, the separate I/O control operations
of (1) initiating the I/O transaction, (2) selecting the target device controller,
and (3) gating data from a processor register onto the I/O data bus can all
be performed concurrently.   The primary requirement for this procedure is
that the I/O bus be expanded to include the address of the device to be
used in the I/O transaction.

Figure 4-9 illustrates a timing scheme that uses four fixed intervals
within a major cycle to coordinate an output data transfer operation.   The

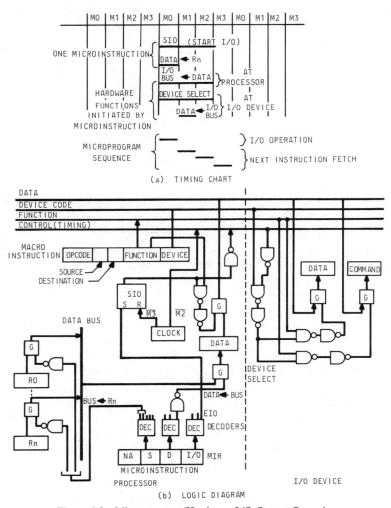

Figure 4-9   Microprogram/Hardware I/O Output Operation

four fixed intervals, M0 through M3, represent microcycles in which a microinstruction may be executed. When an I/O operation is initiated, it is always timed to begin during the M0 microcycle (for instance, a START__ I/O microinstruction would be executed during this interval). Since the START__I/O microinstruction could occur during any microcycle, it is synchronized with the major cycle of the I/O transaction so that each step in the control of an I/O transaction may be carried out properly.

4.7.1 I/O Macroinstruction Format

A typical arrangement of implementing an input data transfer operation to the processor is shown in Figure 4-10. It is assumed that the START__ I/O microinstruction occurs during minor cycle M0. The macroinstruction

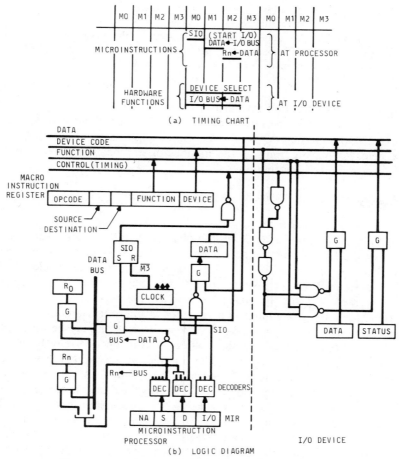

Figure 4-10 Microprogram/Hardware I/O Input Operation

fetched from main storage completely specifies the I/O operation to be performed. The *I/O macroinstruction* consists of the following fields:

1. OPCODE: This specifies that an I/O operation is to be performed and whether it is to be an input data transfer or an output data transfer.
2. SOURCE: This represents the address of the general register (R0 through Rn) that is to act as the source of the data; this data is to be gated onto the I/O bus.
3. DESTINATION: This specifies the address of the general register that is to receive the data word transferred from the I/O device to the processor.
4. FUNCTION: This field identifies the register in the target device controller that is to be used in the I/O transaction and decides whether it is to be used to send or receive data. For example, a data word could be sent from the DATA register or STATUS register of the I/O device; similarly, a data word could be received by the COMMAND register or the DATA register of the I/O device.
5. DEVICE: This field specifies the address of the device controller to be used in the I/O transaction. It is entirely possible that an I/O device may use two or more device controllers. The address of each device controller *must* be unique.

With the macroinstruction format shown in Figure 4-10, the output of the FUNCTION field and the DEVICE field may be used directly as additional control signals on the I/O bus. The direct application of the outputs of these fields to the bus reduces the number of microcontrol steps required to process the macroinstruction.

4.7.2 Macroinstruction-Initiated I/O Output Operation

In the case of a macroinstruction which initiates a data output operation, the data word is transferred from one of the general registers (R0 through Rn) over the I/O bus to the appropriate input register in the target device controller. As shown in Figure 4-9, the data word is directed to the DATA register or COMMAND register of the I/O device by the operation(s) specified by the contents of the FUNCTION field of the macroinstruction. The macroinstruction opcode initiates a sequence of microinstructions which implement the data output operation. A separate opcode may be assigned to specify an output macroinstruction, while another opcode may be used to specify an input macroinstruction. The first microinstruction in the execution sequence shown in Figure 4-9 performs two functions: (1) It sets the START__I/O (SIO) flip-flop, and (2) it transfers the contents of the specified general register into the DATA register of the processor. Setting the SIO flip-flop automatically initiates the hardware control sequence to transfer the contents of the processor DATA register into one of the internal registers of the target I/O device. While the I/O transaction is automatically proceeding to completion under control of the I/O hardware, the microcontrol sequence may concurrently carry out other unrelated operations within the processor such as the FETCH of the next macroinstruction. The output of the SIO flip-flop is set for three microcycles and is used in combination with the output of the FUNCTION field in the macroinstruction register to gate the contents of the DATA register onto the I/O bus. Since the FUNCTION field and DEVICE field outputs are bus signals and are held in a stable condition during the duration of the macroinstruction, the DEVICE SELECT gate in the target I/O device directs the SIO signal to the data transfer logic of the selected device controller. The SIO signal (in conjunction with additional timing pulses) is used to gate the data word on the I/O bus into the DATA register or command register of the selected device controller. When the SIO flip-flop is reset by the M3 pulse from the processor clock circuit, all the control signals associated with the data output operation are terminated. This completes the I/O data transfer specified by the macroinstruction.

4.7.3 Macroinstruction-Initiated I/O Input Operation

The timing and control logic associated with a data input operation initiated by a macroinstruction is given in Figure 4-10. The first microinstruction in the microinterpretation sequence for the data input macroinstruction sets the START I/O (SIO) flip-flop. The output of the SIO flip-flop is placed on the I/O bus and is used by the target device controller to gate the contents of either its DATA register or its STATUS register onto the bus. The specific register in the target device controller is specified by the contents of the function field in the macroinstruction register. A microinstruction strobes the data on the I/O bus into the processor DATA register at M1, and the contents of the processor DATA register are transferred into the general register specified by the DESTINATION field of the macroinstruction during the M2 minor cycle. These two gating signals may also be performed automatically by the I/O hardware. The actual way the gating signals are realized depends on whether the gating signals are implemented in hardware as opposed to the processor using a sequence of microinstructions to specify their occurrence.

4.8 I/O SYNCHRONIZATION OF FIXED CYCLE TIMING

During each microcycle, a set of fundamental timing pulses may be used to control when a specific microoperation or control primitive is enabled. These fundamental timing pulses are generated by the processor clock. Each major cycle is made up of a fixed set of microcycles or a set time interval which is used by all I/O operations. Figure 4-11(a) illustrates how

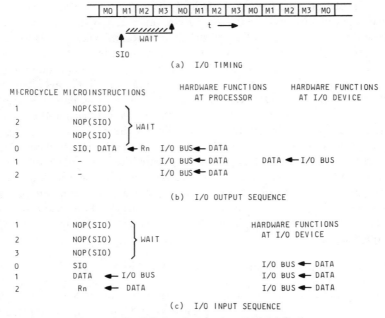

(a) I/O TIMING

MICROCYCLE	MICROINSTRUCTIONS	HARDWARE FUNCTIONS AT PROCESSOR	HARDWARE FUNCTIONS AT I/O DEVICE
1	NOP(SIO) ⎫		
2	NOP(SIO) ⎬ WAIT		
3	NOP(SIO) ⎭		
0	SIO, DATA ◄─ Rn	I/O BUS ◄─ DATA	
1	–	I/O BUS ◄─ DATA	DATA ◄─ I/O BUS
2	–	I/O BUS ◄─ DATA	

(b) I/O OUTPUT SEQUENCE

1	NOP(SIO) ⎫		
2	NOP(SIO) ⎬ WAIT		HARDWARE FUNCTIONS AT I/O DEVICE
3	NOP(SIO) ⎭		
0	SIO		I/O BUS ◄─ DATA
1	DATA ◄─ I/O BUS		I/O BUS ◄─ DATA
2	Rn ◄─ DATA		I/O BUS ◄─ DATA

(c) I/O INPUT SEQUENCE

Figure 4-11 I/O Synchronization of Fixed Cycle

an I/O operation is synchronized with the basic microcycle sequence of a major I/O cycle. The SIO microinstruction that initiates the I/O operation is always executed during the M0 microcycle. Even though the SIO microinstruction can be executed during any microcycle, its execution is delayed by the microcontrol logic until the M0 microcycle. The sequence of microinstructions used to output data to the target device controller is shown in Figure 4-11(b); a similar sequence of microinstructions used to input data to the processor from the target device controller is shown in Figure 4-11(c). The synchronization of the I/O operation with the fixed microcycle sequence used by the processor is achieved by repeatedly executing an NOP microinstruction and by *not* executing the SIO macroinstruction until the M0 interval occurs.

4.8.1   Repetitive Free-Running I/O Cycle Timing

Figure 4-12 illustrates how the microprogram is placed into a WAIT loop. The next address field in the microinstruction register (MIR) contains the address of the current microinstruction (typically an NOP microinstruction). Thus, the same microinstruction is repeatedly executed until the occurrence of the M0 microcyle. The M0 microcycle breaks the WAIT loop by setting

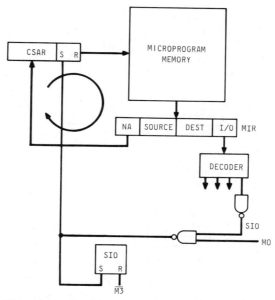

Figure 4-12 Conditional Wait Microprogram Wait Loop

the SIO flip-flop and adding 1 to the contents of the CSAR after the next address field has been loaded into the CSAR. The microcontrol sequence is then directed to the next microinstruction in the sequence. If the microinstruction format does not make use of a next address field, a WAIT loop may be established by inhibiting the increment by one mechanism associated with the CSAR which will then function as a pure binary counter. The inhibition of the increment pulse leaves the address of the current microinstruction in the CSAR and forces the current microinstruction to be repeatedly executed until the occurrence of the M0 microcycle removes the inhibit signal. The timing relationship shown in Figure 4-11(a) is also called a *free-running, fixed I/O cycle.*

4.8.2 Repetitive Non-Free-Running I/O Cycle Timing

A fixed major cycle composed of fixed microcycles results in a microprogram experiencing unnecessary pauses in its microexecution sequence because the I/O bus is not engaged in an I/O transaction or is in the IDLE state. These unnecessary WAIT intervals when the processor executes an NOP microinstruction can be significantly reduced using the I/O cycle timing shown in Figure 4-13(a). Instead of generating a continuous set of timing pulses (M0 through M3), the timing circuitry can be arranged so that the microexecution sequence pauses at the beginning of the M0 microcycle and

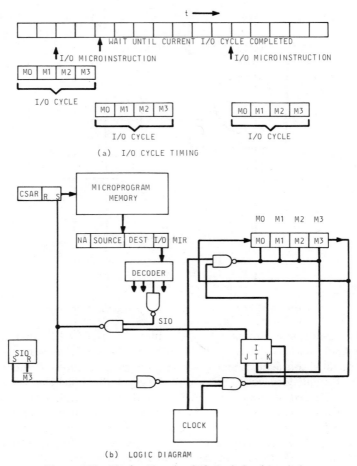

Figure 4-13   Nonfree-Running I/O Cycle Implementation

does not continue until the required I/O operation has been completed (i.e., the C flip-flop is set). When an I/O microinstruction is encountered by the microcontrol logic and an I/O transaction is currently active, the SIO microinstruction will not be executed until the current I/O operation has been completed. If the SIO microinstruction occurs after the previous I/O operation has been completed, the SIO microinstruction will be executed immediately.

Figure 4-13(b) illustrates the implementation of a non-free-running I/O cycle-timing logic. The timing signal is derived from the contents of a 4-bit shift register. When the shift register is in the IDLE state, a 1 is stored in bit 0 (the leftmost bit) with the remaining bits held in the 0 state. So long as the shift register is in the IDLE state, a status bit or IDLE (I) flip-flop is set, indicating that an I/O microinstruction can be executed by the microcontrol unit. As shown in Figure 4-13(b), if the IDLE flip-flop is in the 1s state and an SIO microinstruction is detected in the MIR, the SIO flip-flop will be set. The setting of the SIO flip-flop starts the I/O control cycle and causes the SIO microinstruction to be executed. The execution of the SIO microinstruction clears the IDLE (I) flip-flop and allows the clock signal to advance the 1 in the shift register from bit 0 to bit 1. Each shift defines a new microcycle (M0, M1, M2, M3) until the 1 is circularly shifted back into bit 0. When a 1 is again loaded into bit 0, the IDLE flip-flop is again set. The IDLE flip-flop being in the 1s state inhibits any outputs from the clock from having any effect on the shift register and allows another SIO microinstruction to occur, thus repeating the same sequence of operations (i.e., generating another cycle of timing pulses, M0 through M3).

4.9 SUMMARY

The microprogram control of an I/O transaction is similar to the microprogram control of an access of main storage. In some minicomputers and most second-generation microcomputers, the I/O devices share a common bus with main memory. The I/O devices occupy a portion of the address spectrum of the common bus; the communication sequence that occurs between a selected I/O device functions essentially the same as when main storage is referenced.

A basic aspect of establishing an I/O transaction is for the processor to specify which I/O device is to act as the target peripheral in the information exchange. The processor performs the device selection by transmitting an address and a DS command to all devices in the peripheral environment. The I/O device whose address corresponds to the address sent by the processor accepts the DS command and begins the specified I/O operation.

In general, a microprogram-controlled I/O operation requires that the logic designer be familiar with timing as well as the generation of the individual control signals that implement the data transfer operation. Microprogram-controlled I/O operations may be done with fixed or variable timing signals. In either case, the information contained in the macroinstruction must be used by the sequence of microinstructions that implement the control of the actual I/O operation. Many of these details are a function of the specific application requirements, including precisely how the I/O timing is synchronized with the microexecution timing of a microinstruction.

4.10 REFERENCES

1. Ashok K. Agrawala and T. G. Rauscher, *Foundations of Microprogramming Architecture, Software and Applications* (New York: Academic Press, 1976).

2. H. Y. Chang, R. C. Dorr, and D. J. Senese, "The Design of a Microprogrammed Self-Checking Processor of an Electronic Switching System," in *IEEE Trans. on Comput.,* C-22, No. 5, (May 1973), 489–500.

3. R. W. Cook, W. H. Sisson, T. F. Storey, and W. N. Toy, "Design of a Microprogram Control for Self-Checking," in *IEEE Trans. on Comput.,* C-22, No. 3, (March 1973), 255–262.

4. *HP 2100 Computer Microprogramming Guide* (Cupertino, Calif.: Hewlett-Packard, 1972).

5. S. S. Husson, *Microprogramming—Principles and Practices* (Englewood Cliffs, N.J.: Prentice-Hall, 1970).

6. *Meta 4 Computer System Microprogramming Reference Manual* (Publication 7043MO) (San Diego, Calif.: Digital Scientific, 1972).

7. *Microprogramming Handbook* (Irvine, Calif.: Microdata Corp., 1971).

8. *Model 4 Micro-Programming Reference Guide* (Oceanport, N.J.: Interdata, 1968).

9. R. L. Morris and J. R. Miller, *Designing with TTL Integrated Circuits,* Texas Instruments Electronics Series (New York: McGraw-Hill, 1971).

10. A. B. Salisbury, *Microprogrammable Computer* (New York, Amsterdam: Elsevier, 1976).

11. T. F. Storey, "Design of a Microprogram Control for a Processor in an Electronic Switching System," *Bell Syst. Tech. J., 55,* No. 2 (Feb. 1976), 183–232.

PART II

Fault-Tolerant Design

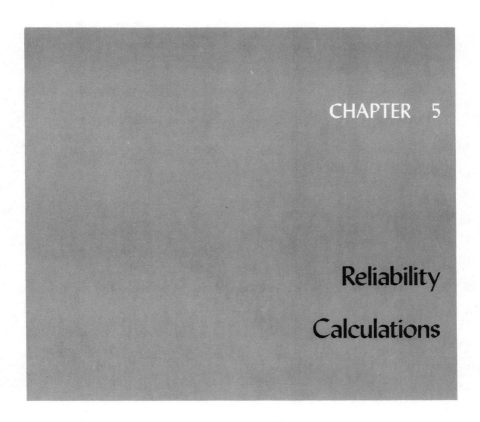

CHAPTER 5

Reliability
Calculations

5.1 INTRODUCTION

5.1.1 Definition of Reliability

The term *reliability* has been used repeatedly in various books and journals to describe qualitatively the performance of a device or system. In common usage, this term's accepted definition does not involve numerical values. The definition of reliability as the characteristic of an item expressed by the probability that it will perform a required function under stated conditions for a stated period of time is commonly accepted in engineering applications. *Probability* is the likelihood of the occurrence of an event. It is a quantitative measure either calculated or derived from experimental observations. It may be a function of time and other parameters determined by the situations being considered. For example, the reliability objectives of a telephone switching office designed for use in the Bell System are (1) a total system downtime of no more than 2 hours during the 40-year life of the switching system and (2) no more than 0.01 percent of the calls should be lost or handled incorrectly during the system's operation. Satisfactory operation, in this case, is not 100 percent; a few incomplete or wrong connections are permissible since the customer is expected to immediately redial and obtain the correct connection. On the other hand, a malfunction in critical equipment, such as underwater amplifiers in the transatlantic cable system, may cause an entire system to become inoperative. In this case, satisfactory operation requires all amplifiers to be working. This situation can be compared to a chain of Christmas lights connected in series; when one light is defective, none of the others will be energized.

The length of time of operation for a telephone switching system is simply the life span of the equipment that makes up the system. The switching system must function continuously, without interruption, until the equipment is replaced at the end of its life or for some other reason. Since service must be provided 24 hours a day, there can be no scheduled system downtime for repair or maintenance.

In contrast, the life span of an airborne missile is equivalent to the duration of its mission, which can be quite short when compared with the 40-year life of telephone switching equipment.

The following parameters can individually or collectively have a marked effect on the reliability of a given system: environmental conditions (temperature, humidity, pressure, vibration, shock, radiation, corrosive atmosphere), operating conditions (voltage, current, and power dissipation), and so on. Some of these factors are more difficult and expensive to control than others, but all of them do contribute to the reliability characteristic of a system.

5.1.2   Failure Rate

When an item no longer works as intended, it has failed to perform its required function. An item may be any part, subsystem, system, or equipment that can be individually evaluated and separately tested. Well-defined failures which are usually both sudden and complete are normally referred to as *catastrophic failures*. Such failures are unpredictable and may not be evident during normal testing procedures. Failures that take place gradually in equipment that is operational are classified as *degradation failures*. Often such failures are partial (i.e., the equipment will function correctly part of the time). Degradation failures are the result of aging, which causes certain characteristics of the equipment under consideration to deviate beyond specified limits. In many instances, failures of this type cause intermittent or marginal conditions that are extremely difficult to isolate. Techniques of *stressing* the operating conditions to force partial failures to become complete failures have been used to identify the weak components before they become troublesome to a working system.

The failure pattern of equipment placed in service can be categorized naturally into three periods of operation. At the very beginning, any inherently weak parts that are the result of improper design, improper manufacture, or improper use usually fail fairly soon. The early failure rate, although relatively high, decreases progressively and eventually levels off as the weak components are replaced. This situation is illustrated in Figure 5-1 and is called the *early life period* of a system. The diagram in Figure 5-1 is commonly referred to as the *bathtub curve*. The curve is divided into three periods. Many early failures can be sorted out by the burn-in test or by 100 percent inspection. Such a practice is common in eliminating all "weaklings" by subjecting components to tests under accelerated conditions. Similarly, systems are operated for a period of time under varying conditions to ensure detection of early failures or potential failures. This practice is certainly a must for equipment aboard airborne missiles and satellites, which are nonrepairable during missions. This type of inspection is also highly desirable for repairable equipment such as undersea transatlantic amplifiers whose repair is a major undertaking and very expensive. For low-cost small computers, a 100 percent burn-in of components may not be economically feasible. However, a certain amount of stressing components by varying the power supply voltages or increasing the clock rate may identify marginal components in a working system.

After the early failures have been replaced, the components settle down to a long, relatively steady period at an approximately constant failure rate. In this period, the failure rate is usually low, and the failures are unlikely to be due to any single cause. This means the failures from a wide variety of causes occur at random and at a uniform rate without any obvious pattern. The normal working life of a system occurs during this interval. This interval is also called the *useful life period* of a system.

In the *wear-out period,* the components rapidly deteriorate, and each component eventually wears out. The failure rate, as indicated in Figure 5-1, rises again. The wear-out failures can be avoided by replacing components before they reach this period. As an example, the wear-out period

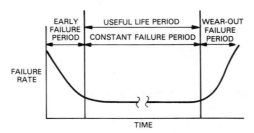

Figure 5-1 Typical Bathtub Curve of Failure Rate Versus Time

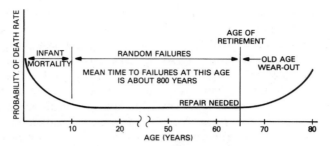

Figure 5-2   Human Life Characteristics

for automobile batteries usually begins at the end of the warranty.   The item must then be replaced in order to ensure continued reliable service.

Human life characteristics closely observe the bathtub curve shown in Figure 5-2.   The first part of the curve is normally referred to as the *infant mortality period.*   Infants unfortunate enough to be born with physical defects or weaknesses die in the early years of life.   After the tenth year, the death rate drops to its lowest level, and a majority of those who survive live to old age.   The deaths occurring during the second period are attributed to a wide variety of causes, occurring on a random basis at a constant rate. In the sixtieth and seventieth years, the curve rises as people begin to die of natural causes.   This is the period of old age.   The risk of death continues to increase with age until everyone in the group is dead.

5.2   RELIABILITY CALCULATION WITH CONSTANT FAILURE RATE

The constant failure rate represented by the useful life portion of Figure 5-1 implies that the probability of failure is independent of age.   This simply means that old equipment that is still operating is just as good as new equipment that has been recently installed.   For any constant failure rate, the value of reliability depends only on time.   A reliability function that is characterized by a constant failure rate is the negative exponential distribution. The negative exponential distribution function has the following form:

$$R = e^{-\lambda t} \tag{1}$$

Where λ = failure rate and t = time.

It is assumed that when a system commences operation (begins its mission time at $t = 0$) all components are operational.   By this assumption, $R(0) = 1$.   Since all components must fail in infinite time, $R(\infty) = 0$.   Figure 5-3 illustrates the negative exponential reliability function for different constant failure rates.   The reliability curve descends more steeply with a larger value of λ (the failure rate), but the general shape remains the same.   The

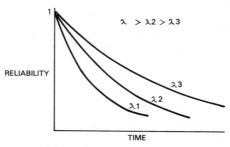

Figure 5-3   Reliability Function with Constant Failure Rate

importance of the negative exponential distribution function is that the reliability is independent of where time $t = 0$ is defined.   If an item of equipment has a failure rate of λ, its reliability for the period of time t is $e^{-\lambda t}$.   If at the end of this time the item is still in the same operating condition, its reliability for the next time period of equal duration is still $e^{-\lambda t}$.   During the interval when the equipment failure rate is relatively constant, the negative exponential function is a good representation of the reliability of the equipment.

The reliability function for a constant failure rate can easily be shown to take on the negative exponential distribution.   Assume that a large number of components are tested.   The reliability at any time t is simply the probability that a device has survived from the time $t = 0$ to time "t" and that the device has functioned properly during that interval of time.   Since the reliability R is a probability, it may also be represented as the ratio of the number of units still operating at time "t," N_S, divided by the total number of units that began the test, N_T.   This ratio may be represented as

$$R = \frac{N_S}{N_T} \tag{2}$$

Since the total number of units that began the test, N_T, is equal to the *sum* of the number of units still operating at time "t," N_S, *and* the number of units that have failed up to time "t," N_F, Eq. (2) may be expressed as

$$R = \frac{N_S}{N_T} = \frac{N_T - N_F}{N_T} = 1 - \frac{N_F}{N_T} \tag{3}$$

By differentiating Eq. (3), the following expression is obtained:

$$\frac{dR}{dt} = -\frac{1}{N_T} \frac{dN_F}{dt} \tag{4}$$

By multiplying both sides of Eq. (4) by N_T/N_S, the result is

$$\frac{N_T}{N_S} \frac{dR}{dt} = -\frac{1}{N_S} \frac{dN_F}{dt} \tag{5}$$

The term dN_F/dt is the frequency at which failures occur. When this term is divided by the number of units still operating, N_S, the expression $(1/N_S)$ (dN_F/dt) is the *instantaneous failure rate* for one component:

$$\frac{1}{N_S}\frac{dN_F}{dt} = \lambda(t) \tag{6}$$

In general, the instantaneous failure rate is a function of time. By combining Eqs. (2) and (6), Eq. (5) may be rewritten as

$$\frac{1}{R}\frac{dR}{dt} = -\lambda(t) \tag{7}$$

or

$$\frac{dR}{R} = -\lambda(t)\ dt \tag{8}$$

Assume that the instantaneous failure rate $\lambda(t)$ is a constant, λ_0. If Eq. (8) is integrated from $t = 0$ to $t = t$ and from $R(t) = R(0)$ to $R(t) = R$, we obtain

$$\int_1^R \frac{dR}{R} = -\int_0^t \lambda_0\ dt \tag{9}$$

Note that the boundary condition $R(0) = 1$ implies that the reliability of all devices included in the test at time $t = 0$ is unity. The resulting integration yields

$$\ln R = -\lambda_0 t \tag{10}$$

Solving for the reliability functions $R(t)$ gives the following:

$$R(t) = e^{-\lambda_0 t} \tag{11}$$

Therefore, for devices with a constant failure rate, the associated reliability function is given by the negative exponential distribution function as indicated by Eq. (11).

A physical system normally consists of many different types of components (i.e., transistors, connectors, switches, etc.). Typically, each type of component has a different instantaneous failure rate. One means of characterizing a physical system is to treat each component as being in *series* with the other components in the system. Consequently, when a single component fails, the entire system fails. The reliability function of the entire system is represented by the product of the individual reliability functions for each component. In making this statement, it is assumed that the reliability of each component is independent of all other components. The overall system reliability function may be represented by the expression

$$R_T = R_1 R_2 * \cdots R_i * \cdots R_n \tag{12}$$

If the reliability function for each component is given by an exponential distribution function, that is,

$$R_i(t) = e^{-\lambda_i t} \tag{13}$$

then Eq. (12) becomes

$$R_T = e^{-\lambda_1 t} e^{-\lambda_2 t} \cdots e^{-\lambda_i t} \cdots e^{-\lambda_n t} \tag{14}$$

Collecting terms and simplifying Eq. (14), yields the following expression:

$$R_T = e^{-(\lambda_1 + \lambda_2 + \cdots + \lambda_i + \cdots + \lambda_n)t} \tag{15}$$

For a *series interconnection* of components whose individual reliability functions are exponential, the failure rate for the total system is the sum of the individual failure rates of each component.

5.3 MEAN TIME BETWEEN FAILURES

The *mean time between failures* (MTBF) may be regarded as the average time an item may be expected to function before it fails. There is no certainty that the item will not break down before the end of this period or, for that matter, that it will not function longer. However, on the average, the interval between failures for a piece of equipment is given by its MTBF.

The MTBF, like any mean value, is the first moment of the parameter being considered. In this case, the mean value can be found by summing the times to failure of all units under consideration and dividing the result by the total number of units N_T as follows:

$$\text{MTBF} = \frac{\displaystyle\sum_{i=1}^{N} \text{times to failure of each unit}}{N_T}$$

$$= \frac{\displaystyle\sum_{i=1}^{N} t_i N_{F_i}}{N_T} \tag{16}$$

where N_{F_i} is the number of units that have failed in time interval "t_i." All units are assumed to operate until failure. Consequently,

$$\sum_{i=1}^{N} N_{F_i} = N_T \tag{17}$$

Eq. (16) defines the average time to failure for one component. N_{F_i} is the number of units failing at time "t," and, in the limit as the number of units being considered becomes very large, N_{F_i} is the same as dN_F/dt, the frequency of failures as a function of t. When dN_F/dt is divided by the total number of units N_T, such a unit failure distribution curve is called a *failure density function*. This can be expressed as follows:

$$f(t) = \frac{1}{N_T} \frac{dN_F}{dt} \tag{18}$$

or, from Eq. (4),

$$f(t) = -\frac{dR}{dt} \tag{19}$$

As the number of units becomes infinitely large, the summation of Eq. (16) becomes an integration process, which can be expressed as follows:

$$\text{MTBF} = \int_0^\infty tf(t)\, dt \tag{20}$$

where $f(t)$ is given by

$$f(t) = \frac{1}{N_T} \sum_{i=1}^N N_{F_i} \to \frac{1}{N_T} \frac{dN_F}{dt}$$

Substituting the expression for $f(t)$ given by Eq. (19) into Eq. (20) yields the following expression for the MTBF:

$$\text{MTBF} = \int_0^\infty t\left(-\frac{dR}{dt}\right) dt = -\int_0^\infty t\, dR \tag{21}$$

If Eq. (21) is integrated by parts, the expression for the MTBF becomes

$$\text{MTBF} = -[tR]_0^\infty + \int_0^\infty R\, dt \tag{22}$$

If it is assumed that the reliability function is given by an exponential distribution function, $R(t) = e^{-\lambda t}$, Eq. (22) becomes

$$\text{MTBF} = -[te^{-\lambda t}]_0^\infty + \int_0^\infty e^{-\lambda t}\, dt \tag{23}$$

Evaluating the first part of Eq. (23) by L'Hospital's rule yields the following:

$$\underset{t\to\infty}{\text{Lim}} [te^{-\lambda t}] = \underset{t\to\infty}{\text{Lim}} \frac{d[t]}{d[e^{\lambda t}]} = \underset{t\to\infty}{\text{Lim}} \frac{1}{\lambda e^{\lambda t}} \tag{24}$$

and

$$\underset{t\to\infty}{\text{Lim}} \frac{1}{\lambda e^{\lambda t}} = 0 \tag{25}$$

$$\text{MTBF} = \int_0^\infty e^{-\lambda t} \, dt \qquad (26)$$

For $\lambda(t) = \lambda_0$, a constant failure rate,

$$\text{MTBF} = -\frac{1}{\lambda_0} [e^{-\lambda_0 t}] \, _0^\infty = \frac{1}{\lambda_0} \qquad (27)$$

In general, the MTBF of a system may be treated as the integral of the reliability function of the overall system:

$$\text{MTBF} = \int_0^\infty R(t) \, dt \qquad (28)$$

The MTBF can also be visualized intuitively by supposing a particular unit has a constant failure rate of 10^{-6} failures per hour. If this unit is tested and replaced by an identical unit every time it fails, the unit will fail, on the average, once every 10^6 hours. Therefore, the MTBF is equal to 10^6 hours. This is just the reciprocal of the constant failure rate for the exponential function, where $\lambda_0 = 10^{-6}$ failure per hour.

The MTBF is a *quantitative* measure of reliability. It gives the average time interval during which equipment is expected to operate without a failure. In some of the literature this interval is also referred to as the *mean time to failure* (MTTF). Technically speaking, MTTF and MTBF are *not* identical. The MTBF can be defined in an alternative form as

$$\text{MTBF} = \text{MTTF} + \text{MTTR} \qquad (29)$$

where MTTR is the *mean time to repair.* If a component or a system is *not repaired* when a failure is experienced, the MTBF and MTTF are the same quantity. In general, MTTF and MTBF have been used interchangeably since MTTR is usually very small in comparison with MTTF.

5.4   REPAIR TIME

The repair time is another factor that materially affects the reliability and the maintainability of a system. When one unit in a duplicated system is defective, the system depends on the second unit to continue operation. If the defective unit is repaired quickly, the chance of the complete system going down becomes quite small because the second unit will operate in such a manner so as to preserve the integrity of the system's operation. Since the system is vulnerable only during the time it takes to repair the defective unit, a short repair time can increase the system reliability tremendously.*

* Fault diagnosis and repair are discussed more fully in Chapter 8.

To design and manufacture a system with a specified value of reliability for a given period of operation, it is essential not only to estimate the failure rate of individual components but also to predict the MTTR for various fault conditions that could occur in the system. Such a prediction is usually based upon the past experiences of the designer and the resources (such as personnel and equipment) that will be available for repair work. The system repair time may be divided into two separate intervals called the *passive repair time* and the *active repair time*. The passive repair time is the time interval measured from the time a fault is first recognized in the system until the time that maintenance personnel arrive to initiate repair work. This interval is determined entirely by the administrative and logistic support provided by the user of the system. An interval of time is required by the maintenance organization to assemble technicians for the task of servicing the faulty system. Additional time is required to transport these personnel and their service equipment to the location of the failing system. This passive time can be reduced by increasing the number of personnel engaged in repair activity. In this case, several individuals may function "on call" to provide an immediate response to a service request. The improvement in the repair time is achieved at the expense of the salaries paid to the additional service personnel. A trade-off thus exists between the ease with which a system may be maintained in an operational state and the cost of providing the required support environment.

The active part of the repair time is the actual time required by the maintenance personnel to recognize, isolate, and correct the trouble condition in the faulty system. This time is directly affected by the equipment design and may be further subdivided into the following intervals:

1. *Fault detection interval:* The period of time between the occurrence of a failure and when the system recognizes that a failure has occurred.
2. *Fault diagnosis interval:* The period of time required by the maintenance personnel to isolate the trouble to a few replaceable circuit boards. This interval is a function of both the sophistication of the equipment design and the technical skill of the maintenance personnel.
3. *Repair interval:* The time period required by the maintenance personnel to carry out the replacement of any suspected faulty circuit boards. This interval is also intimately related to the equipment design and the technical skill of the repair personnel.
4. *Verification interval:* The amount of time required by the maintenance personnel to verify that the repair of the fault has been effective in correcting the trouble condition and that the system is fully operational.

Again, the active repair time can be reduced by improvement of both the hardware and software designs, with an eye toward *minimizing* the maintenance skills required to support the system. In view of the continued increase in labor costs, this is a particularly worthwhile philosophy to observe.

5.5 AVAILABILITY

The *availability of equipment* may be defined as the probability of the equipment operating satisfactorily at any point in time while the equipment is used under stated conditions. The concept of availability is used in measuring system effectiveness. Both reliability and maintainability are combined in the concept of availability. This relationship may be expressed as follows:

$$\text{Availability} = \frac{\text{Total time}}{\text{Total time} + \text{Total downtime}}$$

$$= \frac{\text{Total time}}{\text{Total time} + (\text{Number of failures} \times \text{MTTR})}$$

$$= \frac{\text{Total time}}{\text{Total time} + (\lambda_0 \times \text{Total time} \times \text{MTTR})}$$

$$= \frac{1}{1 + \lambda_0 \times \text{MTTR}} \qquad \text{if MTTF} = \frac{1}{\lambda_0}$$

$$= \frac{\text{MTTF}}{\text{MTTF} + \text{MTTR}} \tag{30}$$

where the reliability function is assumed to be an exponential distribution $R(t) = e^{-\lambda_0 t}$.

Since MTTF is a measure of reliability and MTTR is a measure of maintainability, a trade-off between the two can be arranged to realize a given availability. As the MTTF (reliability) increases, the MTTR can also increase. This means a more reliable system can tolerate a longer repair time. A trade-off might be made in which ease of maintenance and/or repair would be enhanced at the expense of reliability. In this case, both the MTTR and the MTTF would be reduced to retain the same availability.

5.6 SERIES SYSTEMS

The reliability of a system can be derived from a knowledge of the reliability of each of its components. The components are interconnected to form functional units which, in turn, are configured into systems. The ultimate concern of both the designers and users of such systems is the reliability of the total system. A large system may be functionally partitioned into smaller

parts.   These smaller parts can be analyzed individually to determine their
separate reliabilities.   These individual parts can then be considered from
the point of view of how they are interconnected.   This allows a measure
of reliability for the entire system to be calculated.   The two basic interconnection arrangements of such system components are the *series logic system*
and the *parallel logic system*. The mathematical model for the reliability of
a series logic system is based upon the multiplication law of probability,
which covers the occurrence of two independent events.

If A and B are two independent events having probabilities P_a and
P_b, then the probability that both A and B will occur simultaneously
is the product $P_a P_b$.

As an example, consider a system consisting of two units A and B functionally
connected together as shown in Figure 5-4.   This combination will result
in an overall system failure if either unit fails.   This means both units must

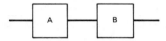

Figure 5-4   Series System

operate satisfactorily in order for the system to be considered operationally
correct.   The reliability of this system, R_{ab}, may be expressed as

$$R_{ab} = R_a R_b \tag{31}$$

Using a similar line of reasoning, the reliability of a system consisting
of a series interconnection of n units may be expressed as

$$R_{an} = R_a R_b \cdots R_n \tag{32}$$

This expression can be rewritten in a more compact form as

$$R_{an} = \prod_{i=a}^{n} R_i \tag{33}$$

where the symbol Π represents the product of all R_i terms from the initial
value a to the final value n.

The reliability function R_a may be regarded as a measure of the probability that a system *will not* fail in a given period of time.   Similarly, the
unreliability function Q_a may be regarded as a measure of the probability
that the system *will* fail in the same period of time.   This period of time t_n
is often called the system's *mission time* and is measured from the time the
system is placed in service ($t = 0$) until the end of the mission ($t = t_n$).
It is assumed that at $t = 0$ the reliability of the system is unity; i.e., $R(0)$
$= 1$.

Since the system must either fail or operate successfully during its mission time, the following relationship exists between the reliability function R_a and the unreliability function Q_a:

$$R_a + Q_a = 1 \tag{34}$$

or

$$R_a = 1 - Q_a \tag{35}$$

where Q_a is the probability of a failure occurring in system A. Substituting this relationship into Eq. (31) yields the following result:

$$R_{ab} = 1 - Q_{ab} = (1 - Q_a)(1 - Q_b) \tag{36}$$

which can be written as

$$Q_{ab} = Q_a + Q_b - Q_a Q_b \tag{37}$$

Equation (37) gives the relationship of unreliabilities for a series system of two units. The system unreliability is the probability of either or both of the units failing.

As indicated previously, for constant failure rates λ_a and λ_b, the reliability expression may be written as

$$R_{ab} = R_a R_b = e^{-\lambda_a t} e^{-\lambda_b t}$$
$$= e^{-(\lambda_a + \lambda_b)t} \tag{38}$$

and

$$\lambda_{ab} = \lambda_a + \lambda_b \tag{39}$$

Since the failure rate is still a constant, the MTBF is

$$\text{MTBF} = \frac{1}{\lambda_a + \lambda_b}$$
$$= \frac{1}{2\lambda_0} \quad \text{if } \lambda_a = \lambda_b = \lambda_0 \tag{40}$$

Note that the reliability of the system is the product of the reliabilities of its individual units. Consequently, its overall reliability can be quite low when a large number of units are interconnected in a series arranagement. For example, for 40 units in series, each with a reliability of 0.9, the system would have a reliability of about 0.015. Consequently, *to achieve high reliability, individual units must, of necessity, be of very high reliability.*

A central processor of a computer system may be considered divided functionally into several units: the arithmetic unit, the control unit, and the input/output (I/O) unit. They are essentially interconnected in series insofar as reliability is concerned since a failure in any one unit would cause the processor to malfunction.   Similarly, within each unit, all components may be regarded as interconnected in a series configuration since the failure of a single component will cause an error in the given unit unless the component is a redundant element.   The reliability of the entire processor may be calculated by (1) summing the total failure rates for each unit, (2) calculating the reliability for each unit, and then (3) multiplying the reliability of the individual units to obtain the overall reliability figure.

Component failure rates on the order of 10^{-5} failures per hour would be regarded as poor; 10^{-8} failures per hour would be regarded as acceptable for high-reliability applications; 10^{-9} failures per hour would be considered very reliable.   The unit most frequently used to express failure rates is *percent failures per* 10^3 hours or *failures per* 10^5 hours. This unit is fairly convenient for expressing mechanical assembly failure rates, but when used for devices incorporating integrated electronic parts, the numbers become quite small and inconvenient.   For this reason, the failure rate is expressed in *FITS*. One FIT corresponds to one failure per 10^9 hours.   This unit is especially convenient in expressing the failure rates for electronic systems for the reason mentioned above.

5.7   PARALLEL SYSTEMS

In a simple parallel system, two units are connected so that if one unit fails, the system does not fail (see Figure 5-5).   Both units must fail to cause the system to fail.   This mode of operation is normally referred to as *active redundancy*.   The mathematical model for the reliability of a parallel system is based upon the *law of probability*.   The law of probability requires that the probabilities of two nonmutually exclusive events be treated as follows:

If A and B are events which are not mutually exclusive, then the probability of either event occurring separately or both events occurring together is expressed as $P_a + P_b - P_{ab}$, where P_a and P_b are the probabilities of the occurrence of event A and event B. $P_a P_b$ is the probability of both events occurring simultaneously.

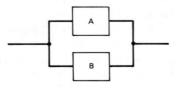

Figure 5-5   Parallel System

The reliability function for the parallel system may be expressed as

$$R_{ab} = R_a + R_b - R_a R_b \qquad (41)$$

Since the unreliability function Q was defined earlier as the complement of the reliability function, the reliability for a parallel system may be rewritten as

$$R_{ab} = 1 - (1 - R_a)(1 - R_b)$$
$$= 1 - Q_a Q_b \qquad (42)$$

In general,

$$R_{an} = 1 - (1 - R_a)(1 - R_b) \cdots (1 - R_n)$$
$$= 1 - Q_a Q_b \cdots Q_n \qquad (43)$$

The probability of an overall system failure (or the unreliability function) is given by the product of the probability of failure for each individual unit. This is analogous to the probability of success (or the reliability function) for a series system. However, for constant failure rates of λ_a and λ_b, the parallel system no longer has a constant failure rate when the reliability function is exponential; that is, $R = e^{-\lambda t}$. For this case, the reliability of the overall system may be expressed as

$$R_{ab} = e^{-\lambda_a t} + e^{-\lambda_b t} - e^{-(\lambda_a + \lambda_b) t}$$
$$= 2e^{-\lambda_0 t} - e^{-2\lambda_0 t} \qquad \text{if } \lambda_a = \lambda_b = \lambda_0 \qquad (44)$$

The expression for R_{ab} as given in Eq. (44) may be integrated from 0 to ∞ to obtain the expression for the MTBF of a parallel system with an exponential reliability function:

$$\text{System MTBF} = \int_0^\infty R_{ab} \, dt$$

$$= \int_0^\infty (2e^{-\lambda_0 t} - e^{-2\lambda_0 t}) \, dt$$

$$= \frac{3}{2\lambda_0} \qquad (45)$$

The inverse relationship between the MTBF and the failure rate which existed for a series system does *not* hold true for a parallel system. One cannot take the reciprocal of $3/2\lambda_0$ to obtain the equivalent failure rate for a parallel system. The failure rate must be calculated through the use of Eq. (7):

$$\lambda(t) = -\frac{1}{R} \frac{dR}{dt} \qquad (46)$$

Substituting $2e^{-\lambda_0 t} - e^{-2\lambda_0 t}$ for R and taking the derivative of R with respect to t, the system failure rate $\lambda_{ab}(t)$ is obtained:

$$\lambda_{ab}(t) = \frac{2\lambda_0 e^{-\lambda_0 t} - 2\lambda_0 e^{-2\lambda_0 t}}{2e^{-\lambda_0 t} - e^{-2\lambda_0 t}}$$

$$= \frac{2\lambda_0 e^{-\lambda_0 t}(1 - e^{-\lambda_0 t})}{2 - e^{-\lambda_0 t}} \tag{47}$$

Figure 5-6 shows the failure rate for a two-unit parallel system as a function of time. This failure rate approaches the constant value of a one-unit parallel system as the time t is allowed to go to infinity.

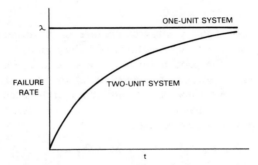

Figure 5-6   Failure Rate of Two-unit Parallel System

5.8   SERIES-PARALLEL CONFIGURATIONS

The reliability of a block of n series units with m parallel elements in each unit, as shown in Figure 5-7, is

$$R_T = [1 - (1 - R)^m]^n \tag{48}$$

where R is the reliability of each element. The equation is obtained by combining Eq. (43) for the parallel case and Eq. (33) for the series case.

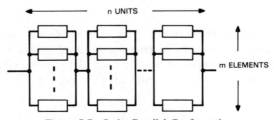

Figure 5-7   Series-Parallel Configuration

Let

$$R_T = R_1 R_2 \cdots R_j \cdots R_n = \prod_{i=1}^{n} R_i \qquad (49)$$

The reliability of the jth series element is given by

$$R_j = 1 - Q_{j1} Q_{j2} \cdots Q_{jm} = 1 - \prod_{k=1}^{m} Q_{jk} \qquad (50)$$

Then the resulting system reliability is given by

$$R_T = \prod_{i=1}^{n} \left(1 - \prod_{k=1}^{m} Q_{jk} \right) \qquad (51)$$

Each element has the same reliability, $R_i = R$, so that

$$Q_{ik} = 1 - R_i \quad \text{and} \quad R_T = \prod_{i=1}^{n} [1 - (1 - R_i)^m] \qquad (52)$$

$$R_T = [1 - (1 - R)^m]^n \qquad (53)$$

It can readily be seen that the system reliability R_T increases with m, the number of units in parallel, and that it decreases with n, the number of elements in series.

Similarly, the reliability of a block of m parallel paths, each with n elements, as shown in Figure 5-8, is

$$R_T = 1 - (1 - R^n)^m \qquad (54)$$

In practice, a system is normally represented by a combination of series and parallel units. The precise arrangement depends largely on the system's operational characteristics. In effect, individual units can be considered to be in parallel whenever an alternative interconnection path exists between the units which enables the system to function properly even if one or more units have failed. Similarly, individual units will be considered to be in series whenever it is necessary for *all* units to function correctly *simultaneously* for the system to function properly.

Consider the simple case of a two-unit configuration, which is shown

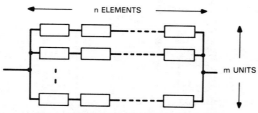

Figure 5-8   Parallel-Series Configuration

in Figure 5-9(a). Unit A is connected in series with unit B, and, for reliability, both units have been duplicated. Units A and B may be the CPU and the memory of a computer system. They form a single functional block which will fail if any component within the block experiences a failure. The entire system will work if either A_1 and B_1 both work *or* if A_2 and B_2 both work.

Although there are two CPUs and two memories, it is possible for the overall system to fail if a bad CPU is encountered in conjunction with a bad memory. This situation is reached if the two faulty units are represented either by the combination A_1 and B_2 or the combination A_2 and B_1. If either CPU is allowed to work with either memory, four workable configurations for the CPU and memory are available instead of two. Figure 5-9(b) illustrates the physical arrangement of the CPUs and memories. This arrangement permits the additional working modes. Assume for a moment that the added flexibility requires no additional hardware and that the reliability R for each unit is 0.9. In this situation, the reliability for the case in which each CPU must work *only* with its own main memory is given by

$$R = 1 - (1 - R^2)^2$$
$$= 1 - (1 - 0.9^2)^2$$
$$= 0.96 \tag{55}$$

If the CPU is allowed to work with *either* its own main store or the main store of its mate, the associated reliability is given by

$$R = [1 - (1 - R)^2]^2$$
$$= [1 - (1 - 0.9)^2]^2$$
$$= 0.98 \tag{56}$$

An improvement in reliability is realized with the second arrangement. However, additional hardware is required to enable each CPU to work with either memory unit. The increase in the number of components would naturally increase the failure rate and decrease the reliability. This may cause the net gain in reliability between the two arrangements to be negative, meaning that the second arrangement is less reliable than the first. A more thorough analysis of each specific case would reveal the exact behavior of the reliability of each overall system.

Figure 5-9   2 x 2 Series-Parallel and 2 x 2 Parallel-Series Configurations

5.9 STANDBY REDUNDANCY

It has already been shown that the overall reliability of a system can be improved by adding redundancy so that if one unit fails, there is another unit to carry on the work. There are active and standby types of redundancy. The parallel configuration described previously in Sec. 5.8 is the active type in which the redundant elements are continuously energized and used to perform the required circuit or system function(s). Standby redundancy is the condition used in a system where the additional units are activated only when needed. The spare tire in a car represents a form of standby redundancy. The spare is used only when one of the mounted tires fails. In this example, the spare unit remains new and unused until placed in service, rather than being used continuously and wearing out while the currently active tires are being used. The advantages of active and standby redundancy can be expressed in terms of the MTBF. (See Table 5-1.)

The MTBF for the standby case assumes that the standby unit does not malfunction during the period that the on-line unit is functioning properly. Furthermore, this MTBF calculation assumes that the failure statistics of the standby unit do *not* start until the standby unit has been switched into operation to replace the failed active unit. Therefore, the MTBF of the standby configuration is twice the value of the one-unit system configuration. Comparing the MTBFs of the three system configurations given in Table 5-1, the standby configuration appears to be the favorable one. This conclusion is based upon the following two assumptions about the failure characteristics of the standby configuration:

1. The failure rate of the inactive standby unit is 0, and the equipment remains in perfect working condition, ready for immediate use. That is, the standby unit does not fail during the period of correct operation of the active unit.

TABLE 5-1 MTBF of Different Redundant Processor Configurations

CONFIGURATION	MTBF
ONE UNIT, NO REDUNDANCY	$\dfrac{1}{\lambda_0}$
TWO UNITS, ACTIVE REDUNDANCY	$\dfrac{3}{2\lambda_0}$
TWO UNITS, STANDBY REDUNDANCY	$\dfrac{2}{\lambda_0}$

NOTE: *IT IS ASSUMED FOR EACH PROCESSOR CONFIGURATION THAT THE RELIABILITY FUNCTION IS REPRESENTED BY AN EXPONENTIAL DISTRIBUTION FUNCTION.*

2. The fault detection logic and the hardware necessary to switch the previously active unit out of the system and replace it with the standby unit will *always* function perfectly. The reliability of this subsystem is 1.

For many systems, particularly in the electronics field, the failure rates of nonenergized components are normally lower than for those components exposed to normal operating conditions. A failure rate of 0, of course, is somewhat unrealistic. Even an unused component may have an appreciable failure rate while waiting to be used, and the longer it remains on standby, the greater the risk of its failing when it is finally required. With active redundancy, as in the case of a duplicated computer system, the spare unit can be constantly checked by itself or by the working unit to ensure that the spare is in perfect working condition at all times.

The switching equipment for a processor configuration employing standby redundancy is perhaps the most critical part of the system. Functionally, as shown in Figure 5-10, the task of switching from the main unit to

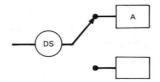

Figure 5-10   Standby Redundancy

the standby is simple. However, the switching subsystem hardware is not an easy circuit to implement with extremely high reliability. The difficult functions of detecting and deciding when to perform the switching operation is embedded in the block designated as DS, as shown in Figure 5-10. In addition, a means of energizing the standby must be provided so as to avoid hazardous "transients" during the switching operation (stray power surges are likely to wander and damage circuits). Obviously, many factors must be taken into account in the switching logic design. Consequently, the physical implementation of the switching logic required for a standby redundancy configuration can introduce a high degree of unreliability into the overall system.

5.10   REPAIRABLE SYSTEMS

In general, commercial computers normally fall into the category of *repairable systems*. If a failed unit can be repaired while a redundant unit has taken over the task of providing continuous operation, the system reliability is improved. The system MTTF, a measure of reliability, depends largely on the failure rate and the repair time. Both contribute to the calculation of the MTTF and influence the system design in terms of the reliability objectives.

A short repair time reduces the probability of the substitute unit failing before the original unit is restored to service. This is also true for low failure rates. Hence, the proper choice of components and maintenance procedures is essential to achieving high reliability.

Maintenance actions can be divided into two types: *preventive* and *corrective*. The preventive maintenance actions eliminate potential sources of failures *before* the failures occur. The difficulty of this technique is predicting when to carry out the action and what criterion to use in replacing components. Also, the replacement process should not interfere with the normal operation of the system. Corrective maintenance actions are represented by the repair steps required to restore a failed unit to its normal operational state.

In computer systems, it is difficult and expensive to employ a thorough philosophy of preventive maintenance since such a philosophy requires manual interaction with the system. Manual interaction, unless it is very simple, often causes more difficulties than it solves. Moreover, with the continuing rise in the cost of labor, it becomes financially impractical to require periodic manual maintenance actions. However, many routine maintenance procedures can be automated using computer programming techniques and simple preventive maintenance strategies. The overall maintenance plan *must* be integrated into the system structure to allow some preventive maintenance procedures to be automated. For example, many faults in the detection hardware do not trigger alarms to indicate that a fault has occurred. A system which will indicate a failure any time a fault is detected is called a *fault-secure system.* A fault-secure system will always generate an error output for every occurrence of a fault but does not necessarily compensate for the fault. A fault-secure system provides a detection mechanism for all faults which occur. These faults merely disable the detection circuitry from detecting system failures. This is a particularly *dangerous situation* since the effect is to conceal or mask further failures. Routine checking procedures that result in the identification of these so-called *dormant faults* will improve reliability. To carry out these routine checks, some hardware must be added to simulate fault conditions that are extremely difficult to set up artificially in the existing system. By appropriately establishing the proper test condition(s) and applying a well-designed test sequence, the detection circuitry can be checked on a periodic basis to ensure its proper functioning. Thus, routine checking for dormant faults can be carried out as an automatic preventive maintenance activity without any manual interaction being required by the system. Similarly, certain degradation failures can also be identified automatically by *stressing* the operating conditions near the upper or lower limits of the various subsystems. Such "stress" procedures can involve varying the power supply voltages or adjusting the system clock rate according to a test program which is run on the processor itself.

Corrective maintenance can increase system reliability tremendously. A duplicated system that maintains a redundant or backup copy is subject to a *complete system failure* only when (1) the on-line system has taken a hard fault which has caused (2) the backup system to be switched on-line as the active unit, and (3) the backup unit is undergoing repair.

Consequently, a duplicated redundant system can be said to be *vulnerable* to total system failure only when the original active unit has failed and is undergoing repair.   The reliability is therefore related not only to the failure rate but also to the repair rate or to the rate at which the failure is corrected.   If μ is the *repair rate* or the *reciprocal of the repair time,* the system MTTF of a duplicated redundant system is expressed by

$$\text{MTTF} = \frac{3\lambda_0 + \mu}{2\lambda_0^2} \tag{57}$$

for active redundancy and by

$$\text{MTTF} = \frac{2\lambda_0 + \mu}{\lambda_0^2} \tag{58}$$

for standby redundancy, where λ_0 is the failure rate of *each unit.*   Eqs. (57) and (58) are derived in Appendix A, under the assumption that the failing unit is repaired as soon as it fails.   If no repair is carried out, the repair time is infinite, and $\mu = 0$, the two expressions reduce to $(3/2\lambda_0$ and $2/\lambda_0$, respectively, which are the same as those derived previously in Sec. 5.9.   Usually μ is much greater than λ_0 (that is, repair time is usually much smaller than the mean time to failure).   Therefore, Eqs. (57) and (58) reduce to

$$\text{MTTF} \approx \frac{\mu}{2\lambda_0^2} \tag{59}$$

for active redundancy and to

$$\text{MTTF} \approx \frac{\mu}{\lambda_0^2} \tag{60}$$

for standby redundancy.

Table 5-2 summarizes the MTTF for the two cases with and without repair.   If $\mu = 0.25$ repair per hour (4 hours per repair) and $\lambda_0 = 10^{-5}$ failure per hour (mean time to failure of 10^5 hours), Table 5-2 yields the following results:

Active redundancy: MTTF $= 1.25(10)^9$ hr with repair
MTTF $= 1.5(10)^5$ hr without repair
Standby redundancy: MTTF $= 2.5(10)^9$ hr with repair
MTTF $= 2.0(10)^5$ hr without repair

TABLE 5-2 MTTF of Active and Standby Redundancy

REDUNDANCY	MTTF WITH REPAIR	MTTF WITH NO REPAIR
ACTIVE	$\left(\dfrac{\mu}{2\lambda_0^2}\right)$	$\left(\dfrac{3}{2\lambda_0}\right)$
STANDBY	$\left(\dfrac{\mu}{\lambda_0^2}\right)$	$\left(\dfrac{2}{\lambda_0}\right)$

5.11 SYSTEM DOWNTIME

If the faulty component is repaired shortly after its fault has been detected, a significant increase in reliability can be achieved in both the active and standby redundancy configurations for a given system. Specifically, if the failure rate λ_0 is kept low and the repair rate μ is kept high, the system can exhibit a remarkable increase in its MTTF.

System downtime, another measure of reliability, is a criterion used in designing reliable systems for real-time* applications such as telephone systems. In a redundant system, assuming that the repair rate or the MTTR (mean time to repair) is the same with one unit failed or with two units failed, the downtime is essentially the repair time required to restore one unit to full operation. Over the life of the system (i.e., its mission time), the total downtime is expressed by

$$DT = \text{Number of failures over its life multiplied by MTTR}$$

$$= \frac{L}{\text{MTTF}}\,\text{MTTR} \tag{61}$$

where L = life of the system or total operational time. In the case of active redundancy, total system downtime can be expressed as

$$DT = \frac{2\lambda_0^2}{\mu} L \frac{1}{\mu}$$

$$= \frac{2\lambda_0^2}{\mu^2} L \tag{62}$$

For standby redundancy, total system downtime can be expressed as

---

* James Martin in *Design of Real-Time Computer Systems* (Englewood Cliffs, N.J.: Prentice-Hall, 1967) gives the following definition of *real time:* "A real-time computer system may be defined as one which controls an environment by receiving data, processing them, and returning the results sufficiently quickly to affect the environment at that time."

$$\text{DT} = \frac{\lambda_0^2}{\mu^2} L \tag{63}$$

For telephone systems, as mentioned previously, the reliability requirement set by the Bell System is a system downtime of less than 2 hours over the system's 40-year life span. These requirements establish the value for DT and L in a telephone office. To meet this objective, the system must be designed with the appropriate values for λ_0 and μ. The failure rate λ_0 of one unit may be regarded as the summation of failure rates of all components within the unit (a series interconnection of components).

Since the downtime varies directly with λ_0^2, it is desirable to keep this parameter small by using as few components as possible and ensuring that each component is highly reliable. As the number of parts increases, the risk of one becoming defective increases. To reduce the repair time, additional circuitry is required to facilitate detection of failures and isolate the faulty parts so that troubles can be recognized and corrected quickly. As a result, the *reduction of repair time may cause an increase in the number of parts and, hence, the failure rate.* A good engineering design should attempt to obtain *subsystem* values for both a longer MTTF and a shorter system downtime. The trade-off between λ_0 and μ is both a technical and economic choice which is conditioned by how well the system can meet its reliability objective.

5.12   COST OF RELIABILITY

The most important consideration in the design of any equipment or system is usually cost—specifically the initial cost of the equipment. Nevertheless, the heavy emphasis on initial cost is very often a mistake. Maintenance cost should also be considered before the equipment has been designed or purchased. The maintenance and repair costs depend on the reliability of the equipment. As the reliability increases, maintenance costs decrease. However, the initial cost of the equipment will be higher since some form of hardware redundancy must be used to obtain the higher reliability. Usually more skilled, and therefore more highly paid, technicians must be employed to repair and maintain highly sophisticated modern computer systems. Therefore, a trade-off exists between the ongoing maintenance costs of a system (i.e., how often must it be serviced and by what caliber of service personnel) and the initial cost of the computer system.

The most significant factor in selecting a given system with a high-reliability requirement should *not* be the initial cost of the system but the overall expense of operating and maintaining the system *after* its initial purchase. If the proper maintenance features have been added to the system, the actual total expense (initial cost *plus* ongoing maintenance charges) can be held down significantly. By paying more initially to obtain more reliable

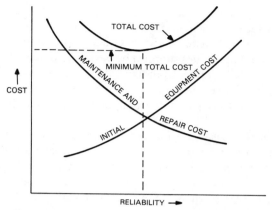

Figure 5-11 Variation of Total Cost with Reliability

equipment, maintenance costs can be made lower, and the total cost of purchasing and operating the system is reduced. The effect is shown in Figure 5-11, where the initial cost rises as reliability increases, and at the same time, maintenance and repair costs decrease. The total cost of purchasing and maintaining a system first falls with increasing reliability and then rises again, showing that the *most cost-effective* system is at the minimum point represented by the dashed lines in the figure. In practice, the *optimum economic reliability* is difficult to realize because it involves many elusive variables in estimating production and maintenance costs.

Optimum economic reliability can be achieved with any reasonable accuracy only if there is a considerable amount of *previous experience* by the designers from which they can draw. In some cases, the minimum total cost is not always the determining factor in deciding the degree of a system's reliability. If the results of a failure are likely to be serious, it may be necessary to provide *more redundancy* to ensure continuous and reliable operation. In the other extreme, it may be necessary to reduce reliability to a minimum acceptable level for the buyer whose main consideration is initial cost. This, then, is the challenge: to design computer systems, particularly small computer configurations, which satisfy a wide range of applications with different reliability requirements.

5.13 AN EXAMPLE OF RELIABILITY PREDICTION

Reliability calculation is essentially a prediction for a given system based upon probabilities of events which may or may not occur during the system's mission time. Many variables and unknowns may influence the outcome. During the development of a system, considerable attention must be directed to the selection and/or testing of components. The failure rates of standard components are usually available from manufacturers. When new components are used, they must be *exhaustively tested* under stressed and accelerated conditions to determine their performance. From the results of these tests, a fair estimate can be made of the new component failure rates. Using these test values and the values supplied by device manufacturers, calculations can be made of the failure rates of individual circuits, subsystems and, finally, the entire system. These calculations are valuable in deciding on the extent and type of redundancy required to attain the desired reliability in the overall system.

As an example, consider using a small computer that employs a semiconductor main memory consisting of 32,768 words, each word being 18 bits long. This hypothetical small machine is to be used in a telephone switching application and must meet the Bell System reliability requirement of a total system downtime of less than 2 hours over a period of 40 years. Tables

TABLE 5-3 Failure Rate of Components in CPU

COMPONENT	NUMBER	FAILURE RATE IN FITS*	
		A	B
BIPOLAR INTEGRATED CIRCUIT CHIPS	3,000	60,000	120,000
CAPACITORS	200	2,000	4,000
RESISTORS	200	400	2,000
SOLDER CONNECTIONS	75,000	37,500	75,000
CONNECTOR TERMINALS	5,000	5,000	10,000
TOTAL	83,400	104,900	211,000

* 1 FIT = 1 FAILURE PER 10^9 HOURS

TABLE 5-4 Failure Rate of Components in Main Memory

COMPONENT	NUMBER	FAILURE RATE IN FITS*	
		A	B
BIPOLAR INTEGRATED CIRCUIT CHIPS	500	10,000	20,000
MOS INTEGRATED CIRCUIT CHIPS	576	28,800	57,600
CAPACITORS	200	2,000	4,000
RESISTORS	150	300	1,500
SOLDER CONNECTIONS	20,000	10,000	20,000
CONNECTOR TERMINALS	1,500	1,500	3,000
TOTAL	22,926	52,600	106,100

* 1 FIT=1 FAILURE PER 10^9 HOURS

TABLE 5-5 Grand Total of Failures in CPU Main Memory

	FAILURE RATE IN FITS★	
UNIT	A	B
CPU	104,900	211,000
MAIN MEMORY	52,600	106,100
TOTAL	157,500	317,100

★ *1 FIT = 1 FAILURE PER 10⁹ HOURS*

5-3, 5-4, and 5-5 list the components used to configure the central processing unit (CPU) and main memory. Each table also gives two predetermined failure rates representing the possible range of values of the failure rates for each of the component populations. Each failure rate is given in column A and column B.

Consider Table 5-3; the number of bipolar integrated circuit chips (this is the population of this specific component) used to build the CPU is given as 3000. The number of failures experienced by this population is shown as 60,000 failures in 10^9 hours. The more pessimistic failure rate is assumed to be twice the failure rate of the most optimistic case. Consequently, column B for the population of bipolar integrated circuit chips gives a failure rate of 120,000 failures in 10^9 hours. Table 5-4 gives the failure rates of the hardware used to build main storage. The overall failure rates for the CPU and main memory may be obtained by *summing* the failure rates of each of the individual components used in each unit (i.e., the components are treated as being in series for the reliability calculation). With this approach, Table 5-5 gives the failure rates of the CPU and main memory for an active

TABLE 5-6 Assumed Failure Rate per Component

COMPONENT	FAILURE RATE IN FITS ★	
	A	B
BIPOLAR INTEGRATED CIRCUIT CHIPS	20	40
MOS INTEGRATED CIRCUIT CHIPS	50	100
CAPACITORS	10	20
RESISTORS	2	10
SOLDER CONNECTIONS	0.5	1
CONNECTOR TERMINALS	1	2

★ *1 FIT=1 FAILURE PER 10⁹ HOURS*

redundancy configuration and a standby redundancy configuration.   Table 5-6 lists the assumed failure rate per component for two cases: A (optimistic) and B (pessimistic).

The component failure rates listed in columns A and B of Table 5-5 result in an MTBF ($1/\lambda_0$) for the combined CPU and main memory of 3153 hours and 6349 hours.   This range represents the most pessimistic value and the most optimistic values for the failure rates of the individual components.

Figure 5-12 shows the system downtime as a function of the MTTF for a single unduplicated unit.   As a means of comparison, Figure 5-12 also includes the downtime as a function of a duplicated unit.   The MTTF for the duplicated system is a measure of the time during which *both* the

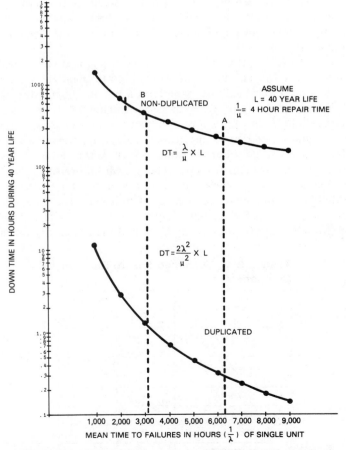

Figure 5-12   Reliability Comparison Between Nonduplicated and Duplicated Systems

active and standby units have sustained failures. The MTTF for this condition is given by $\mu/2\lambda_0^2$. This expression was derived in Sec. 5.10 as Eq. (59). As shown in Figure 5-12, the variation in system downtime is substantial between the duplicated and unduplicated systems. Points A and B in Figure 5-12 represent the results of calculations which were made for two different failure rates. For the unduplicated unit, the downtime calculations yield values of 222 hours for point A and 444 hours for point B. These results may be compared with the values of 0.29 hour for point A and 1.1 hour for point B generated by the duplicated system. The component failure rates that will *actually* be experienced will fall somewhere between these two points. Since the reliability objective of this design example is a downtime of less than 2 hours, the duplicated system satisfies the condition; the nonduplicated unit does not.

Figure 5-13 shows how the repair time affects the system downtime when a duplicated unit is employed. *As the repair time is shortened, the downtime is reduced.* This, of course, is rather obvious since the duplicated units are active and operate independently. Also, it is assumed that the failed unit is quickly repaired so that a failure in the second unit is not likely to occur when the first unit has also experienced a failure. The probability of both units failing simultaneously exists only during the repair interval.

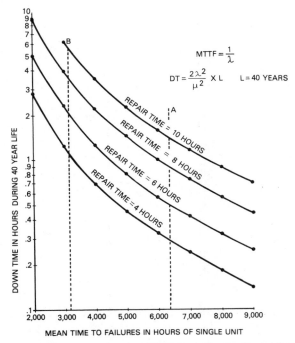

Figure 5-13   Downtime Versus MTTF for Active Duplicated System

Of course, when both units have failed, the system will be down during repair. If the failure rate increases, the system downtime can be maintained by increasing the repair rate (μ). This means that if *less reliable components* are used in the implementation of the system but the required repair techniques have been *improved,* then the system downtime can be maintained at the same level as a system built with *more reliable components* but one that requires a longer repair time because *inferior* repair techniques are used to service the system.

An alternative used to represent the reliability of a system is the MTTF associated with the system. Figure 5-14 shows the variation in the MTTF between the duplicated and the nonduplicated systems. A substantial increase in reliability is obtained with duplication. Points A and B again represent the result of calculations that were made for two different sets of failure

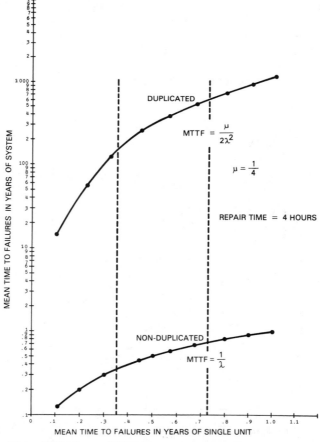

Figure 5-14 System MTTF Versus Single-Unit MTTF

rates, except in this example the time scale is expressed in years rather than in hours. For the nonduplicated system, the MTTF calculations are 0.72 year for point *A* and 0.36 year for point *B*. These values may be compared with 600 years for point *B* for the duplicated system. If the repair time (μ) is assumed to be 4 hours, an order of magnitude improvement is realized with duplication.

Reliability calculation is a process of predicting from available failure rate data the achievable reliability of a part, subsystem, or system and the probability of meeting the reliability objectives for a specified application. These calculations are most useful at the early design stages of a project. The use of pure numerical values for the reliability of various components generally will provide little benefit in evaluating the initial system design. However, such figures can be extremely valuable when it is necessary for a designer to select from a number of alternative designs. The designer may be able to make such a selection based upon a particular type of system redundancy and its associated reliability.

5.14 RELIABILITY DEMONSTRATION

Predicted reliability, as described in the previous section, is the estimated reliability of fully developed, operational equipment. Predicted reliability is the *expected value* after the early failure period has passed and most of the weak components have been eliminated and design errors have been corrected. To demonstrate that the predicted reliability has been met, it is necessary to verify the predicted value by testing the equipment under standard operating conditions.

Such tests tend to be expensive and quite difficult to conduct, especially when the inherent reliability of the equipment is reasonably high. For example, the failure rate of an electronic part might be of the order of 20 FITs. This means that on the average the part will operate for 50 million hours (approximately 5708 years) before a failure occurs. Clearly, it is an impossible task to operate a system over such an extended period of time. The time interval, however, can be reduced by testing a group of similar parts together. This group is sometimes called a *population*. If 10,000 parts are tested together, 50 million test hours can be accumulated in 0.57 year, assuming that the failure statistics of the group are the same as the failure statistics of its individual members. This, however, is the time interval during which only one failure is expected. Consequently, a considerably longer test interval is required to obtain a significant number of failures in order to place any confidence in the accumulated failure measurements.

Since most electronic components are quite reliable, testing under normal operating conditions usually involves testing a large number of parts and employing long testing intervals. One method of reducing the very long test times is to use an *accelerated test*. The idea is that the normal life span of the item under test can be compressed into a much shorter time interval using the concept of a sample population. For example, experimental data accumulated by various semiconductor manufacturers indicates that a relationship exists between the stress applied to an electronic part and its failure rate. This relationship normally would differ between various types of devices and between different manufacturing methods. Most electronic parts such as resistors, capacitors, or semiconductor devices exhibit physical changes in their operating characteristics as a function of temperature (i.e., the current and/or voltage can change radically). Therefore, by increasing the ambient temperature a device is exposed to, its associated failure rate also increases. In this way, the testing interval for a population of components can be shortened substantially from many years to a few weeks. This, in turn, reduces the cost of component evaluation.

Another example of the reliability evaluation of a device is the testing of a mechanical OFF-ON switch. Assume the expected life of such a switch is 300,000 operations. Under normal conditions, the switch is operated on the average 20 times per day in a typical system. This means the expected life of the switch is about 40 years. For testing purposes, the switch can easily be given 300,000 operations in the course of 50 hours when it is actuated at the accelerated rate of 100 operations per minute. After 50 hours, the switch will continue to be tested until it fails. Hence, a life span test, representing more than 40 years of life, can be completed in several days. Although the life of a typical component was compressed into a short time, the conditions of use are kept approximately normal. Under these circumstances, the results of the life span test can be regarded as highly indicative of how the component will fail in its normal operating environment.

Reliability demonstration on a system-wide basis in which a number of subsystems or components are interconnected is much more difficult and costly. This situation is complicated even more as the complexity of interconnections and the number of components increase. In general, a test on 1000 or even 100 complete systems will not be practical unless they are very small. The real test of a complete system is that carried out by the customer in the course of normal operations. A well-planned strategy of recording all maintenance activities performed on all machines supplied by a specific manufacturer would facilitate reliability calculations. It is expected that during the first year of operation the maintenance activities on such new machines will be high due to design bugs and weak components which have not been detected in the factory testing (quality control). Sometimes customers are hesitant to be the first ones to try a system until the design has more or less stabilized. In the small computer field, when new software has been designed in conjunction with the introduction of a new machine, considerably *more* difficulties may be expected in the use and operation of the system. Many software bugs are extremely difficult to isolate and therefore have an adverse effect on the reliability of the system. Until most design bugs in both the hardware and the software have been eliminated, the maintenance activities corresponding to the early failure period will be high. Such maintenance actions reduce gradually as more and more machines are used in different applications. Through the actual operation of such systems, large amounts of meaningful data can be accumulated to predict the reliability of the system. At this point one may ask, "Then what good are the reliability calculations?" Primarily, they serve several important functions. First, they help to verify whether the system has met its reliability design objective. If not, the deficiencies and shortcomings of the system can be determined and perhaps corrected. Even if the machines are already in production, further improvements in the reliability can be realized by examining the statistics and characteristics of system failures. For example, assume that the user has found the electrical interconnections between the CPU and the peripheral units to be intermittent. One solution would be for the user to replace the faulty connector with a more reliable one. In other cases, the user may want to collaborate with the manufacturer to determine the trouble and correct the shortcoming.

Another important function of reliability measurements is to accumulate sufficient data and experience so that the next generation of machines will be better designed. Consider again the example of the connector problem just discussed. If the solution has not substantially improved the machine's performance, this factor should be considered to be significant in designing the next machine. The new design could be structured to eliminate or minimize the number of connectors or the number of leads interconnecting the various functional units. The reliability measurements, in general, will provide insight to the potentially weak points in the system and will also allow the designers to monitor continuously the performance of the machines.

5.15 SUMMARY

The concept of reliability was defined in this chapter, and its evaluation for specific systems was discussed. In particular, the exponential distribution function was shown to characterize the reliability of a system with a constant failure rate. The distinction between the terms *mean time between failures* (MTBF) and *mean time to failure* (MTTF) was outlined as well as the concept of repair time and system availability. The case of standby redundancy was developed in terms of the reliability such a configuration exhibited. Various procedures for using redundancy in repairable systems were discussed, with the cost of maintenance being a specific item that was examined. Finally, an example using a CPU and main memory was developed to predict the actual reliability exhibited by a physical system.

5.16   REFERENCES

1. R. E. BARLOW and F. PROSCHAN, *Mathematical Theory of Reliability* (New York: Wiley, 1965).

2. I. BAZOVSKY, *Reliability Theory and Practices* (Englewood Cliffs, N.J.: Prentice-Hall, 1961).

3. S. R. CALABRO, *Reliability Principles and Practices* (New York: McGraw-Hill, 1962).

4. R. W. DOWNING, J. S. NOWAK, and L. S. TUOMENOKSA, "No. 1 ESS Maintenance Plan," *Bell Syst. Tech. J., 49* (Sept. 1964), 1961–2019.

5. N. W. ROBERTS, *Mathematical Methods in Reliability Engineering* (New York: McGraw-Hill, 1964).

6. M. L. SHOOMAN, *Probabilistic Reliability, an Engineering Approach* (New York: McGraw-Hill, 1968).

7. D. J. SMITH, *Reliability Engineering* (New York: Barnes & Noble, 1972).

CHAPTER 6

Maintenance Design

Considerations

6.1   THE IMPORTANCE OF RELIABILITY

The reliability requirements can vary considerably from application to application. For example, in the transatlantic telephone cable system, underwater amplifiers or repeaters, designed as an integral part of the cable, must operate with a very high probability of no failures for 20 years. This is necessary because of the cost involved in sending a cable ship to the site, locating the defective amplifier unit under several miles of ocean water, bringing the defective part of the cable aboard ship, installing a new amplifier, returning the cable to the ocean floor, and returning the ship to port. The repair cost may amount to $1 million in addition to the loss of revenue while the cable is being repaired and carrying no messages.

In the case of computers aboard unmanned missiles or spacecraft, defective units cannot be repaired. Therefore, continuous operation is essential to a successful mission. Even aboard a manned spacecraft, an astronaut, already burdened with many more urgent tasks, cannot take on the additional task of repairing a defective computer. Therefore, the techniques used to achieve ultrahigh reliability during short missions are quite different from the techniques used in repairable systems.

Nearly all commercial computers are accessible to maintenance personnel. When a fault occurs, the system must detect the trouble quickly and then shut down to await repair. For most scientific or accounting problems, the interruption of operation is annoying but not catastrophic. Inconveniences result from having a system out of commission 6 or more hours at a time, in which case the entire operating procedures of the installation could be disrupted. One maintenance objective of both scientific and business machines is to reduce drastically the maximum length of repair time. This objective requires fault diagnosis techniques that can isolate the trouble to within a few replaceable units or circuit packs.

For real-time applications, such as telephone switching or process control, uninterrupted operation is essential, requiring the system to function correctly even when a fault is present and maintenance is being performed. One approach to providing continuous operation is the use of redundant machines. In electronic telephone switching systems, the central processor is duplicated, and both units process the same input data. The outputs are taken from the active (on-line) machine. If the on-line machine fails, the outputs are promptly switched to the standby machine. The defective unit is then repaired and put back into operation. The system is completely shut down *only* if both machines are faulty. In the process control industries, ultrahigh reliability may be obtained by having *more than two machines* operating independently, processing the same input data. In this case, the system is inoperative only if all machines are faulty.

Standby machines do not produce or contribute any useful work except in emergencies. In an earlier telephone switching system, the No. 5 Crossbar System, the electromechanical relays used in the system were several orders of magnitude slower than the electronic devices used in an *electronic switching system* (ESS). The organization of this electromechanical system required many processors operating in a multiprocessing mode (i.e., the processors were executing concurrently running tasks) in order to handle the volume of calls experienced by the system. The development of ESSs, which benefit by the high speed of electronic components, has moved in the direction of using a single high-speed processor. This high-speed processor can handle the traffic (volume of calls) that formerly required many slower electromechanical processors. For reliability, a standby processor is provided to take over if the working processor fails. In such a case, service is not affected. However, the No. 5 Crossbar System, with a multiplicity of markers (processors), decreases its traffic handling capacity when one or more markers become defective, resulting, perhaps, in a degradation of service or call-handling capability.

6.1.1 The Reliability Needs of Minicomputers and Microcomputers

The development of low-cost, small computer systems has expanded at a phenomenal rate. The hardware cost of a *central processing unit* (CPU) was significantly reduced through the remarkable developments in integrated circuit technology. As a result, the use of minicomputers and microcomputers has spread to many areas of process control, data processing, telecommunication, automated testing, device control, and so on. The reliability needs are different for each of these various applications. For real-time systems such as a computer-controlled chemical process or some complex industrial process, there must be a reasonably high probability that no faults will occur, since such failures may result in defective products and a reduction in output at considerable cost to the company. In this type of application, it is also desirable to have continuous performance with minimal interruption. Consequently, fault recovery techniques developed for telephone systems are also applicable to many real-time industrial control systems.

Reliability considerations were *overshadowed* in the design of the early small computers by the marketing requirements of (1) reducing the hardware cost of the CPU and (2) improving the throughput capability of the processor. The neglect of the maintenance problem has produced some rather disgruntled users of small machines. As the cost of labor continues to rise, maintenance has become an important factor in choosing a minicomputer. More automatic methods have had to be provided to detect and diagnose faults in minicomputer systems, allowing less skilled technicians to repair defective units quickly. The additional hardware and/or software for reducing the cost of repair and system downtime is a wise investment since maintenance costs represent a substantial portion of the operating costs of a small computer system.

In addition to providing check logic circuitry for detection and fault isolation, techniques have had to be developed to allow continuous operation even in the presence of a defective unit for some real-time control systems. This means that backup redundancy in the form of duplication is designed to assume full system control automatically when an error is detected.

There are many sophisticated proposals for achieving high reliability, particularly in special spaceborne computers. For example, in short-term missile flights, exceedingly high reliability can be obtained through the use of triplication and voting. In this scheme, each circuit is triplicated, and majority voter circuits are used to assign the correct output for each triplicated unit.   The concept of triplication and majority voting can be extended to include the entire system.   For longer missions that can include extended real-time systems and/or space flights, the use of multiple processors configured to perform concurrent processing and load sharing can provide an extremely high-capacity computing system with high-reliability features.   When a hardware error is detected, the faulty processing unit is switched out of service.   In this mode, it will perform *no* processing, and the remaining processors will automatically be reconfigured by the system fault recovery software to handle the processing load.   If there are a sufficient number of processing units in the arrangement of multiple processors, the whole system may not even feel the impact.   In the worst case, the remaining processors would have to perform more tasks than were originally assigned to them when no faults existed in the system, thereby reducing the system's performance.   However, for repairable commercial systems, the straightforward *active standby concept,* which was discussed earlier, has been used and proven effective in real-time telephone applications for many years.

Reliability-oriented design techniques have been characterized by the high cost of hardware to provide reliability and therefore have been used only in extremely critical applications.   The additional hardware required to achieve reliability causes the required circuitry to double or triple its usage of components; this also increases the cost and complexity of the particular application.   The advent of Medium Scale Integrated (MSI) and Large Scale Integrated (LSI) circuits makes possible the implementation of high-reliability logic circuitry with only a relatively small increase in overall system cost.   Also, the high cost of maintenance can be reduced drastically, since the system can be repaired easily and quickly.

6.2   REDUNDANCY FOR FAULT-TOLERANT COMPUTING

If a computer were fault-free, the hardware and software would always behave in a predicted way.   In the environment of everyday computer usage, however, the perfect computer has not yet been designed and built, and failures in both hardware and software *do* occur.   Hardware failures may affect the control sequence or data words within the machine.   This results in errors of two types: (1) The program sequence may be unchanged, but the failure affects the outcome of the final results, or (2) the program sequence is altered, and the program executed is no longer the specified algorithm.   Software faults are the result of improper translation or implementation of the original algorithm.   The flow of instruction execution deviates from the correct control sequence.   In many instances, unfortunately, hardware and software faults are indistinguishable. *Fault-tolerant computing* is defined as the ability to compute correctly in the presence of a failure, regardless of the source of the errors.

6.2.1   Protective Redundancy

Fault-tolerant computing requires redundancy to bypass an error so that the final results are correct. This redundancy, know as *protective redundancy,* consists of either hardware redundancy, software redundancy, time redundancy, a combination of any two of these types, or all three types. *Hardware redundancy* consists of additional components or circuits required for error detection and correction. *Software redundancy* consists of the additional programs required to reestablish an error-free working system under trouble conditions. It may include fault detection and diagnostic programs to periodically test all logic circuits of the computer for possible hardware faults. *Time redundancy* consists of a retry of an erroneous operation. It includes the repetition of a program or segment of a program immediately after detection of an error. The retry is often done by hardware. The automatic reread of a memory location in which a parity failure is detected can be initiated by the hardware error detection logic.

Although protective redundancy is functionally classified into three separate types, the types do overlap in the sense that one type encompasses one or both of the other types. In the case of software redundancy, the control program requires both memory space (hardware) and execution (time). Each of these types of redundancy and their various combinations have been employed in the design of fault-tolerant computing; the choice depends on the user application and the associated reliability requirements.

6.2.2   Basic Hardware Redundancy Techniques

Redundant hardware structures that provide fault-tolerant computing fall into two basic categories: *static redundancy* and *dynamic redundancy.* Both of these may play a roll in the same system. The first method, also known as *fault masking,* involves "masking" or concealing the fault by reconfiguring the system around the fault with additional components or circuits. These circuits are an integral part of the structure; error correction is done automatically since the error is masked out by the redundant logic, making the error transparent to the system. The dynamic technique generally requires two sequential steps: *detection* and *correction.* A fault is first detected, and then recovery action corrects the error. The fault is partitioned out of the operational part of the system by substituting a fault-free unit.

6.2.3 Static Redundancy

The static approach to redundancy uses massive replication of each component, circuit, or subsystem. Error correction occurs automatically. However, if the fault is not susceptive to masking and causes an error, the fault will go undetected and not be corrected.

In the case in which the most frequently encountered failure in a component is an open circuit, redundancy is introduced by paralleling two of the components. Figure 6-1(a) shows a parallel connection of diodes. The failure of a single open circuit diode would not influence the circuit operation. In the other case, in which the dominant failure mode is the short circuit condition, a *series configuration of the components* is necessary—see Figure 6-1(b)—to compensate for a short circuit failure. If the probability of failure is equal for both modes, a combination of the series and the parallel arrangements is the best method for correcting single errors; see Figure 6-1(c).

Fault detection is extremely difficult when static redundancy is applied at the component level since the component fault is masked out by the redundant hardware (components). For a repairable system design, this method of fault correction appears to be undesirable from the viewpoint of fault isolation (i.e., a fault cannot necessarily be recognized at the system level and isolated to a specific unit). On the circuit level, one of the fault-correcting techniques is the use of quadded logic. This scheme is based upon quadruplication of circuitry whereby the error is corrected within two or three levels of the logic beyond the fault that caused it. Correction is accomplished by logically combining signals from circuits that have not failed with the signal from the faulty circuit (see Figure 6-2). Obviously, this technique makes use of a massive replication of logic gates and is rather complicated. Again, fault detection is inherently difficult because the redundant hardware conceals the faults.

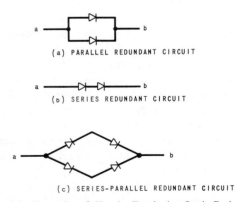

(a) PARALLEL REDUNDANT CIRCUIT

(b) SERIES REDUNDANT CIRCUIT

(c) SERIES-PARALLEL REDUNDANT CIRCUIT

Figure 6-1 Examples of Circuits Employing Static Redundancy

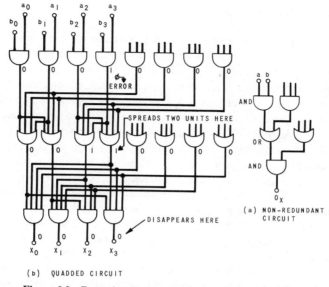

(a) NON-REDUNDANT CIRCUIT

(b) QUADDED CIRCUIT

Figure 6-2   Example of a Circuit Employing Quadded Logic

On the subsystem level, John von Neumann's original concept of *majority logic* has been widely studied and enlarged upon by many reliability designers, particularly for military applications. This technique involves triplication of the functional blocks and voter circuits (see Figure 6-3). Voter circuits restore the proper output when a fault is present in one of the functional blocks. To safeguard against failure in the voter circuit, the majority logic concept is applied to the voter circuits as well.

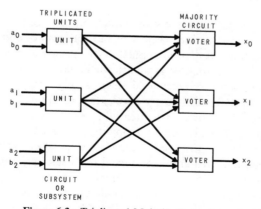

Figure 6-3   Triplicated Majority Redundancy

6.2.4 Dynamic Redundancy

Dynamic redundancy requires additional parts or subsystems to serve as spares within the system. This technique is also referred to as *selective redundancy* since the redundancy is judiciously chosen to give the most effective protection against failures. In response to an error, the faulty unit is automatically (or manually) replaced with a good unit to correct the trouble. The selected circuit, prior to its use, may be active (powered) or passive (unpowered). There are three necessary steps in this procedure. First, the error must be detected quickly. This is the foremost step in the procedure. If the fault detection logic points to a fault within a single replaceable unit, then the second step of diagnosis is not needed. On the other hand, if the fault detection logic embraces a number of replaceable units, the second step of diagnosis must be initiated to pinpoint the faulty unit. In diagnosis, the fault is analyzed either by special hardware or by software diagnostics; the result is an assignment of the fault to a specific device or unit. The third and final step is recovery action to eliminate the fault by replacing the offending unit with a working unit. In addition, for a real-time control system, if the error occurs in the midst of an operation, some program *rollback* is necessary to discard the bad data and to recover as much good data as possible. A rollback operation makes use of the concept of *checkpoints*. A checkpoint is a scheduled point in the execution sequence when the state of the system is saved. Program rollback forces execution to restart at the last checkpoint and to begin processing the data saved at that checkpoint since the data is assumed to be unmutilated. This means recovery must involve both hardware and software to ensure continuity of operation, or, at least, to minimize the disturbance to the system.

6.2.5 Coding Techniques

Coding has been used extensively in telecommunications and telemetry for error detection and correction. Many of the concepts of coding theory used in telecommunications have been applied in the implementation of data transfer operations within computer systems, particularly data transfers between main storage and various peripheral devices (e.g., tape units and disks). Cyclic redundancy codes and parity checks (see Chapter 7) have been widely used for checking data stored in sequential-access bulk memory devices such as 9-track magnetic tape drives and floppy disks. Similarly, for main storage operations, error-detecting and -correcting codes have been used. Their applications have been effective and economical in protecting information stored in main storage against transient or permanent errors.

Within the processor, the data signals are processed by various arithmetic operations or logical functions. The data undergoes a computational process of modification; the original data is transformed by the processor into a numerical result. The normal parity-check bits are not preserved in any consistent manner for the resultant data. Thus, parity checking of the result is not a meaningful approach to assessing the validity of the computation. However, there are special codes belonging to classes of residue codes that have the property of having check codes preserved under a transformation such as a computation. Extensive work has been done with arithmetic codes for checking arithmetic operations. In general, the encoders and decoders are rather complex when the codes have to be preserved by going through arithmetic or logical functions. These subjects are covered in greater detail in Chapter 7.

Both static and dynamic redundancy structures are methods of providing spare parts to enable the system to tolerate failures. Figure 6-4 shows the general types of redundancy and their functional relationship. In the static case, the spare units (components, circuits, or subsystems) are a permanent part of the unit; they either correct the error or mask the error to prevent it from spreading into parts that will be visible or harmful to the system. The masking function takes place automatically; corrective action is immediate and "wired in." However, the *major drawback* of this structure

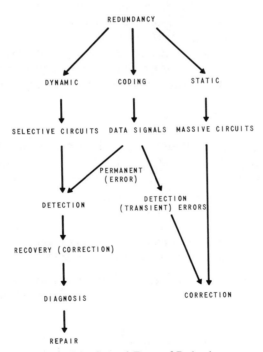

Figure 6-4 General Types of Redundancy

is that the fault cannot be identified.   This leads to difficulties in testing and repairing.   Consequently, static types of redundancy have been used primarily in military applications that require high reliability for a short duration.

For commercial applications, the cost of massive redundancy has been too extensive to justify its use except in special situations.   Instead, the machines used in commercial applications must be repairable.   This implies that a dynamic type of redundancy, including coding techniques, is more suitable for commercial applications.   The remainder of this chapter will be concerned with the implementation of fault detection as opposed to fault masking since the ability to detect and isolate faults is the most important aspect of fault-tolerant design of computers.   Fault diagnosis will also be covered since it is essential to achieve a highly maintainable system.

6.3   MAINTAINABILITY

Maintainability is defined as the probability of a failed unit being restored to full operational effectiveness within a given time.   It is a measure of the speed with which loss of performance is detected, diagnosed, and repaired.

A relationship exists between maintainability and reliability as well as between the repair rate of a system and its failure rate.   These relationships can be derived as follows: Let M represent the maintainability measure or the probability of all components being in the operational state (i.e., none have experienced a failure), and let F represent the probability at any time that the failed components will not have been restored to fully operational service:

$$M = 1 - F \qquad (1)$$

If F is equal to 0—that is, all failed components are repaired instantaneously (zero repair time)—M is equal to 1 or 100 percent.   The factor F at time t may be expressed by

$$F = \frac{N_F}{N_T} \qquad (2)$$

where N_T = total number of units which initially failed
  N_F = number of units still inoperative at time t

Since the number of units restored to proper operation plus the number of units which are still inoperative equal the total number of units which have failed, Eq. (2) may be expressed as

$$F = \frac{N_F}{N_T} = \frac{N_T - N_G}{N_T} = 1 - \left(\frac{N_G}{N_T} \right) \qquad (3)$$

where N_T = total number of units which initially failed
N_F = number of units still inoperative at time t
N_G = number of units restored to proper operation at time t

Equation (3) may be differentiated and expressed as

$$\frac{dF}{dt} = \frac{1}{N_T} \frac{dN_G}{dt} \tag{4}$$

By multiplying both sides of Eq. (4) by N_T/N_F, the following expression is obtained:

$$\left(\frac{N_T}{N_F}\right)\frac{dF}{dt} = \left(\frac{1}{N_F}\right)\frac{dN_G}{dt} \tag{5}$$

The term dN_G/dt is the frequency at which the defective units are being restored to service. When this term is divided by the number of units that are still inoperative at time t, the instantaneous repair rate for one unit can be determined. This can be written as

$$\left(\frac{1}{N_F}\right)\frac{dN_G}{dt} \tag{6}$$

Hence,

$$\left(\frac{1}{N_F}\right)\frac{dN_G}{dt} = \mu(t) \tag{7}$$

where $\mu(t)$ is the instantaneous repair rate for one unit.
By combining Eqs. (2) and (7), Eq. (5) becomes

$$\left(\frac{1}{F}\right)\frac{dF}{dt} = -\mu(t) \tag{8}$$

or

$$\frac{dF}{F} = -\mu(t)dt \tag{9}$$

Assuming that $\mu(t)$ = constant = μ_0, integrating both sides of Eq. (9) results in

$$\int_0^F \frac{dF}{F} = -\int_0^t \mu_0\, dt \tag{10}$$

or

$$\ln F = -\mu_0 t \tag{11}$$

Solving for *F* gives

$$F = e^{-\mu_0 t} \tag{12}$$

By substituting $e^{-\mu_0 t}$ for *F*, Eq. 1 becomes

$$M = 1 - F = 1 - e^{-\mu_0 t} \tag{13}$$

or

$$M = 1 - e^{-(t/\mathrm{MTTR})} \tag{14}$$

where $\mu_0 = 1/\mathrm{MTTR}$ and MTTR = the mean time to repair for each of the components.

The *mean time to repair* (MTTR) and the repair rate (μ) are related to maintainability *(M)* as indicated by Eq. (13). The time *(t)* is the permissible time constraint for the maintenance action. For a smaller *t*, the maintainability is lower for a given MTTR. Similarly, increasing the MTTR will also decrease *M*.

MTTR is the length of time between failure and restoration to full operation. This includes fault detection, diagnosis, and repair time. Before any maintenance action can be initiated, the fault must first be detected. This is perhaps the most important aspect of design for reliability. For ordinary applications, maintainability is beneficial because it increases system availability by reducing the downtime for repair. In fault-tolerant systems, for critical applications in which the essential parts are replicated to tolerate a failure, a failure must be detected and repaired before a second intolerable failure occurs.

6.4 FAULT CHARACTERISTICS AND ASSUMPTIONS

Hardware failures are generally classified into two types: *permanent* (solid) or *transient* (intermittent). A failure may cause the logic values at one or more points of the logic circuitry to become opposite to the specified values. This symptom is normally referred to as a *logic fault*. A logic fault may or may not cause an immediate error in the result of a computation. In many logic circuits, the outputs are controlled directly by the macroinstruction sequence so that a fault will propagate as an error *only* if that portion is used in the computation. The more frequently used portion of the machine will recognize faults more quickly. Eventually, however, a logic fault will result in an error either in the program sequence, or in the data produced by the computation, or both.

The exact nature of a fault generally depends on whether the failure is a fixed or intermittent malfunction of a component or a circuit. A fixed failure usually causes the logic value at certain outputs or inputs to be *stuck-*

at-1 or *stuck-at-0.* When a program sequence is repeated with the same set of initial conditions, the results are the same for any permanent failure if there are no *race* conditions generated because of the fault. That is, timing relationships have *not* been changed by the fixed fault so that transient faults are produced. It is easier to design a program sequence to detect permanent *stuck-at* faults when the test outputs are repeatable.

Transient faults are intermittent and a great deal more difficult to isolate. They may be caused by a number of different situations. A transient error may be an error in an intermittent device, such as a resistor that opens when it heats up and then returns to its normal state when the device is turned off. A transient error may also be an error in a poorly designed circuit that behaves marginally under certain operating conditions. Another cause of transient faults is noise induced into the system because of external interferences. External interference may be caused by irregularities in the power and ground system, stray electromagnetic fields, or other severe environmental conditions. In these cases, the faults introduced are temporary, and their occurrence is unlikely to be detected by any periodic check-out program which examines the hardware for faults.

There are other types of failures that are catastrophic and immediate. Power supplies and clock signals, which fan out or are distributed to many parts of the system, are good examples of elements that may create this type of error. A degradation in the waveshape of clock signals or a reduction of power supply voltages below design limits may create marginal circuit operation, resulting in faults of a transient nature.

Software faults can also cause problems in a system. Program errors exist even in small, relatively simple systems. They may be caused by improper translation of the functional specification or algorithm into a sequence of machine instructions. Program errors may also be caused by improperly handling or even overlooking all possible system conditions that may influence the execution of program sequences. Software faults sometimes cause symptoms similar to hardware faults. The solid type of software errors are repeatable, particularly when the algorithm is implemented incorrectly. The transient types of errors are intermittent because they are sensitive to the system state or to *data* and therefore not easily reproduced. In many instances, software errors occur very far upstream in the program sequence and are not recognized immediately. For these reasons, software faults are at times more difficult to detect and isolate than hardware faults. Further, certain hardware and software faults are indistinguishable. However, when a program has been "repaired," it will remain "fixed," as opposed to hardware that is subject to physical deterioration and other related problems. The same hardware fault may recur again and again. Unfortunately, the task of eliminating all software faults from any sizable program is not as easy as it sounds, particularly when the program undergoes continuous changes.

6.5 SUMMARY

Reliability requirements for the performance of digital systems have steadily increased with the proliferation of computing machines. As the small computer has become widely utilized in a variety of applications, the cost of maintaining the system to keep it operational has become an item of great concern to the user community. This concern has manifested itself in the manufacturers' beginning to develop machines that (1) have fault detection capabilities and (2) may be quickly repaired. Redundancy has been the primary approach taken to achieve high availability or uptime in a digital system. In general, the redundancy used has taken the form of protective redundancy which can be broken down further into the categories of (1) hardware redundancy, (2) software redundancy, and (3) time redundancy. These categories can overlap; the precise way that they are employed is a function of the computing requirements of the application.

In general, the most effective use of protective redundancy is to provide a mechanism for detecting the occurrence of faults *and* indicating the location of the faults at the macrosystem level. Repair may proceed automatically by the system compensating for the failure, or repair may be done by manual intervention. The final resolution and repair of a subtle system fault *must* be left to the ingenuity of the highly skilled craftspersons responsible for maintaining the system.

In designing any fault detection software and/or hardware, it is desirable from a maintenance point of view to include as many test sequences as possible so that the fault(s) may be isolated and quickly identified. In general, such software can be designed by assuming that the classical stuck-at-1 or stuck-at-0 faults will occur in their logic. However, real-world systems experience a range of faults considerably beyond the two classical fault types. In particular, multiple fault occurrences in the same system and transient faults are two examples of nonclassical fault types. Nonetheless, the classical stuck-at-1 and stuck-at-0 faults represent a practical model that is quite straightforward to implement. In a majority of system faults, the classical approach to fault detection has proven quite adequate.

6.6 REFERENCES

1. A. AVIZIENIS, "Fault-Tolerant Systems," *IEEE Trans. Comput.*, C-25, No. 12 (Dec. 1976), 1304–1312.
2. T. E. BROWNE, T. M. QUINN, W. N. TOY and J. E. YATES "No. 2 ESS Control Unit System" *Bell Syst. Tech. J.*, 48, No. 8 (Oct. 1969), 2619–2668.
3. W. C. CARTER and W. G. BOURICIUS, "A Survey of Fault-Tolerant Architecture and its Evaluation," *Computer*, 4, No. 1 (Jan. 1971), 9–16.

4. W. C. CARTER and C. E. MCCARTHY, "Implementation of an Experimental Fault-Tolerant Memory System," *IEEE Trans. Comput., C-25,* No. 6 (June 1976), 557–568.

5. H. Y. CHANG, R. C. DORR and D. J. SENESE, "The Design of a Micro-Programmed Self-Checking Processor of an Electronic Switching System," *IEEE Trans. Comput., C-22,* No. 5 (May 1973), 489–500.

6. H. Y. CHANG and J. M. SCANLON, "Design Principles for Processor Maintainability in Real-Time System," *AFIPS Conf. Proc., 35* (1969), 319–328.

7. A. D. FRIEDMAN and P. R. MENON, *Fault Detection in Digital Circuits* (Englewood Cliffs, N.J.: Prentice-Hall, 1971).

8. F. MATHUR and A. AVIZIENIS, "Reliability Analysis and Architecture of a Hybrid-Redundant Digital System: Generalized Triple Modular Redundancy with Self-Repair," *AFIPS Conf. Proc., 36* (1970), 375–383.

9. T. R. N. RAO and O. N. GARCIA, "Cyclic and Multi-Residue Codes for Arithmetic Operations," *IEEE Trans. Inf. Theory, IT-17,* No. 1 (Jan. 1971), 85–91.

10. T. F. STOREY, "Design of a Microprogram Control for a Processor in an Electronic Switching System," *Bell Syst. Tech. J., 55,* No. 2 (Feb. 1976), 183–232.

11. J. G. TRYON, "Quadded Logic," in *Redundancy Techniques for Computing Systems,* eds. R. H. WILCOX and W. C. MANN (New York: Spartan, 1962), 205–228.

12. J. F. WAKERLY, *Error Detecting Codes, Self-Checking Circuits and Applications* (New York: Elsevier North-Holland, 1978).

CHAPTER 7

Fault Detection

7.1 FAULT DETECTION: A COMMENTARY

In general, error detection can be accomplished through the use of hardware, firmware (microprograms), and software only or a combination of all these methods. The type of checking circuitry used depends on the logical structure of the machine as well as the operational and the functional use of the data and the control signals.

Error detection codes can be effectively used to represent information symbols transmitted within the machine itself. A bus-oriented data structure which is used to transfer information with one or more parity-check bits appended to the bus can be engineered to provide high error detectability through the use of parity checking circuits, strategically located in the processor.

Arithmetic or logical operations modify data signals as the information flows through a computer. Coding schemes must be chosen to be compatible with the arithmetic functions that are to be performed. Extensive research has been done in the area of using residue codes for arithmetic operations. While these codes seem to provide the most elegant means of error detection during arithmetic operations, parity prediction has also been used and studied extensively. The designer's prime objective is a unified, simple parity check throughout the entire machine. With the continuing cost reduction in hardware, the best and the most complete fault detection technique may be the *brute force* method of duplicating each logical unit and matching the outputs of the two units after each control step has been executed.

Control circuits usually differ in their logical implementation from processor to processor. This irregularity of implementation makes the control logic the most difficult portion of a computer system to test and diagnose, requiring a great deal of special hardware for fault detection. The use of microprogramming provides a good, systematic approach to implementing control logic. The regularity of the control store structure and its associated addressing logic makes it particularly easy to check for errors. Additional error detection hardware may be readily incorporated as part of the control store logic.

Fault detection may be performed under program control by having an error detection program apply a series of output signals to a circuit. The error detection program also monitors the output(s) of the circuit for each series of input signals. The outputs are compared against a *table of expected values* by the error detection program to determine if a fault has occurred. To design a complete test sequence for a specific circuit, the test conditions must be oriented toward checking the circuit at the level of the components themselves rather than at the level of the macroinstruction set.

A logic gate with N inputs does *not require* that 2^N input combinations be applied to the gate to verify that it is operating correctly or without the occurrence of any faults. In most cases, it is sufficient to check the output behavior for each input. As an example, the input/output sequence shown in Table 7-1 is sufficient to completely check a three-input AND gate for the occurrence of any errors.

In many computers, program-controlled test sequences are applied to check out the system on a periodic (scheduled) basis. If a failure occurs in the interval during which the test sequences are not being run and the failure is not detected by the fault detection hardware, the computer will produce erroneous results during this period. To minimize the likelihood of this happening, the frequency at which the machine is periodically tested by an error detection program may be increased. The approach adopted by the designers of the Bell System No. 2 Electronic Switching System (No. 2 ESS) is based on the *duplication and match* philosophy. In this approach, both central processors handle the same input information and run in synchronism with each other. Critical outputs from each machine are matched against one another at the completion of each internal machine control opera-

TABLE 7-1 Sufficient Input Test Sequence for a 3-Input AND Gate

INPUT SEQUENCE			OUTPUT	COMMENT
A	B	C		
1	1	1	1	TEST OUTPUT FOR ERROR
0	1	1	0	TEST INPUT A IN CONTROLLING OUTPUT
1	0	1	0	TEST INPUT B IN CONTROLLING OUTPUT
1	1	0	0	TEST INPUT C IN CONTROLLING OUTPUT

$$(A\ B\ C) = f$$

NOTE: FOR AN n-INPUT GATE, n+1 TEST INPUT COMBINATIONS ARE ADEQUATE.

tion. Only one machine, called the *on-line machine,* actually handles the call processing. The second machine functions as a *shadow processor* to the on-line machine so that matching may be performed. The peripheral equipment is controlled by the on-line machine. When the outputs from the two machines mismatch, a fault detection program is called in to determine which machine is faulty.

7.2 ERROR DETECTION CODES

7.2.1 Error Detection Concepts

The basic idea of error detection codes is to add additional information (bits) to a data word so that if errors occur they can be detected. These additional bits are also called *check bits.* The error detection capability of this approach is a direct function of the number of check bits included in a word. A good error detection code will allow multiple-bit errors to be detected in the data word. If the detected error(s) can be uniquely identified and the check bits allow the original error-free data word to be reconstructed, the error detection code is then not only capable of error detection but also *error correction.*

For data words that are transmitted over a long distance, the data words may be subjected to various noise sources that are transient in nature and may cause one or more bits of data to be mutilated. A burst of noise in a serial transmission channel may take the form of bipolar voltage spikes that swing from a positive voltage level to a negative voltage level and back again. This bipolar noise voltage may extend for many bit intervals, causing multiple bidirectional bit errors (a 1 changes to a 0, and a 0 changes to a 1). Extensive error detection and correction schemes have been developed in the communication field to combat such data errors. Some of these checking techniques are also applicable to data transmission within the computer, particularly on words fetched from main storage and placed in an internal processor register. Similar checking schemes may be associated with input/output transfers occurring between the processor and a peripheral device.

Errors in computer circuits, however, are more likely to be the result of circuit failures rather than a noisy environment. Further, circuit faults usually affect a signal or a data word in *one particular direction* (this is called a *unidirectional fault*). For example, a circuit failure may change a 4-bit data word from 0110 to 1111 or 0000 but not to 1001. One of the requirements for selecting an error-detecting code is that the fault characteristics of the code must be easily recognized to allow detection of those errors most likely to occur. Another requirement is that the checking procedures associated with the code for encoding and decoding data words must be as simple and fast as possible. The cost-effectiveness of any error-detecting code requires that a given degree of detection (the number of types of errors that may be detected) be achieved with a *minimum* number of check bits. The cost of error detection has two interrelated components: the complexity of the associated checking hardware and the time required by the checking logic to determine what error(s), if any, have occurred.

7.2.2 Parity Checking

Parity checking is the most widely used code for error detection within a computer system. It is a code that requires a minimum number of check bits and provides a good error detection capability. Parity checking is accomplished by assigning a parity bit to a data word. An odd-parity check requires that the total number of bits in the 1s state in the data word *plus* the check bit must be an *odd* number. An even-parity check requires that the total number of bits in the 1s state in the data word *plus* the check bit must be an *even* number. For example, data words 10110100 and 10101000 contain four 1s (an even number) and three 1s (an odd number), respectively. For an odd-parity check, the check bit must be set to 1 in the first data word and 0 in the second data word; that is, 101101001 and 101010000, respectively. In this example, the check bit occupies the least-significant bit position of each data word. For an even-parity check, the check bit must be set to 0 in the first data word and to 1 in the second data word. Any single-bit faults or odd-multiple-bit faults are detectable by a single parity-check bit. However, faults caused by an even number of bits being in error will not be detected by the parity checks since an even number of faults will appear transparent to the parity generation logic.

Parity checking for binary data may be expressed mathematically as follows:

$$P(N) = \left[\sum_{i=0}^{n} a_i \right] \bmod 2$$

$$= a_n \oplus a_{n-1} \oplus \cdots \oplus a_1 \oplus a_0 \qquad (1)$$

where

$$N = a_n(2^n) + a_{n-1}(2^{n-1}) + \ldots + a_1(2^1) + a_0(2^0)$$

The symbol $\oplus$ represents the modulo 2 addition operation or the exclusive-OR function and

$$a_i = \begin{cases} 0 \\ 1 \end{cases}$$

For example, if $N = 101101001$, with the most-significant bit being the parity bit (chosen to give N odd parity), the operation of a parity check gives

$$P(N) = 1 \oplus 0 \oplus 1 \oplus 1 \oplus 0 \oplus 1 \oplus 0 \oplus 0 \oplus 1 = 1 \qquad (2)$$

If any single-bit error (or odd number of bit errors) occurs in N, the result of $P(N)$ would be 0 instead of 1, indicating an error had occurred in the parity generation procedure.

7.2.3 Residue Codes

Residue codes belong to a class of codes that detects (or corrects) errors in the results produced by an arithmetic unit as well as errors that have been caused by faulty data transfer or storage operations. The unique property of this class of codes is that the codes are preserved during arithmetic operations.

As in the case of parity checking, residue codes are also *separable codes.* That is, the data part of a word is separated from the check bits in the encoded representation of the word. This allows the data word and the check bits to be handled separately. The residue $R(N)$ of a number N may be formulated as follows: Let the number N be given by

$$N = a_n r^n + a_{n-1} r^{n-1} + \ldots + a_0 r^0$$

$$= \sum_{i=0}^{n} a_i r^i, \qquad \text{where } 0 \le a_i < r \qquad (3)$$

The residue $R(N)$ can then be expressed as

$$R(N) = \left[\sum_{i=0}^{n} a_i r^i \right] \bmod m, \qquad \text{where } 0 \le R(N) < m \qquad (4)$$

This expression for the residue function differs from the expression for the parity-check function in that the residue is over the weighted value of the radix r as opposed to the unweighted binary digits used in the parity check.

The residue of a number N can be calculated by *dividing* N by the modulus m. The quotient will consist of an integer term K and a remainder term. The remainder term is the residue. This mathematical operation may be expressed as follows:

$$\frac{N}{m} = K + \frac{R(N)}{m} \tag{5}$$

For example, consider the decimal number system with $r = 10$, $N = 233$, and $m = 7$; the residue function of 233 modulo 7 is determined as follows:

$$\frac{N}{m} = \frac{233}{7} = K + \frac{R(N)}{7}$$

$$= 33 + \tfrac{2}{7} \tag{6}$$

The remainder term, or residue modulo 7, is

$$R(N) = 2 \tag{7}$$

For binary systems, the residue modulo 2 can be calculated in an entirely similar manner. When the checking modulo is chosen to be of the form $m = 2^n - 1$, that is, 3, 7, 15, . . . ($n = 2, 3, 4, . . .$), then the logic implementation of the checking circuit can be simplified relative to the checking logic required by other moduli *not* generated by the formula $2^n - 1$. When the values for m (3, 7, 15, 31, . . .) are used, the residue function $R(N)$ can be represented by r bits; the actual calculation of the residue does not require the extended process of division. For example, consider the binary number N:

$$N = a_n(2^n) + a_{n-1}(2^{n-1}) + . . . + a_0(2^0)$$

$$= \sum_{i=0}^{n} a_i(2^i), \quad \text{where } a_i = \begin{cases} 0 \\ 1 \end{cases} \tag{8}$$

This binary number can also be represented by n/r digits, where the quotient is rounded off to the *next highest* digit and each digit is r bits wide (composed of r bits). This representation for N can be expressed as

$$N = \sum_{i=0}^{(n/r)-1} b_i(2^r)^i \tag{9}$$

where b_i is the ith digit representing r bits of the number N, with b having a value between 0 and r. That is,

$$0 \le b < r \tag{10}$$

For example, if $N = 01101110$ and $r = 3$, then the 8-bit binary representation of N may be divided into three separate digit groups as follows:

$$N = \underbrace{01}_{b_2}\ \underbrace{101}_{b_1}\ \underbrace{110}_{b_0} \tag{11}$$

or

$$
\begin{aligned}
N &= \sum_{i=0}^{2} b_i(2^3)^i \\
&= b_2(2^6) + b_1(2^3) + b_0(2^0) \\
&= (1)2^6 + (5)2^3 + (6)2^0
\end{aligned} \tag{12}
$$

Since

$$
\begin{aligned}
R(2^r) &= (2^r)\bmod(2^r - 1) = 1 \\
R(2^r)^i &= (2^r)^i \bmod(2^r - 1) = 1
\end{aligned} \tag{13}
$$

and

$$R[b_i(2^r)^i] = b_i(2^r)^i \bmod(2^r - 1) = b_i \tag{14}$$

the residue of N may now be expressed as

$$
\begin{aligned}
R(N) &= N \bmod(2^r - 1) \\[4pt]
&= \sum_{i=0}^{(n/r-1)} b_i(2^r)^i \bmod(2^r - 1) \\[4pt]
&= \sum_{i=0}^{(n/r-1)} b_i \bmod(2^r - 1)
\end{aligned}
\tag{15}
\tag{16}
$$

The final expression is the modulo $2^r - 1$ summation of b_i digits. Each digit is r bits wide and has a form that is similar to that in the parity calculation. For the parity calculation, $r = 1$, and a digit consists of one bit; the modulo addition is referred to base $m = 2$.

Residue codes are *separable codes* as are the parity-check codes. The major difference between the two code categories is that the residue codes are preserved under arithmetic operations. For residue codes, the operands x, y and their check symbols x', y' are handled separately; x, y generate the result z, while x', y' generate check result z'. The checking algorithm computes the residue from the result z, as shown in Figure 7-1, and compares the residue with the check result z'. If the two values match, no error is detected. A disagreement between the two values is detected as a fault in either the main arithmetic unit or in the check circuit.

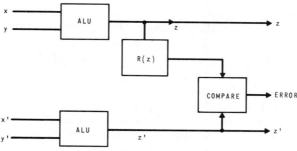

Figure 7-1 Residue Checking

7.2.4 Fixed-Weight Codes

Encoded binary signals used in a computer system represent basically two types of information: data or control. The data signals, in turn, represent a variety of entities: numbers, characters, addresses, and labels, for example. These entities may be used directly without any modification, or they may be operated on by any of the arithmetical or logical functions available on the processor to compute specific values needed by the currently executing program. Separable error detection codes *(systematic codes)* such as parity and residue codes allow the original data to be determined without any additional decoding. This characteristic is quite convenient for processing and handling data signals within the computer system. For control functions, the binary encoded signals may similarly employ separable error detection codes. However, these signals are usually decoded at their destinations (i.e., the logic gates that *generate* each of the control signals). Therefore, nonseparable error detection codes with special characteristics may be used to realize more effective error detection when *individual* control signals are required to be checked for errors.

The *fixed-weight* or *m-out-of-n code* is an important type of nonseparable code. In coding theory, the weight of a code word is defined as the number of *nonzero components* in the code word. For a binary word, the weight is the number of 1s in the code word. Therefore, a fixed-weight code has a fixed number of 1s. Its unique property is its ability to detect all *unidirectional multiple-bit errors.* This type of error occurs when a fault causes *all* the data bits *in error* to either change from the 0 state to the 1 state or from the 1 state to the 0 state, but error transitions may not occur in both directions simultaneously. Therefore, any unidirectional type of error will cause the code word to have a *different weight;* this characteristic results in the errors being detectable by the checking logic. For an undetectable error, the fault must cause compensating errors; that is, when one bit is changed from the 0 state to the 1 state, another bit will be changed from the 1 state to the 0 state. This gives the appearance of maintaining the fixed weight of the data word. In most situations, the probability of such compensating errors occurring would be quite small. This characteristic of detecting all multiple unidirectional errors makes the fixed-weight code an important type for error detection within the computer.

The 2-out-of-5 code shown in Table 7-2 has been widely used to represent decimal digits. The 5-bit code has 10 binary combinations, each having exactly two 1s. To define 10 numbers, a minimum of four binary bits is required to uniquely represent each number; six binary bit patterns are treated as unused combinations. An additional parity-check bit could be added to provide error detection over each binary coded digit. However, the usage of the check bit would bring the total number of bits required in a binary coded digit to five bits, which is the same number as required by an encoded representation using the 2-out-of-5 code. The 2-out-of-5 code gives a greater error detection capability. However, which code is chosen to encode the decimal digits depends largely on how the coded information is to be used by the digital machine. The usage of special codes for error checking will be discussed in more detail in the following sections.

As an aside, there are an infinite number of fixed-weight codes. The number of code words in a binary m-out-of-n code is given by

$$\frac{n!}{m!\,(n-m)!} \tag{17}$$

where

TABLE 7-2 2-out-of-5 Code Representation of Decimal Digits

DECIMAL DIGIT	BINARY CODE				2-OUT-OF-5 CODE				
0	0	0	0	0	0	0	0	1	1
1	0	0	0	1	0	0	1	1	0
2	0	0	1	0	0	1	1	0	0
3	0	0	1	1	1	1	0	0	0
4	0	1	0	0	1	0	0	0	1
5	0	1	0	1	0	0	1	0	1
6	0	1	1	0	0	1	0	1	0
7	0	1	1	1	1	0	1	0	0
8	1	0	0	0	0	1	0	0	1
9	1	0	0	1	1	0	0	1	0

NOTE: BINARY COMBINATIONS 1010, 1011, 1100, 1101, 1110, 1111 ARE NOT USED.

n = total number of bits in a code word
m = total number of bits that *must* be in the 1 state in a code word
$n! = n(n-1)(n-2) \cdots 2(1)$

The maximum number of code words for a given n occurs when $m = n/2$. For example, the 4-out-of-8 code, commonly used as an error detection code, has 70 possible combinations. This represents the maximum number of code word combinations that are available when any of the other seven m-out-of-8 codes are considered.

7.3 CHECKING DATA TRANSFER PATHS

7.3.1 Sources of Error in the Data Transfer Path

The primary function of a data processing system is to handle binary data. Normally, fast-access storage in the form of flip-flop registers provides short-term storage for information being used in current data processing operations. The data paths handle not only data but also instructions and control information up to the physical locations in the digital machine where the control and/or data signals are decoded for internal use by the machine. It is necessary for efficient system operation that the CPU allow rapid transfer of information from any register to any other register and also between main memory and any register. This is usually accomplished by transferring the required information on one or more data buses.

Most of the information which is handled within the digital machine normally passes through main storage. An additional parity bit may be appended to all data words and checked at the end of each data transfer. The parity bit is normally sufficient to detect *all* single-bit errors in a data word. If this parity bit is carried throughout the data processing part of the system, all single-bit faults, not only in memory but also in the flip-flop registers and their associated logic circuitry, will be detected.

When data words undergo any arithmetic or logical operation, the simple parity bit is *not* preserved. Instead, the parity bit must be regenerated after the arithmetic or logic operation. The amount of hardware required to perform the parity regeneration depends on the type of error detection code selected to be used with each data word. In choosing an error detection design, the cost of the checking hardware, the impact of error detection on system performance, and the degree of error detectability must be considered in order to realize the best possible overall system performance.

The logical design of the data path circuitry also plays an important part in determining which faults can be easily detected and require a *minimum* amount of error checking hardware. It is possible to logically structure the data path circuitry such that a specific circuit failure can be caused to occur repeatably when the same set of operating conditions arises. (This characteristic is sometimes used to define such circuit faults as being *deterministic.*) This characteristic also limits the fault from affecting more than a certain number of bits in a data word. Therefore, the designer of the data transfer circuit must consider the logic structure of the circuit as well as the error detection code used so as to achieve the most efficient circuit design from the viewpoint of both error detection and diagnosis.

7.3.2 Register Data Cell with Race Condition Faults

Data cells or flip-flop elements are used as the basic building blocks in forming data registers. Data words of appropriate size can be temporarily stored in these flip-flop registers to facilitate data processing. Since a large portion of logic circuitry within a processor consists of these flip-flop circuits, it is essential to design a register structure in which faults may be easily detected and diagnosed.

Figure 7-2 shows how two commonly used data transfer circuits under certain logic faults will result in a *race* condition being present in the circuit. As indicated in Figure 7-2(a), a stuck-at-1 output of data inverter I or an open circuit input to gate R will cause an erroneous output from gate R. This erroneous output will occur whenever the input DATA signal is a 1

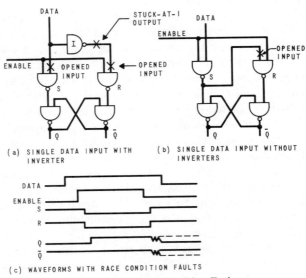

(a) SINGLE DATA INPUT WITH INVERTER

(b) SINGLE DATA INPUT WITHOUT INVERTERS

(c) WAVEFORMS WITH RACE CONDITION FAULTS

Figure 7-2   Race Condition Faults

and the ENABLE control signal is in the 1 state. Under these input conditions, both gate S and gate R become active (enter the 0 state) simultaneously. This condition causes simultaneous SET and RESET signals to be applied to the flip-flop. The net result is that both output Q and $\overline{Q}$ will be held in the 1 state. The same situation exists for the circuit shown in Figure 7-2(b) with the data input an open circuit. When the ENABLE control signal returns to its normal or 0 state, the flip-flop is left in an unstable condition. The flip-flop will eventually settle into either the 0 state or the 1 state; these are the flip-flops two *stable* states. The final state of the flip-flop depends largely on the logic signal delay of the two data paths, gate S to the asserted output *(Q)* of the flip-flop and gate R to the negated output *($\overline{Q}$)* of the flip-flop. If the delays through these two paths are similar, then the final state of the flip-flop cannot be precisely determined. The flip-flop may oscillate, as indicated in the timing diagram of Figure 7-2(c), with the output finally settling in either the 0 state or the 1 state. Both final states are equally likely. The consequence of indeterminate final states occurring in a system gives the appearance of the system containing a transient error. A transient error gives inconsistent diagnostic results; it can not be absolutely identified. If the fault cannot be absolutely identified and corrected, the machine could be restored to operation with the fault unresolved. This could cause further maintenance trouble responses by the system. It is important, therefore, to eliminate such unresolved faults from the processor logic wherever possible by anticipating such faults in the original logic design and removing them before they are ever "set in hardware."

7.3.3 Register Data Cell with Diagnostic Control

There are several possible solutions to the race problem and its associated inconsistent diagnostic results. One solution is to provide separate and independent ENABLE signals to control the two data paths which SET and RESET the flip-flop. During a normal data transfer operation, both ENABLE signals are activated simultaneously to gate the data into the flip-flop. This situation is illustrated in Figure 7-3(a). When an error is detected by a parity check or some other error-checking techniques, a diagnostic test sequence can be applied to enable one gating path at a time. This procedure will check the operation of the flip-flop in response to the SET and RESET inputs being applied separately and eliminates the possibility of having both signals applied to the flip-flop simultaneously under any single fault condition. The same result can be achieved by using a special maintenance access control signal to isolate either data path (SET or RESET signal path) independently. Figure 7-3(b) illustrates this maintenance situation. Typically, such maintenance control signals are derived from special status flip-flops which are

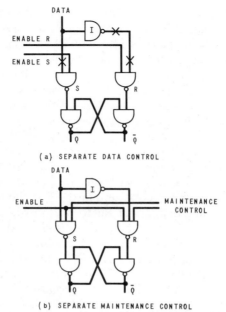

(a) SEPARATE DATA CONTROL

(b) SEPARATE MAINTENANCE CONTROL

Figure 7-3   Register Data Cell with Diagnostic Control

under control of the processor fault diagnosis program.   In the case of separate
ENABLE signals applied to the SET and RESET logic gates, the ENABLE
signals could be derived from separate control fields in the microinstruction;
separate maintenance control signals could be used with the SET and RESET
gates to validate the behavior of each gate.

It is obvious that the approach of separate control signals requires
additional circuitry in terms of logic gates, terminals, and interconnections.
A more desirable solution would be to modify the data transfer logic so
that any faults would result in a deterministic (repeatable) error without
the need for additional circuitry.

7.3.4   Register Data Cell without Race Condition

The difficulty with the structure of the previous data transfer circuits is that
a fault can occur which could result in *both* the SET and RESET signals
being applied simultaneously to the flip-flop; they both can then be removed
but not necessarily at the same time.   This situation gives rise to a race
condition, with the final state of the flip-flop *equally likely* to settle in either
the 0 state or the 1 state.   Figure 7-4(a) illustrates a solution to this problem
which eliminates failures of the race condition type.   For all logic faults

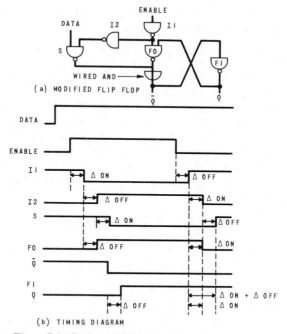

Figure 7-4 Register Data Cell without Race Condition

that might occur under different input conditions, the data cell (flip-flop) outputs Q and $\overline{Q}$ will be stable. This means that an input fault is repeatable (deterministic) and that consistent diagnostic results will be obtained when the circuit is subjected to a sequence of test inputs (vectors).

The data transfer capability of the circuit shown in Figure 7-4(a) takes advantage of the collector-tie capability of the NAND logic gates. The SET and RESET signals are applied to both the input stage and output stage of the flip-flop on the $\overline{Q}$ side of the data cell. When data is transferred into the flip-flop, the ENABLE signal resets the flip-flop, holding the F0 gate in the high state. If the data is a 0, gate S is also held in the high state. This action produces a high voltage level at the $\overline{Q}$ output and a low voltage level at the Q output. These voltage levels represent a 0 being stored in the data cell (flip-flop). If the data is a 1, the output of gate S is held at a low voltage level. Although the gate F0 is in the high potential state, the resultant output $\overline{Q}$ is at a low potential. This behavior is characteristic of the logic wired-AND function in which the output from several logic gates are tied together. The data cell (flip-flop) shown in Figure 7-4(a) is set to the 1 state by the action of the wired-AND logic. The timing diagram of a logical 1 being transferred into the data cell is shown in Figure 7-4(b).

When the ENABLE signal becomes active, it is propagated through the logic chain formed by the following gates:

$$\text{Gate I1} \rightarrow \text{Gate I2} \rightarrow \text{Gate S} \rightarrow \text{Gate F1}$$

A time delay is experienced by the signal that sets the flip-flop because of the logic chain the signal must pass through. When the ENABLE signal returns to the inactive or 0 state, the output of gate F0 and gate S will switch to the opposite state. To keep the flip-flop stable with the output $\bar{Q}$ remaining at low potential, the output of gate F0 must go low before the output of gate S goes high. For this condition to be met, the maximum propagation delay through gate F0 must be less than the minimum delay formed by the logic chain of gate I2 and gate S. This relationship may be expressed mathematically as

$$(\Delta_{ON})_{MAX} < (\Delta_{ON} + \Delta_{OFF})_{MIN} \tag{18}$$

where

$$\Delta_{ON} = \text{gate turn-on delay}$$
$$\Delta_{OFF} = \text{gate turn-off delay}$$

Typically, the value of Δ_{OFF} is larger than the value of Δ_{ON}. This condition is easily satisfied with typical *transistor-transistor logic* (TTL) gates. Any logic faults occurring with the circuit shown in Figure 7-4(a) will be deterministic (repeatable). This circuit does not require any additional control signals or gates to solve the race condition problem. The first inverter, gate I1, is not required if the ENABLE signal is considered to be in the active state when it is at a low potential or in the logical 0 state. If gate I1 is provided, its output can be used to directly control other flip-flops which form the data register.

7.3.5   Fault Characteristics of Data Transfer Circuits

To provide the most effective checking technique for detecting an error in a logic circuit, the effects of *all* possible faults associated with the logic circuit must be considered by the designer. For data transfer operations, the data cell (flip-flop) is used as the basic logic circuit for information transfer. Data registers can be formed by cascading two or more flip-flops. A bank of data registers is illustrated in Figure 7-5. A data word is transferred from the DATA-IN bus to one of the registers in a bit-parallel operation in which all bits in the data register can be changed simultaneously. Similarly, the data stored in a register is strobed from the source register onto the DATA-OUT bus as a bit-parallel operation.

The control signals for reading from or writing into a data register

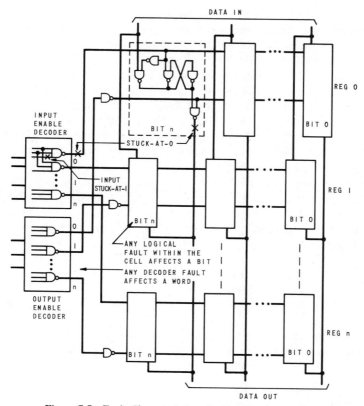

Figure 7-5 Fault Characteristics of a Data Register Bank

are common to all bit positions. The INPUT-ENABLE decoder and the OUTPUT-ENABLE decoder allows the source register and the destination register to be selected as members of the data register bank. This behavior is implemented by taking the outputs of the source register, inverting the outputs through the use of additional logic gates, and feeding the resultant signals back as inputs to the DATA-IN bus.

The data transfer circuit shown in Figure 7-5 consists of two basic parts: the data cell (flip-flop) elements and the decoding logic which forms the access circuitry of the data register bank. Any logic fault within a flip-flop affects only one bit in a data word. Consider the case in which the output gate of bit n in register 0 is stuck-at-0. The bit n positions for all registers appear to be stuck-at-0 since the bit n outputs of all the registers are connected to a common bus lead. This type of fault creates a situation in which the fault diagnosis program cannot distinguish which output gate on the bit n bus is exhibiting a stuck-at-0 fault. However, the fault characteristics associated with a decoder error affect all bits within a data word rather than a single bit. For example, the stuck-at-0 fault occurring on the decoder output shown in Figure 7-5 will cause the data word in register 0 to follow the data on the DATA-IN bus; the stuck-at-0 fault condition enables the data on the DATA-IN bus to be continuously gated into register 0.

This means all bits in register 0 may be in error. Similarly, the stuck-at-1 fault at the input to the INPUT-ENABLE decoder would result in multiple outputs being generated from the decoder. The stuck-at-1 fault appears as a "don't care" condition at the input to the INPUT-ENABLE decoder. This "don't care" condition permits the first decoder gate to be selected whenever the second decoder gate with all its inputs active (except for the input in error) is selected. This situation causes both gates to be active in gating the input data into register 0 *and* register 1. Again, a single fault affects the entire data word. Errors which occur in the data transfer logic circuits can be readily diagnosed as belonging to either of the following two categories:

1. Faults that cause the same bit to appear to be in error in *all* registers in the data register bank
2. Faults that cause one or more bits in the same data register to be in error

The fault detection hardware can be organized to take advantage of these two fault categories that occur in data transfer circuits.

7.3.6 Separate Checks for Control and Data Circuits

Since the faults that occur in a data register bank may be identified with (1) a specified bit position associated with all registers, (2) a specific register itself, or (3) the decoding and control logic used to access a target register, separate error-checking schemes can be used to detect data faults and control signal faults. Figure 7-6 shows the implementation of separate checking schemes for control signals and data; a single parity-check bit may be used to detect all single-bit errors within a register. It is assumed that any faults occurring within the register will *only* affect one bit. The input data to a destination register in the register bank is checked for correct parity, and an error indication is generated by the parity-check logic when wrong parity is encountered. The parity-check logic validates that the data word has been gated out *unmutilated* from the source register and placed on the INPUT DATA bus. The parity-check logic does *not* validate that the data is gated into the destination register correctly. Any bit error which occurs during the transfer of the data from the INPUT DATA bus to the destination

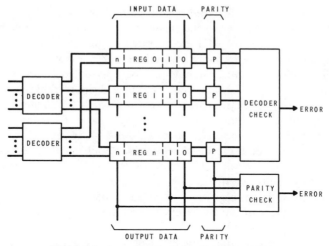

Figure 7-6 Separate Check for Control and Data

register will be caught when the current destination register is used as the source register in a subsequent data transfer operation.

For decoder faults affecting a single word of data, the faults may *not* be detected by the parity check. The control leads from the decoder can be checked as a group to verify that *only one* control lead from each decoder is active at any given time. Any error introduced by a decoder fault (multiple control signal outputs) will be detected immediately; individual bit errors will be detected when the data word is read out from the source register. A more detailed description of decoder checks and parity checks is given in later sections.

7.3.7 Combined Check for Control and Data

The decoder check eliminates the need for detecting multiple-bit errors in a data word. This leads to the simple single-bit error detection scheme shown in Figure 7-6. However, if the error detection capability of the check code is expanded to include the entire word (i.e., a *simple* parity check is no longer used), the decoder check is not required. Decoder faults are manifested as *multiple data-bit errors* in a word and are detectable by the use of an expanded check code. The control logic for the check code must be replicated at each bit position to ensure independence between the data and its check code. This approach eliminates the possibility of decoder faults causing the input data with its correct check code to be gated into one or more additional registers in the data register bank *besides* the correct destination register. Such a fault will not be manifested as a detectable data error unless the checking logic for the input data and the checking logic for the decoder control circuitry are kept separate.   Typically, multiple-bit errors occur because all bits in a register are operated on simultaneously by common control signals—and one or more of the common control signals may be in error.   The common control signal may be eliminated by replicating the decoding logic on a *per-bit basis* and forcing a decoder fault to affect *only* one bit in a word.   This approach is referred to as *bit-slicing* the register bank; that is, all logic circuitry associated with a specific bit position in all the registers is placed in a *single* functional unit.   The register bank is then made up of a chain of these bit-sliced units.   Such a bit-sliced unit could be a single integrated circuit (IC) chip, or it could be made from several IC chips.   Any faults within the bit-sliced unit would affect the same bit position in one or more registers.   A single parity-check bit as shown in Figure 7-7 will detect *all* faults within the bit slice regardless of decoder or data faults.

If a combined checking scheme is used to detect errors in both the individual data words and the control signals emanating from the decoder logic, it is necessary to replicate the access decoders for each bit position. In a semiconductor memory, one of the commercially available 4K memory chips is organized on a bit slice, which contains 4K words with one bit in each word (4K × 1 RAM).   The primary purpose of this RAM structure

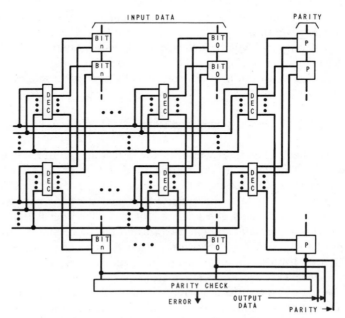

Figure 7-7   Combined Check for Control and Data

is to minimize the number of *external* leads going off the chip. This, in turn, reduces the physical size of the chip. Because of the number of individually selectable data bits (4K), the access decoder becomes more efficient in addressing a single bit from an address which is a large number (such as a 12-bit address required by the 4K × 1 RAM). However, if the 4K × 1 RAM chip were to be used as a bit-sliced building block for the data register bank within the processor, the replication of the access decoders for a relatively small number of words (16 or less) is somewhat excessive and expensive on a bit-sliced basis. Consequently, commercially available bit-sliced devices which may be used to build a register bank are organized on a *nibble* (4-bit) basis: sixteen words with four bits in each word (16 × 4 RAM) or 64 words with four bits in each word (64 × 4 RAM). This arrangement shares the access circuitry among four bit positions to reduce the amount of replication.

If data registers are made up of these 16 × 4 or 64 × 4 register building blocks, the check code must be capable of detecting 4-bit errors since a decoder fault may manifest itself as a 4-bit error in the data. An additional 4-bit nibble, as shown in Figure 7-8, can be used to provide a sufficient number of bits in a check code to detect *all* faults within the 4-bit register building block. The choice of the check code depends on the error-checking technique to be used in fault detection. An interleaved parity check is shown in Figure 7-8. A parity bit is assigned to cover one bit from each 4-bit

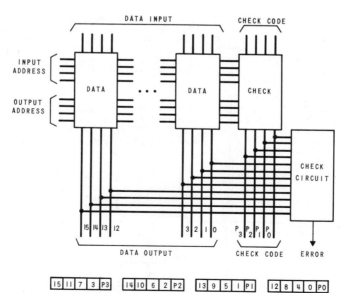

Figure 7-8 Interleaved Parity Check

register building block.   Any faults within a nibble can then be detected by the four parity-check bits.

7.3.8   Data Check by Repeated Operation (Echo Check)

Thus far, the consideration of fault detection during data transfer operations has been centered on the use of parity-check bits.   Instead of employing check codes, the data transfer operations within the processor can be checked by repeating each data transfer operation.   In this case, additional time is used to match the results of the repeated data transfer operations as opposed to employing additional check bits with each data word.

Figure 7-9 shows a method of checking data by repeating each data transfer between a source register and destination register.   A decoder check is necessary to ensure that the control signals are generated properly to perform the data transfer.   If a decoder check is not performed, a decoder fault may cause a data word to be transferred into one or more unspecified registers in the register bank as well as into the correct destination register. The result of this fault is that the contents of the unspecified registers may be changed when the contents should have remained unmodified.   This type of fault can occur without being detected—unless a decoder check is per-

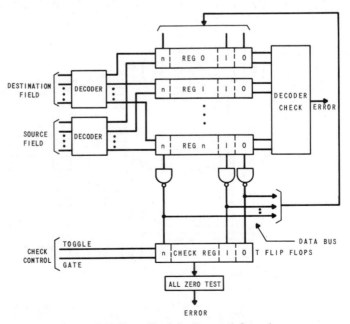

Figure 7-9   Data Check by Repeated Operation

formed on each data transfer operation. The data check, as shown in Figure 7-9, consists of an additional step which checks the contents of the destination register to determine whether the data has been transferred correctly. This is done by incorporating a *check register* as part of the data transfer circuitry. The control sequence to perform an echo check data transfer operation using the implementation shown in Figure 7-9 is as follows:

1. The data from the source register is gated onto the data bus and from the data bus into the destination register.
2. At the same time, the data on the data bus is also gated into the check register; separate check control logic is used to perform this data transfer.
3. The new data in the destination register is then gated onto the bus and toggled into the check register. If a data bit is a 1, the corresponding bit in the check register is toggled to the opposite state. If the data bit is a 0, the state of the corresponding bit in the check register is left unchanged.
4. The net result of gating the new contents of the destination register to the check register is that if the contents of the destination register and the check register are identical, the check register will contain all 0s when the operation is completed. A T-type flip-flop should be used to implement the check register since the T flip-flop inherently possesses the ability to complement its output state when a trigger (T) input is applied to the data cell. If any error occurs during the data transfer operation which uses an echo check, the check register will contain a non-0 word, and an error indication will be given.

7.3.9 Single-Bus Arrangement with Check Register

The data check by repeated operation (as shown in Figure 7-9) is concerned with validating the integrity of data transfers within a block of registers. The registers are interconnected by a data bus; data flows from a source register to a destination register via this common bus. Since data is transferred over a single bus, the use of a check register is adequate to check all data transfers which occur between registers in the register block. A more complete processor structure which uses the single-bus arrangement with a common check circuit is shown in Figure 7-10.

The data transfer operations considered up to this point have dealt with operations in which the data flow within the processor is from one register (a source) to another register (a destination). Typically, the registers found in a processor may be divided into two types: *general registers,* which perform multipurpose accumulator-type functions, and *special registers,* which perform specific functions. A data transfer operation between the processor and main storage or a peripheral device usually involves dedicated registers,

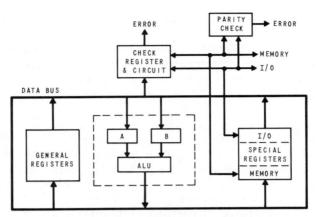

Figure 7-10 Single Bus with Check Register

such as the program address register, memory data register, input buffer register, and so on.   To ensure that the data is transferred from a peripheral device or main storage to the processor without error, the information transfer must be verified.   As shown in Figure 7-10, the assumption is made that a parity-check bit is carried with each main storage data word or I/O data word.   As the data enters the processor from either main storage or a peripheral device, the data is checked for correct parity and gated into both the check register and the appropriate dedicated register.   At this point, if the data passes the parity check, the data is assumed to be correct, and the parity bit is no longer included in the data word.   To ensure that error-free data enters into a dedicated register correctly, the data must be gated onto the common bus and compared with the same data stored in the check register.   A single fault which could occur when the data word is gated into either the check register or a dedicated register will result in a data word mismatch (an error condition).   This type of data transfer is done on a synchronous basis.   For asynchronous data transfers between the processor and a peripheral unit, a separate check register buffer is required to temporarily hold the data from the peripheral unit until the processor is ready to perform the checking operation.*   When the processor is ready to process the data, it transfers the contents of the check register buffer into the check register and performs the data check with the contents of the dedicated register used in the asynchronous I/O operation.

Similarly, data transfers from the processor to its peripheral units are checked by the check register.   This is done to ensure that the data is error-

---

* An asynchronous data transfer involving the processor and a peripheral device implies that data can be gated into or out of a dedicated register with *no* fixed time relationship to the processor clock.

free prior to the generation of the parity-check bit. A logical or arithmetic operation is performed on data directed to the *arithmetic logic unit* (ALU) portion of the processor. The checking of the ALU output is covered more extensively in later sections.

When the parity check is extended over the data bus within the processor, a parity checker attached to the data bus checks all data transfers which occur over the data bus. Figure 7-11 illustrates a single-bus architecture with a common parity-check circuit used to validate all data transfers over the data bus. It is not necessary for the check logic to confirm that the data reaches the destination register correctly. If an error occurs in transferring the data from the bus into the destination register, this error will be caught later when the data is processed. As indicated in Figure 7-11, the data to, or from, a peripheral device is buffered temporarily in a dedicated register. The data in the dedicated register is checked when the contents of the data register are gated onto the bus and then to a general register. However, instruction words and data words are transferred from main storage at a relatively high transfer rate. In most instances, the instructions are used to perform specific operations in which no error checking is done. If a data word is to be checked by the common parity checker, the data word must be gated onto the bus. This, of course, requires an additional step in the instruction execution sequence and, consequently, penalizes the performance of the processor. A separate parity checker that is dedicated to checking data received by the processor from main storage, as shown in Figure 7-11, eliminates the need to use the parity checker attached to the data bus on an instruction FETCH. The employment of a separate parity

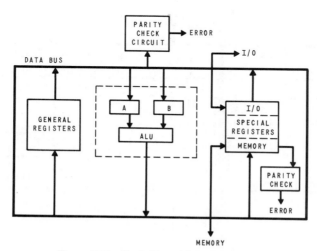

Figure 7-11 Single Bus with Parity Check

checker simplifies the error-checking logic used by data transfer operations involving accesses of main storage.

7.3.10   Multibus Structure with Parity Check

The single-bus structure offers a common point at which the data flow between two processor registers can be easily checked.   However, in most processors, the data transfer circuitry is arranged to handle arithmetic functions which use two operands.   In such processor structures both operands are presented *simultaneously* to the ALU; the result of the ALU operation is then directed either to a dedicated register used as an accumulator or to one of the general registers.   An ALU operation, such as binary addition, can be done in one or two control steps when the two operands are supplied simultaneously to the ALU inputs as opposed to the three control steps required by the single-bus processor structure.   To check the data flow in a multibus structure, more check hardware is required.   Figure 7-12 shows a three-bus structure with the necessary checkers to simultaneously check separate data words which are appearing concurrently on all three buses.   The additional checkers, one attached to each of the three buses, can each perform a simple parity check.   However, the validation of the parity checkers to ensure that they are performing properly is a much more complex logic operation.   The considerations involved in checking the parity-check logic circuits will be discussed in a later section.

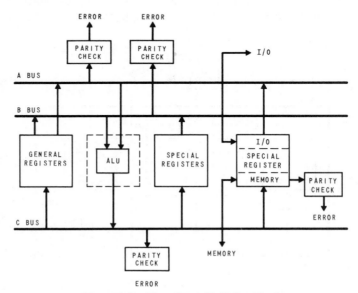

Figure 7-12   Three-Bus with Parity Check

7.3.11 Code Conversion

The error characteristics of a logic circuit depend to a large extent on the structure of the devices (such as gates) used to implement the logic circuit. The current semiconductor devices available for use as building blocks in implementing memory units are organized as bit-sliced structures in order to keep the number of external terminals to a minimum. This results in a smaller physical chip size being required by a memory unit. Because of the large number of words normally associated with main storage, the cost of main storage is usually *higher* than the cost of the processor. It is economically attractive to keep the number of check bits associated with a data word to a minimum. This is equally true when a bit-sliced structure is considered. In particular, for a bit-sliced structure a single parity bit per byte (eight bits) appears quite adequate for checking data words fetched from main storage.

However, the hardware registers within a processor are typically constructed from bit slices that contain four bits for each register position (16-word × 4-bit register slice). These register slices are used to form, as an example, 16 registers of 16 bits each. Consequently, only four address leads are required to reference the individual registers in the group, and more data leads may be brought off a chip. To check an individual register, it may be more convenient to use another register slice as opposed to a single parity-check bit for the whole word. If a large number of circuits are put on a chip, as in the case of a microprocessor on a chip, the most straightforward means of checking the behavior of the chip may be to match its outputs against another chip performing the same logical operation.

Because of the nature of hardware implementation, the methods used to generate the check bits for main storage and the internal data paths of the processor may be different. As information is transferred from main storage to the internal register of the processor, the check code being used to validate the current data transfer must be translated (converted) to agree with the hardware being used. Figure 7-13 shows the sections in the processor at which code conversion logic must exist to properly check the current data transfer operation. A data word which is transferred from a peripheral device to an internal processor register may use one check code to validate the data transfer from the peripheral device register to the internal processor register and *another* check code to validate a data transfer between two internal processor registers. Similarly, one check code may be used to validate a data word fetched from main storage, and another check code might be used by the processor to validate a data transfer between the MDR and an internal register. If a different check code is used to validate arithmetic and logic operations, an additional code conversion is required to convert from one check code used to check both ALU inputs and another check

237

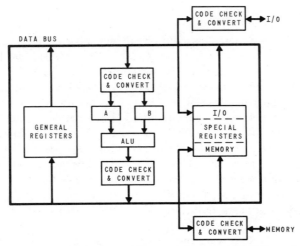

Figure 7-13   Code Conversion Between Memory and I/O Operations

code used to validate the ALU output. In many cases, each unit may be more efficiently validated using one specific type of code. For example, the arithmetic functions are more efficiently checked with residue check codes, while main memory is better checked by a simple parity check. The choice of one check code over another cannot be determined solely by the requirements of a specific application; the requirements of the *total* system structure must also be considered. Otherwise, the conversion logic required to convert between widely diverse coding schemes can become highly complex and can add *excessive* logic delays to internal data transfers within the processor. In addition, the communications between the processor and main storage, as well as the processor and its peripheral devices, can be severely slowed down.

7.4   CHECKING CONTROL PATHS

7.4.1   Control Signal Encoding and Decoding

There are two types of leads that interconnect the various parts of a data processing system: those which carry data signals and those which carry control signals. These leads may carry serial communications signals, the leads may be arranged to transfer all information in bit-parallel fashion, or a combination of the two approaches may be used. The choice depends on system requirements and cost. Within a central processor or any functional unit where the leads lengths are relatively short, the bit-parallel method is used for transmitting both the data and the control signals.

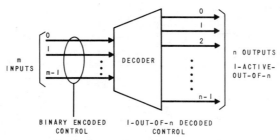

Figure 7-14 Flow of Control Signals

The control signals, in many instances, are treated in the same manner as regular data words. For example, the opcode and control fields of a macroinstruction are typically encoded into more compact binary fields in order to keep the macroinstruction within a certain word size. Insofar as the memory system is concerned, macroinstruction words and data words are treated as binary data when fetched from main storage and placed in the MDR to be used by the processor. However, after the macroinstruction words are loaded into the MDR, they are moved to the IR where they are interpreted as a machine command; the interpretation operation requires that the opcode field and the associated operand fields be decoded. The process of decoding binary data and checking that the decoding operation has been properly performed is an *important* part of error detection.

Figure 7-14 gives a functional diagram of how the binary encoded control signals are translated into a more compact binary representation in which one output is active in a field of n possible outputs (1-active-out-of-n translation). For an m-bit binary input field there are n possible output signals—only *one* of which can be active at any given time. Several binary encoded fields can be decoded simultaneously using separate decoders to generate concurrently active control signals. It is attractive to maintain the control signals in the *binary encoded form* up to the point in the logic where the physical control signals are actually interconnected to their control pins. A decoder would be used to generate a 1-active-out-of-n control signal which would be attached by a single, physical lead to the appropriate control pin. This approach greatly simplifies the number of physical leads that have to be carried through a processor structure and provides a simple means of checking the validity of the control signals (if two signals from a decoder are active, an error has occurred).

7.4.2 Binary Decoder Fault Characteristics

The binary decoder has a straightforward logical structure. Figure 7-15 illustrates the implementation of a 3-bit to 1-out-of-8 output signal translation using NAND logic gates. The decoder transforms a 3-bit input to eight

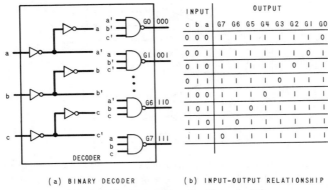

(a) BINARY DECODER   (b) INPUT-OUTPUT RELATIONSHIP

Figure 7-15 Binary Decoder Characteristics

digital outputs with only one of the eight outputs permitted to be in the active or 0 state at any time. For any single logic fault of the type stuck-at-0 or stuck-at-1, the errors introduced at the decoder outputs are mostly unidirectional. The errors may take one of two forms:

1. The *selected* output experiences a transition from the 0 state to the inactive or 1 state. This would imply that no active output was supplied by the decoder when a 1-out-of-8 translation was performed.
2. An *unselected* output experiences a transition from the 1 state to the 0 state. Normally, this would represent a *multiple-output error.*

Table 7-3 gives an example of each of these fault conditions. Table 7-4 indicates the type of output errors which can occur in a binary decoder under various types of input and output fault conditions. There are several single faults that can cause the same wrong output *(bidirectional compensating errors).* If the input inverter gates are *not* included as part of the decoder, then there is *no* decoder fault that would affect the outputs *bidirectionally*

TABLE 7-3 Typical Unidirectional Faults Experienced by a Binary 1-Active-out-of-8 Decoder

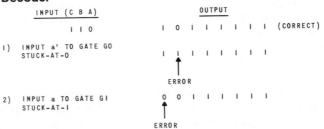

TABLE 7-4 **Error Characteristics of a Binary Decoder**

GATE	FAULTS	ERROR RESULTS		
		NO OUTPUT	MULTIPLE OUTPUTS	WRONG OUTPUT ONLY
FIRST INVERTER	INPUT STUCK-AT-1			✓
	INPUT STUCK-AT-0			✓
	OUTPUT STUCK-AT-1			✓
	OUTPUT STUCK-AT-0			✓
SECOND INVERTER	INPUT STUCK-AT-1	✓		
	INPUT STUCK-AT-0		✓	
	OUTPUT STUCK-AT-1		✓	
	OUTPUT STUCK-AT-0	✓		
DECODER	INPUT STUCK-AT-1		✓	
	INPUT STUCK-AT-0	✓		
	OUTPUT STUCK-AT-1	✓		
	OUTPUT STUCK-AT-0		✓	

to give a wrong output. Although it is not indicated in the table, correct output occurs when a stuck-at-0 or a stuck-at-1 fault presents the correct input or output to the decoder gates. In that case, the fault does not cause any error in the output.

7.4.3 Decoder Check Circuits

There are numerous ways of checking the decoder circuit for errors. The brute force approach is to simply duplicate the decoder and match the outputs of the two decoders. This situation is illustrated in Figure 7-16. If a fault exists in either decoder, the fault will be detected by the comparator. The

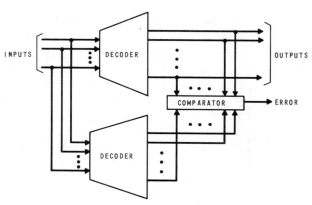

Figure 7-16 Duplicate and Match Logic

major drawback associated with such a detection technique is the large-size comparator required to check all the outputs and the difficulty of checking the comparator to ensure that *it* is functioning properly.

A reduction in the size of the comparator can be obtained by reducing the number of leads that are used as inputs to the comparator. This can best be done by reencoding the output leads of the 1-active-out-of-*n* translator and regenerating the associated binary input value. This regenerated binary input can then be matched against the original binary input value to validate the operation of the 1-active-out-of-*n* translator. This procedure is illustrated in Figure 7-17. The Boolean logic expressions for the output signal *(A, B, C)* of the encoder used to regenerate the original binary input signals are

$$A = \overline{G1} + \overline{G3} + \overline{G5} + \overline{G7} \tag{19}$$

$$B = \overline{G2} + \overline{G3} + \overline{G6} + \overline{G7} \tag{20}$$

$$C = \overline{G4} + \overline{G5} + \overline{G6} + \overline{G7} \tag{21}$$

Unfortunately, the error detection capability of this encode-and-match scheme is inadequate. Certain fault conditions will not be detected. For example, when $abc = 111$ and input a' is held in a stuck-at-1 fault condition as an input to gate G6, the decoder output will be 00111111 instead of 01111111, which represents a multiple-output error. The regenerated binary signal fed back to the comparator will be 111; this is the same as the original binary input. Hence, the stuck-at-1 fault for a' will not be detected. This result can readily be seen from an examination of the Boolean equations for *A, B,* and *C*. When G7 = 0, *A, B,* and *C* are 1s, regardless of the state of the other inputs. The encoder maps the error output into a legitimate

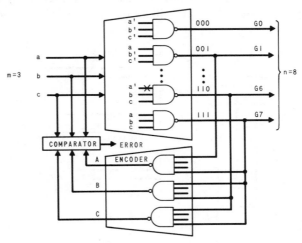

Figure 7-17 Encode and Match Logic

input code word. This problem can be eliminated by expanding the encoder outputs to include *both* the primed values *(A', B', C')* and unprimed values *(A, B, C)*. Essentially, the outputs are mapped into a 3-out-of-6 code as shown in Table 7-5. The encoded outputs for each bit position used as an input to the comparator are *two-rail* (i.e., both the asserted and negated values of each variable are passed to the comparator). This means that for *each* bit position output from the encoder the binary values of 10 or 01 are *legitimate;* the 00 and 11 output values are *error conditions*. If the input inverters shown in Figure 7-15 are *not* included in the encoder logic, the fault detection procedure can be simplified. The decoder error conditions, in which either no output is supplied by the decoder when a translation is performed *or* multiple outputs are supplied by the decoder, can be checked by a *bit-by-bit comparison* of the duplicated encoder outputs *only*. Figure 7-18 gives a logical implementation of this bit-by-bit comparison procedure. The encoder is replicated so that both the primed values of the inputs *(A', B', C')* and the unprimed values *(A, B, C)* can be supplied to a comparator. The comparator checks each bit position for the 00 or 11 bit patterns; this implies that the primed and unprimed values of the same variables are in the same state, which is an error condition. If the inverters used to produce the primed values of each input variable are included as part of the 1-active-out-of-*n* decoder, then the set of unprimed encoder outputs *(A, B, C)* must be compared with the binary input data to ensure that the right 1-active-out-of-*n* translation has occurred. This check scheme can be simplified by examining the fault characteristics of the 1-active-out-of-*n* decoder circuit. As indicated previously, a single logic fault (with the exception of faults in the input inverters) will be reflected in the decoder output as one of two types of faults: Either the decoder has produced *no output,* or the decoder has produced *multiple outputs*. A number of faults can occur in the 1-active-out-of-*n* decoder logic which will cause a *second* output to become active as well as the correct output. For example, if the input *a* to gate

TABLE 7-5 Encoder with Two-Rail Outputs

INPUTS			DECODER OUTPUTS								ENCODER OUTPUTS					
c	b	a	G7	G6	G5	G4	G3	G2	GI	G0	C'	C	B'	B	A'	A
0	0	0	I	I	I	I	I	I	I	O	I	O	I	O	I	O
0	0	I	I	I	I	I	I	I	O	I	I	O	I	O	O	I
0	I	0	I	I	I	I	I	O	I	I	I	O	O	I	I	O
0	I	I	I	I	I	I	O	I	I	I	I	O	O	I	O	I
I	0	0	I	I	I	O	I	I	I	I	O	I	I	O	I	O
I	0	I	I	I	O	I	I	I	I	I	O	I	I	O	O	I
I	I	0	I	O	I	I	I	I	I	I	O	I	O	I	I	O
I	I	I	O	I	I	I	I	I	I	I	O	I	O	I	O	I

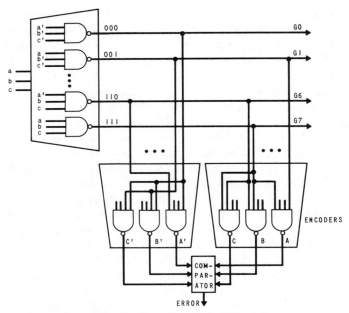

Figure 7-18 Replicate Encoder and Match Logic

G7 in Figure 7-18 is stuck-at-1 and the input vector to the decoder is $a'bc$, gate G7 will produce an active output in addition to the correct output supplied by gate G6. The corresponding input vectors to produce active outputs from gate G6 and gate G7 are, respectively, 011 and 111. These input vectors differ by the value of only one bit and are said to be separated by a distance of one bit in code space (this difference is also referred to as a *unit distance* error). If input a to gate G7 was stuck-at-0 instead of stuck-at-1 and the input vector to the decoder is abc, the error condition—in which the decoder does *not* produce an output for a legitimate input vector—will exist. To further refine the error-detecting capability of the 1-active-out-of-n decoder, the decoder outputs can be sorted into two groups: One group will contain all decoder outputs which possess an odd number of binary 1s, and the other group will contain all decoder outputs which possess an even number of 1s. The first group checks those decoder outputs which legitimately contain an odd number of 1s for *odd parity;* the latter group checks the remaining decoder outputs for *even parity.* Figure 7-19 illustrates this decoder checking scheme for the 1-active-out-of-8 decoder. Any decoder outputs checked by the same parity gate differ in their binary representations by at least two bits. As a result, for most multiple-output conditions, the output in error belongs to the other parity group; this means multiple outputs will provide an output vector at the parity gates whose binary value is 11.

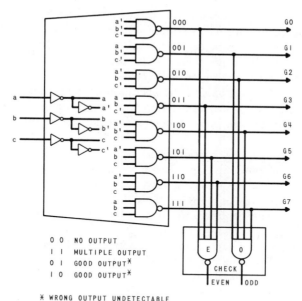

0 0	NO OUTPUT
I I	MULTIPLE OUTPUT
0 I	GOOD OUTPUT*
I 0	GOOD OUTPUT*

* WRONG OUTPUT UNDETECTABLE

Figure 7-19 Simple Decoder Check Logic

The 11 output corresponds to a multiple-output error condition, while the 00 output corresponds to the fault condition in which the decoder has produced no output for a legitimate binary input vector. The 01 and 10 output vectors from the parity gates represent error-free operation of the decoder—provided the input inverter faults are neglected.

There is a class of decoder faults that may not be immediately detected. When a decoder output is stuck-at-0, it is permanently active for *all* input combinations to the decoder. Thus, it will not only produce an output for the correct input vector but for *all* other input vectors as well. It is possible in this situation that both the correct output *and* the stuck-at-0 output may belong to the same parity group. In this case, the output error will *not* be detected. As soon as an input vector is applied to the decoder that produces a correct output whose parity is different from that of the stuck-at-0 output, the output fault will be detected by the parity logic. In some cases, it may be necessary to apply several different input vectors to the decoder before the output fault results in a detectable error.

The simple parity-check circuit which tests for odd and even parity is also *self-testing* in that any fault in the parity-check logic is also propagated to the output of the parity detector as an error. Stuck-at-0 or stuck-at-1 faults at the inputs to the parity-check logic will result in an error output vector with a value of 00 or 11 for some input vectors. No special input vector to the 1-active-out-of-n decoder is required to test either the decoder or the parity-check logic. Both logic circuits are *actively* monitored by the checking logic during normal operation of the 1-active-out-of-*n* decoder.

The two outputs from the parity-check circuit (odd parity and even parity) must merge at some point in the processor logic to give an error indication. The error indication will then enable the appropriate fault recovery action such as (1) halting the operation of the processor, (2) causing an error interrupt, (3) restarting the processor by forcing the system to go through a reinitialization, or (4) reconfiguring the system into an error-free environment.

Because the error conditions detected by the parity-check logic are represented by an output vector with a value of either 00 or 11, a single exclusive-OR (XOR) circuit may be used to distinguish between a fault condition and the proper functioning of the decoder and its parity-check logic. The overall checking configuration of the 1-active-out-of-*n* decoder and its parity-check logic is shown in Figure 7-20. XOR gate is not a self-testing circuit in that certain faults within the XOR gate will mask out any error-indicating signal from the parity check circuit. For example, if the output of the XOR gate is permanently stuck-at-1 (which indicates error-free operation of the decoder logic and its parity-check circuit), an error, whether it is in the decoder or in the parity-check logic, will not be recognized. Therefore, it is essential that the XOR circuit be checked periodically to ensure that it is working properly. An input vector must be applied to the XOR gate to verify that the XOR gate will generate a correct error indication. The input vector for this situation should take either the value 00 or 11— the error vector values generated by the parity-check logic. The output of the XOR gate may be validated by applying a special TEST signal to the output of the parity-check logic and the XOR gate which generates both

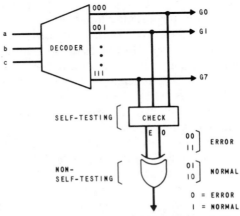

Figure 7-20 Two Rails to Single Output Logic

input error vectors to the XOR gate. Figure 7-21 illustrates the mechanism used to validate (check) the operation of the *non-self-testing* logic circuitry associated with a 1-active-out-of-8 decoder. Under normal operating conditions, the TEST input is held in the 0 state. This allows the 01 and 10 output vectors from the parity-check logic to be passed directly to the inputs of the XOR gate. The output of the XOR gate will be placed in the 1-active state for either of the legitimate input combinations. To determine that the XOR gate will respond correctly to the two input sequences (00 and 11, which represent an error in the parity-check logic), the TEST input is set to a 1. If the input vectors 01 or 10 are applied to the XOR gate during this TEST time, the XOR gate *actually* sees the input vectors 00 or 11, respectively. The output of the XOR must respond with a 0 state output, which indicates that the XOR gate has recognized the test input vectors correctly.

The decoder error check described thus far is used mainly to validate the correct operation of the decoder circuitry. It is assumed that the binary data presented to the decoder logic is *without error*. To validate the integrity of the binary data prior to the decoder logic, the binary data may be transmitted with a parity bit; the parity bit may be checked *prior* to the binary data being used by the decoder, or the parity check may be combined with the overall checking logic used by the decoder. The basic idea is to extend the parity-check logic used with the decoded outputs to include the parity bit associated with the input vector applied to the decoder. Figure 7-22 illustrates the implementation of this combined parity and decoder check logic. The 1-active-out-of-8 decoder performs the *dual* functions of translat-

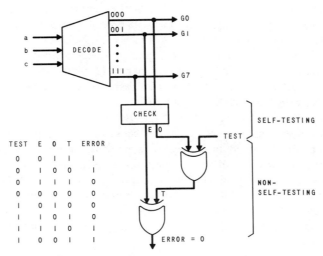

Figure 7-21 Test of Error Output Circuit

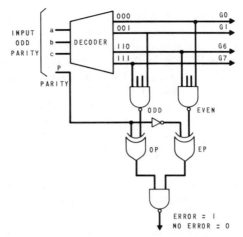

Figure 7-22   Combined Parity and Decoder Check Logic

ing the binary input vector into a single active output *and* checking the parity of the output signal in conjunction with the parity of the binary input vector. The outputs from the odd-parity gate and even-parity gate are compared with the parity bit of the binary input vector. The comparison operation is performed by XOR gate OP and XOR gate EP. The XOR gate will produce an error output if an *inconsistency* is found in the combined parity check. As an example, assume that the data word 0010 *(abcP)* fetched from main storage is correct but that an error was introduced into the data word by a hardware fault in the data transfer path. Let the data word be altered to the binary value 0000. When this binary value is applied as an input vector to the decoder, gate G0 will produce an active output instead of gate G1. This behavior results in the EVEN NAND gate producing an input of 1, while the ODD NAND gate produces an output of 0. If the original data was encoded using odd parity $(P = 0)$, the inputs to XOR gate OP and XOR gate EP are 00 and 11, respectively. The resultant outputs from XOR gate OP and XOR gate EP are each 0. This provides an input vector of value 00 to the output ERROR NAND gate and produces an ERROR output signal equal to 1. For those decoder faults which produce no output when a valid input vector is present, or a wrong output for a valid input vector, or multiple outputs for a valid input vector, one of the two XOR gates will propagate a 0 output to the ERROR NAND gate. This 0 output will be interpreted as an error. The combined parity and decoder check circuit tests to see that a valid binary code word is present at the input to the decoder and that the input data is correctly translated by the decoder.

7.4.4 Decoder Timing Problem

As in any logic design, the static case of decoder outputs is easily analyzed because the static decoder outputs do not present any timing difficulties. However, in the case where the outputs of the decoder can change dynamically since the binary input data is changing dynamically, several outputs from the decoder may be simultaneously active for a brief interval of a few nanoseconds. This behavior, which can produce *spikes* in the decoder outputs, is due to variations in the logic delays experienced by the logic gating chains in the decoder. These *unwanted* spikes normally appear in some of the unselected outputs of the decoder. As an example, consider the case when the binary input vector of value 111 is replaced by an input vector of value 000. Because of the difference in logic delays in the data paths, the data arriving at the decoder may make the following state transitions:

$$\boxed{\text{START}} \quad 111 \;\rightarrow\; 110 \;\rightarrow\; 010 \;\rightarrow\; 000 \quad \boxed{\text{END}} \qquad (22)$$

In this situation, *two spikes* will be generated from the decoder, as shown in the timing diagram of Figure 7-23. During the state transition sequence which proceeds from an input vector of value 111 to an input vector of value 000, spurious outputs from the 110 and 010 decoder gates (G6 and G2, respectively) are generated. It is possible to eliminate these unwanted spikes by not combining any processor timing pulses with the decoder outputs until *farther along* in the processor logic chain. Under this condition, no additional steps are required to eliminate the spikes. However, for certain control functions, it is desirable to use the decoder outputs directly without introducing any delayed timing signals. Since any improper decoder output can cause an error in the system behavior, the spikes must be eliminated by *inhibiting the decoder outputs* during the period when the binary input data is being changed. The logic for this inhibit function is shown in Figure 7-24(a). The inputs to the decoder are normally supplied by a data register

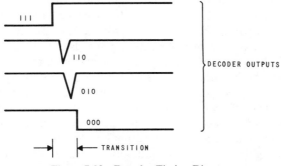

Figure 7-23 Decoder Timing Diagram

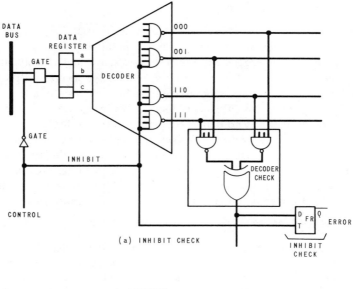

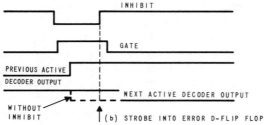

Figure 7-24   Logic Spike Elimination Using a Decoder Inhibit Signal

in the processor. The same control signal that enables the data transfer from an internal processor register to the data register which feeds the decoder can also be used to disable the decoder from generating an active output. If the disabling input is effective in controlling the decoder output gates, no spurious spikes will be produced during the data transfer. However, if a stuck-at-1 fault occurs on any one of the inhibit inputs of the decoder output gates, the faulty input may cause a spike at the output of that gate. Detection of such a condition is rather difficult in view of the *transient nature* of the output error. However, the stuck-at-1 fault can be identified during normal operation of the decoder. In this case, when the decoder gate with the stuck-at-1 fault is selected, the output of the gate will become active *earlier* than the outputs in which the inhibit signal is functioning properly. The inhibit signal will delay the appearance of the decoder outputs, as shown in Figure 7-24(b). This means that the decoder check circuit output will also settle in the 1s state earlier than it would with the inhibit signal functioning properly at the input to the decoder. Under this condition the decoder check output can be gated into an edge-triggered D flip-flop to store the error indication. The positive edge of the inhibit signal can be used for the gating signal associated with the D flip-flop. This check scheme validates only the correct behavior of the inhibit signal. Other types of decoder faults require that the output from the decoder check logic be ignored during the time in which the inhibit signal is applied to the inputs of the decoder.

7.4.5 The Use of Multiple Stages of Decoding and Checking Logic

There are logical and/or control functions which require an output from one decoder to act as an enable input to another decoder. A tree structure can be formed by using the outputs of the decoders which appear *earlier* in the tree as the enable inputs for decoders which appear later in the tree. A good example of a tree structure formed from decoders is the addressing logic used to reference locations in main storage. Typically, the main storage address is divided into two sections. The precise way the address is divided depends on how the main storage modules are partitioned. The higher-order address bits are decoded to select a particular memory module, and the low-order address bits are decoded at *each* module to select a word from the module. Another example of a decoder tree is found in the decoding of a macroinstruction. The output of the final decoder may be used to perform specific control operations such as setting and clearing individual bits of a specific processor register. Figure 7-25 illustrates a logic arrangement which incorporates multiple stages of decoding logic. Several decoder outputs are used to enable auxiliary decoders. The checking of each decoder can be done individually. However, it is always more desirable to extend the checking logic to include as much hardware as possible. To do this, it is necessary to examine decoder outputs which can be nested deep within the decoder tree. This includes faults associated directly with the common enable lead within each auxiliary decoder which would not be covered otherwise. As shown in Figure 7-25, each auxiliary decoder is checked by use of a combined parity and decoder logic circuit in order to detect the occurrence of all possible single faults. The checking of the auxiliary decoder is done only when it is selected (not shown in Figure 7-25). The decoder check logic associated with the main decoder checks to see that *only one* output is active from the group of auxiliary decoders and the direct outputs of the main decoder. The outputs from each of the decoder check logic circuits associated with the auxiliary decoders are *brought back* as inputs to the main decoder check logic. These outputs represent the decoded output of

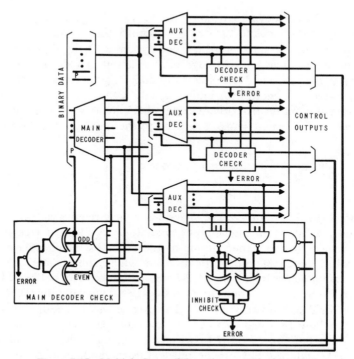

Figure 7-25   Multiple Stage of Decoding and Checking Logic

the main decoder after the decoded output has propagated through the auxiliary decoders.

7.4.6   I/O Device Select Check Logic

A common technique for selecting a peripheral device is to distribute the actual decoding of a device address *to* the control logic associated with each peripheral. Typically, the address of a peripheral device is transmitted over an I/O bus which is shared by all peripherals. An address decoder gate is situated within each peripheral that translates the address transmitted on the I/O bus. Figure 7-26 illustrates this peripheral device addressing scheme. The binary address specifies one peripheral among all the peripheral devices which are connected to the I/O bus. To check that the correct peripheral device has been selected, a decoder check can be employed which requires that the peripheral device addresses be sorted into two groups: a group in which the total number of 1s in the address is an odd number (odd-parity group) and a group in which the total number of 1s in the address is an even number (even-parity group). The decoder located at each peripheral device generates an odd-parity or even-parity signal when the address of

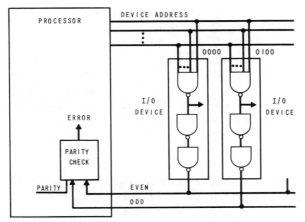

Figure 7-26 Device Select Check Logic

the target peripheral is decoded. An odd-parity bus and an even-parity bus are returned to the processor; the decoder at each peripheral device is connected to either the odd-parity bus or the even-parity bus. At the processor, the parity signals are checked with the original parity of the device address to see if both the odd-parity signal and even-parity signal are active concurrently. This condition indicates that two or more peripheral devices have been selected and is called a *multiple device selection error*. The target peripheral device, in this case, may have been correctly selected as well as one or more unwanted peripheral devices.

7.4.7   *m*-out-of-*n* Codes

For many of the logic faults which can occur in a digital circuit, the data word, in most instances, appears to experience *unidirectional errors*. These types of errors result in all the bits in error in a data word undergoing either a $0 \rightarrow 1$ transition or a $1 \rightarrow 0$ transition. The two error transitions are *not* intermixed in a data word. For example, the data word 1100 would be changed to 0000 for unidirectional errors of the type $1 \rightarrow 0$; the data word 1100 would be changed to 1111 for unidirectional errors of the type $0 \rightarrow 1$. The error word 1010 would be assumed to not occur since it involves the transitions $0 \rightarrow 1$ and $1 \rightarrow 0$ occurring simultaneously. A class of error-detecting codes called *m-out-of-n codes* has the property of being able to detect all unidirectional errors that occur in a code word. The redundancy of such codes is embedded in the code. *m*-out-of-*n* codes are also referred to as *nonsystematic codes*. When the information is needed in another form elsewhere in the computer system, a code translator must be used to convert the coded data word into the required format. An important advantage of systematic codes is that the information and check bits are separable; the data word may be readily obtained by ignoring the check bits. Data manipulation is more easily handled when a systematic code is used to represent the individual data words since error detection and correction procedures are simplified. *m*-out-of-*n* codes can be used to great advantage in encoding the control field of a microinstruction because of their ability to perform error detection. A more detailed discussion on this application of *m*-out-of-*n* codes will be given in later sections.

7.4.8 *m*-out-of-*n* Decoding

Figure 7-27 shows a procedure for decoding an *m*-out-of-*n* code to 1 active output in a group of 20 outputs. For simplicity, a 3-out-of-6 code is used as an example. Only 20-out-of-64 possible binary combinations have three 0s and three 1s. Each gate contains six inputs; a gate defines one of the 20 legitimate 3-out-of-6 code words. For any unidirectional error which causes the input vector to have other than three 1s, none of the 20 gates will produce an active or 0 output. Under the condition of *no* active output, the error gate shown in Figure 7-27 will produce an ERROR signal. In the case of a fault in the decoding circuitry, such as input *f* to the first gate experiencing an open circuit, the input error is masked by the redundant input. This error can be considered a "don't care" input for the first gate

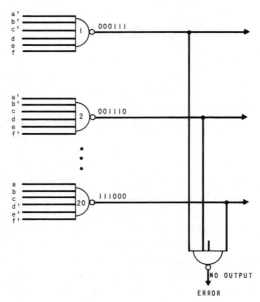

Figure 7-27   m-out-of-n Decoding Logic

since the output will be a function only of the inputs a', b', c', d and e. However, if a decoder output is stuck-at-0 (this represents an active output), the error gates will *not* detect this fault condition, nor will the **ERROR** gate detect it. A more effective error detection scheme and a simpler method of implementing the decoder is more desirable than the logic arrangement shown in Figure 7-27.

The key to simplifying the 3-out-of-6 decoder circuitry is to eliminate the redundant inputs. As shown in Figure 7-27, there are six inputs per gate; half these inputs are redundant. The redundant inputs are the so-called *primed* input set (a', b', c', d', e', and f'), where the prime (') sign represents the complement of the input variable. If the primed inputs are removed, a substantial savings in logic gating is achieved since simpler input gates may be used, and the complex interconnection pattern of the logic gates is simplified. This also simplifies the overall fault detection procedure for the 3-out-of-6 decoder circuit.

When only m inputs are used per gate, an error occurring in the m-out-of-n code word can produce one of two possible fault conditions: The decoder will produce *no output* for a legitimate input m-out-of-n code word, or the decoder will produce one or more outputs in addition to the correct output. The precise way these faults are detected depends on whether the decoder error has changed the number of 1s in the code word to be less than m or greater than m. If the number of 1s is one greater than m, there will be $m + 1$ outputs generated from the decoder instead of the one legitimate output. This can readily be seen by examining the number of possible groups of m inputs that may be formed from a set of $m + 1$ inputs:

$$C_m^{m+1} = \frac{m+1}{m!(m+1-m)!} = m + 1 \tag{23}$$

For reasons of simplicity, consider the 3-out-of-6 code as an example. Assume that the correct code word is 00111 and that a decoder fault causes the code word to change to 001111. Under this condition, as shown in Figure 7-28, the top four gates having inputs $----111$, $--1-11$, $--11-1$, and $--111-$ will respond, each with an active output. The dash (–) indicates the absence of an input variable or a "don't care" condition. (The input variable may be either in the 0 or the 1 state.) A more effective check scheme for m-out-of-n decoding which uses *no* redundant inputs may be implemented by dividing the decoder outputs into two or more groups. The grouping criterion cannot be the same as that used with the binary decoding scheme since the parity of all the legitimate m-out-of-n code words is the same. The philosophy observed in the m-out-of-n code grouping method is to ensure that multiple gate outputs do not all belong to the same group. For example, Figure 7-28 shows the decoder outputs partitioned into two groups in which the two check gates (GP1 and GP2) have *no*

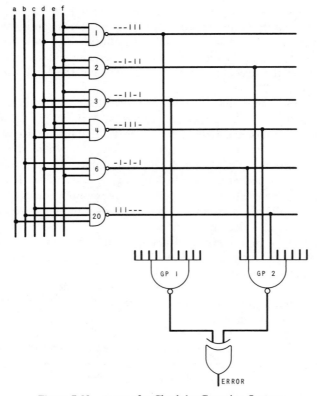

Figure 7-28   m-out-of-n Check by Grouping Outputs

inputs in common so that the previous fault conditions can be recognized (i.e., – – –111, – –1–11, – –11–1, – –111–).   In general, there are many ways to partition the outputs of a decoder into groups so that the decoder may function as a self-testing logic unit.   One possible partition of the decoder outputs is shown in Figure 7-29.   Here, code words whose three high-order bits are identical are assigned to different check groups.   Outputs whose three low-order bits are identical are also assigned to different check groups. Using this approach, all unidirectional faults affecting a 3-out-of-6 code word will be detected.   However, certain faults within the decoder circuitry will not be caught instantaneously.   For example, an output stuck-at-1 or an input with an open circuit may cause multiple outputs to occur within the same group.   For the case of a stuck-at-1 output, the fault will not be recognized until an output is generated in the other group.   If it is equally likely that the next code word will belong to either check group 1 or check group 2, then the stuck-at-1 output fault can be detected quickly.   On the other hand, the fault condition in which an input to the decoder has experienced

CODE A B	DECIMAL REPRESENTATION A	B	GROUP 1	GROUP 2
--- I I I	0	7	✓	
-- I - I I	1	3		✓
-- I I - I	1	5	✓	
-- I I I -	1	6		✓
- I -- I I	2	3	✓	
- I - I - I	2	5		✓
- I - I I -	2	6	✓	
I --- I I	4	3		✓
I -- I - I	4	5	✓	
I -- I I -	4	6		✓
- I I -- I	3	1	✓	
- I I - I -	3	2		✓
- I I I --	3	4	✓	
I - I -- I	5	1		✓
I - I - I -	5	2	✓	
I - I I --	5	4		✓
I I --- I	6	1	✓	
I I -- I -	6	2		✓
I I - I --	6	4	✓	
I I I ---	7	0		✓

Figure 7-29 Grouping Outputs into Two Groups

an open circuit may go undetected for a considerable length of time. As an example, refer again to Figure 7-28. If input *c* to gate 3 is an open circuit, whenever gate 1 is activated, gate 3 will also become active. This produces multiple outputs in the *same* check group. To detect this particular fault, gate 6 must be selected. A quicker detection may be realized by partitioning the outputs into more groups.

7.4.9 Reencode and Match Check Logic

Instead of using an approach which divides the decoder outputs into disjoint check groups, a more complete and faster decoder error check would be one in which each decoder output gate generates the complement of its input code word. The complementation procedure supplies an *m*-out-of-*n* code word which is unique; that is, for any error occurring in the decoder, the output will be a code word that *does not belong* to the *m*-out-of-*n* code used by the decoder. As an example, consider the reencode and match-checking logic shown in Figure 7-30. If input *c* to gate 2 experiences a stuck-at-1 fault, then gate 2 will supply an active output whenever gate 1 is activated by the input logic signal $d'c'ba$ (this corresponds to the binary number 0011). In the 2-out-of-4 encoder circuit, the output of gate 1 is reencoded as the logic signal $DCB'A'$ (this corresponds to the binary number 1100). In the 2-out-of-4 encoder circuit, the output of gate 2 is reencoded as the logic signal $DC'BA'$ (this corresponds to the binary number 1010). If gate 2 has a stuck-at-1 input error, as previously described, such that

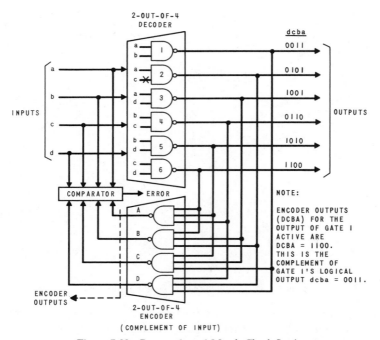

Figure 7-30   Re-encode and Match Check Logic

gate 2 will supply an active output when gate 1 supplies an active output, the resultant logical output from the 2-out-of-4 encoder is $DCBA'$, which corresponds to the binary number 1110. The error output is generated by the 2-out-of-4 *encoder* forming the *inclusive-OR* of the separate 2-out-of-4 decoder outputs. The comparator matches the two data words *dcba* and *DCBA* on a bit-by-bit basis to determine whether any corresponding bits are alike. In this example, bit *b* in the decoder output and bit *B* in the encoder output are alike. Therefore, an error indication will be supplied by the comparator. For the same stuck-at-1 fault, gate 2 will also be active whenever gate 3 is activated by its input logic signal, $dc'b'a = 1001$. The net effect of multiple decoder outputs is to cause the individual *m*-out-of-*n* code words associated with each active decoder output to be inclusive-ORed together at the input of the 2-out-of-4 encoder. This, of course, generates an output code word from the 2-out-of-4 encoder which has more than two bits in the 1s state. Consequently, the error in the decoder will be detected by the comparator.

In a similar fashion, the above scheme will detect faults which result in no output being supplied by the decoder. For example, an error may affect the data in such a manner that the number of bits in the 1s state in the output code word *(dcba)* is *less* than *m* in the *m*-out-of-*n* code. Under this condition, none of the decoder outputs will be in the active state. As a result, the outputs from the m-out-of-n *encoder* circuit will all be in the 0 state. Since the output data word must contain at least $n - m$ 0s, $n - m$ bits in the output from the encoder will be identical to the input code word; this situation represents an error condition detectable by the comparator. All unidirectional faults affecting either the input code word to the decoder or the decoder circuitry itself will be detected by the comparator at the time of their occurrence.

7.4.10 m-out-of-n Self-checking Checker

A *totally self-checking circuit* gives an error indication during normal operation whenever a fault occurs in either the normal logic circuit or the check circuit itself. A totally self-checking circuit never allows an erroneous output to occur without generating an error signal. The self-testing circuit described previously that was to be used with the binary decoder check circuit does *not* totally self-check itself. An output error may not be detected immediately, but there is at least one normal input code word which will detect the output fault condition. The choice between self-testing and totally self-checking circuits depends on the reliability requirements of the total system and how much money the system designer wishes to spend to implement that reliability. In general, totally self-checking circuits will be *more expensive* than self-testing circuits.

To satisfy the requirement that a check circuit be totally self-checking, it is essential that the check circuit have at least two outputs. The reason for this, as pointed out previously, is that if the single output is stuck in the state which indicates an error-free condition in the check circuit, any faults occurring within the decoder will be ignored. The output from the check circuit, which indicates an error, must be validated during normal operation to achieve total self-checking behavior. The *error-free output vectors* from a totally self-checking checker with two outputs are 01 and 10. Under normal operation, the checker must be exercised by forcing its output vector to change from the 10 value to the 01 value. Noncode inputs, or any faults within the normal logic circuit or the check circuit, will map into an error output of either 00 or 11.

For many applications, it is desirable to have as many code words available as possible when an m-out-of-n code is employed. The *maximum* number of code words that may be obtained for an m-out-of-n code occurs when n is equal to $2m$. Anderson has shown in his thesis* that a checker implemented using sum-of-product terms (minterms) will be self-checking

---

* D. A. Anderson, "Design of Self-checking Digital Networks Using Coding Techniques," Ph.D. thesis. Urbana, Ill.: University of Illinois, 1971.

for all possible single faults only if the input code words are expressed in an m-out-of-$2m$ code. Consequently, the design of self-checking check circuits will be restricted to only those check circuits associated with m-out-of-$2m$ decoders.

As an example, consider the design of a totally self-checking 3-out-of-6 code check circuit. The first step in the design is to divide the bits in the input data word into two equal groups of m bits each. Each group of three bits must be sorted into four logic groups, as shown in Figure 7-31. These subgroups will generate an output for each of the following conditions:

1. The number of bits in the 1s state in the input data word is greater than or equal to 0; the notation for this group is given by

$$\geq 0(1) \tag{24}$$

2. The number of bits in the 1s state in the input data word is greater than or equal to 1; the notation for this group is given by

$$\geq 1(1) \tag{25}$$

3. The number of bits in the 1s state in the input data word is greater than or equal to 2; the notation for this group is given by

$$\geq 2(1) \tag{26}$$

4. The number of bits in the 1s state in the input data word is greater than or equal to 3; the notation for this group is given by

$$\geq 3(1) \tag{27}$$

With the exception of the "$\geq 0(1)$" subgroup, more than one subgroup will produce an active output for a given input data word. Consider the input data word with a value of 111. In this case, all subgroups will produce an active output since the number of bits in the 1s state in the input data word meets the following conditions:

1. The input data word has at least one bit in the 1s state; the "$\geq 0(1)$" subgroup will produce an active output.
2. The input data word has at least two bits in the 1s state; the "$\geq 1(1)$" subgroup will produce an active output.
3. The input data word has at least three bits in the 1s state; both the "$\geq 2(1)$" subgroup and the "$\geq 3(1)$" subgroup will produce active outputs.

As a point of interest, for a given number of bits in the 1s state in the input data word, the subgroup with the *same* number of 1s and *all* subgroups with a fewer number of bits in the 1s state will give active outputs. Similarly, the remaining three bits in the input data word are sorted into four logic subgroups; each subgroup is again defined by the number of bits

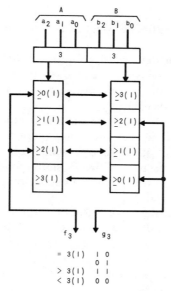

Figure 7-31 Functional Diagram of a 3-out-of-6 Checker

in the 1s state in the input data word for which the subgroup checks. An output is generated from each of these subgroups for the same conditions, as shown in Figure 7-31. The subgroups are paired—one subgroup in the pair coming from each 3-bit partition of the input data word. The number of bits in the 1s state represented by each pair must be exactly three. This means the legitimate pairs for the 3-out-of-6 code input data word are given by the sets

$$[\geq 0(1) \longleftrightarrow \geq 3(1)], \quad [\geq 1(1) \longleftrightarrow \geq 2(1)] \qquad (28)$$

$$[\geq 2(1) \longleftrightarrow \geq 1(1)], \quad [\geq 3(1) \longleftrightarrow \geq 0(1)] \qquad (29)$$

where the first element in each set represents the subgroup from the *A* partition of the input data word; the second element in each set represents the subgroup from the *B* partition. It is a characteristic of these pairings that *only* one pair will produce an active output for a given 3-out-of-6 input data word. The set of subgroup pairs may be further combined to form the following two groups:

$$[\geq 0(1) \longleftrightarrow \geq 3(1)] + [\geq 2(1) \longleftrightarrow \geq 1(1)] = f \qquad (30)$$

$$[\geq 1(1) \longleftrightarrow \geq 2(1)] + [\geq 3(1) \longleftrightarrow \geq 0(1)] = g \qquad (31)$$

Since only *one* pair will produce an active output in the *f* and *g* group for a correct 3-out-of-6 input data word, the correct values for the outputs of *f* and *g* treated as a binary number are either 10 or 01. If the input data word is other than a legitimate 3-out-of-6 code word, the *fg* outputs will be either 11 or 00.

Consider the input data word given by 110011. The $\geq 2(1)$, $\geq 1(1)$, and $\geq 0(1)$ subgroups of *both* the *A* and *B* partitions of the input data word will produce active outputs. As a consequence, two pairs of subgroups will produce active outputs—specifically, the $[\geq 1(1) \leftrightarrow \geq 2(1)]$ subgroup in the *g* logic *and* the $[\geq 2(1) \leftrightarrow \geq 1(1)]$ subgroup in the *f* logic. This check scheme ensures that when an input data word has more than three bits in the 1s state, the resultant output of the *fg* logic will be 11. If the input data word contains fewer than three bits in the 1s state, none of the four pairs for either the *A* or *B* partition will produce an active output. Hence, the output from the *fg* logic will be 00.

Consider the input data word given by 011000. For this code word, the $\geq 2(1)$, $\geq 1(1)$, and $\geq 0(1)$ subgroups of the *A* partition will produce an active output as well as the $\geq 0(1)$ subgroup of the *B* partition. None of these outputs belongs to a pairing in either the *f* logic *or* the *g* logic. Consequently, the *fg* output is 00, which corresponds to an input combination with less than three 1s.

The $\geq 0(1)$ subgroup is redundant since it is true for *all* input data words. The pairing or set $[\geq 0(1) \leftrightarrow \geq 3(1)]$ does not need to include the 0(1) subgroup at all. It can simply be ignored in the actual implementation of the totally self-checking 3-out-of-6 code checker.

Figure 7-32 illustrates the logical implementation of the totally self-checking 3-out-of-6 code check circuit. The logical expressions for an active output to be generated by each subgroup are as follows:

1. *A* partition (a_2, a_1, a_0):

$$[\geq 1_a(1)] = a_0 + a_1 + a_2$$
$$[\geq 2_a(1)] = a_0a_1 + a_0a_2 + a_1a_2$$
$$[\geq 3_a(1)] = a_0a_1a_2 \tag{32}$$

2. *B* partition [b_2, b_1, b_0]:

$$[\geq 1_b(1)] = b_0 + b_1 + b_2$$
$$[\geq 2_b(1)] = b_0b_1 + b_0b_2 + b_1b_2$$
$$[\geq 3_b(1)] = b_0b_1b_2 \tag{33}$$

The notation $[\geq 2_a(1)]$ is read as the subgroup of the *A* partition *(a_2, a_1, a_0)* of the input data word in which the number of bits in the 1s state is greater than or equal to 2.

The input data word is given as the following sequence of binary digits:

$$(a_2, a_1, a_0, b_2, b_1, b_0)$$

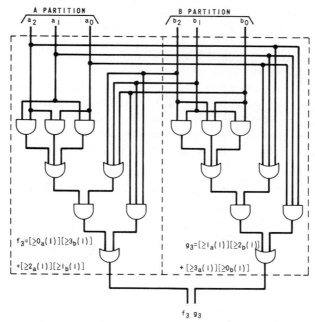

Figure 7-32   Totally Self-Checking 3-out-of-6 Checker

The logical expressions for an active output to be produced by the paired subgroups (f_3 and g_3) are as follows:

$$f_3 = \{[\geq 0_a(1)][\geq 3_b(1)]\} + \{[\geq 2_a(1)][\geq 1_b(1)]\}$$
$$= b_0 b_1 b_2 + (a_0 a_1 + a_0 a_2 + a_1 a_2)(b_0 + b_1 + b_2) \tag{34}$$

$$g_3 = \{[\geq 1_a(1)][\geq 2_b(1)]\} + \{[\geq 3_a(1)][\geq 0_b(1)]\}$$
$$= (a_0 + a_1 + a_2)(b_0 b_1 + b_0 b_2 + b_1 b_2) + a_0 a_1 a_2 \tag{35}$$

where the notation (f_3 and g_3) implies that the output functions are active *only* if three or more bits in the paired subgroups are in the 1s state.

If a general m-out-of-$2m$ code is used, the logical expressions for the f_m and g_m outputs become

$$f_m = \sum_{i=0}^{m} [\geq i_a(1)][\geq (m-i)_b(1)],$$

where $i = 0, 2, 4, \ldots,$ an even number   (36)

$$g_m = \sum_{i=0}^{m} [\geq i_a(1)][\geq (m-i)_b(1)],$$

where $i = 1, 3, 5, \ldots,$ an odd number   (37)

A self-checking circuit is realized by subdividing the checker into two separate independent subcircuits. Each subcircuit generates a single output. Those output values are complementary for a normal *m*-out-of-2*m* input code. (That is, the *fg* outputs will be either 01 or 10.) For any errors in the input code word or in the check logic, the two outputs will take on the same value (that is, the *fg* outputs will be either 00 or 11). A totally self-checking checker has the advantage of not requiring periodic testing; any faults occurring in the logic circuits will be detected immediately. The previous checking scheme for an *m*-out-of-*n* code required that the outputs from the decoder be encoded to regenerate the original input code word. A comparison of the regenerated code word and the original code word was then

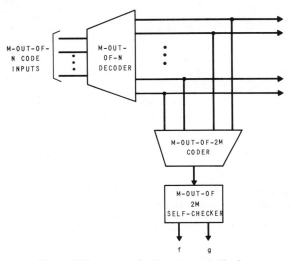

Figure 7-33   m-out-of-n Decoder and Checker

performed by matching the individual bits in the two code words. A simple comparator can be made from XOR gates to perform the matching function. However, the XOR gate realization of an *n*-bit comparator is *not* a self-testing design. The XOR gate realization requires periodic testing to ensure its proper operation. A self-checking comparator is a much more complex design than the logic realization which uses XOR gates. Instead of comparing the reencoded outputs with the input, the decoder outputs can be checked directly with a self-checking *m*-out-of-2*m* checker, as shown in Figure 7-33. If the number *n* in the *m*-out-of-*n* decoder is not equal to 2*m,* the decoder outputs can be encoded into a *k*-out-of-2*k* code. The self-checker logic will then completely check not only the input code but also any faults occurring in the *m*-out-of-*n* decoder, the *k*-out-of-2*k* encoder, and the checker itself.

7.4.11 Elimination of Decoder
Timing Problems

Timing problems are encountered when a normal binary decoder is used because transient output combinations may be generated. Since all binary input combinations to a binary decoder are legitimate input code words, output transitions may be generated during the interval in which the input code word is settling into a stable state. Consequently, when the input code word is changed from one binary value to another binary value, there is a finite transition period during which the input variables can undergo state changes which can represent many different legitimate input code words. This behavior is primarily due to the variations in logic gate delays encountered by the individual variables in the input code word; the result of this behavior is that spurious decoder outputs can occur during the transition period of the input variables. These undesirable outputs (spikes) are normally masked by a clock pulse or other control signals, either at the decoder or farther downstream in the output logic chain. The use of an m-out-of-n code can simplify the resolution of input timing problems which result in spurious output signals from the decoding logic.

Since an m-out-of-n code contains a fixed number of bits in the 1s state, a sufficient means of eliminating decoder spikes is to keep the number of bits in the 1s state at the input to the decoder to less than the value m during the transition period of the input code word. This procedure can be implemented quite easily if the data register which supplies the input to the m-out-of-n decoder is cleared prior to the new input code word being gated into the data register. As an example, assume that the initial code word in the data register is 111000 and that the new code word to be gated into the data register is 000111. The inputs to a 3-out-of-6 decoder may go through the following transitions as the new input code word settles in the data register:

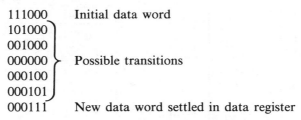

Note that in the transition sequence which changes the initial data word (111000) to the new data word (000111), none of the input code words to the decoder are 3-out-of-6 code words. Hence, no spurious spikes will be generated in the outputs of the 3-out-of-6 decoder.

The elimination of potential erroneous spikes in the output logic of the 3-out-of-6 code decoder simplifies the logic design of the decoder.   In addition, the necessity of inhibiting any outputs from the decoder during the period in which the input code word is being changed is eliminated.

7.5   MICROPROGRAM CONTROL CHECK

7.5.1   Microinstruction Error
Detection Techniques

A simplified functional diagram of the interpretation sequences for a series of macroinstructions is shown in Figure 7-34.   Each macroinstruction is interpreted by a separate, independent microinstruction sequence.   The length of a microinstruction sequence depends on the complexity of the function to be performed by the macroinstruction.   The length of a microinstruction sequence can vary considerably depending on the control function to be performed, such as interrupt identification and servicing and control of the system display panel.   Each microinstruction sequence (microprogram) can be thought of as existing independently of any other microinstruction sequence which is invoked by a macroinstruction opcode.   The control operation which directs a macroinstruction to invoke a microinstruction sequence which interprets the macroinstruction is called the macroinstruction-to-microinstruction interface or the *macro-to-micro interface.*   It is essential that the correct microinstruction sequence be selected; otherwise, an entirely different macroinstruction will be interpreted. The execution of the *correct* microinstruction at each step in the microprogram is controlled by the *micro-to-micro*

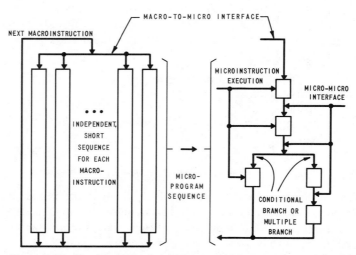

Figure 7-34   Simplified Functional Diagram of Microprogram Sequence

interface which determines the address of the next microinstruction to be executed. To validate the correct operation of the microprogram control section, the microcontrol may be divided functionally into three parts: the macro-to-micro address sequencing part, the microinstruction execution part, and the micro-to-micro sequencing part. The proper behavior of the microcontrol section during each of these functions may be checked to ensure that the current macroinstruction is being properly interpreted. Prior to specifying what error detection techniques should be used during each of these execution phases, it is advantageous to evaluate the possible fault types that could occur. Once the fault types have been identified, the appropriate error detection schemes can be devised. The basic facility which determines the behavior of the microprogrammed control implementation is the organization and physical operation of the control memory. The functional details of the control memory need to be considered in order to develop an effective error detection and maintenance scheme.

7.5.2 Control Store ROM Circuit Chip and Its Fault Characteristics

A typical 512-word × 8-bit ROM circuit chip is shown in Figure 7-35. The memory elements are arranged in a 64 × 64 transistor array with a bit of information stored in each transistor if the emitter of the transistor is connected to the vertical bit line (this connection represents a 1 stored in the transistor). The bit is in the 0 state if the transistor is *not* connected to the vertical bit line. A square array gives the best packing density in terms of the silicon area required for implementing the memory bits and their interconnections. The partitioning of the 4096 bits on the circuit chip into 512 words by 8 bits gives an adequate word length for many applications: The memory structure is easily expandable into a longer word length through the use of additional ROM chips. It is not necessary that the number of bits in a memory word be divisible by 8 to perform this expansion in word length. The 512-to-8 ROM chip is of sufficient width so that if all 8 bits in the expansion ROM are not used, the amount of memory wasted (that is, unused) is not significant. More importantly, the number of leads going off the integrated circuit chip must be kept to a minimum to keep the size of the DIP (dual in-line package) small. This allows a higher packing density of DIPs on a circuit board. The decoding circuitry is arranged to select an 8-bit word from the 64 × 64 array in the following manner:

1. The higher-order six bits of the control store address are used to select *one* of the 64 rows in the array.
2. The least-significant bits of the control store address are used to select one group of eight bits out of the eight 8-bit groups on the LSI chip.

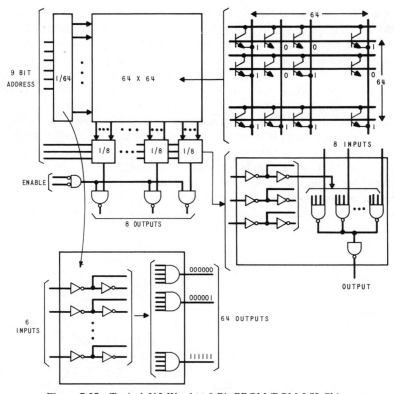

Figure 7-35 Typical 512-Word × 8-Bit PROM/ROM LSI Chip

As shown in Figure 7-35, the 1-out-of-8 binary decoder is structurally the same as the decoder discussed in the previous section. Any single logical fault results in *one* of the following two error conditions appearing at the decoder output:

1. No output is produced.
2. More than one output is produced, including the correct active output.

If the first set of address inverters experiences either a stuck-at-0 fault or a stuck-at-1 fault, the fault will cause a decoder output fault of the form no output, the wrong output, or multiple outputs. The no-output condition is easily detectable since no data will be read from the control store on a memory FETCH operation. In the case of multiple outputs from the address decoder, two or more control store locations are accessed concurrently; the contents of the referenced location are ORed together in the Control Store Data Register (CSDR). A fault of this type typically produces *unidirectional errors* in the contents of the CSDR. Consider the following example:

10001 . . . 000101	Correct word in control store to be accessed
01100 . . . 101100	Concurrently accessed word in addition to correct word
11101 . . . 101101	Resultant output formed by the bit ORing of the previous two outputs

The errors introduced for this fault condition are unidirectional in that the 0s are changed to 1s but not vice versa. Similarly, for the no-output condition, all outputs will be in the 0 state. In this case, the decoder errors change the 1s to 0s in the resultant data word from control store since the no decoder output fault corresponds to *no* reference being made to any location in control store. The errors are again unidirectional.

In the 64 × 64 memory array, any single fault would tend to affect a single crosspoint or a row or column of crosspoints. By the nature of its construction, an open circuit at the base of a crosspoint transistor would cause all bits in the memory beyond the transistor to be in the stuck-at-0 fault condition. Two transistor base circuits shorted together would result in a multiple access of control store. Again, the error characteristic of faults which affect more than one bit in the control store ROM is that such faults tend to cause unidirectional errors in the contents of the CSDR.

The selection of a particular group of eight outputs is done using eight 1-out-of-8 decoders as shown in Figure 7-35. The 64 possible outputs of the LSI ROM chip are divided into eight groups, with eight bits in each group. For a given combination of the three least-significant bits in the control store address, one bit from *each* of the eight output groups is selected to construct the 8-bit output word. In other words, a row consisting of 64 bits contains eight 8-bit words. The three least-significant bits of the address select one of the eight words in the row specified by the six most-significant bits of the control store address. The 1-out-of-8 decoder is replicated eight times, for each of the outputs. Any faults affecting a single decoder would affect only a single output bit.

Using the LSI ROM chip just described, control memories of different sizes can be designed and implemented quite easily. As an example, Figure 7-36 shows a control memory structure with the dimensions of 4K words × 32 bits; the control memory was built using the 512-word × 8-bit ROM chip as a building block. For reasons of simplicity, the fan-out requirements of the address bits and the chip enable signals have been ignored. In the implementation given in Figure 7-36, it is assumed that the signal leads are capable of driving all the 512 × 8 ROM chips which make up

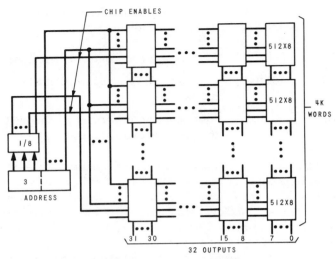

Figure 7-36   4K-Word × 32-Bit ROM Diagram

the control store.   In practice, if the fan-out requirements for the individual signal leads are exceeded, additional drivers must be provided to furnish the extra drive capability.   As shown in Figure 7-36, the low-order address leads fan out to every ROM chip in the control memory.   This permits one 8-bit word to be selected from *each* of the 512 × 8 ROM building blocks.   There are eight rows of the 512 × 8 ROM chips; each row consists of four ROM chips.   Consequently, the number of bits in a control store word is given by 4 × 8 = 32 bits.   The nine least-significant control store address bits therefore select one 32-bit word from *each* of the eight rows of 512 × 8 ROM chips.   The three most-significant address bits are decoded by a 1-out-of-8 binary decoder to select a specific row.   This final translation results in the selection of one specific 32-bit control store word.   Although there are two enable leads shown in the ROM chip of Figure 7-35, only one lead is used as an address enable signal.   The other lead could be used for strobing the output so that the spurious outputs which can occur during the time interval the address bits are changing are masked out.   However, it is quite difficult to check this timing signal since it is applied to *all* the 512 × 8 ROM chips.   A better solution to removing spurious decoder outputs would be to inhibit the control store outputs until the address bits have settled.   The fault characteristics associated with this control memory implementation, in addition to the faults identified with the 512 × 8 ROM chips, are errors associated with the 1-out-of-8 decoder.   A multiple decoder fault would affect the output data word fetched from the control store.   For instance, two or more data words could be read from the control memory simultaneously.   The resultant data word would be the inclusive-OR of the individual data words. Similarly, when a wrong 1-out-of-8 decoder output is activated, the selected address will differ from the correct address by one bit, but the bit in error could correspond to *any* of the eight binary input combinations formed by the three most-significant bits of the control store address. If the chip enable decoder is replicated to meet the fan-out requirement (for example, one decoder could drive one-half of the ROM chips, and another decoder could drive the other half), then any fault associated with one decoder would affect only one-half of each word in the 4K $\times$ 32 ROM rather than the full words in the control memory.

The error characteristics of a microprogram memory constructed from 512 $\times$ 8 LSI ROM chips used as building blocks may be summarized as follows:

1. Single- or multiple-bit errors can occur in the output data word.
2. Unidirectional errors can occur in the output data word.
3. If the errors are not unidirectional, then the control store address is incorrect.
4. Typically, errors will be localized to a 512 $\times$ 8 ROM chip or to a group of 512 $\times$ 8 ROM chips; the errors will normally not be scattered in any random fashion throughout the 4K $\times$ 32 control memory.

These types of errors are characteristic of a memory structure built using either **LSI ROM** chips or **LSI RAM** chips as building blocks. However, in the case of a memory built from **LSI RAM** chips, the faults which can occur during a memory **WRITE** operation must *also* be considered.

7.5.3   Control Field Checks

The control memory contains basically two types of data which are stored as encoded information in the individual microinstructions. This encoded data consists of *control information* (i.e., what control primitives are to be activated by the current microinstruction) and *sequencing information* (i.e., the address of the next microinstruction to be executed). Typically, the encoded control information is immediately decoded to activate the necessary control primitives. No further code conversion is required to obtain the appropriate control primitives. Consequently, there is *no* constraint placed on the encoding of the control information: Either a separable code or a nonseparable code may be used. The choice of the type of code to be used must be based upon how effective a given code is in detecting the faults which are associated with the control logic implementation. The simplest choice is to use parity-check bits with one parity bit assigned to each control field in the microinstruction. On the other hand, m-out-of-n codes provide maximum protection against multiple-output errors and unidirectional bit errors. The redundancy in an m-out-of-n code is greater than the redundancy supplied by a checking scheme which employs a single parity-check bit. For example, the maximum number of legitimate code words associated with a 4-out-of-8 code is 70. If less than 64 code words are needed, a 6-bit binary code word is sufficient. If error detection is to be performed, a single additional parity-check bit may be employed; this gives an overall binary code word length of seven bits, which is only one bit less than that required by a 4-out-of-8 code word. However, if the number of binary code words exceeds 64 *and* is less than 71, the number of bits in the binary code word and the number of bits in the 4-out-of-8 code word are equal. In general, an m-out-of-$2m$ code is *highly efficient* when compared to other codes since the check bits and the information bits are combined into an efficient nonseparable code. The m-out-of-$2m$ code provides a maximum capability for error detection at the *least* possible cost in hardware.

A microinstruction is normally partitioned into several control fields to facilitate the selection of the necessary control primitives. The simplest operation to be performed at the microcontrol level is the control of a data transfer from one register to another. It is possible to visualize an entire microprogram control sequence organized as a sequence of data transfer microinstructions. For any arithmetic operation, the operands are directed to the ALU as data transfers with a few additional signals used to specify the desired ALU operation. The result of the ALU operation can then be directed to any internal register as another data transfer. The degree of parallelism in a microinstruction is determined by the number of control points which may be simultaneously activated by the microinstruction. Parallel or concurrent operation at the microinstruction level implies additional hardware and more check circuitry. Typically, a single data transfer microinstruction consists of two fields: one to specify the *source* of the data and the other to specify the *destination* to which the data is directed. Figure 7-37 gives a functional diagram for a microinstruction which uses two control fields to specify a data transfer; the first field specifies the source (FROM field), while the second field specifies the destination (TO field). The content of each field is encoded in an m-out-of-$2m$ code, where the value of m is determined by the maximum number of control points required in *each* of the two fields. The fields may not necessarily be of the same size. The decoders and checkers used with each field are of the type described in the previous sections. Although the decoder outputs are checked directly, a more complete check can be performed if the control signals can be reencoded into their original values and *brought back* from as far along the control logic chain as possible. The regenerated values for each of the control fields would then be matched against their original values to determine if any errors had occurred in the translation process. The major difficulty in implementing this checking technique is the large number of leads that must be brought back to a common point in the processor logic for checking. In

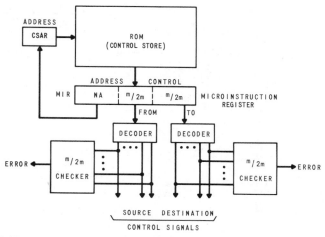

Figure 7-37 A Single Data Transfer Microprogram Control Field

many instances, control signal errors will manifest themselves as data errors at the destination register where the errors will be detected by a data check.

The use of m-out-of-$2m$ codes to encode the information contained in the control fields of a microinstruction not only provides a means of checking the contents of the microinstruction read out of control storage but *also* validates that the information was transferred correctly into the MIR and then properly decoded. In other words, any faults with the control store ROM result in a code word which is not an m-out-of-$2m$ code word. The only exception to this statement is when the wrong data word is read from the control ROM.

The timing involved in executing a microinstruction is an important consideration in ensuring that any faults will manifest as solid logic errors. Clock signals can often be used to mask spikes or race conditions that are present in the microcontrol logic. As indicated in the previous section, the use of m-out-of-n codes can eliminate any decoder spikes during the transition period when the next microinstruction is gated into the MIR. This is done by having the microcontrol logic clear the MIR prior to the next microinstruction being gated into the MIR. In some instances, the decoder spikes may not be harmful if the decoder outputs are used in control signals farther along in the control logic gating chain. Figure 7-38 gives the timing diagram of a polyphase clock system which generates the timing signals for the decoding and execution of a typical microinstruction. In Figure 7-38, the timing signals shown control a single data transfer between a SOURCE register and a DESTINATION register, with the data being moved over a common bus. The SOURCE field of the microinstruction specifies *where* the data that is gated onto the bus is coming from; the DESTINATION field directs

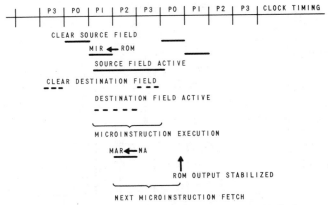

Figure 7-38   Microinstruction Execution and FETCH Timing

the data from the bus into a specific register. The control signal which gates the data from the bus into the DESTINATION register must be disabled before the data appearing on the bus is removed. If there are sufficient delays through the control logic to guarantee that the gate-in signal to the DESTINATION register is removed, the transition of data on the bus while the DESTINATION register input gates are still enabled is avoided. Otherwise, a clock signal may be used in conjunction with the gate-in signal to strobe the data from the bus into the DESTINATION register. It is quite difficult to check for the presence *or* correct occurrence of this clock signal since a clock pulse error will result in the marginal behavior of the data transfer operation; such marginal behavior can appear to be the result of a number of different logic faults.

A simple solution to this clock problem is shown in the timing diagram of Figure 7-38. If the DESTINATION field in the microinstruction register is cleared by an earlier clock phase P3 instead of clock phase P0 (shown as a dashed line in Figure 7-38), the control signal for the DESTINATION field may be shortened to the interval specified by clock phase P1 *and* P2 instead of the interval P1 *and* P2 *and* P3. This timing arrangement guarantees that the data is stable on the bus when the gate-in signal for the DESTINA-TION register is returned to the inactive state. The MIR is cleared and the next microinstruction loaded into the MIR during clock phase P1. If the MIR is not loaded with a legitimate microinstruction, the m-out-of-$2m$ code used for the contents of the SOURCE and DESTINATION fields in the microinstruction will detect an error in the microinstruction read from control store.

Buffering the outputs of the microprogram memory serves the dual functions of eliminating any need for internal timing for the control store outputs and allowing the parallel execution of the *current* microinstruction while the *next* microinstruction is fetched from control store during the same period. The outputs from a ROM structure may undergo some noticeable transitions during the period the control store address bits are settling. These output transitions can be masked out by gating the outputs of the control ROM into the MIR *after* the control store address bits have stabilized. As shown in Figure 7-38, the control store output is gated into the MIR on the leading edge of the P1 clock phase: edge-triggered flip-flops are used as storage elements in the MIR. Any malfunction of the clocking operation will result in a data word in the MIR that is not an *m*-out-of-*n* code word and will therefore be detected later by the decoder check logic attached to the control field of the microinstruction. Immediately after the memory output has been gated into the MIR, the address of the next microinstruction can be set up. This action can take place during the decoding and execution phases of the current microinstruction. The overlap operation of the current microinstruction and the next microinstruction is referred to as a *pipelining operation*. Pipelining yields a higher execution rate for the microinstructions and increases the macroinstruction execution rate of the processor.

7.5.4 Next Address Field Checks

The usage of an *m*-out-of-*n* code is quite suitable for a microinstruction control field in which the contents of the control field are immediately decoded and the decoded outputs used directly as control primitives within the processor. In some cases, it is either not convenient or not desirable to use an *m*-out-of-*n* code to encode the contents of a field in a microinstruction. Typically, two reasons for *not* using an *m*-out-of-*n* code are as follows:

1. The valid code word combinations are rather small for a given number of total bits *(n)* in the code word.
2. A conversion from the *m*-out-of-*n* code to another code may be required in the control logic of the processor; this code conversion can often be very complex and can introduce additional potential faults in the system.

For the next address field of a microinstruction, it is desirable to maintain the contents of the next address field in binary form so that the contents may be used *either* as the address of the next microinstruction to be executed *or* as binary data for internal processing at the microcontrol level. Consequently, the use of a *separable code* for encoding the contents of the next address field is an appropriate choice in terms of the flexibility offered by a separable code.

The simplest separable code is one which associates a single parity-check bit with the contents of the next address field. It offers the attractive feature that the single parity bit will detect all single-bit errors that occur in the next address field and all errors which involve an odd number of bits being in error.   Since the fault characteristics of a binary coded field may produce multiple-bit errors in which an even number of bits may be in error, a single check bit is not adequate.   An expanded parity-check scheme may be used with additional check bits associated with the data word in order to detect a larger class of failure conditions.   An expanded parity-check method can be used to detect an *even number of unidirectional errors* in a code word.   This scheme can be described as follows.   Assume a binary number expressed as

$$N = A_0(2^0) + A_1(2^1) + \cdots + A_i(2^i) + \cdots + A_n(2^n),$$

$$\text{where } A_i = \begin{cases} 0 \\ 1 \end{cases} \quad (38)$$

A parity-check character P can be developed by forming the expression

$$P = \left| C + \sum_{i=0}^{n} A_i \right|_m$$

where "$|\,|_m$" is the residue of the quantity inside the vertical brackets to modulo m and C is a constant.

If $m = 2$, the ordinary binary parity-check character is generated by forming the modulo 2 sum of the bits in the number N *and* the constant C.   The value of C will be either 0 or 1; its specific value is determined by the requirement that the overall parity of the check character plus the number N must be either odd (in which case $C = 0$) or even (in which case $C = 1$).

When m is greater than 2, the check character P can take on values greater than 0 or 1.   For example, if $m = 4$, the value of the check character can be either 0, 1, 2, or 3; these values require two bits in the encoded data word to properly represent the check character.   A 2-bit, modulo 4 residue check character will detect all unidirectional errors in a data word, but it will *not* detect unidirectional errors in which the number of bits in error is a multiple of 4.   For m greater than 4, an even larger class of unidirectional errors may be detected.

To maximize the detection capability of an expanded parity check, the errors which occur must affect either the data bits or the check bits in a specific data word but not *both*.   Using a modulo 4 parity check, certain faults which cause a single check bit and a single data bit in the same word to be in the wrong state may not be detected, for example,

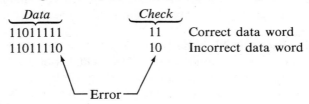

Data	Check	
11011111	11	Correct data word
11011110	10	Incorrect data word

A fault in the data word which causes one data bit to be in error and one check bit to be in error, as shown above, will be undetectable with a modulo 4 check character. However, if it is recognized that the errors are all unidirectional, the undetectable errors can be eliminated by *generating the check character from the 0s in the data word instead of using the 1s.* For the previous example:

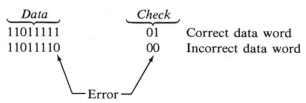

Data	*Check*	
11011111	01	Correct data word
11011110	00	Incorrect data word

The check code (00) detects the error. Any unidirectional errors affecting both the data bits and the check bits would not result in a correct check code being generated.

As the number of check bits increases, the complexity of the additional logic circuitry necessary to generate the check character also increases. While a single parity bit does not permit the detection of any fault in which an even number of bits in the data word are in error, the single parity bit is still the simplest *and* most widely used check scheme. Advantage can be taken of the fact that multiple-bit errors tend to affect *adjacent bits* instead of being randomly dispersed throughout the encoded data word. Adjacent-bit errors can be readily detected if the bits in the binary encoded next address field are interleaved with the bits from the control field of the microinstruction. Figure 7-39 illustrates this interleaved coding scheme in which the control field is encoded in an *m*-out-of-*n* code. Any multiple adjacent-

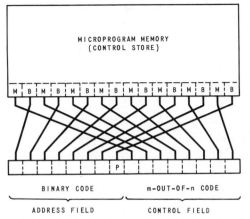

Figure 7-39 Interleaved Coding Technique

bit faults will affect both the binary next address field and the *m*-out-of-*n* code word in the control field. Consequently, a single parity-check bit is adequate to detect single-bit errors in the binary field; multiple adjacent-bit errors will be detected by the *m*-out-of-*n* code check. The probability of faults causing an even number of bit errors which occur only in the binary field is quite small. The interleaved coding technique does not require any additional hardware to perform error detection. It does, however, provide additional protection against multiple errors since errors in adjacent bits can be detected. It will be assumed, in any further discussions, that the interleaved coding technique is used when a microinstruction is considered that consists of a binary code next address field and a control field encoded using an *m*-out-of-*n* code.

7.5.5 Microinstruction-to-Microinstruction Sequence Interface

Two parity-check bits may be used in each microinstruction to check that the microcontrol unit is sequencing correctly from one microinstruction to the next microinstruction. One parity-check bit can be used to represent the parity of the address of the current microinstruction; the other parity-check bit can be used to represent the parity over the contents of the next address field in the current microinstruction. Since the contents of the next address field are used to fetch the next microinstruction, the parity bit associated with the next address field may be compared with the parity bit *calculated* for the address of the next microinstruction. If the two parity bits agree, then the sequencing from one microinstruction to its successor appears to be correct. Figure 7-40 illustrates the microinstruction sequence check scheme. Each microinstruction is required to contain two parity-check bits. P_{NA} is the parity bit of the next address field, and P_A is the parity of the address of the current microinstruction. The P_{NA} bit of the present microin-

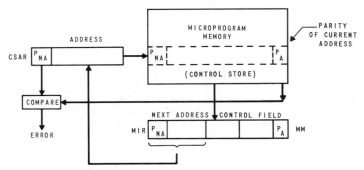

Figure 7-40 Microinstruction-to-Microinstruction Sequence Check with Next Address Field

struction is compared with the stored P_A of the address of the current microinstruction. It checks the linkage from one microinstruction to its successor. It includes the control memory output and validates that the next microinstruction is accessed correctly in order for a string of microinstructions to be executed in their proper sequence. A decoder fault in the access circuitry of the control memory which results in the selection of the wrong microinstruction will be detected by this sequence check.

If a binary counter is used to generate the address of the next microinstruction by adding 1 to the address of the current microinstruction, the parity over the next address must be calculated by the processor hardware. In this case, a parity prediction scheme may be used to compute the parity of the address of the next microinstruction. For this case, each microinstruction will contain only one parity-check bit—the parity bit for the address of the current microinstruction. This arrangement is shown in Figure 7-41, with a binary counter used to generate the address of the next microinstruction. While the CSAR is used to access the next microinstruction, the control store address counter is incremented by one to point to the next sequential address in control memory. At the same time, the parity is predicted by the logic attached to the CSAR so that the next control store address and its associated parity-check bit are generated independently. This procedure avoids the occurrence of any fault which might affect *both* the parity-check bit and the new address in the counter in a compensating fashion; the parity-check bit would mask out any binary counter address error. When the microinstruction fetch is completed, the program counter is gated to the address register to repeat the same sequence of operations. The sequence check is performed by comparing the stored parity bit in the microinstruction with the parity bit generated by the parity predict logic to ensure that the proper control store word is accessed.

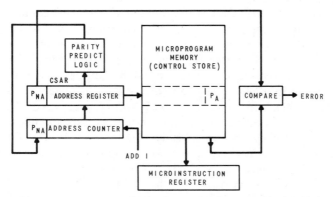

Figure 7-41 Microinstruction-to-Microinstruction Sequence Check with Sequential Address Generation

7.5.6 Conditional Branch Microinstructions

The ability to execute a conditional transfer of control at the microinstruction level is one of the basic operations required in a microprogram. When a conditional branch microinstruction is executed, the microprogram typically may transfer control to one of two alternative addresses in control store. The actual control store address is determined by specific conditions which have occurred in the system. To validate that the correct branch address in control store has been taken by the microcontrol logic, it is necessary to arrange the conditional branch addresses in such a manner that any fault in the conditional branch logic will result in a microinstruction sequencing error being detected by the control logic.

A possible scheme for validating the conditional operation when the next address field is provided as part of the microinstruction is as follows: To facilitate this operation, it is assumed that many of the conditional results of various data manipulations or arithmetic operations—such as a register containing all 0s, the occurrence of a carry overflow from the ALU, and so on—have been established prior to the execution of a conditional microinstruction. These conditions are stored in status flip-flops within the processor. A microprogram can individually test these status bits and perform a conditional branch operation on their content. The conditional branch microinstruction specifies the conditions to be tested and provides the hardware to derive the appropriate branch address. Typically, the address of the next microinstruction is selected to fall on an even-numbered location in control store when a conditional branch microinstruction is used. When the contents of the next address (NA) field is gated from the microinstruction register (MIR) into the CSAR, the state of the condition bit to be tested is typically gated into the least-significant bit of the CSAR. If the condition bit is in the 1s state, the address of the next microinstruction appearing in the CSAR is the *sum* (INCLUSIVE-OR) of the contents of the NA field and the value 1; otherwise, the address of the next microinstruction is just the contents of the NA field of the current microinstruction. The use of even addresses in a conditional branch microinstruction simplifies the hardware implementation of branch address logic. Instead of additional logic circuitry being required, if the address of the next microinstruction is generated by the NA field, a simple logical gating arrangement is all that is required. The generation of the parity-check bit for the next address is also simplified from that required by the binary counter scheme. Figure 7-42 illustrates the logical implementation of the checking scheme for a conditional branch microinstruction that employs a next address field. The logic that tests the status bits is duplicated so that the address bits in the CSAR and the parity bit associated with the CSAR may be generated independently. A fault occurring in either duplicated logic block will result in an address in the CSAR with its parity

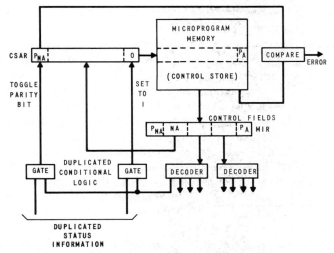

Figure 7-42 Conditional Branch Microinstruction with Next Address Field

bit in error. As the next microinstruction is fetched from control store, the error will be detected by the sequence check logic which compares the parity bit in the CSAR with the parity bit stored in the next microinstruction. To provide additional error detection capability, the setting of the least-significant bit in the CSAR and the toggling of the parity bit in the CSAR can be arranged to be complementary. When the least-significant address bit is changed by the conditional branch logic, the parity bit is not changed and vice versa. This essentially gives a two-rail, self-detecting error check when the next address is modified in the least-significant bit position. If *both* the least-significant address bit *and* the parity bit change concurrently, a hardware fault has occurred. In addition, any parity error in the CSAR will be caught by the comparison of the parity-check bit in the CSAR with the parity-check bit incorporated in the microinstruction that is loaded into the MIR.

7.5.7 Macroinstruction-to-Microinstruction Sequence Interface

Each macroinstruction is interpreted on the hardware of the host machine by a sequence of microinstructions called a *microprogram*. The starting address of the microprogram is determined by the value of the macroinstruction opcode. The different techniques that may be used to generate the starting address of the interpretive microprogram for a macroinstruction have been discussed in Chapter 2. Typically, the macroinstruction opcode is gated directly into the k least-significant bits of the CSAR; the $n - k$ most-significant bits have previously been loaded with a base address for an area in control store. In some implementations, the opcode may be translated through use of a read-only memory (ROM) and mapped into a starting address which could be anywhere in control store. Figure 7-43 shows one possible implementation of the translation procedure for a macroinstruction opcode. Each macroinstruction is fetched from main memory and placed in the macroinstruction register (IR), where the IR, the CSAR, the parity generation logic, and associated gating paths (called the *macro-to-micro interface logic*) translate the macroinstruction opcode into the starting address in control store of a microprogram. To initiate the translation of the next macroinstruction in the main program, the last microinstruction in the interpretation sequence for the current macroinstruction must indicate that a new macro-opcode translation may be performed. Typically, the last microinstruction will contain all 0s in the next address (NA) field. The use of the all-0s value is a convenient way for the microcontrol sequencer to be alerted that the opcode of the next macroinstruction should be gated into the CSAR.

There are several errors that can occur in the sequencing operation as the microcontrol sequencer *completes* the interpretation of the current macroinstruction and *begins* the interpretation cycle of the next macroinstruction. First, errors may occur when the output of main storage is loaded into the macroinstruction register (IR). If the opcode field includes a dedicated parity bit, a validity check of the macroinstruction opcode can be performed when the entry address into control memory in generated. In

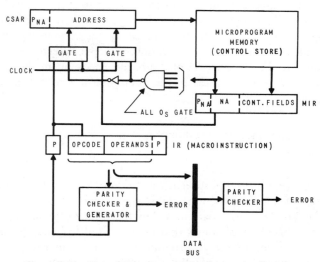

Figure 7-43   Macroinstruction-to-Microinstruction Interface

general, the opcode is normally not assigned a separate parity-check bit. Consequently, the verification of the macroinstruction opcode must be done *prior* to the generation of the entry address in control store; this verification validates the data transfer of the macroinstruction into the IR. A separate parity checker may be used to monitor the IR for correct parity over the new macroinstruction. This arrangement is shown in Figure 7-43. An alternate check procedure would involve having the IR gated onto the data bus *after* the new macroinstruction has been loaded in the IR; the contents of the IR would then be checked for errors by the parity checker attached directly to the data bus.

A second type of error occurs when the contents of the IR have been verified to be correct but the gating of the macroinstruction opcode into the CSAR has been done incorrectly. This situation typically results in an odd number of bits being in error which will be detected by a normal parity sequence check. If an even number of bits are in error, then the fault will not be detected.

A third type of error results when the all-0s detection gates are enabled prematurely due to an input fault (for example, an open circuit at one of the input gates). Instead of gating the contents of the next address field of the current microinstruction into the CSAR, the opcode associated with the next macroinstruction is gated into the CSAR. This type of error causes the microprogram sequence to terminate prematurely, resulting in an incomplete execution of the current macroinstruction.

Although it is possible for a single fault in the sequencing logic to produce multiple-bit errors in the data path, this type of fault is usually associated with the common control portion of the gating path which affects all bits connected to the same control signal. Typically, the number of bit errors will depend on the data pattern. It is possible that a simple parity check of the data word will *not* immediately detect a fault in which a multiple number of bits in the data word are in error. However, the fault should be detected within a few data transfer operations by the microsequence check logic. This fault detection behavior is normally quite satisfactory since the mutilation of a few data words should not seriously affect the application. But more importantly, this approach avoids adding *excessive* fault detection hardware solely to detect faults at the time of their initial occurrence.

The type of error which the sequence check logic will *not* detect is a fault that causes a new microprogram sequence to be initiated before the old microprogram sequence has completed. This means that the previous macroinstruction is not completely executed before a new macroinstruction interpretation sequence is begun. A relatively small number of faults will cause this type of trouble. It may be advantageous to check for these faults on a periodic basis using a special test sequence to ensure that the faults will be recognized within a certain time interval after their first occurrence.

The microinstruction sequence check can be extended to include faults which prematurely initiate a microprogram sequence. One such scheme is indicated in Figure 7-44(a) in which the parity bit of the address of the *previous* microinstruction is also provided as part of the current microinstruction. This allows both a backward check and a forward check of the sequence of microinstructions which have recently been executed. The parity of the address of the *current* microinstruction P_A is compared with the parity check bit P_{NA} for the address of the microinstruction. The address of the microinstruction is obtained either from the macroinstruction opcode or from the next address field of the *previous* microinstruction. The comparison of the values for P_A and P_{NA} corresponds to a forward sequence parity-check operation. This situation is shown in Figure 7-44(b). The P_A bit from the previous microinstruction is also stored temporarily in a local flip-flop (data cell). The current microinstruction contains a third parity check bit P_P which corresponds to the parity bit of the address of the previous microinstruction. P_P should be the same as the value of P_A for the previous microinstruction. A backward sequence check is performed by comparing P_A and P_P to determine whether the current microinstruction is properly *linked* to the previous microinstruction. In most cases, the premature termination of a microprogram sequence will be detected by this backward sequence check.

The implementation of the extended sequence check logic is shown in

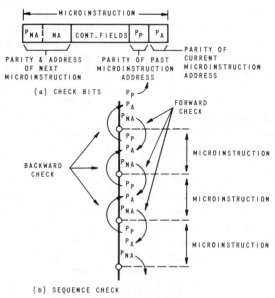

(b) SEQUENCE CHECK

Figure 7-44 Extended Sequence Check

Figure 7-45. The forward check logic is performed by comparing the P_A of the current microinstruction with the parity bit of the CSAR. The backward sequence check requires that the P_A bit be temporarily stored in another flip-flop so that it can be compared with the P_P bit of the next microinstruction. At the end of each microprogram sequence, the next macroinstruction is initiated by having the microcontrol sequencer gate the opcode into the CSAR; the opcode defines the starting address in control store of a new microprogram sequence. This action is equivalent to executing a conditional branch microinstruction, with a multiplicity of possible addresses in control store being available to function as the address of the next microinstruction. This implies that a multiplicity of microprogram sequences can be initiated—depending on the value of the macroinstruction opcode. As indicated in Figure 7-46(a), the first microinstruction of each microprogram sequence must contain the parity bit P_P of the address of the last microinstruction to ensure that the *micro-to-macro interface* is correctly maintained. When several microinstructions branch into a common location, as shown in Figure 7-46(b), the addresses of each of the branch microinstructions which occur in the separate microprogram sequences must have the same value for the P_A check bit. This permits a backward sequence check to be consistent with the value of the P_P check bit found in the microinstruction located at the entry address of the common microprogram. This restriction is not severe if each microinstruction contains a next address field. The usage of a next address field allows any address in control memory to be specified as the address of the next microinstruction with the correct parity check bit assigned.

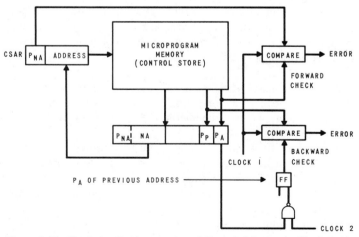

Figure 7-45   Hardware Implementation of Extended Sequence Check Logic

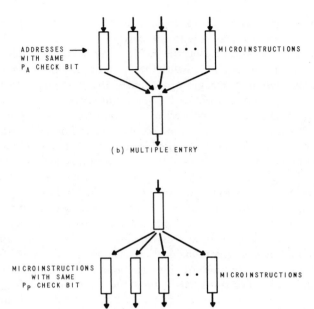

Figure 7-46   Restriction in Extended Sequence Check Operation

7.5.8   Macroinstruction Operand Field Processing

A macroinstruction is normally divided into several fields in order to specify the different addressing modes, operands, and conditions to be used in the execution of the macroinstruction.   For example, a simple data transfer macroinstruction which uses two internal processor registers may consist of the following information fields:

1. The opcode which specifies that a data transfer operation is to be performed
2. The source operand (the internal register which is to supply the data)
3. The destination operand (the internal register which is to receive the data)

Within a processor, there are usually a large number of data registers. Some are general-purpose registers, which provide convenient and quick-access data storage to facilitate programming.   Other registers are dedicated to specific hardware functions and perform as program counters, error registers, timing counters, and so on.   Conventional programming such as programs written for data processing operations only make use of the general-purpose registers.   However, for system programming or maintenance programming, both the general-purpose registers and the special registers may be involved. Consequently, there may be three different formats for a register-to-register data transfer macroinstruction: *register-to-register, register-to-special-register,* and *special-register-to-register.* There is a fourth format for a data transfer macroinstruction, *special-register-to-special-register,* but the fourth format is not used since the operation specified by the fourth format can be done by a combination of the other data transfer formats (for example, a special-register-to-register operation followed by a register-to-special-register operation). As an illustration, assume there is a processor which contains a set of 16 general-purpose registers and another set of 16 special registers. A possible 16-bit macroinstruction format for a simple register-to-register data transfer operation may consist of an 8-bit opcode field and two 4-bit operand fields. The opcode defines the machine operation, and the two operands specify the source and the destination register which are to participate in the data transfer operation. To identify one of the three data transfer operations, a unique opcode is assigned to *each* of the three formats. Therefore, in a data transfer instruction, the opcode identifies which combination of the two sets of registers (general-purpose or special) is involved, and the operand fields specify one of the 16 registers within each of the designated register sets.

When a new macroinstruction is transferred into the IR for processing, the integrity of the macroinstruction must be checked, preferably by a separate hardware checker. If a separate checker is *not* used, then the macroinstruction must be gated from the IR onto the data bus and the checking logic associated with the bus used to validate the integrity of the macroinstruction. In addition, separate parity bits can be associated with each field of the macroinstruction. This permits each field to be used individually and a separate error check performed on the contents of each field.

Figure 7-47 illustrates one possible implementation of the register-to-register data transfer macroinstruction. It is assumed that the SOURCE operand X and the DESTINATION operand Y each contain four bits, while the operand fields in a microinstruction are encoded in a 4-out-of-8 code. An output from *each* of the 4-out-of-8 decoders shown in Figure 7-47 is used to enable two 1-out-of-16 decoders associated with the macroinstruction register (IR). The active outputs from each of the 1-out-of-16 decoders are used to generate the control signals to transfer a data word from any SOURCE register to any DESTINATION register. This is the standard procedure used to generate the microcontrol signals associated with a data transfer operation, since 1-out-of-n decoder circuits are normally part of the access circuitry of a register array or stack. Decoder checking must be included as part of the overall data transfer validation check.

The binary decoders associated with the SOURCE field X and DESTINATION field Y can be considered redundant in that the same control signals can be obtained directly from the outputs of the SOURCE field and

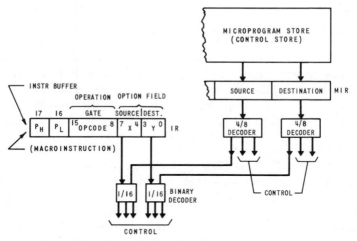

Figure 7-47   Register to Register Gating Macroinstruction

the DESTINATION field decoders associated with the microinstruction. If the operand fields of the macroinstruction can be translated and gated to the SOURCE and the DESTINATION fields of the microinstruction register (MIR) at the same time, the control store outputs are gated to the MIR; then the 1-out-of-16 decoders are not needed.

The conversion of a 4-bit binary code word to a 4-out-of-8 code word is a straightforward process. The conversion can be performed using a single, simple gating operation in which a bit in the binary code will be translated to the 2-bit representation 10 if the binary bit is a 1 and will be translated to the 2-bit representation 01 if the binary bit is a 0. The Y field of the macroinstruction may be translated into its equivalent 4-out-of-8 code word in the following manner:

1. The all-0s code word appearing in the DESTINATION field of the microinstruction is treated as a special condition used by the microcontrol sequencer.
2. When the microinstruction is fetched from control memory and the all-0s code word is recognized as being present in the DESTINATION field, the content of the macroinstruction Y field is automatically gated into the DESTINATION field in the MIR.

Similarly, the presence of the all-0s code word in the SOURCE field of a microinstruction can be used to automatically translate the binary contents of the macroinstruction X field into its equivalent 4-out-of-8 code and gate the result into the SOURCE field of the MIR.

Figure 7-48 illustrates this translation logic. The main disadvantage of this approach is that if the special-register set is to be enabled, an additional set of binary to 4-out-of-8 translators is required since the special registers

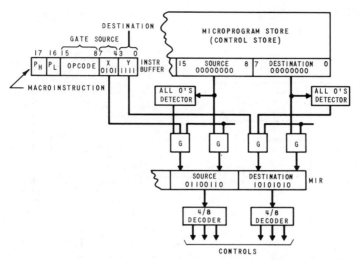

Figure 7-48 Another Method of Implementing a Register Gating Macroinstruction

cannot be translated into the same 4-out-of-8 code words as the general-register set. Moreover, additional control signals are necessary to provide the selection of each set of translators.

A more flexible arrangement uses the combination of a binary translator and the control memory itself to provide the valid 4-out-of-8 code for both the SOURCE and the DESTINATION control fields in the MIR. That is, the control store provides a 1-out-of-2 code word for the two most-significant bits of the 4-out-of-8 code word in the MIR; the binary translator converts the 4-bit binary code found in the X or Y fields of the macroinstruction into a 3-out-of-6 code word which is inserted in the six least-significant bits of the 4-out-of-8 code word in either the SOURCE or DESTINATION fields of the MIR. Figure 7-49 illustrates this translation procedure. If the contents of either the SOURCE or DESTINATION field are binary 01000000, then the general-register set of the processor is to be used in the interpretation of the macroinstruction; if the contents of either of these fields are 10000000, then the special-register set is to be used. Since the microinstruction that contains the SOURCE and DESTINATION fields is read from control store before it is gated into the MIR, the six least-significant bits in each of these fields will contain all 0s. Two all-0s detectors may be used: one detector to check for all 0s in the SOURCE field and the other to check for all 0s in the DESTINATION field. The presence of all 0s in the SOURCE field will gate the contents of the X field in the IR through the binary to 3-out-of-6 translation logic and into the six least-significant bits of the MIR. A similar translation takes place when all 0s are detected in the DESTINA-

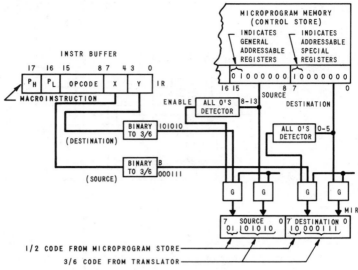

Figure 7-49   Macroinstruction Operand Translation

TION field of the microinstruction. This procedure allows any general addressable register to be gated to any special register and vice versa without the use of any additional control logic. It should be noted that no additional error-checking circuitry is required to validate the behavior of the 3-out-of-6 or 1-out-of-2 translators since the resultant microinstruction in the MIR is checked by the 4-out-of-8 decoders attached to the MIR.

7.5.9   Microprogram Mode Change

Thus far, the discussion of fault detection has been concerned with the use of hardware redundancy to detect errors at the time of their occurrence. In most instances, the redundant hardware does *not* degrade the performance of the processor, and immediate error detection is achieved. Fault detection may also be implemented by the use of software or firmware in which a program designed to exercise a specific piece of hardware is run on a regularly scheduled basis by the operating system. In this method, faults may *not* be caught immediately. However, if the fault detection program is run on a sufficiently frequent basis (i.e., every 10 milliseconds, etc.), then faults which occur in the hardware will be detected before they will have caused serious problems in the correct function of the processor.

Another fault detection technique which makes use of firmware is to use a *mode bit* in conjunction with the macroinstruction opcode to derive the entry address in control store of the microprogram which interprets the macroinstruction. This technique uses time redundancy to increase fault detection capability; it consists of *two* complete sequences of microinstructions for each macroinstruction. One sequence of microinstructions is arranged to give the *best possible performance* in terms of execution speed for each macroinstruction sequence, while the second sequence is designed to ensure that the operations performed by the microinstructions are done correctly *(fault detection mode).* The use of two interpretation sequences per macroinstruction results in an implementation of the macroinstruction set in which performance may be traded off for additional execution time. This arrangement allows the processor to perform fault detection when execution time is not critical.

Figure 7-50 describes the implementation of a microprogram mode change scheme. Each macroinstruction opcode has two microcode sequences associated with it. The precise microcode sequence selected is dictated by the mode bit *M*. The use of the mode bit keeps the two microcode sequences physically separated. When the mode bit is *not* set, the entry address associated with the macroinstruction opcode will point to the lower half of the control memory. When the mode bit is set, the entry address will point to the upper half of the control memory.

This method of generating the entry address into control store permits interpretive microprograms for the *different* target machines to be stored in the same control memory. In fact, programs that execute on different target machines can be run interchangeably using this scheme by having the operating system change the state of the mode bit to point to the appropriate microcode block in control store.

In the fault detection mode, the interpretive microprogram may take twice as much space in control store as the high-performance microprogram so that each control step in the microprogram may be validated. For example, consider the operation of the following simple ADD macroinstruction:

$$\text{ADD R1,R2} \qquad (39)$$

In this macroinstruction the contents of general register R2 are added to

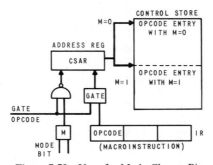

Figure 7-50 Use of a Mode Change Bit

the contents of general register R1, with the sum stored back in general register R1. This machine operation may also be written in the following notation:

$$R1 \leftarrow R1 + R2 \qquad (40)$$

The ADD macroinstruction will be implemented on the common bus structure shown in Figure 7-51. The microcontrol steps required to interpret the ADD macroinstruction are shown in steps 1 through 6; in each case, error checking is performed on the control operation that was executed:

1. $A \leftarrow R1$: The contents of general register R1 are transferred to internal register A for temporary storage via the common data bus. A parity check is done on the data as the data is transferred over the bus to ensure that R1 contains the correct data. No check is made to determine whether the data is gated into A correctly.
2. $BUS \leftarrow A$: The contents of A are gated onto the bus for a parity check. If the parity check passes, it ensures that the data was gated into A correctly.
3. $B \leftarrow R2$: This control operation is the same as step 1 except that the contents of general register R2 are transferred to internal register B for temporary storage.
4. $BUS \leftarrow B$: The contents of B are gated out onto the common bus and checked by the bus parity checker.
5. $R1 \leftarrow SUM$: The ALU result (SUM) is gated into R1. It is assumed in this implementation that the parity-check bit is generated with the SUM. When the SUM is gated onto the common bus, the SUM is checked for correct parity.
6. $BUS \leftarrow R1$: The contents of R1 are gated onto the common bus and checked by the bus parity checker.

In this microprogram sequence every other microinstruction is inserted to check that the data word reaches the destination register without any error.

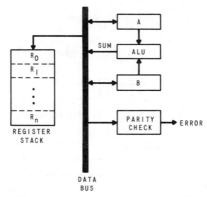

Figure 7-51 Use of a Common Bus for the ADD Operation

This is done by gating the contents of the destination register onto the common bus after the data word has been placed in the destination register. The data word is then validated by the parity checker associated with the common bus. If the destination register check is *not* done, the microprogram sequence can be shortened to the following three microinstructions:

1. A ← R1
2. B ← R2
3. R1 ← SUM

The execution time of the microprogram is shortened if a complete check of each data transfer operation in the microprogram is *not* provided.

If the mode bit is set to either 1 or 0, the **ADD** macroinstruction is interpreted by one of the two microprogram sequences previously described. Both microprograms generate the same result—the **ADD** macroinstruction is executed—but the microprogram which performs error checking takes *additional time*. Any fault that occurs is detected, essentially, as soon as it occurs. An interesting use of the mode bit is to allow it to be toggled periodically to activate the high-performance microcode. The mode bit would be left in the high-performance state for a period of time and then toggled again to allow the microcode with built-in self-checking features to be executed. This alternating action allows the execution speed of the microcode to be interleaved with the fault detection capability. In addition, the mode bit may be under control of the operating system such that when the system is busy, the mode bit is set to allow the *fast version* of the microcode sequences to be executed. However, when the system is *not* busy, the mode bit is set to allow the microcode routines which incorporate self-checking to be executed. The system software keeps track of the state of the mode bit and the processor work load. The macroinstructions are normally interpreted by the self-checking microcode sequences. When the system software determines that the processor work load has reached a preestablished level (the system is busy), the mode bit is set to allow the high-performance microprograms to be executed. In this fashion, the system performance may not be degraded at all.

7.6 ERROR DETECTION IN ARITHMETIC AND LOGIC OPERATIONS

The basic arithmetic operations performed by a small computer are binary addition and shifting. For subtraction, 2's-complement addition is commonly used. The conversion of a negative number into 2's-complement form is easily done by complementing every bit in the number (forming the 1's-complement) and then adding 1 to the result. Most machines perform this conversion in a single step. Multiplication and division can be accomplished by the repeated use of the basic arithmetic operations. Such an iterative process is implemented in software or firmware. However, as the scale of integration continues to increase and the cost of hardware continues to decrease, hardware MULTIPLY and DIVIDE packages offered optionally for many small machines will become more attractive in small systems which require high-performance arithmetic operations. For many dedicated functions, such as process control, high-performance arithmetic operations are not really needed. In the discussion which follows, only methods for detecting errors in the basic arithmetic and logic operations will be considered.

7.6.1   Parity Prediction in Binary Counting

Binary counting is one of the more important operations within a processor. The program counter (PC) is typically implemented as a forward binary counter. The PC normally contains the address of the next macroinstruction in the main program sequence.

The binary counting function can be performed using the addition capability of the ALU and a register which functions as an accumulator. To perform this function, several control steps are required:

1. The contents of the PC must be gated into the accumulator.
2. The contents of the accumulator must be gated into the ALU and 1 added to the contents.
3. The result is gated back into the accumulator.
4. The new contents of the accumulator are gated back into the PC.

This sequence of events is probably quite satisfactory for small machines in which the serial operation eliminates the need for circuitry required to increment the PC were it to be implemented as a binary counter. However, the serial operation requires additional time when compared to the usage of a parallel binary counter. For larger machines, the overhead of performing the serial binary *additions* operation for every macroinstruction (except for those macroinstructions which represent branching operations) becomes an important factor in determining the throughput capability of the processor. Consequently the PC is typically implemented as a dedicated hardware register that can also function as an incrementable forward binary counter.

If addresses in main storage carry along a parity-check bit for fault detection, the parity bit *may or may not* undergo a change when the address is incremented by 1 (for example, when 1 is added to the contents of the program counter). Whether the parity bit changes or not depends on the number of bits in the main storage address which change during the increment-by-1 operation. If an even number of bits are affected, the parity bit remains unchanged; otherwise, the value of the parity bit is complemented. The parity of the main store address is checked when the address is used to reference a location in main storage. If the parity is correct, the main store address is utilized to predict the parity of the next address. After the PC had been incremented by 1 and the new parity bit has been generated, the value of the new parity bit is compared to the value of the predicted parity bit. If the two do not match, an error in the increment-by-1 operation of the PC is indicated.

The standard procedure for predicting the parity of a binary counting sequence can be determined by examining Table 7-6. Table 7-6 exhibits the relationship of the present binary number to the next binary number is a forward counting sequence and the behavior of the parity bit over the counting sequence. If Table 7-6 is rearranged to generate Table 7-7, the characteristics of the parity bit during the binary counting sequence become more obvious. Table 7-7 has the 4-bit binary numbers (counts) grouped according to the number of bits that change state in proceeding from the present count to the next count (i.e., 1 is added to the present count to generate the next count). All the present counts whose least-significant bit is 0 are grouped together; there are eight in this category. Note that the values of the next count for these same eight present count values have only their least-significant bit changed from a 0 to a 1. The other three bits remain unchanged. Since only one bit has changed in progressing from the present count to the next count, the parity bit of the present count must also be changed. The next grouping of counts in Table 7-7 is arranged so that the *two* least-significant bits in the present count are in the 01 state; there are four counts in this category. In progressing from the present count

TABLE 7-6 Binary Counting
Parity Changes

PRESENT COUNT	NEXT COUNT	PARITY CHANGE
0 0 0 0	0 0 0 1	YES
0 0 0 1	0 0 1 0	NO
0 0 1 0	0 0 1 1	YES
0 0 1 1	0 1 0 0	YES
0 1 0 0	0 1 0 1	YES
0 1 0 1	0 1 1 0	NO
0 1 1 0	0 1 1 1	YES
0 1 1 1	1 0 0 0	NO
1 0 0 0	1 0 0 1	YES
1 0 0 1	1 0 1 0	NO
1 0 1 0	1 0 1 1	YES
1 0 1 1	1 1 0 0	YES
1 1 0 0	1 1 0 1	YES
1 1 0 1	1 1 1 0	NO
1 1 1 0	1 1 1 1	YES
1 1 1 1	0 0 0 0	NO

TABLE 7-7 Binary Counts
Grouped According to the Number
of Bits Changed

PRESENT COUNT	NEXT COUNT	PARITY CHANGE
0 0 0 0	0 0 0 1	YES
0 0 1 0	0 0 1 1	YES
0 1 0 0	0 1 0 1	YES
0 1 1 0	0 1 1 1	YES
1 0 0 0	1 0 0 1	YES
1 0 1 0	1 0 1 1	YES
1 1 0 0	1 1 0 1	YES
1 1 1 0	1 1 1 1	YES
0 0 0 1	0 0 1 0	NO
0 1 0 1	0 1 1 0	NO
1 0 0 1	1 0 1 0	NO
1 1 0 1	1 1 1 0	NO
0 0 1 1	0 1 0 0	YES
1 0 1 1	1 1 0 0	YES
0 1 1 1	1 0 0 0	NO
1 1 1 1	0 0 0 0	NO

to the next count, the values of the *two* least-significant bits are changed
from the 01 state to the 10 state.   Since an even number of bits in the
present count have been changed, the parity bit remains unchanged for the
next count.   Similarly, the other present count values are arranged such
that an increasing number of bits are changed as the present count is incremented to the next count.   Table 7-8 shows the bit patterns of the groupings
associated with the present count and the next count; the dash in this table
represents the bits which remain unchanged when the present count is incremented to the next count.   When a 1 is added to a binary number, the
rightmost 0 and all preceding 1s are complemented to form the next count.
For example,

$$0101001111 + 1 = 0101010000$$

The bits in boldface type are the bits changed by the complementation operation to generate the next binary count.

TABLE 7-8 Abbreviated Binary
Counts Grouped According to the
Number of Bits Changed

PRESENT COUNT	NEXT COUNT	PARITY CHANGE
- - - 0	- - - 1	YES
- - 0 1	- - 1 0	NO
- 0 1 1	- 1 0 0	YES
0 1 1 1	1 0 0 0	NO
1 1 1 1	0 0 0 0	NO

For a backward (decrement-by-1) binary counter, the present count column and the next count column in Table 7-8 are *interchanged*. In the decrement-by-1 operation, when a 1 is subtracted from a binary number, the rightmost 1 in the binary number and all preceding 0s are complemented to form the difference number. For example,

$$0101010000 - 1 = 0101001111$$

This is the reverse of the procedure used in the previous example.

Parity prediction takes advantage of the following characteristic of the binary groups formed in Table 7-8: When the next binary count is formed, the only bits to change state are (1) the bit in the present count which contains the *rightmost 0* and (2) all bits which precede the rightmost 0 bit.

Assuming the least-significant bit of the present count is in the 0 state, an odd number of bits in the present count will change state only if the rightmost 0 occurs in an even-numbered bit position. Hence, in this situation *only,* the predicted parity of the next count is the complement of the parity for the present count. If the rightmost 0 occurs in an odd-numbered bit position, the increment-by-1 operation will cause an even number of bits to change state. Therefore, the parity of the next count will remain unchanged from the parity of the present count. Figure 7-52 illustrates the implementation of the parity predict logic for a forward binary counter. The function of the rightmost 0 detector is to determine if the first 0 in the present count is located in an *even*-numbered bit position. If it is, a signal is generated to toggle the parity-check bit (complement the bit) when the increment-by-1 function is performed. For simplicity, the full details of the binary counter circuit are *not* shown in Figure 7-52.

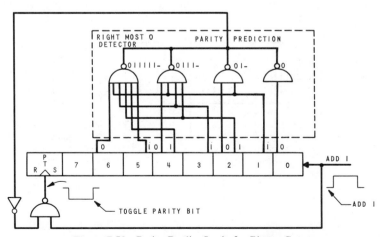

Figure 7-52   Parity Predict Logic for Binary Counter

To provide the maximum error detection capability, the binary counter design must be arranged so that all faults which can occur will result in a single-bit error in the next count or in an odd number of bit errors in the next count. Otherwise, the single parity-check bit which detects only single-bit errors or an odd number of bit errors will not be able to determine that an error has occurred. For example, consider the binary ripple counter with a stuck-at-1 fault as shown in Figure 7-53. The next count will be

$$01111 + 1 \rightarrow 01000$$

instead of the correct value, 10000. The parity of the next count that is in error is the same as the parity for the correct value of the next count; conse-

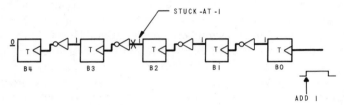

Figure 7-53   Binary Ripple Counter Fault

quently, the error will *not* be detected by the parity check. This means that for certain faults the errors which can occur are data-dependent and may not be detected by the parity-check logic. A design which can immediately detect all single faults is illustrated in Figure 7-54. In this arrangement, which represents a parallel binary counter, any faults in the counter affect only one bit and are therefore detectable by the associated parity-check logic.

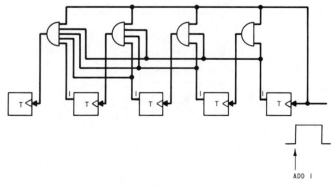

Figure 7-54   Parallel Binary Counter Logic

7.6.2 Parity Prediction in Binary Addition

The binary adder is the basic building block of the arithmetic section of a processor. Typically, the binary adder is implemented as a ripple-carry type or with carry-look-ahead logic. In some cases, the binary adder may be constructed using both of the previous implementations. The choice of which implementation is to be used is dictated by the cost of the associated hardware and the speed of the arithmetic operation required. The error characteristics of a binary adder depend heavily on the logic structure of the implementation. The fault detection scheme must therefore take into consideration the resultant errors caused by logic faults within the binary adder itself.

The use of a single parity-check bit per data word is a very efficient method of performing single-bit error detection. However, the parity bit is not preserved by arithmetic operations; that is, when the sum of two data words is generated, the associated parity bit is not, in general, the correct parity for the result. For systematic codes, the data part of the sum is correct, but the resultant parity-check bit may be incorrect. It is possible to predict the new parity bit for the sum on the basis of the parity bits for each of the input operands and the carry signals produced during the addition process.

7.6.3 Parity-Check Adder

The parity of the sum of two operands can be calculated by exclusive-ORing the bits in the sum as follows:

$$P_s = S_{n-1} \oplus S_{n-2} \oplus \cdots \oplus S_1 \oplus S_0 \tag{41}$$

where the notation $\oplus$ represents the exclusive-OR operation and the sum is given by binary number $S = S_{n-1}S_{n-2} \cdots S_1S_0$. Substituting the logic expression for the generation of the ith sum bit,

$$S_i = a_i \oplus b_i \oplus c_{i-1} \tag{42}$$

where a_i and b_i are the operand digits and c_{i-1} is the incoming carry from the preceding $(i-1)$th binary adder stage. From this the following equation is obtained:

$$P = a_{n-1} \oplus b_{n-1} \oplus c_{n-2} \oplus a_{n-2} \oplus b_{n-2} \oplus c_{n-3} \oplus \cdots$$
$$\oplus a_1 \oplus b_1 \oplus c_0 \oplus a_0 \oplus b_0 \tag{43}$$
$$= (a_{n-1} \oplus a_{n-2} \oplus \cdots \oplus a_1 \oplus a_0)$$

$$\oplus (b_{n-1} \oplus b_{n-2} \oplus \cdots \oplus b_1 \oplus b_0) \tag{44}$$
$$\oplus (c_{n-2} \oplus c_{n-3} \oplus \cdots \oplus c_1 \oplus c_0)$$

$$P_s = P_a \oplus P_b \oplus P_c \tag{45}$$

where P_a and P_b are the parity-check bits of the input operands and P_c represents the parity of *all* the carry signals generated in the addition process.

From Eq. (45) the parity-check bit for the sum can be predicted by exclusive-ORing the parity bits of each input and the parity bit formed by all the carries. The results of the addition process can be checked for error by calculating the parity of the sum according to Eq. (41) *and,* separately, according to Eq. (45). The two calculations should agree; otherwise, an error has occurred in either the adder *or* in the check circuit. Figure 7-55 gives a general block diagram for the use of parity prediction logic in the checking scheme for a binary adder.

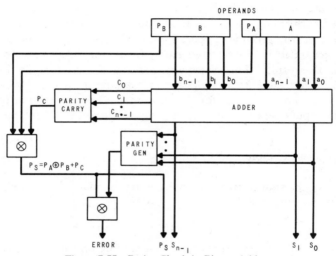

Figure 7-55   Parity Check in Binary Adder

7.6.4   Ripple-Carry Adder Error Characteristics

The *ripple-carry adder* is a binary adder in which a carry can propagate serially from the least-significant bit through each intermediate stage to the most-significant bit. The carry circuitry forms a serial string, with the carry from the $(i-1)$th stage acting as an input to the carry generation logic of the ith stage. Single failures in the adder logic may result in a single sum-bit error, or a burst of sum- and carry-digit errors may occur as the carry propagates. Figure 7-56 shows the logical implementation of the ripple-carry adder. The carry output from the $(i-1)$th adder stage feeds the ith adder stage to generate both the ith sum bit and the carry bit *from* the ith adder stage. Any faults in the sum circuit affect only the sum output; a parity check over the sum will detect these single-bit errors. However, faults in the carry circuit will cause a burst of sum- and carry-digit errors

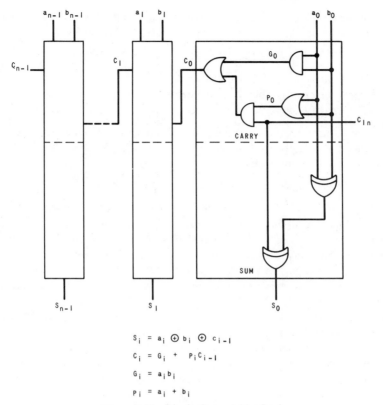

$$S_i = a_i \oplus b_i \oplus c_{i-1}$$

$$C_i = G_i + P_i C_{i-1}$$

$$G_i = a_i b_i$$

$$P_i = a_i + b_i$$

Figure 7-56 Ripple Carry Adder Logic

because of the way the carry propagates from one adder logic stage to the next. For example, consider the behavior of the ripple-carry adder shown in Table 7-9. In this example, a fault in the logic which generates the carry from the fourth adder stage (C_4) causes the error to propagate to the carry

TABLE 7-9 **Errors in Ripple-Carry Adder**
Output Caused by Errors in Carry Propagation
Logic

VARIABLE	BINARY VALUE	PARITY BIT
A-INPUT VECTOR	1 0 1 1 1 0 0 1 0 0 1 1 0 1 1 0	1
B-INPUT VECTOR	0 0 0 0 0 1 1 1 1 1 0 0 0 0 0 1	0
CARRY VECTOR	0 0 1 1 1 1 1 1 1 1 1 1 0 0 0 0	0
SUM VECTOR	1 1 0 0 0 0 0 1 0 0 0 0 1 0 1 1 1	1

NOTE: THE BITS IN ERROR ARE UNDERLINED.

logic for generating carries C_5, C_6, and C_7. The value of the parity bit *predicted* by using Eq. (45) for the adder output is given by

$$P_s = P_A \oplus P_B \oplus P_C = 1 \oplus 0 \oplus 0 = 1 \tag{46}$$

where P_A = parity over the A input vector
P_B = parity over the B input vector
P_C = parity over the carry vector

The error pattern in the carry bits C_4, C_5, C_6, and C_7 is reflected in the errors which have appeared in the sum bits S_5, S_6, S_7, and S_8. The parity calculated from the sum outputs is

$$P_s = S_0 \oplus S_1 \cdot \cdot \cdot \oplus S_{n-1} = 1 \oplus 1 \oplus \cdot \cdot \cdot \oplus 1 = 1 \tag{47}$$

This agrees with the parity predicted by using Eq. (45) since the errors in the carry bits cause the same *number* of bits in the sum to be in error. Therefore, the errors in both the carry bits and the corresponding sum bits affect the parity calculations for the carry input vector and the sum in the *same* direction; hence, the errors are *undetectable* by the parity-check scheme. A single fault in the carry circuit can cause any number of carry errors to occur in succeeding ripple-adder stages. This means that if an error in the carry logic for the ith stage causes C_i to be in error and the C_i error causes the $(i + m)$th adder stage to generate an error in C_{i+m}, all carries which are generated from the adder stages between the ith and the $(i + m)$th stages will also be in error. A burst of $m + 1$ carry errors results in a burst of $m + 1$ sum-digit errors, as previously shown. This can be seen by examining the expression of the ith sum digit:

$$S_i = A_i \oplus B_i \oplus C_{i-1} \tag{48}$$

Whenever the carry from the preceding stage, C_{i-1}, is in error, the ith sum bit S_i will also be in error. The total number of bits in error in both the carry input vector *and* the sum produced by the ripple-carry adder will always be an even number.

7.6.5 Parity Check by Carry Duplication

A standard approach taken to avoid the problems associated with the ripple-carry logic is to duplicate the carry circuit. This approach isolates the parity prediction logic from the adder logic. For the ripple-carry adder circuit shown in Figure 7-56, the carry out of the ith adder stages is given by

$$C_i = G_i + P_i C_{i-1} \tag{49}$$

where $G_i = a_i b_i$ and $P_i = a_i + b_i$. The logic expression for the duplicated carry out of the ith stage is given by

$$C_{di} = G_{di} + P_{di} C_{i-1} \tag{50}$$

where $G_{di} = a_{di}b_{di}$ and $P_{di} = a_{di} + b_{bi}$, where the subscript denotes that the variable is associated with the duplicated logic circuit.

From the previous two sets of equations, it can be seen that an error in G_i or P_i *cannot* cause an error in C_{di} because C_{di} is independent of both G_i and P_i. However, an error in the C_{i-1} term is common to both the logical expression for C_i and the logical expression for C_{di}.

As an example, consider the behavior of a ripple-carry adder which uses the duplicated carry propagation logic shown in Table 7-10. An error in the carry generation logic which occurs in the fourth stage of the adder causes the error to propagate to the carry generation logic for the fifth, sixth, and seventh stages of the regular carry circuits. However, only the fifth, sixth, and seventh stages of the duplicated carry logic are affected; the fourth duplicated carry stage is not affected. The parity for the sum using the duplicated carry output is

$$P_s = P_A \oplus P_B \oplus P_{dc} = 1 \oplus 0 \oplus 1 = 0 \tag{51}$$

where $P_A =$ parity of the A input vector
$P_B =$ parity of the B input vector
$P_{dc} =$ parity of the duplicated carry vector
$P_C =$ parity of the sum vector

The parity of the sum calculated using the individual bits in the sum is given by

$$P_s = S_0 \oplus S_1 \oplus \cdot \cdot \cdot + S_{n-1} = 1 \oplus 1 \oplus \cdot \cdot \cdot \oplus 1 = 1 \tag{52}$$

An error due to a fault in the ripple-carry logic is therefore detected by the use of a duplicated ripple-carry circuit. A burst of errors consisting of $m + 1$ consecutive bits being in error in the sum caused by an error in the carry generation logic for C_n will cause all the duplicated carries $C_{d,n+1}$ through $C_{d,n+m}$ to be in error. The total number of errors in the overall duplicated carry C_d is always one *less* than the total number of errors in the overall carry C. The *resultant* number of bits in error when both the

TABLE 7-10 Errors in Ripple-Carry Adder Output with Duplicated Carry Propagation Logic

VARIABLE	BINARY VALUE	PARITY BIT
A-INPUT VECTOR	1 0 1 1 1 0 0 1 0 0 1 1 0 1 1 0	1
B-INPUT VECTOR	0 0 0 0 0 1 1 1 1 0 0 0 0 0 1	0
CARRY VECTOR	0 0 1 1 1 1 1 1 <u>1 1 1 1</u> 0 0 0 0	0
DUPLICATED CARRY VECTOR	0 0 1 1 1 1 1 1 <u>1 1 1</u> 0 0 0 0 0	1
SUM VECTOR	1 1 0 0 0 0 0 1 <u>0 0 0</u> 1 0 1 1 1	1

NOTE: THE BITS IN ERROR ARE UNDERLINED.

overall sum vector and the overall carry vector are considered together is always an odd number. Consequently, the errors are detectable by using a parity check.

Figure 7-57 shows the duplicated carry circuit for a binary adder which will detect all carry errors caused by a single fault in either the adder or the carry logic. The regular carry logic expression is common to both the logic expression for the next sum digit and the duplicated carry circuit. This arrangement is necessary to ensure that the *total* number of sum-digit errors plus the errors which occur in the duplicated carry digit will *always be odd*. If the duplicate carry digit is implemented using the following logic expression,

$$C_{d,i} = G_{d,i} + P_{d,i}C_{d,i-1} \tag{53}$$

in which the duplicate carry circuit will be completely independent of the binary adder circuit, an error in the carry digit will *not* cause an error in

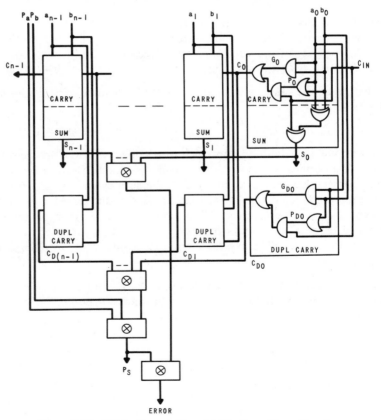

Figure 7-57   Ripple Carry Adder with Duplicate Carry Circuit

the duplicate carry digit. Consequently, a carry fault will cause an even number of sum-digit errors to pass undetected since the duplicate carry digits will contain no errors.

7.6.6 Look-ahead Carry Adder Error Characteristics

The *look-ahead carry structure* is a parallel logic arrangement in which *all carries* are generated simultaneously and independently. Speed is obtained by generating the carry from the current stage and not waiting until the carries from the previous counter stages have had sufficient time to ripple through to the current stage. The equations for the carry look-ahead are given in Table 7-11.

The implementation of a look-ahead carry circuit using the previous logic equations is shown in the top portion of Figure 7-58. As shown in Figure 7-58, each sum output is independently generated. Any faults affecting either the carry from the ith adder stage or the sum logic circuit will cause a single-bit error. However, the P_i and G_i logic outputs are shared among the individual carry circuits. Faults affecting the P_i and G_i outputs may cause a burst of error to appear in both the carry outputs and the sum outputs. A parity check that employs the individual duplicated carry outputs will detect these errors just as the parity check used by a ripple-carry binary counter would. Consider the faults indicated in the adder logic shown in Table 7-12.

An error in bit P_2 will cause the fault to propagate from bit C_2 through bit C_6 in the carry vector outputs. However, the fault propagates *only* from bit $C_{d,3}$ through bit $C_{d,6}$ of the duplicated carry vector outputs. If the total number of bits in error in the sum vector is *added* to the total number of bits in error in the duplicated carry vector, an odd number will *always* be obtained. The faults are therefore detectable by a simple parity check.

TABLE 7-11 Logic Equations for the Generation of the Individual Look-Ahead Carries

$$C_0 = G_0 + P_0 C_{in}$$

$$C_1 = G_1 + P_1 G_0 + P_1 P_0 C_{in}$$

$$C_2 = G_2 + P_2 G_1 + P_2 P_1 G_0 + P_2 P_1 P_0 C_{in}$$

$$C_i = G_i + P_i G_{i-1} + P_i P_{i-1} G_{i-2} + P_i P_{i-1} P_{i-2} G_{i-3} + \cdots + P_i P_{i-1} P_{i-2} \cdots P_i P_0 C_{in}$$

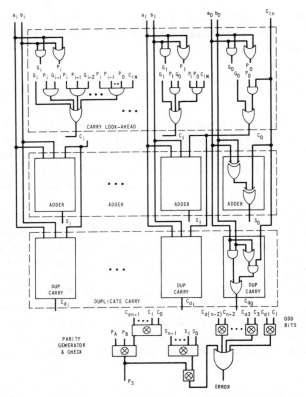

Figure 7-58 Carry Look-Ahead Adder with Duplicate Carry Circuit

TABLE 7-12 Parity Checking to Detect Errors Using Duplicated Carry Outputs in a Look-Ahead Adder

VARIABLE	BINARY VALUE	PARITY BIT
A-INPUT VECTOR	1 0 0 1 1 0 0 1 1	1
B-INPUT VECTOR	0 0 1 0 0 1 0 0 1	1
P-VECTOR	1 0 1 1 1 1 1 1 1	0
G-VECTOR	0 0 0 0 0 0 0 0 1	1
CARRY VECTOR (C)	0 0 1 1 1 1 1 1 1	1
DUPLICATED CARRY VECTOR (C_d)	0 0 1 1 1 1 0 1 1	0
SUM VECTOR	1 1 0 0 0 0 1 0 0	1

NOTE: THE BITS IN ERROR ARE UNDERLINED.

$$P_i = a_i + b_i \text{ AND } G_i = a_i b_i$$

TABLE 7-13 Effect of Faults in Carry Logic Circuit

VARIABLE	BINARY VALUE	PARITY BIT
A-INPUT VECTOR	1 0 0 1 1 0 0 1 1	1
B-INPUT VECTOR	0 0 1 0 0 1 0 0 1	1
CARRY VECTOR (C)	0 0 0 0 0 0 <u>1</u> 1 1	1
DUPLICATED CARRY VECTOR (C_d)	0 0 0 0 0 <u>1</u> 0 1 1	1
SUM VECTOR	1 0 1 1 1 <u>0</u> 1 0 0	1

NOTE: THE BITS IN ERROR ARE UNDERLINED.

This is also true when an error occurs in G_i. Since each individual carry circuit is independent of both the previous sum outputs and the earlier carry generation logic, any fault in a specific carry circuit will affect *only* the output of the single carry bit. This single carry-bit error will be reflected as an error in the sum bit produced by the following adder stage. However, the carry output for the ith adder stage drives the duplicated carry circuit $C_{d,i+1}$; this circuit also produces an output error in $C_{d,i+1}$.

Consider the fault behavior shown in Table 7-13. Note that, in general, an error in C_i causes an error in $C_{d,i+1}$ *and* S_{i+1} since C_i acts as an input to both the $(i+1)$th stage of the duplicated carry generation logic *and* the $(i+1)$th adder stage. In Table 7-13, bit C_2 is in error; this causes bit $C_{d,3}$ to be in error in the duplicated carry vector and results in bit S_3 of the sum being in error. The sum of the number of bits in error in the sum vector and duplicated carry vector is 2, which is an even number. A simple parity check will *not* detect faults affecting the C_i logic circuits. This type of fault results in two pairs of carry outputs C_i, $C_{d,i}$ and C_{i+1}, $C_{d,i+1}$. An additional error check of the carry faults requires only that outputs from each pair be compared. If the outputs differ, an error has occurred. The complete checking scheme for the look-ahead carry adder is shown in Figure 7-58.

7.6.7 Group Look-ahead Carry Adder

Large binary adders which are implemented with full look-ahead carry logic circuits become very expensive in terms of the fan-out and fan-in requirements of the circuits needed to implement the successive look-ahead carry logic stages. A procedure for achieving a good compromise in cost is to incorporate the use of group look-ahead schemes in which an *n-bit-word* is divided into *m b-bit groups*. The look-ahead carry concept can be applied *to* the groups as a whole, to bits *within* a group, or to both categories concurrently. The types of single faults that can occur depend largely on the logic structure employed. A supplementary check must be performed on the hardware, in addition to the parity checks, to establish that the group look-ahead carry logic is *fault-secure* for all single faults. That is, the group look-ahead carry logic can detect all single faults. However, parity checks which use the duplicate carry logic will detect a majority of single faults in the adder circuit. The small percentage of remaining faults may require special checking procedures.

7.6.8 Residue-Checked Binary Addition

The parity-checked adder is normally used to check for an odd number of bit errors in the sum vector. A residue code may be used when a greater degree of error detectability is desired. The residue-code-checking logic functions completely independently of the adder logic circuit. The residue-code-checking logic depends only on the inputs to the adder (the addend and augend) and the output from the adder (the sum). Consequently, the error detection capability of the residue-code-checking logic is independent of the adder structure whether the adder structure is of the ripple-carry type or the look-ahead carry type.

In a residue code with a number base m, the check symbol of an operand A is generated by long division; that is, the quotient of $A \div m$ is formed. The remainder of this division operation is the *residue of A to the base m*. In residue codes which do not require a great deal of detection logic (low-cost codes), the number base is typically taken to be of the form

$$m = 2^n - 1 \tag{54}$$

where n is greater than 1.

The residue of the code word (operand) A is obtained by performing a modulo $2^n - 1$ addition of the n bits in the code word. This procedure may be simplified if the n bits are divided into k groups in which each group contains $l = n \div k$ bits. The quotient $n \div k$ must be an integer. If these k groups are formed, then a modulo $2^l - 1$ addition of the l bits for each of the k groups can be used to generate the residue of A.

For example, to calculate the check symbol or residue of A (where $A = 1010111001011001$), the 16 bits must be divided into four 4-bit groups. The groups must then be added together in a 4-bit binary adder with an end-around carry. This technique is illustrated in Figure 7-59. Using this technique, the residue R is given by

$$\begin{aligned} R &= 1010 + 1110 + 0101 + 1001 \\ &= 1001 + 1110 = 1000 \end{aligned} \tag{55}$$

The arrangement shown in Figure 7-59 is called a *modulo 15 residue tree*

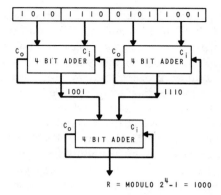

$$R = \text{MODULO } 2^4 - 1 = 1000$$

Figure 7-59   Modulo-15 Residue Tree

structure. Instead of using the three 4-bit adders, the same result can be obtained with a single adder in which each addition operation is performed separately on the single 4-bit adder.

The residue generated by the adder circuit in Figure 7-59 has two different, legal representations for the 0 residue: the binary number that contains all 0s *or* the binary number that contains all 1s. The residue check logic must recognize that these two representations of the 0 residue are equivalent. The checking logic can map the all-0s binary number into the all-1s binary number, or vice versa, in order to establish their equivalence.

In a residue check of binary addition, the check symbol must either be furnished as part of the input data or be derived directly from the data. Figure 7-60 gives an arrangement in which the residue check symbols are

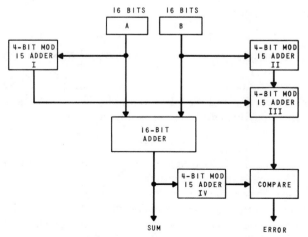

Figure 7-60   Low-Cost Residue Check

calculated.   The data bits and check bits are processed *independently* by the 16-bit adder and the four 4-bit adders.   The sum output from the 16-bit adder is used to generate a residue check symbol which is *compared* with the check symbol produced by the modulo 15 adder III.   If an error has occurred in the addition process, the two residues will *not* be identical.

It can be seen from the diagram in Figure 7-60 that the logic delay through the residue check circuits (adder I, adder II, and adder III) is greater than the logic path delay generated by a standard binary addition of two 16-bit numbers.   This means that the residue-checking arrangement shown in Figure 7-60 adds delay to the binary addition operation.   Alternatively, the addend *(A)* and the augend *(B)*, as well as the sum, may be buffered in data registers to allow additional time for residue checking.

7.6.9   Parity Check of Logic Functions

A very flexible and useful set of operations for manipulating data is the 16 Boolean functions of two variables.   These functions are obtained by logically combining the corresponding bits of two variables A and B.   The individual bits may be represented by the notation A_i and B_i, where the subscript i represents the ith bit of either variable A or variable B.   The four minterms associated with two Boolean variables A_i and B_i can be generated as follows:

$$m_0 = \overline{A}_i \, \overline{B}_i$$
$$m_1 = \overline{A}_i \, B_i$$
$$m_2 = A_i \, \overline{B}_i$$
$$m_3 = A_i \, B_i$$

where m_0, m_1, m_2, and m_3 are the four minterms formed from two Boolean variables.   Any Boolean function of two variables may be represented by the following expression:

$$f(A_i, B_i) = S_0 \overline{A}_i \overline{B}_i + S_1 \overline{A}_i B_i + S_2 A_i \overline{B}_i + S_3 A_i B_i \qquad (56)$$

where S_0, S_1, S_2, and S_3 are Boolean constants and may take on either the value 0 or the value 1.

Various logic functions of two variables may be obtained by specifying the values of S_0, S_1, S_2, and S_3.   For example, if $S_0 = S_3 = 1$ and $S_1 = S_2 = 0$, the following Boolean function is obtained:

$$f(A_i, B_i) = \overline{A}_i \, \overline{B}_i + A_i \, B_i \qquad (57)$$

This function can be used to compare two bits to determine if the two bits match (have the same value) or are different.

Figure 7-61 shows the logic circuitry which will implement any of the 16 Boolean functions of two variables; the values specified for S_0, S_1, S_2, and S_3 determine the exact function that will be realized.   The control bits (S_0, S_1, S_2, and S_3) are common to each of the two variable Boolean

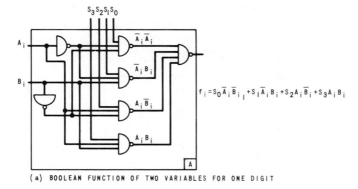

$$f_i = S_0 \overline{A}_i \overline{B}_i + S_1 \overline{A}_i B_i + S_2 A_i \overline{B}_i + S_3 A_i B_i$$

(a) BOOLEAN FUNCTION OF TWO VARIABLES FOR ONE DIGIT

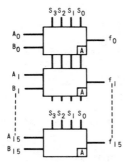

(b) DISTRIBUTION OF CONTROL BITS (S_0, S_1, S_2, S_3) TO EACH LOGIC MODULE

Figure 7-61   Boolean Function of Two Variables

logic modules associated with each bit position of the vector variables A and B.   The distribution of the control bits to each Boolean logic module is shown in Figure 7-61(b).   The 16 possible Boolean functions of two variables are tabulated in Table 7-14.

A parity check may be performed on the 16 Boolean functions, but the results are somewhat unique to each logic operation.   The XOR operation is perhaps the most straightforward logic operation to perform a parity check on since the parity of the result can be predicted by XORing the input variables together.   The parity of the result can be found as follows:

$$P(A) = A_{n-1} \oplus A_{n-2} \oplus \cdots \oplus A_1 \oplus A_0 \tag{58}$$

$$P(B) = B_{n-1} \oplus B_{n-2} \oplus \cdots \oplus B_1 \oplus B_0 \tag{59}$$

$$P(A \oplus B) = A_{n-1} \oplus B_{n-1} \oplus A_{n-2} \oplus B_{n-2} \oplus \cdots \oplus A_0 \oplus B_0 \tag{60}$$

$$= (A_{n-1} \oplus A_{n-2} \oplus \cdots \oplus A_0) \oplus (B_{n-1} \oplus B_{n-2} \oplus \cdots \oplus B_0)$$

$$= P(A) \oplus P(B)$$

TABLE 7-14 Control Bit Assignments for 2-Variable Boolean Functions

CONTROL S_3 S_2 S_1 S_0	LOGIC FUNCTION f
0 0 0 0	0
0 0 0 1	$\overline{A}\,\overline{B}$
0 0 1 0	$\overline{A}B$
0 0 1 1	$\overline{A}\,\overline{B} + \overline{A}B = \overline{A}$
0 1 0 0	$A\overline{B}$
0 1 0 1	$\overline{A}\,\overline{B} + A\overline{B} = \overline{B}$
0 1 1 0	$\overline{A}B + A\overline{B} = A \oplus B$
0 1 1 1	$\overline{A}\,\overline{B} + \overline{A}B + A\overline{B} = \overline{A} + \overline{B}$
1 0 0 0	AB
1 0 0 1	$\overline{A}\,\overline{B} + AB = \overline{A \oplus B}$
1 0 1 0	$\overline{A}B + AB = B$
1 0 1 1	$\overline{A}\,\overline{B} + \overline{A}B + AB = \overline{A} + B$
1 1 0 0	$A\overline{B} + AB = A$
1 1 0 1	$\overline{A}\,\overline{B} + A\overline{B} + AB = A + \overline{B}$
1 1 1 0	$\overline{A}B + A\overline{B} + AB = A + B$
1 1 1 1	1

For example, let the *A* and *B* input variables be represented by the following binary vector:

$$A = 10100011 \tag{61}$$

$$B = 01101000 \tag{62}$$

The XOR function of *A* and *B* is given by

$$A \oplus B = 11001011 \tag{63}$$

$$P(A) = 1 \oplus 1 \oplus 0 \oplus 0 \oplus 0 \oplus 0 \oplus 1 \oplus 1 = 0 \tag{64}$$

$$P(B) = 0 \oplus 1 \oplus 1 \oplus 0 \oplus 1 \oplus 0 \oplus 0 \oplus 0 = 1 \tag{65}$$

$$P(A \oplus B) = P(A) \oplus P(B) = 0 \oplus 1 = 1 \tag{66}$$

P(A) is the parity bit of input *A,* and *P(B)* is the parity bit of input *B; P(A ⊕ B)* is the predicted parity of the result when even parity is used. If odd parity is used in the parity-check logic, the predicted parity bit for the result will be given by

$$P(A \oplus B) = P(A) \oplus P(B) \oplus 1 \tag{67}$$

or

$$P(A \oplus B) = P(A) \oplus \overline{P(B)} \tag{68}$$

or

$$P(A \oplus B) = \overline{P(A)} \oplus P(B) \tag{69}$$

The parity relationship of several logic functions can be derived from a direct examination of Table 7-15. For example, the parity calculation for the OR function can be obtained by recognizing from Table 7-15 that

$$A + B = (A \oplus B) \oplus (AB) \tag{70}$$

$$P(A + B) = P(A \oplus B) \oplus P(AB) \tag{71}$$

The compare function is simply the complement of the XOR function $\overline{A \oplus B}$. For an even number of bits in the data word the parity of $\overline{A \oplus B}$ is the same as for $A \oplus B$.

The other Boolean functions listed in Table 7-15 employ variations of the AND and OR functions in which both the asserted (uncomplemented) and negated (complemented) values of the input variables A and B are present. These Boolean functions can be checked for errors by employing additional logic to determine the correction to the check bit(s) when the complemented as well as the uncomplemented values of the A and B variables are supplied as inputs to the logic that generates the desired Boolean function.

The error-checking logic required to validate such Boolean functions must be considered separately from the logical implementation of the Boolean function. By examining the generalized logic for implementing any Boolean function of two variables shown in Figure 7-61(a), some interesting properties of the exclusive-OR function $A \oplus B$ and its complement $\overline{A \oplus B}$ can be observed:

1. The function $A \oplus B$, when it is behaving properly, will produce an output from the $\overline{A}B$ gate, or the $A\overline{B}$ gate, or the function will produce *no* output at all.
2. The function $\overline{A \oplus B}$, when it is behaving properly, will produce an output from the $\overline{AB}$ gate or from the AB gate, or the function will produce *no* output at all.

The function $A \oplus B$ and its complement are capable of exercising every input and output signal in the logic circuit shown in Figure 7-61(a) provided the proper sequence of input values for the A and B variables are supplied. Any logic faults will eventually propagate to the output as an error and can be detected by a parity check. Consequently, the parity check for each

TABLE 7-15 Relationships of Several Logical Functions of Two Variables

INPUT VALUES		LOGICAL FUNCTIONS			
		AND	EXCLUSIVE OR	INCLUSIVE OR	COMPARE
A	B	AB	A $\oplus$ B	A+B	$\overline{A \oplus B}$
0	0	0	0	0	1
0	1	0	1	1	0
1	0	0	1	1	0
1	1	1	0	1	1

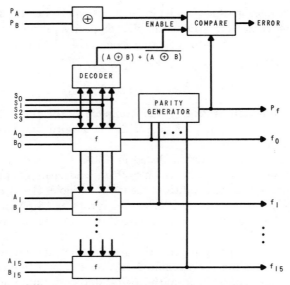

Figure 7-62 Parity Check of Boolean Logic Function

Boolean logic function needs to be performed *only* on the XOR function $A \oplus B$ and its complement $\overline{A \oplus B}$. This simplifies the hardware implementation of the parity-check logic for the Boolean logic functions, as shown in Figure 7-62. This implementation, however, will *not* immediately detect the occurrence of a fault.

7.6.10 Duplication and Matching of the ALU Results

Consider the 4-bit ALU logic circuit shown in Figure 7-63(a), which is the logical equivalent of an MSI chip supplied by commercial companies (the 54/74181). It is a common MSI chip, costing only a few dollars. Rather than providing a separate logic package to check each ALU function, a more complete check of the entire ALU can be accomplished by duplicating the ALU circuit and matching the outputs of the two ALUs at the conclusion of each ALU operation.

Figure 7-64 illustrates an arrangement in which the ALU is duplicated and the outputs of the two ALUs are matched after each ALU operation. A single data bus is used to gate the outputs from ALU I to the comparator where the output from ALU II is matched against the output from ALU I. If a parity bit is associated with each data word, the data is checked as the data word is gated onto the bus by a bus parity check. The parity bit does *not* ensure that the data word reaches the destination register correctly. In the case of data to be used by the ALU, the operands are buffered in separate, duplicated data registers (the *A* and *B* registers shown in Figure

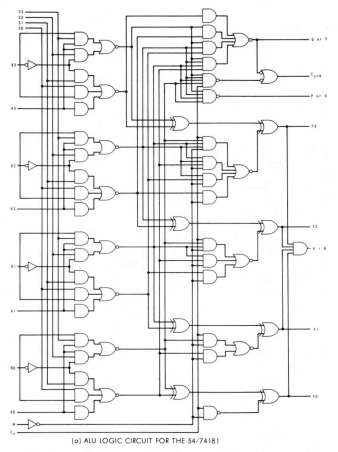

(a) ALU LOGIC CIRCUIT FOR THE 54/74181

SELECTION				ACTIVE-HIGH DATA		
				M = H	M=L; ARITHMETIC OPERATIONS	
S3	S2	S1	S0	LOGIC FUNCTIONS	C_n = H (NO CARRY)	C_n = L (WITH CARRY)
L	L	L	L	F = $\overline{A}$	F = A	F = A PLUS 1
L	L	L	H	F = $\overline{A+B}$	F = A+B	F = (A+B) PLUS 1
L	L	H	L	F = $\overline{A}B$	F = A+$\overline{B}$	F = (A+$\overline{B}$) PLUS 1
L	L	H	H	F = 0	F = MINUS 1 (2's COMPL)	F = ZERO
L	H	L	L	F = $\overline{AB}$	F = A PLUS A$\overline{B}$	F = A PLUS A$\overline{B}$ PLUS 1
L	H	L	H	F = $\overline{B}$	F = (A+B) PLUS A$\overline{B}$	F = (A+B) PLUS A$\overline{B}$ PLUS 1
L	H	H	L	F = A $\oplus$ B	F = A MINUS B MINUS 1	F = A MINUS B
L	H	H	H	F = A$\overline{B}$	F = A$\overline{B}$ MINUS 1	F = A$\overline{B}$
H	L	L	L	F = $\overline{A}$+B	F = A PLUS AB	F = A PLUS AB PLUS 1
H	L	L	H	F = $\overline{A \oplus B}$	F = A PLUS B	F = A PLUS B PLUS 1
H	L	H	L	F = B	F = (A+$\overline{B}$) PLUS AB	F = (A+$\overline{B}$) PLUS AB PLUS 1
H	L	H	H	F = AB	F = AB MINUS 1	F = AB
H	H	L	L	F = 1	F = A PLUS A	F = A PLUS A PLUS 1
H	H	L	H	F = A+$\overline{B}$	F = (A+B) PLUS A	F = (A+B) PLUS A PLUS 1
H	H	H	L	F = A+B	F = (A+$\overline{B}$) PLUS A	F = (A+$\overline{B}$) PLUS A PLUS 1
H	H	H	H	F = A	F = A MINUS 1	F = A

(b) ALU LOGIC FUNCTIONS FOR THE 54/74181

Figure 7-63 Logic Diagram of the 54/74181 ALU

315

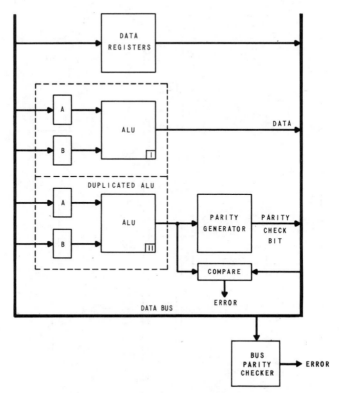

Figure 7-64 Duplicated ALU and Matching Logic

7-64). Under the assumption that only a single fault will occur, the independent data paths into each ALU guarantee that one of the two ALUs will be functioning correctly. The independent data paths eliminate the need to check whether or not the operands arrived at the ALUs in an error-free condition. The outputs from ALU I are used as the actual source of the ALU results to the rest of the processor logic. When the outputs from ALU I are gated onto the bus, the data is moved into the comparator and matched against the outputs of ALU II. This completely checks the results of the ALU operation. The parity of the result can be generated from the output of ALU II, as shown in Figure 7-64.

7.7 SELF-TESTING CHECK CIRCUITS

7.7.1 Self-testing Parity Checker

As discussed in the previous sections, the parity-check circuit determines whether the number of bits in the 1s state in a data word is an odd or even number. A parity-check bit appended to a data word is generated such that the total number of bits in the data word in the 1s state plus the parity bit is either an odd or even number. For example, the odd-parity check of a 16-bit data word $(D_{15} D_{14} D_{13} \cdot \cdot \cdot D_1 D_0)$ plus its associated parity bit P must satisfy the following equation:

$$D_0 \oplus D_1 \oplus \cdot \cdot \cdot \oplus D_{14} \oplus D_{15} \oplus P = 1 \qquad (72)$$

Figure 7-65 illustrates the implementation of this parity checker using XOR gates. The implementation forms a tree structure in which five different levels of XOR gates are used to generate the parity signal. Each level successively reduces the number of outputs that must be examined by a factor of 2. Consequently, standard two-input XOR gates may be used to implement the parity-check logic. The final output will equal 1 if the parity over the data word *and* its parity bit P is odd; otherwise, the final output will equal 0. The logic delay through the parity-check circuit depends on the speed of the XOR gate and the number of levels in the check circuit. When a data word is transferred over a common data bus, it is desirable for the data to be checked *on the fly* as the data flows over the bus. A data register

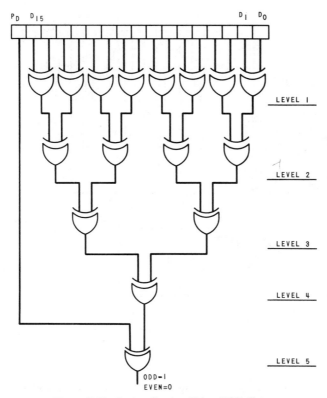

Figure 7-65 Parity Checker Using XOR Gates

can be provided to hold the data word until the parity check is completed. The primary purpose for using a bus data register is to extend the parity-checking interval. This allows the bus gating logic to have a clearly defined gating path established from the SOURCE register over the data bus and into the DESTINATION register. Additional time is also allowed for the data on the bus to stabilize. If the parity check over a data word requires still more time than is available on the processor, a faster check circuit should be implemented using faster logic gates.

Alternatively, the parity check can be accomplished by having each level in the logical implementation examine three outputs at a time rather than the two outputs at a time used by the XOR realization. Figure 7-66 illustrates the three-input parity checker and the usage of the three-input checker to generate the parity for a 16-bit data word plus its parity bit *P*. The total logic delay for this implementation is *less* than the total logic delay of the XOR implementation.

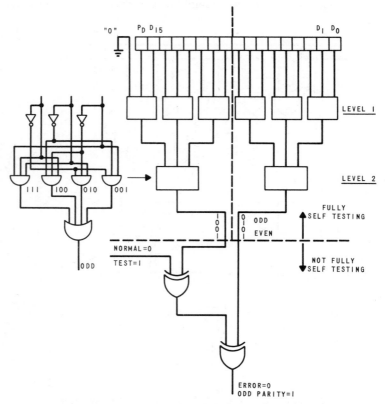

Figure 7-66 3-Input Parity Check Building Block Realization

Another important factor in the implementation of any error-checking logic is the *self-testing property* of the check circuit. One of the necessary requirements for self-testing is that the check circuit may be partitioned such that the asserted values of the outputs are dual rail, 10 or 01. Figure 7-66 indicates that the parity-check logic is divided into two halves. If odd parity was correctly calculated, the correct output combinations for the two pairs of outputs that occur on level 2 are either 10 or 01. Any single fault within the error-checking logic will cause the level 2 output combinations to become either 00 or 11. Both these states indicate that an error has occurred in the check logic. The final stage combines the two output signals from level 2 to generate an error signal. In the figure, the checker is implemented such that correct parity is odd parity. This means the final stage will produce an output of 1 if odd parity is generated; otherwise, it will produce an error signal of 0. A fault in the last stage may cause the output to be permanently stuck-at-1. When this happens further faults in the check logic will be masked and left undetected. An additional XOR gate is inserted in the left half of the parity tree to allow the behavior of the output gate to be validated through the application of a special TEST signal. This TEST signal could be supplied by a fault recognition program, in performing fault diagnosis.

7.7.2 Procedure for Checking a Match Circuit

In the error-checking scheme that requires that the unit to be checked be duplicated and a match of the outputs be performed after each control operation involving the unit (this is also called the *duplication and match check mode*), the matcher is an important part of the checking logic. Figure 7-67 gives the logical implementation of a matcher constructed from XOR gates that performs a bit-by-bit comparison of two 16-bit data words. When the two inputs to the XOR gate are the same ($a_i = b_i = 0$ or $a_i = b_i = 1$), the output of the XOR gate is 0; this represents the match condition. When the two inputs to the XOR gate are not the same ($a_i = 1$, $b_i = 0$ or $a_i = 0$, $b_i = 1$), the output of the XOR gate is a 1. This logical 1 is propagated to the output OR gate as an error condition. For the two 16-bit data words shown in Figure 7-67, unless the words match on an individual bit basis (i.e., $a_i = b_i$), the output OR gate will indicate an error.

The difficulty with this checking arrangement is that many of the logic faults that occur within the matcher will *not* be exposed using any self-testing schemes. For example, if any of the XOR gates are stuck with their outputs in the 0 state, the faults will not be detected. To ensure that the matcher is working properly, it must be periodically tested using test input combinations in such a manner that the error conditions may be *recognized*. This means that the inputs must be varied on a bit-by-bit basis to generate the

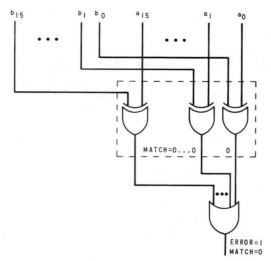

Figure 7-67   Matcher with XOR Gates

error (mismatch) states 01 and 10; this procedure ensures that any single-bit mismatch will cause an error signal.

A self-checking match circuit that compares two binary data words can be designed using the m-out-of-$2m$ check circuit described in Sec. 7.4.10. This is done by complementing one of the input data words. A double-length data word is then formed by appending the complemented code word to the original code word. This concatenation forms a new code word which is an m-out-of-$2m$ code word since a code word concatenated with its complement will yield a new code word with half of its bits in the 1s state and the other half of its bits in the 0s state. As an example, consider the following 16-bit data word:

$$1001111010001010$$

To form a 16-out-of-32-bit code word, the complement of the 16-bit data word must be generated and concatenated with the 16-bit data word. The 16-out-of-32 code word for this data word is give by

Original 16-bit data word   Complement of 16-bit data word

Figure 7-68 shows the two input data words (the A inputs are complemented by inverters) fed into a 16-out-of-32 checker. The outputs from the checker (f_{16}, g_{16}) will either be 10 or 01 if exactly 16 of the 32 inputs are in the 1s state; otherwise, the outputs will be 00 (when there are *more* than 16 inputs in the 1s state) or 11 (when there are *less* than 16 inputs in the 1s state.

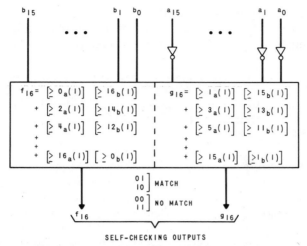

Figure 7-68 Self-Checking Matcher Using 16-out-of-32 Checker

7.8 SOME HARDWARE CHECKS FOR SOFTWARE BUGS

7.8.1 Handling Program Bugs

Aside from hardware faults, program faults (bugs) can also cause errors in the system. However, program bugs may be much more difficult to handle than hardware faults, particularly when seldom-used branches in a program are executed or when the data relevant to a program is mutilated in a subtle and nonobvious manner. Hardware-checking procedures, such as those discussed in the previous sections, are designed specifically to detect physical circuit faults in the ALU, the data path(s), or the control section. In general, hardware error checks will not be capable of detecting software faults. Even when two processors are running in synchronism and are matched for error detection, the same bug may appear in the program executing in the on-line machine *and* in the copy of the program executing in the standby machine and may therefore go undetected. In real-time applications, it is desirable to recognize software bugs *as rapidly as possible* and then take the necessary corrective action to remove the bug from the system. Although the program fault cannot be corrected immediately, restarting the program at a prescribed location (check point) and reinitializing some of the system data are usually sufficient to temporarily correct the difficulty in the software.

7.8.2 Use of a Watchdog Timer

In a computer, the operating system normally oversees and coordinates the activities of the system. For some applications, such as the control of a telephone office, the operating system is cyclic in nature; that is, the operating system program always returns to its basic starting point upon completion of the scheduled tasks. For this discussion, a task may be regarded as an executable module of code that has the following properties:

1. A system name (task-ID) that is created in the operating system data tables.
2. A priority number which is used by the operating system scheduler program.
3. Various additional pieces of linkage information that allow a task to execute under the operating system and communicate with other tasks that also exist under the operating system.

The main program is normally exercised and debugged to a high degree before it is integrated into a system load. In many cases, however, every alternate path in the program has *not* been exhaustively checked out under all possible operating conditions. Consequently, some of the less traversed branches of the main program may contain subtle logic faults which would sidetrack the main flow of execution and never permit the execution sequence to return to the main program. This situation, of course, could be due to undetected hardware faults as well as program bugs.

A hardware timer is used in Bell System Electronic Switching Systems to guard against program faults from which the system cannot recover. The concept is relatively simple: A hardware timer is run continuously in the processor; the timer is periodically reset by the main program if nothing unusual occurs to deflect the main program from its normal execution sequence. If for some reason (such as a software bug or a hardware fault) the execution sequence never returns to the main program, the timer will *not* be reset. The hardware timer will issue a high-priority interrupt request since it was not reset within a prescribed time interval and will take the necessary action to reinitialize the system. The interrupt will direct execution to begin at a preestablished point in the main program. This is sometimes called a *checkpoint.* When a hot-standby processor is provided in the system, the timer interrupt may automatically cause control to switch to the standby machine in an attempt to recover from the system error.

Although the operation of a hardware timer is quite simple to implement in most processors, the actual function of the timer must be *carefully integrated* with the software structure of the system to provide adequate safeguards in generating timer reset signals. The hardware timer must be reset *only* when the system is performing properly; otherwise, the timer should be allowed to request a reinitialization. For example, the system control program (main program) may take the path of a large circle, as shown in Figure 7-69. The time required to complete one complete cycle may vary depending on the number of tasks active on the system and the length of time each task is given to execute. The timer is initialized to the maximum cycle time required by all the tasks currently defined as active on the system. To ensure

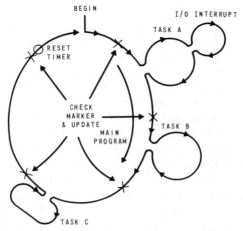

Figure 7-69   Safeguard (or Watchdog) Timer Operation

that the main program cycles through all program segments and/or tasks correctly, a record may be kept in memory of those segments which have been executed.   This record is sometimes called a *marker;* as the main program proceeds along the main cycle, the marker is updated at several preselected points in the cycle.   Figure 7-69 marks the locations in the main program cycle with *X*s where the markers are updated.   If the marker information does not appear to be correct to the main program, the main program may call in a maintenance program in an attempt to diagnose the behavior of the system; if a duplicate processor (hot standby) exists, the maintenance program may switch the hot-standby unit in to replace the faulty on-line machine.   An appropriately placed marker ensures that the main program cycles through the system operation correctly *before* any timer resets can be generated.   Whenever the program wanders off its prescribed path as a result of a software bug or hardware fault, the timer will not receive its periodic reset signal.   Instead, the timer will generate an interrupt request in an attempt to bring the system back into a sane and viable working mode.

7.8.3   Branch-Allowed Check Bit in Program Execution

It is unlikely that software bugs will appear in program modules which consist of consecutive lines of source code that do not involve any branch macroinstructions.   The address assignments for the individual macroinstructions and the location of each data element are assigned automatically by the assembler with virtually no manual specification of the absolute values of the addresses coming from the programmer.

   If a branch macroinstruction is given in the source program, the target location is normally specified by the programmer; in some instances, the determination of the effective address of the target location can involve complex address calculations which are dependent on the peculiarities of the architecture of the host machine. Software errors still occur in "exhaustively" debugged program modules—often because an improper branch operation was performed. Again, this type of software error is very difficult to detect and to isolate once the error has been detected.

A means of detecting the execution of an improper branching operation was implemented on several of the Bell System Electronic Switching Systems. Figure 7-70 illustrates this scheme. A check bit, called a *branch-allowed* (BA) *bit,* is assigned to each word in main memory. If the BA bit contains a 0, the contents of that location in main memory may *not* be referenced by any branch instruction; the location, however, may be referenced by the PC in its normal sequential addressing mode in which the PC is incremented by 1 to point to the location of the next macroinstruction. If the BA bit contains a 1, the contents of that location may be referenced by *any* branch instruction located anywhere in main memory. If a branch instruction is being executed in a normal program sequence, the BA bit of the target location will be checked to see if a branching operation may reference the contents of the target location. If the BA bit is in the 0 state, an improper branch has been executed, and the BA checking logic will indicate that an error has occurred.

In addition to recognizing the branch-allowed error, the address in the program sequence at which the improper branch macroinstruction occurred is *exceptionally useful* in identifying the cause of the branching error. Whenever a branch operation is executed, the address of the location in main storage which contains the branch instruction can be stored in a dedi-

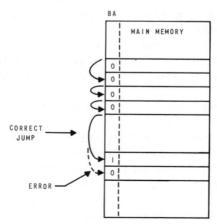

Figure 7-70 Branch-Allowed Check

cated processor register. The additional control steps required to save the address of the branch instruction can be executed while the processor is waiting for the next macroinstruction to be fetched from main storage. If an improper branch has been taken in the normal program execution sequence, the address of the last macroinstruction which causes a branch operation to be executed and the address of the current macroinstruction being executed are available for analysis. These addresses are valuable aids in debugging the currently executing program.

The probability of detecting branch-allowed errors is determined by the distribution of the number of BA bits in the 1s state and the number of BA bits in the 0s state. If 20 percent of the BA bits are in the 1s state and 80 percent are in the 0s state, the probability that an improper branch occurred in the program and was detected would be $P = 0.8$. If the distribution of the number of 1s and 0s is reversed (that is, 80 percent of the BA bits are in the 1s state and 20 percent of the BA bits are in the 0s state), the probability of detecting a branch-allowed error becomes $P = 0.2$. In this case, the use of a BA bit may *not* be cost-effective.

7.8.4 Different Parity Check for Macroinstructions and Data Words

Both macroinstructions and data words are stored in main memory. It is possible that as a result of a software bug or a hardware fault a macroinstruction FETCH may be directed to the location of a data word or vice versa. Obviously, the execution of a data word as a macroinstruction would result in some highly unpredictable program sequences.

If a parity-check bit is assigned to each location in main storage, the parity bit can be used to distinguish between a macroinstruction and a data word. This can be done by assigning odd parity, for example, to a macroinstruction and even parity to a data word. Figure 7-71 shows a layout of main storage consisting of blocks of macroinstructions and blocks of data words in which this parity convention has been observed. These blocks may be interleaved in any manner, including alternating the contents of adjacent main memory locations in the following order: macroinstruction, data word, macroinstruction, data word, and so on. The parity-check scheme is still valid. Since the processor control logic contains the information, implicitly, that the main memory FETCH operation is either for data or for a macroinstruction, it is the control logic that performs the even- or odd-parity check on the information received from main storage.

The parity-checking logic used on data words and macroinstructions overlaps, to a certain extent, the errors introduced into the execution of a program because of errors in the effective address calculations. The usage of a branch-allowed bit, odd parity over macroinstructions, and even parity

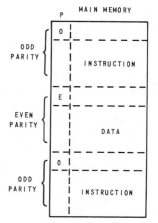

Figure 7-71   Different Parity Check for Macroinstructions and Data Words

over data would detect any software errors that would cause the program to execute in an improper branch operation.   It is quite difficult to anticipate the type of software bugs one might expect in a well-debugged system. Many software errors are highly data-dependent; they occur very infrequently and under abnormal operating conditions.   Therefore, these software errors are *not* caught when standard program debugging procedures are used. These software errors represent the most difficult types of faults to isolate. A primary objective in the use of the BA bit and complementary parity for data words and macroinstructions is to provide the processor with an *early* detection mechanism for these software bugs so that the source(s) of these bugs can be isolated and corrected.

7.9   SUMMARY

The detection of faults is critical to the design of logic circuits that will both function correctly over long periods of time and be easily serviceable when a fault does occur because the fault is quickly identified.   A basic approach to detecting errors (faults) quickly is to use some form of an error detection code.   The simplest form of an error detection code is the use of a single parity-check bit; the parity bit is appended to the data word so that the number of bits in the 1s state in the data word plus the check bit is an odd (even) number. Another error detection code is a residue code, also called a separable code, because the data portion of the code word is kept separated from the check bits associated with the code word.   The major characteristic of residue codes is that they are preserved under arithmetic operations.   A third error detection code is called the fixed-weight or *m*-out-of-*n* code. The fixed weight codes are nonseparable codes with a legitimate code word containing *exactly* *m* bits in the 1s state.

To adequately check the processor for the occurrence of errors, various portions of the processor must be checked independently. The major portions of the processor that must perform independent fault detection are (1) the data transfer paths, (2) the control signal paths, (3) the sequencing of the microcontrol unit, (4) the arithmetic and logic unit (ALU), and (5) the macroinstruction-to-microinstruction interface.

The data transfer paths may be checked using a single parity bit for the data word. Separate checks may be performed on the data word using a parity bit and a 1-active-out-of-*n* decoder for the control signals. This means if more than one decoder output is active at the same time, the hardware will recognize the multiple outputs as a control signal error. Data transfers may be checked for errors by repeating the operation (this is also called an echo check operation), and a separate parity checker may be associated with the internal data bus of the processor so that the parity of the data word being transferred can be checked on the fly as the data word is gated onto the data bus from an internal processor register.

Control signals may be treated in the same manner as data words. In general, however, control signals are encoded such that a decoder output will produce a 1-active-out-of-*n* signal when the control logic is functioning properly. For many logic faults—including those which occur in the control section of a processor—the data appears to undergo unidirectional errors. Such errors occur when *all* the bits in error in a data word appear to undergo either a $0 \leftarrow 1$ transition or a $1 \leftarrow 0$ transition. The class of error-detecting codes called *m*-out-of-*n* codes has the property of being able to detect all unidirectional errors which can occur in a code word. Such *m*-out-of-*n* codes are used to check the behavior of control signal decoders.

The primary reasons for checking the microcontrol logic for improper behavior are (1) to ensure the proper microinstruction-to-microinstruction sequencing, (2) to validate the control word fetched from control store, (3) to check for the proper translation of the individual control fields in a microinstruction, and (4) to ensure that the macroinstruction opcode selects the correct sequence of microinstructions (microprogram) so that the macroinstruction is properly executed. Typically, *m*-out-of-*n* codes are used to check the control field translations, while parity-check bits over the address of the current microinstruction and over the next address field in the microinstruction are used to check the sequencing of the microcontrol unit which governs what microinstruction is executed after the current microinstruction. Checking is performed on the macroinstruction as it is gated into the IR to ensure that the opcode is correct before the interpretive microprogram is initiated by the opcode. A microprogram mode bit may be used in which the executive control program or the craftsperson may select which one of two versions of the interpretive microprogram is to be executed: a fast, high-throughput version with no error detection capability or a much slower version that performs elaborate fault checks on each microcontrol step.

Parity prediction may be used to check for the correct operation of a binary counter, a ripple-carry adder, and a group look-ahead carry adder. Other logic circuits may also use parity prediction to check for errors during the execution of each microcontrol step. In particular, checking the performance of the arithmetic and logic unit (ALU) can be quite difficult. An effective approach to checking the ALU is to use a duplicate ALU and match the outputs of the two units after each ALU operation. This approach appears to be much simpler and more cost-effective than designing an elaborate ALU with built-in fault detection logic since the latter approach requires a special LSI development.

Program faults or software bugs often have all the appearances of hardware faults. In fact, it is often impossible to distinguish between the two fault categories. A watchdog timer is typically used to prevent a program from branching into a segment of code from which no return to the main program is ever made. To protect against improper program branches being taken by the execution sequence, a branch-allowed bit can be assigned to every location in main storage. If the BA bit is set, any branch instruction located anywhere in main storage is permitted to branch to that particular location. If the BA bit is reset, only the normal increment-by-1 operation of the program counter is allowed to reference that location. Finally, separate and different parity checks may be used for macroinstructions and data words. In this case, the control sequence can immediately determine if it is about to execute a data word as a macroinstruction which would be a macroexecution sequence error.

7.10 REFERENCES

1. D. A. ANDERSON, "Design of Self-checking Digital Networks Using Coding Techniques," Ph.D. thesis. Urbana, Ill.: University of Illinois, 1971.

2. D. A. ANDERSON and G. METZE, "Design of Totally Self-Checking Check Circuits for m-out-of-n Codes," *IEEE Trans. Comput.*, C-22, No. 3 (March 1973), 263–268.

3. A. AVIZIENIS, "Arithmetic Error Codes: Cost and Effectiveness Studies for Application in Digital System Design," *IEEE Trans. Comput.*, C-20 (Nov. 1971), 1322–1330.

4. A. AVIZIENIS, "Fault-Tolerant Computing—An Overview," *Computer* (Jan.–Feb. 1971), 5–8.

5. E. R. BERLEKAMP, *Algebraic Coding Theory* (New York: McGraw-Hill, 1968).

6. H. J. BEUSCHER, G. E. FESSLER, D. W. HUFFMAN, P. J. KENNEDY, and E. NUSSBAUM, "Administration and Maintenance Plan," *Bell Syst. Tech. J.*, 48 (Oct. 1969), 2765–2816.

7. H. J. BEUSCHER and W. N. TOY, "Check Schemes for Integrated Microprogrammed Control and Data Transfer Circuitry," *IEEE Trans. Comput.*, C-19 (Dec. 1970), 1153–1159.

8. W. G. Bouricius, W. C. Carter, D. C. Jessep, P. R. Schneider and A. B. Wadia, "Algorithms for Detection of Faults in Logic Circuits," *IEEE Trans. Comput., C-20,* No. 11 (Nov. 1971), 1258–1264.

9. T. E. Browne, T. M. Quinn, W. N. Toy, and J. E. Yates, "No. 2 ESS Control Unit System," *Bell Syst. Tech. J., 48* (Oct. 1968), 2619–2668.

10. W. C. Carter, "A Survey of Fault Tolerant Computer Architecture and Its Evaluation," *Computer* (Jan.–Feb. 1971), 9–16.

11. W. C. Carter, "Theory and Use of Checking Circuits," in *Computer System Reliability* (Maidenhead, England: Infotech Information, Ltd., 1974), 413–454.

12. W. C. Carter, K. A. Duke, and D. C. Jesse, "A Simple Self-Testing Decoder Checking Circuit," *IEEE Trans. Comput., C-20* (Nov. 1971), 1300–1305.

13. W. C. Carter, G. R. Putzolu, A. B. Wadia, W. G. Bouricius, D. C. Jessep, E. P. Hsieh and C. J. Tan, "Cost Effectiveness of Self-Checking Computer Design," *Proc. FTCS, 7* (June 1977), 117–123.

14. W. C. Carter and P. R. Schneider, "Design of Dynamically Checked Computers," *IFIP, 2* (Aug. 1968), 878–883.

15. H. Y. Chang, R. C. Dorr, and D. J. Senese, "The Design of a Microprogrammed Self-Checking Processor of an Electronic Switching System," *IEEE Trans. Comput., C-22,* No. 5 (May 1973), 489–500.

16. H. Y. Chang, G. W. Heimbigner, D. J. Senese, and T. L. Smith, "Maintenance Techniques of a Microprogrammed Self-Checking Control Complex of an Electronic Switching System," *IEEE Trans. Comput., C-22,* No. 5 (May 1973), 501–512.

17. R. W. Cook, W. H. Sisson, T. F. Storey, and W. N. Toy, "Design of a Self-Checking Microprogram Control," *IEEE Trans. Comput., 22* (March 1973), 255–262.

18. J. A. Harr, F. F. Taylor, and W. Ulrich, "Organization of No. 1 ESS Central Processor," *Bell Syst. Tech. J., 43* (Sept. 1964), 1961–2020.

19. G. G. Langdon and C. K. Tang, "Concurrent Error Detection for Group Look-Ahead Binary Adders," *IBM J. Res. Dev., 14* (Sept. 1970), 563–573.

20. S. Lin, *Introduction to Error Correcting Codes* (Englewood Cliffs, N.J.: Prentice-Hall, 1970).

21. E. F. Moore, and C. E. Shannon, "Reliable Circuits Using Less Reliable Relays," *J. Franklin Inst., 262* (Oct. 1956), 281–297.

22. W. W. Peterson, *Error Correcting Codes* (Cambridge, Mass.: M.I.T. Press, 1961).

23. W. W. Peterson, "On Checking an Adder," *IBM J. Res. Dev., 2* (April 1958), 166–168.

24. F. F. Seller, Jr., M. Y. Hsiao, and L. W. Bearson, *Error Detection Logic for Digital Computers* (New York: McGraw-Hill, 1968).

25. R. A. Short, "The Attainment of Reliable Digital Systems through the Use of Redundancy— A Survey," *Comput. Group News* (March 1968), 2–17.

26. S. Y. H. Su and R. J. Spillman, "An Overview of Fault-Tolerant Digital System Architecture," *AFIPS Conf. Proc., 46* (1977), 19–26.

27. W. N. Toy, "A Novel Parallel Binary Counter Design with Parity Prediction and Error Detection Scheme," *IEEE Trans. Comput., C-20* (Jan. 1971), 44–48.

28. W. N. Toy, "Modular LSI Control Logic Design with Error Detection," *IEEE Trans. Comput., 20* (Feb. 1971), 161–166.

29. J. G. TRYON, R. H. WILCOX, and W. C. MANN, *Redundancy Techniques for Computing System* (New York: Spartan, 1962).

30. F. S. VIGILANTE, "Detection of Erroneous Data Processing Transfers," U.S. Patent No. 3,283,307, issued Nov. 1, 1966.

31. J. VON NEUMANN, C. E. SHANNON, and J. MCCARTHY, *Probabilistic Logics and Synthesis of Reliable Organisms from Unreliable Components, Automata Studies* (Princeton, N.J.: Princeton University Press, 1950).

32. J. F. WAKERLY, "Low-Cost Error Detection Techniques for Small Computers," Ph.D. thesis. Stanford, Calif.: Stanford University, 1974.

33. J. F. WAKERLY, "Microcomputer Reliability Improvement Using Triple-Modular Redundancy," *Proc. IEEE, 64,* No. 6 (June 1976), 889–895.

34. J. F. WAKERLY, "Partially Self-Checking Circuits and Their Use in Performing Logical Operations," *IEEE Trans. Comput., C-23,* No. 7 (July 1974), 658–666.

35. S. WINOGRAD, "Coding for Logical Operation," *IBM J. Res. Dev., 6* (Oct. 1962), 430–436.

CHAPTER 8

Fault Diagnosis

8.1 FAULT DIAGNOSIS CONCEPTS

Fault detection determines whether or not a circuit is behaving correctly; *fault diagnosis* localizes or pinpoints the failure to a replaceable unit. The *replaceable unit* may be a component, a circuit, or a subsystem. The fault diagnosis routine utilizes fault detection hardware and test sequences to facilitate the task of locating the defective unit. When the replaceable unit is the logical entity indicating the detected fault, no other diagnostic action may be required since the fault may be corrected by the simple replacement of the bad unit. However, if the detection circuit or diagnostic routine must examine a number of replaceable units, the fault diagnosis routine may be called in to further isolate the offending unit.

In a duplex arrangement, as in the case of the Bell System's No. 2 ESS for real-time control of telephone systems, the *central control* (CC) is duplicated and normally running in synchronism. Both CCs are matched at the maintenance center for fault detection purposes. The mismatch condition indicates that an error has occurred. When a mismatch occurs, it is *not* known which CC has taken a fault. The diagnostic routine must be run at this point to attempt to identify the faulty CC. The diagnostic routine is divided into two parts. The first part, which is the more urgent and essential task, is to determine quickly which CC contains the fault. The quick identification of the faulty processor allows the system to recover with a minimum disturbance. Tests are run by the diagnostic in a sequence that examines as much circuitry as possible as quickly as possible. These *quick tests* can be performed rapidly since the fault resolution of the diagnostic is the CC itself and *not* one of its interior logic circuits. Once the faulty CC has been identified and switched to the off-line state (i.e., the unit is no longer involved in real-time control operations—its healthy duplicate has taken on the processing responsibilities), the requirement that must be met by the diagnostic in terms of real time is relaxed considerably. For example, if the on-line CC is determined to contain the fault, the system would reconfigure itself by switching the standby CC to the on-line state and placing the former on-line CC in the off-line state. However, while the real-time response requirement of the diagnostic has been reduced, the fault resolution of the diagnostic has been increased a great deal so that the diagnostic may isolate a fault to one or a few replaceable units such as a circuit board. The second part of the diagnostic routine makes use of *off-line diagnostics* as opposed to CC quick tests. Typically, off-line diagnostics may be stored in low-cost bulk memory units (i.e., tapes or disks) and brought into main memory when the need arises.

If the CCs are designed to be self-checking in a duplex system, the two processors do not have to be run in the synchronous match mode for fault detection to be performed. The hardware check circuitry both detects a fault and identifies the defective unit down to the circuit board level. On-line diagnostics, in this case, are not necessary to determine which one of the two CCs contains the fault. The self-checking hardware provides the diagnostic information without further testing.

The modern packaging technique of using MSI and LSI* circuits to implement both memories and processors has encouraged the use of large-size circuit boards to house the associated electronics. If the standard repair procedure to be observed by a craftsperson when a fault occurs is the *replacement* of the circuit board containing the fault, fault resolution is considerably simplified. First, a processor is typically implemented on one or two large-size circuit boards. If a fault occurs and is isolated to one of the two processor boards, repair by replacement is a quick, simple, and highly cost-effective approach to servicing the faulty unit. The cost of replacing an entire circuit board is justified when the advantages of (1) a faster repair time for the

---

* MSI, medium-scale integration; LSI, large-scale integration.

faulty unit and (2) the cost savings of not having to develop additional fault diagnosis hardware and software are considered.

When the *detailed* fault resolution requirement is relaxed because of the use of large-size boards in the processor's implementation, a basic problem still exists. Namely, after the faulty unit has been repaired by replacement of the faulty board(s), the integrity of the replacement unit must also be verified to establish that the replacement unit does not also possess a fault. It is necessary for the complete system, including the replacement unit, to be exercised exhaustively to ensure that the difficulty has been corrected. This may often amount to a complete diagnostic test sequence being applied to the repaired system. Even though additional logic is incorporated in the processor hardware to act as an aid in detecting faults and isolating the faults to a specific unit in the processor, a complete evaluation of the hardware by the processor diagnostic program is still required for error-free logic verification of the system.

A logic circuit is tested through the use of a diagnostic either to verify the logical integrity of the circuit (i.e., it performs its prescribed logical function under all possible sequences of inputs) or to detect any fault that may be present in the circuit. A diagnostic test that detects a specific fault corresponds to a combination of input signals that cause an incorrect output from the logic circuit if the fault is present. Any nonredundant logic circuit with n inputs can be completely tested by applying all 2^n possible input combinations to the circuit. As n becomes large, this procedure becomes very inefficient. By examining the physical behavior of the circuit, a smaller set of tests may often be identified which will be *sufficient* to detect all faults that are *likely* to occur.

For example, the input combinations required to completely check out a three-input AND gate is shown in Figure 8-1. The classical faults associated

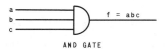

AND GATE

INPUT			OUTPUT	FAULTS								OUTPUT
a	b	c	f	a S-a		b S-a		c S-a		f S-a		f
				0	1	0	1	0	1	0	1	
1	1	1	1	✓		✓		✓		✓		0
0	1	1	0		✓						✓	1
1	0	1	0				✓				✓	1
1	1	0	0						✓		✓	1

Figure 8-1 Input Combinations Required for Checking AND Gate

with a logic gate are the stuck-at-1 and stuck-at-0 faults for each of the inputs and the output. In general, there are 2 $(n + 1)$ possible faults for an *n*-input gate, and $n + 1$ input combinations are required to detect these faults. As indicated in Figure 8-1, the all-1s input will detect any input or output stuck-at-0 faults. The other input combinations check each input's ability to cause the output to change to the opposite state. For an OR gate, the set of input combinations are the *complement* of those for checking the AND gate.

A logic circuit such as an arithmetic unit is made up of logic gates interconnected in a specified manner so that the desired logic functions are realized. The complete circuit can be verified by applying an input sequence that permits the inputs and the output of *each* gate to assume states required to completely check the fault-free operation of the gate. Many of the internal gates are not directly influenced by variations in the input signals and the output. The control of the inputs and the observation of the output must therefore be done indirectly. This indirect evaluation involves examination of logic signals in the logic chain from the input leads through the entire logic chain to the output lead. For example, to check gate X in the circuit shown in Figure 8-2, the three input combinations must be generated by appropriately setting the other inputs in the circuit. The output of gate X is allowed to propagate to the output OR gate for observation. To do this, the other input to the output OR gate must be held in the 0 state. The input combinations check the behavior of gate X completely; they also check faults along the logic gating chain shown in Figure 8-2 from the input signals to the output of the final OR gate.

Test generation for digital logic circuits has been studied extensively since the mid-1960s. The objective of these studies has been to develop a systematic procedure that will allow a designer to derive a set of tests that

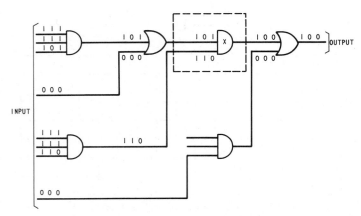

Figure 8-2   Test Inputs Required to Check Gate X

will expose *all* possible faults in a logic circuit. The basic philosophy observed by such test sequence designers has been to apply an input sequence (test vectors) to a specific logic circuit that will cause the output(s) to differ from that of a normal, fault-free condition. The identification of the appropriate test sequences for a complex LSI logic circuit can be a highly laborious procedure—even with the use of sophisticated computer programs. There are essentially four techniques that have been used extensively: the path sensitizing technique, the *D*-algorithm technique, the Boolean difference technique, and Poage's technique. These procedures have been described in considerable detail in several excellent references.*

One of the more important aspects of diagnostic design, especially in the early planning stage, is the specification of features to be incorporated in the hardware (test points, observation points, private control ports) that the diagnostic can use to evaluate the hardware. These features must be specified during the hardware design phase by *both* the logic designer and the diagnostic programmer working together. The following sections cover some of the techniques used to provide control facilities and access ports for diagnostics to be used on specific logic circuits as well as systems.

8.1.1 Fault Diagnosis Starting with the Processor Hardcore

A commonly used procedure in performing fault diagnosis is based upon the bootstrap approach. A small portion of the computer, referred to as the *hardcore,* must be established as functioning correctly before the diagnostic test procedure is initiated. One of two philosophies may be observed in establishing the integrity of the hardcore portion of the processor. The designer may implement the hardcore using sufficiently reliable components that the diagnostic may assume the hardcore is fault-free and can immediately proceed to examine the rest of the system. This, in general, is a very *poor* assumption since it may be assumed that all electronic equipment will fail at sometime during its functional life. The alternative and more realistic philosophy is to require that the hardcore must *first* be validated either by manual intervention or, automatically, by an independent processor that may peer into the operational internal logic of the hardcore. The bootstrap approach of fault diagnosis starts from the point where the integrity of the hardcore has been ensured. The bootstrap approach involves using the hardcore portion of the processor to start the diagnostic evaluation of another portion of the machine and to expand this validation process to the subsystem level as each successively larger level is found to be fault-free. The basic idea is to start evaluating a small section of the processor and to expand

---

* M. A. Breuer, and A. D. Friedman, *Diagnosis and Reliable Design of Digital Systems* (Woodland Hills, Calif.: Computer Science Press, 1976), and H. Y. Chang, E. G. Manning, and G. Metze, *Fault Diagnosis of Digital Systems* (New York: Wiley-Interscience, 1970).

the diagnostic process to include more and more hardware with each succeeding step until the entire machine has been completely tested.

In a simplex system, the use of a hardcore as the hub about which fault diagnosis begins in a processor is an undesirable approach. A simplex system will require the hardcore to be validated by a manual check; there is no backup processor in a simplex arrangement that would allow the hardcore to be automatically evaluated. The use of routine manual procedures to establish the integrity of a machine is not a *mature* system design since an automated recovery procedure would minimize errors introduced by manual mistakes. One of the objectives in system design for fault diagnosis is to *minimize* the amount of hardware in the hardcore while providing a mechanism to facilitate testing the hardcore. The clock circuitry in any processor structure should clearly be assigned to the hardcore, since without the clock signals the system would come to a complete halt. The complexity of the clock is dictated by the number of clock phases required to perform the basic machine cycle. A larger number of clock phases than usual implies that more functions can be carried out within a machine cycle and that the clock circuitry is more complex. For some of the simple microprocessors, a single clock phase is used to step the control sequence along serially. This keeps the clock circuitry as simple as possible but at the expense of using a single clock phase that does not permit concurrent control operations.

The bulk of the processor hardcore is made up of the control circuitry to access main storage, fetch the next macroinstruction, perform the opcode decoding, and then execute the macroinstruction. All these sections must be operational before the diagnostic program(s) can perform useful fault diagnosis. This *essential* operational section includes the portion of main memory which contains the diagnostic programs. Typically, the diagnostic programs are sufficiently large that they are *not* kept as resident code in main storage. Instead, a portion of main storage is built from writable RAM modules; the diagnostic programs are rolled into a paging buffer located in this area of main storage and are saved on a low-cost bulk storage peripheral device such as a 9-track magnetic tape unit or a floppy disk system. Under trouble (fault) conditions the diagnostic programs are paged into main storage to diagnose the trouble or to verify that the system is fully operational.

Figure 8-3 shows the functional diagram of a general diagnostic sequence expanding out to include more and more hardware for a conventionally designed processor. The various functional units as indicated in Figure 8-3 are not shown in proportion to their actual size. In a typical computer, the memory may make up a larger portion of the hardware. *The hardcore can be loosely defined as that part of the hardware that must be functioning correctly in order to initiate any diagnostic functions.* As shown in the figure, the hardcore includes nearly the entire processor when the diagnostic programs are stored off-line in a tape unit.

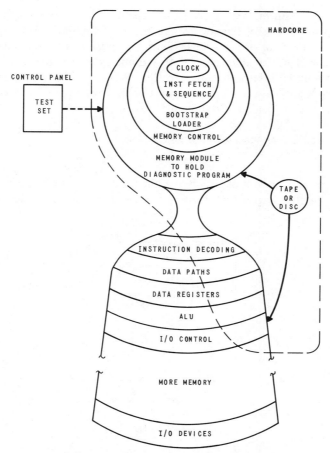

Figure 8-3 Hardcore Diagnosis with Off-Line Diagnostic

When a fault is detected in a simplex system, the simplest and most practical response is for the system to come to a halt and wait to be repaired and returned to the operational state. Testing is usually initiated manually through a test set or the control panel, allowing the maintenance person to "step through" the validation of the integrity of the hardcore. This procedure typically involves manually loading a simple bootstrap loader program into main memory. The bootstrap program will normally contain only a few macroinstructions; otherwise, manually loading the program macroinstruction by macroinstruction through the switches on the control panel would be a tedious *and* highly error-prone job for the craftsperson. The probability of manually inputting a large program into main memory correctly would be quite small. Therefore, a loader program is used to load the diagnostic program into main memory from paper tape, disk, or 9-track magnetic tape. After this is done, the diagnostics can be run to pinpoint the fault in the system.   If the fault affects the bootstrap operation, the diagnostic, in all likelihood, will *not* be able to run.   If it *is* able to run under this condition, the result may be interpreted incorrectly.   When this happens, the maintenance person must use an external test set or the control panel to step through the hardcore and localize the difficulty.

8.1.2 Hardcore Diagnosis with Partial On-Line Diagnostic in ROM

To minimize the amount of circuitry in the hardcore portion of the processor, a portion of the diagnostic program can be stored in ROM and kept on-

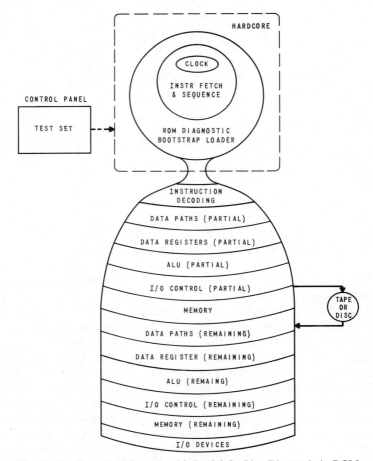

Figure 8-4   Hardcore Diagnosis with Partial On-Line Diagnostic in ROM

line to avoid the necessity of bootstrapping the diagnostics from an I/O device. The portion of the diagnostic placed in ROM should include code that exhaustively validates the circuitry required to transfer the remaining section of the diagnostic into the paging buffer in main storage. The procedure outlined in Figure 8-4 illustrates that the amount of hardware in the hardcore is reduced considerably using this approach since the bootstrap operation is removed from the hardcore validation. Instead, the diagnostic sequence placed in ROM contains the necessary code to check the data paths, registers, the ALU, I/O control, and the main memory modules. When the additional portion of the diagnostic has been rolled into the paging buffer in main storage, the data transfer is verified by the control software to be fault-free. The diagnostic can then be run, at this point, to check out the remaining portions of the processor that were *not* validated during the diagnostic evaluation of the hardcore. As shown in Figure 8-4, this validation is done systematically over all the remaining sections of the processor.

The reduction in the amount of hardware associated with the hardcore simplifies the manual actions that must be taken by a craftsperson to establish the integrity of the hardcore. Consequently, the maintenance person is used mainly to ensure that no unusual problems have occurred in the normal behavior of the hardcore so that the rest of the system can be reliably tested.

8.2 MICROPROGRAM DIAGNOSTICS

8.2.1 Microinstruction Diagnostic Test Points

In a microprogrammed machine, the microinstructions provide access to the individual microoperations or control primitives of the processor. These control primitives represent the *elementary* control signals of the machine. Consequently, if a sequence of microinstructions is used to selectively activate the control primitives, a more detailed evaluation of the hardware may be performed than an evaluation generated by executing a sequence of macroinstructions. For example, in many vertically microprogrammed machines, the basic microinstruction is essentially a data transfer operation from a source register to a destination register. A test sequence (diagnostic) written in microcode can be directed to check the individual hardware control steps. A macroinstruction sequence would be incapable of checking the result at each microstep.

The use of a diagnostic written in microcode can be enhanced further by providing test points in the hardware and along each logic path so that a logic signal may be monitored by the microinstruction sequence as the logic signal propagates through the logic network. Such observation points provide a more efficient means of testing a logic circuit when it is necessary to diagnose the circuit.

To achieve accessibility and controllability of the internal hardware at the logic gate level, excellent fault isolation can be achieved with microprogram diagnostic routines. In a machine with built-in fault detection hardware, microdiagnostics are, in general, much more efficient than diagnostic programs written in macroinstructions. The error indication signals from the detection hardware which may be controlled by a microinstruction provide direct diagnostic information. A microdiagnostic sequence does not need to compare the results of each control operation and analyze internal test points for the occurrence of proper outputs. The microdiagnostic program needs only to interpret the error signal(s) from the detection circuits.

8.2.2 Fault Diagnosis Using Diagnostic Microprograms

The hardcore portion of the processor whose integrity *must* be established before any meaningful fault diagnosis may be performed may be reduced considerably through the use of resident diagnostics written in microcode and stored in the control ROM as part of the microprogram control section. The two units that must be included in the hardcore portion of the processor are the clock generation logic and the microprogram control section. If either unit does not function properly, the microdiagnostics cannot be executed. In a microprogrammed machine, much of the complex sequencing and timing signals of a control section implemented using random logic are replaced by a sequence of microinstructions. This hardware arrangement greatly simplifies the sequencing and timing logic, which results in less control circuitry being included in the hardcore. This accounts for the reduction in the size of the hardcore.

Different types of hardware fault detection checks have been discussed in Chapter 7. It is assumed in all these checking schemes that errors will be caught concurrently with the normal operation of the system; in most instances, the errors will *not* proliferate and contaminate the system before they are detected by the hardware-checking logic. The exact amount of time that may elapse between the occurrence of a fault and its detection is a function of the technique used to detect occurrences of errors: self-checking hardware or scheduled applications of test programs. In general, a combination of the two techniques should be used with the programmed test sequences either stored as resident object code in main memory or as microcode in the microprogram control store. For the purpose of reasonably quick error detection, the fault detection programs are usually stored on-line to facilitate the periodic validation of the system.

From the viewpoint of the overall diagnostic structure, it may not be desirable to store all the diagnostic programs in ROM, particularly when a diagnostic program is relatively large. The previous sections have emphasized the reduction in the amount of hardware associated with the processor hard-core to facilitate the manual effort required to isolate a fault when diagnostics cannot be initiated. However, for small computer systems, even if the hard-core encompasses the entire processor, it involves only one or a few replaceable circuit boards. The major bulk of the hardware and also the less reliable portion of the system consists of the main memory, the I/O environment, and its associated peripheral devices. When self-checking circuitry is integrated into the processor design, the diagnostic microprograms do not need to reside on-line since, typically, they are called in to diagnose the fault under trouble conditions or verify the hardware after the suspected faulty module has been replaced. These checks occur over a much longer interval (weeks or months) than fault detection programs that are executed every so many milliseconds, depending on the application. Consequently, micro-diagnostics need not reside on-line occupying a dedicated area in control store. The microdiagnostics may be kept in an off-line ROM or rolled into a paging buffer in a *writable control store* (WCS).

8.2.3 Microdiagnostics Stored in Off-Line ROM

A maintenance person should normally be present to repair the defective unit when a system detects that a trouble condition exists (i.e., the system has begun to experience hard errors). In this case, the microdiagnostics can function as a tool for the maintenance person to assist in isolating the fault to a single, replaceable module in the system. Since the microdiagnostic is used, in this situation, only as a maintenance aid to be used only when the system has detected a hard fault, the microdiagnostic can be stored in a separate ROM module that does not have to be *permanently* incorporated as part of the control store. Instead, the microdiagnostic module may be kept on a shelf when it is *not* needed and interchanged with a specific ROM module that is normally part of the control store. In other words, the micro-diagnostic ROM module can be physically substituted for a regular ROM module by a maintenance person who will then run the microdiagnostics to locate the system fault.

This type of storage of the microdiagnostics, which might be called the use of an *off-line ROM* module, does *not* dedicate the microdiagnostic ROM module to a single machine. Instead, the maintenance person may carry the microdiagnostic ROM module to other sites to assist in diagnosing the individual machines at each of the sites. The usage of an off-line ROM to store the system microdiagnostics has all the virtues of placing the micro-diagnostics in on-line control storage but limits the amount of hardware associated with the hardcore portion of the processor. If the microdiagnostics require more memory than is available in a replaceable ROM module used in control store, the microdiagnostics may be partitioned into segments and each segment placed in a separate interchangeable ROM module. The maintenance person would then be required to execute each of these segments separately by interchanging the next microdiagnostic segment module with the module that had previously been executed on the processor.

8.2.4 Microdiagnostics Executed from Writable Control Store (WCS)

While the usage of an off-line ROM to store the microdiagnostic programs is attractive from a cost viewpoint, as well as from its simplicity of implementation, a more flexible approach is to execute the microdiagnostic(s) from a writable control store (WCS). The diagnostic tests can be stored on either inexpensive cassette tapes or floppy disks; the size of the WCS can range from 1K to 4K or more control memory locations. The diagnostic tests can be rolled into the WCS from the cassette unit or floppy disk as they are needed. The microdiagnostic would actually consist of a sequence of these tests executed one after the other to validate the integrity of the system. A large portion of the processor must be operational (i.e., the cassette unit or floppy disk controller plus the essential processor timing logic, decoding logic, and data transfer logic) before the microdiagnostics can be run. This requires that additional hardware be included in the processor hardcore portion that must be validated before the microdiagnostics can be executed. Basically, the additional hardware simply increases the repair action to replacing several circuit boards instead of one.

Figure 8-5 gives a functional description of the diagnostic structure of a system employing a WCS. The hardcore portion includes the hardware required to load the microdiagnostic segment into main storage from the bulk storage peripheral (i.e., the floppy disk or cassette units). The bootstrap loader for the bulk storage peripheral would normally be incorporated as an integral part of the ROM control store.

When a hard fault is detected, the microdiagnostic is loaded from the system device into WCS, and execution automatically begins in the first diagnostic test program.

The microdiagnostic programs are most effective in testing the internal logic of the processor. However, as other functional units (i.e., memory modules and I/O devices) are included in the system diagnostics, these units may be *most* effectively diagnosed using macroinstruction sequences rather than microinstruction sequences since the individual microinstructions normally relate to internal processor operations. To use main storage in the fault diagnosis programs, the portion of main storage associated with executing any *macrodiagnostics* (i.e, diagnostics written in assembly language and executed from main storage) must be checked by microdiagnostics prior to the macrodiagnostics being loaded and used to evaluate the remainder of

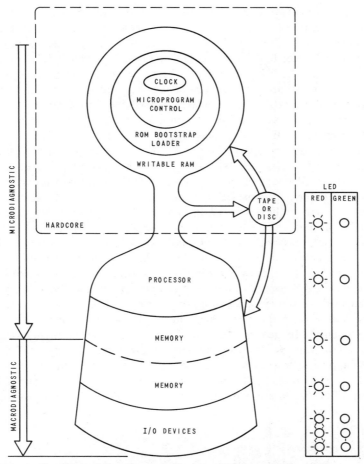

Figure 8-5   Microdiagnostic Structure of a System Using WCS

the system.   As indicated in Figure 8-5, the microdiagnostics cover the processor and part of the memory system, while the remaining memory modules and all the I/O devices are tested by macrodiagnostics.   It is possible to use microdiagnostic programs in conjunction with macrodiagnostics to exhaustively validate a digital system.

8.3   FAULT INDICATION

If hardware fault detection circuits are provided, the error signal from each fault detection circuit provides detailed diagnostic information by setting dedicated flip-flops within the processor.   These flip-flops, in turn, drive *trouble-indicating lights* that show where the faults are located in the system. If a sufficient number of fault detection (hardware check) circuits are used, the information supplied by the check circuits may be detailed enough to localize the suspected fault to one or a few replaceable circuit packs (modules). On the other hand, if the information supplied by the check circuits is *not* adequate, the application of the test sequences contained in the diagnostic procedure will *usually* indicate which replaceable unit contains the fault. Some means of conveying this information to a maintenance person is necessary if corrective action is to take place.   One of the simpler and more direct methods of displaying this information whould be through the use of *light-emitting diodes* (LEDs) mounted on the control panel or on each replaceable circuit board or on both units.   The additional supporting logic circuitry to implement this LED display is quite small.   In addition, the diagnostic data from the dedicated flip-flops can be supplied as output information to be printed on a line printer or teletypewriter.   In the latter case, even if the output devices are not functioning, the LED display will still provide information on the fault condition detected in the system.

Figure 8-5 shows how the diagnostic testing procedure systematically expands outward from the processor hardcore to validate the entire system. The packaging of the system can be organized on a functional unit basis so that the failure of a diagnostic test can be closely associated with a single functional unit.   In general, diagnostic resolution can be highly refined if each functional unit is also a replaceable circuit pack.   Figure 8-6 illustrates a simple approach toward indicating the status of a replaceable circuit pack or module; each replaceable module is provided with a set of two LEDs (one red LED and one green LED).   LEDs may also be grouped together

Figure 8-6   Circuit Pack with LED Indicators

and mounted on a common control panel. Under normal operating conditions, both LEDs on each replaceable module are extinguished. When the diagnostic for the system is manually initiated by a craftsperson pushing a button on the control panel, all the red LEDs are turned on, while all the green LEDs remain in the extinguished or unlit state. The first pair of LEDs shown on the control panel are assigned to the hardcore portion of the processor. A microdiagnostic program initiated by the craftsperson is used to exhaustively validate the hardcore. If the hardcore successfully passes all the microdiagnostic tests so that the hardcore appears to be functioning correctly, the microdiagnostic extinguishes the first red LED on the control panel and lights the corresponding green LED of the pair. The lighting of the green LED is basically a *redundant* action taken by the microdiagnostic since the act of extinguishing the red LED implies the same information. The act of lighting the green LED merely reaffirms the positive action of the microdiagnostic—in this case, that the integrity of the hardcore has been validated by the microdiagnostic. The fault diagnostic procedure then proceeds to evaluate each of the replaceable modules in a preassigned order. As each module successfully passes all the diagnostic tests associated with it, the corresponding red LED is extinguished, and its green LED mate is lit. When the diagnostic procedure detects a fault, the currently executing diagnostic halts all further processor activity; the red LED associated with the faulty module will be lit. It will be the *first* red LED remaining lit in the front panel display; its associated green LED will not be lit. The craftsperson may immediately ascertain (by visual examination of the front panel LED display) which replaceable module is faulty. The replacement of the suspected faulty module should be followed by a reapplication of the diagnostic to verify that the fault has been corrected. If the fault condition is corrected, the system will pass all the diagnostic tests successfully, with all red LEDs extinguished and all green LEDs lit. The system can then be restored to normal operation. If the replacement of the faulty module does *not* correct the error condition, the service procedure must be further refined. Typically, a note might be attached to the control panel next to the LEDs that would instruct the craftsperson performing maintenance to replace the modules on either side of the faulty module. The reason for this approach is that the diagnostic programs are often not capable of isolating certain types of faults to a single replaceable module. This statement is also true about the diagnostic for signals that pass *between* modules. When a fault causes the output signal to be grounded, there is no single technique that may be employed to identify whether the output in the driving module or the input at the driven module is stuck-at-0. The simple solution is to have the craftsperson replace the driving module first. If this approach does not remove the fault, then the driven module must be replaced. If the replacement of the driven module does not eliminate the fault, the diagnostic procedure is probably not adequate to handle the situation and must be *refined* to account for the unresolvable fault condition.

The use of LEDs as fault indicators matches the characteristic of LSI technology quite well in terms of reliability, power requirements, and overall cost. Besides placing the LEDs in a central point such as the control panel, they can also be mounted on each circuit board, as mentioned earlier. Figure 8-6 shows an 8- by 13-inch circuit pack with a red LED trouble (fault) indicator light and a green LED trouble-free indicator light.

8.4 DIAGNOSTIC OBSERVATION POINTS

To isolate the circuit fault to a particular circuit module, the diagnostic program must be capable of obtaining the test result and determining whether any error has occurred. This is relatively simple when the checking is done on data paths or data registers where a *known constant* is gated through the circuit under test. The output result is compared with the original data to determine whether the data has been changed because of faults along the data path. In other logic circuits, the signal may undergo a transformation such as translating a binary number into a 1-active-out-of-m output signal as in the case of a binary decoder circuit. If all outputs are available, they can be gated to a processor register for examination. Any error in decoding can therefore be detected. The difficulty with this procedure is that a large number of output leads must be processed, and the amount of circuitry required to do the processing is greater than that required by the decoder.

Diagnostic observation points, strategically located in a logic circuit, facilitate monitoring the behavior of the circuit. Otherwise, it would be impossible for the diagnostic routines to check out certain portions of the logic. In a self-checking design, the hardware detection circuits clearly are the most appropriate points for observing the behavior of the circuit.

It is necessary to maintain the identity of each error-indicating signal throughout the system. This procedure provides not only useful diagnostic information, but also the error signals serve as observation points for the diagnostic programs. These error signals can be collected throughout the system as the diagnostics are run and stored in one or more dedicated hardware registers. The diagnostic can access the error-indicating registers to determine which of the hardware detection circuits produced an error-indicating signal during the execution of a fault detection test sequence.

Most of the error-detecting circuits described in the previous sections are self-checking so that a single failure in the circuit will generate a fault indication. A completely self-checking circuit requires that two outputs be generated which provide an output signal of the form 1-active-out-of-2. These two outputs are combined to give a single error using the 1-active-out-of-2 encoding if both signals are active or if neither signal is active. The error signal is used to generate an immediate response by the processor. The error signal may (1) interrupt the processor, (2) halt further processing until a craftsperson has manually intervened, and (3) cause the error signal to be stored in a dedicated error register for later analysis by either a craftsperson or an error analysis program. The combining circuit is *not* self-checking in that some fault conditions in the combining circuit will prevent the checking circuitry from giving any error indication; faults normally detected will be ignored. To use the detection circuits as observation points, the non-self-checking portion of the hardware *must be exercised* to ensure that it is fully operational.

Checking the error detection circuits can be done by automatically generating the error condition and observing whether the detection circuit responds to the error condition. For example, in the case of a parity check of a data word, the system can easily create the wrong parity for the data word. Similarly, in checking the response of a circuit using an m-out-of-$2m$ code, noncode words can be used to validate the hardware. Alternatively, it may be desirable to create an error condition using normal data words that are also legitimate m-out-of-$2m$ code words rather than noncode words. This can be done by applying special test signals or stimuli to the check hardware to purposely create the error condition. A special dedicated hardware register and one or more binary decoders can be used for this purpose.

Figure 8-7 shows a general structure for using error signals as observation points. The correct outputs from the self-checking detection circuit are 01 and 10. These two outputs are XORed together to give a single output. To check the XOR gate, another XOR gate is used to form a non-self-testing circuit with the original XOR gate. The second XOR gate is implemented with a test control signal as the second input. The test control signal is normally held in the 0 state. This condition allows the second output from the detection circuit to be passed unchanged to the original XOR gate. If one of the two error conditions 00 or 11 is sensed by this XOR gate, an error signal will be generated that will set a dedicated bit in the error register. If the error signal is not inhibited, it is used to either halt the system or generate a priority interrupt that will be handled by the error detection software. The error register serves the function of storing the information for either visual indication or program interrogation. The test control register allows special conditions to be set up in the system under program control which permit the testing of the fault detection circuit. The test control register may be divided into several fields with each field decoded to generate one active test control signal from each field. Individual bits in the test control register may be assigned to dedicated functions. As indicated in the figure, one bit is used to *inhibit the error signals* from affecting the system. This is necessary for testing the check circuit when

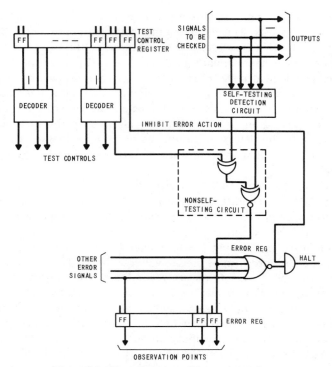

Figure 8-7　Error Signals as Observation Points

an error condition is purposely generated by a diagnostic program. The error register can then be used as an observation point in running the diagnostic program.

8.4.1 Example of a Diagnostic Sequence without Hardware Aids

One of the more difficult circuits to check without using any observation points is the decoder circuit which produces a single active output from m possible outputs. A circuit of this kind is typically used to implement the control logic of a digital machine in a conventional wired logic design. The macroinstruction opcode is normally translated from a binary number to a single active output using such a 1-active-out-of-m decoder. The active output is then combined with the processor clock signals and status flags to generate a sequence of control primitives or microoperations. These control steps provide the sequencing information to fully interpret the macroin-

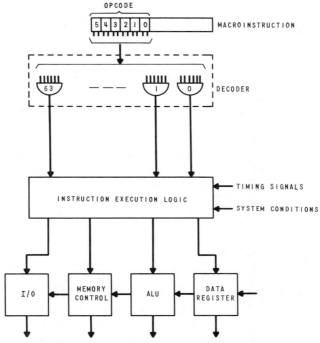

Figure 8-8 Opcode Decoding Circuit

struction opcode on the host machine hardware.   Figure 8-8 illustrates a simplified arrangement of the control logic required to interpret a 6-bit opcode found in the macroinstruction register.   The opcode is decoded using 64 six-input logic gates into the appropriate 1-active-out-of-64 possible outputs. Each of these 64 outputs fans out to all parts of the processor to control the necessary data paths and gating signals required by the macroinstruction. To check if the decoder circuits are functioning properly, each of the 64 decoder gates must be exercised individually.   The major problem in assessing whether the decoder circuitry is functioning correctly is to establish that an unselected gate does *not* become active at the same time as the correct decoder gate.   This is a nontrivial problem and is considerably more difficult to diagnose than the elementary case of establishing that a specific decoder output gate becomes active when it is selected by the translation logic. For example, if the opcode of the macroinstruction is binary 011010 and one of the six input bits in the decoder gate is failing in a *stuck-at-1* fault condition, the following input combinations may be present at the inputs to the decoder logic:

1.	011011	or	011010
2.	011000	or	011010
3.	011110	or	011010
4.	010010	or	011010
5.	001010	or	011010
6.	111010	or	011010

The underlined bit in each input combination represents the bit position in the opcode at which the stuck-at-1 fault has occurred. Note that in each of these six cases it is impossible for the decoder to distinguish between the legitimate macroopcode and the alternate expression shown which would also be decoded by the decoder logic. Thus, it is possible for the decoder logic to generate an entirely correct output for the opcode 011010 *and* an additional output because of the presence of the stuck-at-1 fault. If no direct observation points are provided for the diagnostic to check for multiple outputs from the decoder, the diagnostic program must rely on the indirect technique of observing the response from the decoder for each of the above six input fault cases. To do this, the internal state of the processor must be initialized so that the six separate multiple-output fault cases can be detected. It is entirely possible that it may not be possible for the diagnostic program to initialize the processor so that all six different fault cases can be detected. In this case, the diagnostic must reinitialize the processor for each of these fault conditions in order to obtain any meaningful information on the possible occurrence of these faults. For each of the 64 macroopcodes, this process of initializing the processor and then checking for the occurrence of multiple outputs must be repeated by the diagnostic test program. Consequently, the development of a diagnostic program that will thoroughly check a 1-active-out-of-*m* decoder circuit requires a considerable amount of ingenuity on the part of the diagnostic program designer.

8.4.2   Example of a Diagnostic with a Detection Circuit as an Observation Point

The 1-active-out-of-*m* binary decoder circuit, as mentioned in the previous section, is one of the more difficult logic circuits to check for fault conditions since some faults may not be directly detectable by a diagnostic test sequence. A simple fault detection circuit may be implemented in hardware which can be used to check for multiple outputs from the binary decoder. The fault detection circuit partitions the decoder outputs into two groups: One group generates *even parity* over the outputs from the binary decoder, while the other group generates *odd parity*. Only one decoder output will be active when the binary decoder is functioning in a fault-free manner. Figure 8-9 illustrates the 6-bit macroopcode decoder circuit and its associated fault detec-

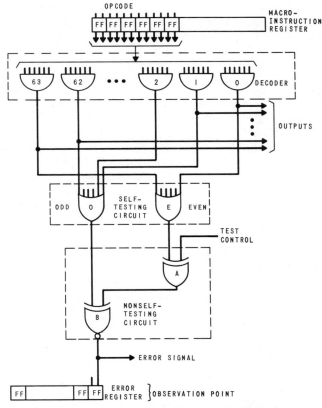

Figure 8-9 Opcode Decoding with Check Circuit

tion logic which uses the odd- and even-parity generation for the binary decoder outputs. The self-testing circuit or fault detection logic consists of an odd (O) parity gate and an even (E) parity gate. The normal or error-free outputs from the O gate and the E gate taken as a 2-tuple are 10 or 01. If a single input fault occurs, such as a stuck-at-1 fault or a stuck-at-0 fault, that forces two outputs to be simultaneouly active, the resultant 2-tuple formed by the O and E gates will be 11. This condition represents the occurrence of a multiple-output condition in the binary decoder circuitry. The outputs from the O and E gates can be XORed together to produce an output signal of 0 from the XOR gate. This output signal can be used to set a flag in the error register and provide an error indication signal. In the figure, an additional XOR gate has been provided with a test control signal which is used to validate the error-indicating circuit.

Prior to the use of the parity detection circuit as a fault observation point, the non-self-testing portion of the circuit must be checked to ensure that it will generate an error signal. This is done by having the diagnostic set the test control signal to the value of 1. The logical signal from gate E is complemented as it is transmitted through gate A. With the test control signal in the 1 state, the normal (error-free) output 2-tuple (01 to 10) from the self-testing circuitry of the binary decoder will be modified by XOR gate A to the values 00 or 11 at the inputs of XOR gate B. These two states (00 and 11) represent the error conditions from the binary decoder for "no output has occurred" and "multiple outputs have occurred." They are sufficient to permit the diagnostic to validate the non-self-testing portion of the binary decoder fault detection circuit.

The validation of the logical gating paths in the binary decoder is quite straightforward. The validation can be done by having the diagnostic cycle the states of the input decoder leads through all 64 allowable binary input combinations. At the end of the input test sequence, the error register is examined to determine whether any errors have been generated. There is *no* need to perform a step-by-step check of each binary input combination as would be required in the case of a binary decoder which had no fault detection hardware.

The use of fault detection hardware to provide diagnostic observation points is also efficient in terms of reducing the number of items of data necessary to characterize a fault. In the case of a 1-active-out-of-64 decoder, the 64 outputs are translated to a single bit in the error register. The diagnostic program may process 1 bit considerably easier than it may process 64 bits.

8.5 MICRODIAGNOSTICS EXECUTED FROM MAIN STORAGE

Typically, most diagnostic programs are seldom used during the normal processing of a digital machine. The diagnostic is invoked when a fault has been detected and fault identification needs to be performed; alternatively, a diagnostic may be invoked to validate that the hardware is fault-free and operating properly. Consequently, a diagnostic does not have to be kept resident in main storage but may be rolled into a paging buffer in main storage *only* when a fault recovery program determines that the diagnostic is needed. Similarly, if diagnostic programs have been written in microcode (microdiagnostics), they do not have to be kept as resident microcode in control store. WCS is used as an integral part of most current microprogrammable machines. Consequently, storing microdiagnostics on a low-cost magnetic cassette unit or floppy disk and rolling the microdiagnostics into WCS on demand comprise an effective approach to not requiring that the microdiagnostics be resident in the microprogram memory.

An alternative to the use of an LSI WCS is to use a portion of main memory as a WCS for diagnostic program execution. Since the LSI WCS is more expensive than main storage, this approach would eliminate the cost of writable microprogram memory. Even though the cycle time of main storage is slower than the cycle time of control store by a factor of from 4 or ·more, this is not an important disadvantage in executing a diagnostic; the diagnostics are not run frequently, and the slower execution time associated with main memory should, normally, not affect the results.

Figure 8-10 illustrates the general procedure for executing a sequence of microinstructions from main memory. A special macroinstruction, called a *microprogram interpret* (MI) macroinstruction, is used to initiate the execution sequence of microinstructions; each microinstruction is fetched from main memory. The opcode of the MI *macro*instruction points to an address in control store which contains an MI *micro*instruction. The MI microinstruction sets up the microcontrol logic to fetch successive words from main storage and allows the microcontrol logic to interpret these words as legitimate microinstructions. The execution of each microinstruction remains the same as if each microinstruction were fetched from control store; however, the control logic must wait for a longer time as each microinstruction is fetched from main storage because of the slower memory cycle time of main storage.

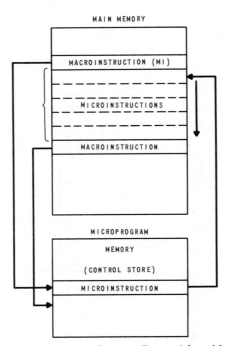

Figure 8-10   Microinstruction Sequence Executed from Main Memory

The number of microinstructions placed in main storage can be arranged to be a variable by having the last microinstruction in the main storage sequence restore the microcontrol logic to its normal mode of fetching microinstructions from control store. Using this approach the sequence of microinstructions placed in main memory can be as long as the software designer deems necessary. The next macroinstruction in the normal main program sequence of macroinstructions can be arranged to immediately follow the last microinstruction in the microprogram placed in main storage. The sharing of main memory for both microinstructions and macroinstructions provides virtually the same capability as the use of a separate WCS but at a much lower equipment cost.

The MI macroinstruction simply puts the microcontrol logic in the *microinterpret mode.* When the processor is in this mode, the microcontrol logic fetches consecutive microinstructions from successive memory locations in main storage. Any number of microinstructions may be executed from main memory until the last microinstruction in the main memory sequence of microinstructions turns off (disables) the microinterpret mode. Figure 8-11 illustrates the logical implementation of the microinterpret macroinstruc-

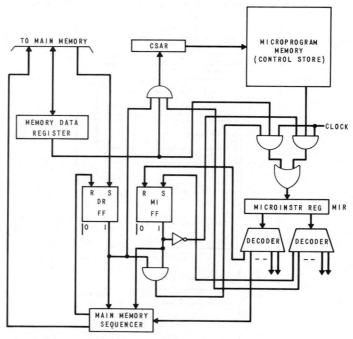

Figure 8-11 Implementation of Microinterpret Macroinstruction

tion. After the MI macroinstruction is fetched from main memory, the opcode portion of the macroinstruction is gated into the *control store address register* (CSAR) to start the microinstruction sequence that interprets the MI macroinstruction. The first microinstruction in the interpretation sequence sets the MI flip-flop. The MI flip-flop being set indicates that all further control store references should be taken from main memory. In addition, the MI flip-flop causes the main store control logic to increment the contents of the MAR by 1 so that the MAR points to the next microinstruction to be executed from main storage. At the completion of the execution of the current microinstruction, the MIR is automatically cleared to the all-0s state. This corresponds to an NOP microinstruction, and the microcontrol logic pauses in a wait loop until the next microinstruction has been fetched from main memory and placed in the MIR. The next microinstruction will be available in the MIR and be ready to be executed by the microcontrol logic when the DATA-READY (DR) flip-flop is set. The contents of the MDR can be gated into the MIR only after the main storage control logic has set the DR flip-flop. The DR flip-flop is cleared when the execution of the current microinstruction is complete. This process is repeated for each new microinstruction so that a stream of microinstructions is fetched from main memory and executed as though the microinstructions had been placed in control store. To terminate the sequence of microinstructions executed from main memory, the last microinstruction in the sequence is required to reset the MI flip-flop. In addition, this last microinstruction has as the contents of the next address field the address of the last microinstruction. This means that the last microinstruction is kept in a wait loop in which the state of the DR flip-flop is continually examined every microexecution cycle. When the DR flip-flop is set, the contents of the MDR contain the next macroinstruction. Its opcode is gated to the CSAR to begin the execution of the next macroinstruction. The resetting of the MI flip-flop directs all further fetches of microinstructions to be made from the control memory and *not* the main memory.

There are certain constraints that must be observed by the logic structure shown in Figure 8-11. One constraint is the word size of the control memory and the word size of the main memory. If both memories have the same number of bits in a memory word, there is a one-to-one correspondence between the number of locations in main memory that are required and the number of microinstructions to be executed from main memory. However, if the control store word contains more bits than a word of main storage, then two or more main storage words are required to configure one microinstruction in main memory. This means that additional sequencing logic is required to read several consecutive main storage locations to configure a microinstruction in the MIR. A difference in word size between the two memories introduces added complexity into the control logic and increases the time interval during which the microcontrol logic is in the wait state after a microinstruction has completed its execution.

Another constraint is that the sequence of main memory microinstructions must be executed in consecutive order. Consequently, each FETCH will cause the contents of the MAR to be incremented by 1. However, no conditional or unconditional branch microinstructions are permitted in the microinstruction sequence stored in main memory. Nonetheless, in many microprograms it is often necessary to execute a conditional branch microinstruction. To perform a conditional operation, it is necessary to use one or more macroinstructions. Whenever a conditional branch is required by the microinstruction sequence, the microinterpret mode is terminated, and a conditional branch is performed by executing a conditional branch macroinstruction. Figure 8-12 depicts a sequence in which macroinstructions are intermixed with the microinstruction sequence placed in main memory. The conditional branch operation is performed by the macroinstructions, after which the system is placed back in the microinterpret mode and a new microinstruction sequence initiated.

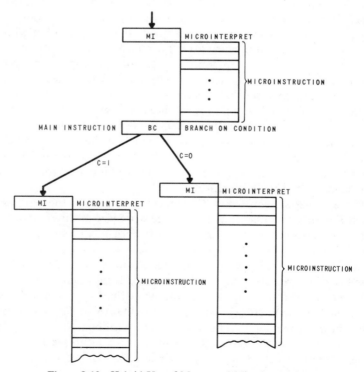

Figure 8-12 Hybrid Use of Macro and Microinstructions

8.6 DIAGNOSTIC TESTING OF MARGINAL CIRCUITS

In any of the previously discussed error operations, it has been assumed that the circuit faults were *hard* faults; that is, the faults were of the stuck-at-0 or the stuck-at-1 types. These faults are always *deterministic* and *repeatable* in the sense that the same errors are *always* generated under the same set of operating conditions. In actual practice, many faults experienced by a system are *not* hard faults that occur suddenly and are easily detectable. Many times a logic gate or circuit begins to fail gradually in that its operating voltage levels and/or current levels no longer continue to fall within specified tolerance levels over a period of time. This gradual degradation creates *marginal operating conditions* within the circuit which cannot be detected when a diagnostic is run since the circuit appears to be functioning correctly most of the time. In addition, such marginal conditions may cause failures which are not repeatable under the same set of test conditions. These types of faults are extremely difficult to identify. The normal procedure for handling marginal errors involves recording all pertinent information when a nonreproducible fault is detected. This information is kept on magnetic tape or disk as an archival file for the system maintenance personnel. The maintenance personnel can use the information in the archival file to arrive at some clues as to the cause of the system transient (marginal) failures. In many cases, the transient failures will eventually be manifested as solid faults. It is desirable from the view of fault diagnosis and repair to eliminate the time interval during which a component experiences transient failures due to marginal operating conditions.

One approach to solving this problem is to stress the component which is experiencing transient failures in such a manner that the component is forced to fail with a *hard fault*. In the actual working environment of a customer installation a wide range of variables can cause marginal component behavior. It is quite difficult to control these variables for testing purposes at the customer site. However, applying electrical signal variations to the circuits to be validated (i.e., increasing or decreasing the power supply voltage or increasing the frequency of the system clock, etc.) will often stress the operating characteristics of many of the circuits in the system. Under this form of stress, marginal conditions or transient failures, in most instances, are forced to become hard faults such as stuck-at-0 or stuck-at-1 faults. This technique was used in the marginal testing of the circuit packs associated with both the call store (data memory) and program store (program memory) of the Bell System's No. 2 ESS processor. As a specific example, the threshold voltage of the sense amplifiers was adjustable to one of two abnormal values. The operating value of the threshold voltage was under control of the diagnostic program. Once the threshold voltage was set to a specific value by the diagnostic, a sequence of diagnostic tests was run to determine if the sense amplifier had sufficient margin to provide a valid readout. Normally, any marginal bits in the sense amplifier readout bus became hard faults. In many instances, potentially marginal sense amplifier boards were also detected during the application of these diagnostic tests.

One of the basic functions performed by the No. 2 ESS sense amplifers was the function of *electrically discriminating* between a logical 0 and a logical 1. Figure 8-13(a) illustrates a typical input waveform as seen by one of these sense amplifiers. There is a considerable variation in the electrical value of the voltages read out from a selection of magnetic cores; these variations are due to differences in the physical properties of the cores themselves. Consequently, due to the differences in the cores, the voltage level for a logical 1 readout can vary considerably—as can the amplitude of the voltage readout for a logical 0. The sense amplifiers, however, were designed to distinguish between a logical 0 and a logical 1 by examining the difference between the maximum electrical signal value for a logical 0 (V_L) and the

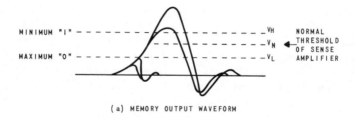

(a) MEMORY OUTPUT WAVEFORM

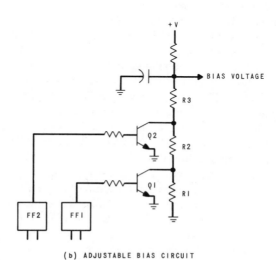

(b) ADJUSTABLE BIAS CIRCUIT

Figure 8-13   Marginal Testing Approach for Memory Circuit

minimum electrical signal value for a logical 1 (V_H). If the sense amplifier is operating properly, the threshold voltage is adjusted to lie in the middle of this voltage range $(V_H - V_L)$ at point V_N, as shown in Figure 8-13(a). This allows approximately an equal voltage margin for a minimum logical 1 readout and a maximum logical 0 readout. A simplified form of the threshold or bias voltage section of the sense amplifier circuit is shown in Figure 8-13(b). Transistors Q1 and Q2 function as switches and control the bias voltage level by shorting either R1 or the series combination of R1 and R2 to ground. Q1 and Q2 are under direct control of the diagnostic program which sets or resets flip-flops FF1 and FF2. Under normal operating conditions, Q1 is on, and the threshold voltage is set at V_N. If a check for marginal behavior is to be performed, the diagnostic program turns off both Q1 and Q2; the result of this action is that the threshold voltage is increased to V_H, the voltage level assigned to a mimimum logical 1. The memory is then cycled through the diagnostic test sequence with the threshold voltage levels of the sense amplifiers set at the value V_H. If the memory readout circuits pass the diagnostic test sequence, it indicates to the diagnostic that the memory is still operating within the tolerance level set for detecting a minimum logical 1. The diagnostic then sets the threshold voltage levels of the sense amplifiers to the value assigned for detecting a maximum logical 0, V_L. The same diagnostic test sequence is reapplied to the memory readout circuits. If the test sequence again passes, it indicates that the readout circuits are operational within the tolerance levels established by the original design. Any marginal conditions should have been detected using these test procedures.

In *dynamic* semiconductor memories, marginal testing can be done by lowering the refresh rate. This has a direct influence on the retention of information by memory cells. Essentially, these cells are capacitors, and the stored charges must be replenished periodically. Otherwise, the information in the memory cells will be lost by the slow discharge of these capacitive memory elements.

Within the processor itself, if the frequency of the clock pulses is increased, an indication of the operating margin observed by the logic circuits can be obtained by observing the clock rate at which the circuits begin to provide incorrect outputs. Figure 8-14 gives the logic diagram of an adjustable clock rate circuit that allows a faster oscillator circuit to be switched into the clock timing logic under control of the diagnostic program. It may be necessary to coordinate when the oscillators' outputs are switched into the clock logic to preserve the continuity of the clock phases and to avoid any spurious clock signals during the interval neither oscillator is in control of the clock logic.

The use of marginal check procedures that test a system for the occurrence of transient faults ensures that the system has an adequate working

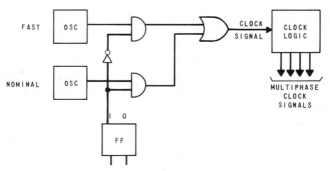

Figure 8-14 Adjustable Clock Rate Circuit

margin for each of the critical variables that influence the circuits' correct behavior. Any potential marginal circuits can be identified before the circuits begin to introduce transient errors in a normal working system—provided that the diagnostics that stress the operating margins of various circuit elements are run on a frequent enough basis. In addition, transient faults caused by circuits operating outside their established margins may be transformed into hard faults by well-designed diagnostic tests that create the appropriate stress conditions on the circuits.

8.7 EXTERNAL DIAGNOSTIC CONTROL

As described in Section 8.1, the hardcore portion of the processor is assumed to be operating properly prior to running any diagnostic tests on the system in a stand-alone environment in which the diagnostics are initiated by a maintenance person. This procedure requires that the hardcore portion be validated prior to running the remainder of the system diagnostics. It is good maintenance design to keep the hardcore portion as small as possible to minimize the amount of hardware that must be manually diagnosed. If faults occur in the hardcore portion of the processor, the maintenance personnel will be required to manually intervene in order to identify what replaceable modules are failing. When failures do occur in the hardcore, manual testing must be performed in which a sequence of diagnostic tests is applied to the hardcore through the control panel or by means of an external test set. The results of these tests, which may be displayed on PASS/FAIL lamps located on the control panel or test set, are used by the maintenance personnel to analyze the fault that has been detected in the processor hardcore. A much quicker method of validating the processor hardcore is to have the necessary diagnostic test sequences automatically run on the hardcore under the program control of another digital machine.

This machine could be a general-purpose small computer or a special-purpose test set; in either case, the hardcore portion of the processor is validated automatically with a minimum amount of manual intervention required by the maintenance people.

For the processor hardcore to be validated or checked by external hardware, access points must be made available in the hardcore that may be used by the diagnostic program to both control the state of the hardcore and monitor the results of each test sequence that is applied to the hardcore. These access points must be integrated into the initial design of the processor hardcore so that the diagnostic program can examine and control the hardcore at the elementary logic gate level, if necessary. With the high cost of labor, the concept of remote and centralized maintenance appears to be an attractive solution. Using this approach, the expertise necessary to perform maintenance of a digital system is *concentrated* at a central location. Instead of dispatching technicians to the site of a faulty machine, fault diagnosis is done *remotely* using serial communication lines that act as data links to the centralized maintenance facility. This method is illustrated in Figure 8-15. The *diagnostic access ports* are used by the central maintenance processor to transmit the diagnostic test sequences to the remotely located processor that needs to be diagnosed and repaired. These diagnostic tests are identical to the tests that would be invoked manually at the site by a local craftsperson except that the tests are *initiated* by the remote centralized maintenance processor. The results of the diagnostic tests are *returned* to the maintenance processor for analysis by the maintenance specialists concentrated in the centralized facility.

The remote application of diagnostics to a faulty processor can be imple-

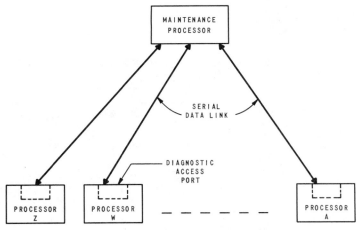

Figure 8-15 Remote Processor Diagnosis via Data Links

mented as shown in Figure 8-16. A serial digital communication link is established between the faulty processor and the centralized maintenance processor. This serial link is used to pass messages between the two machines. Interfaces are required at both the remote processor and the centralized maintenance machine to convert the digital signals from the serial data link to the proper data format at a preestablished data rate. Each message that is transmitted between the central maintenance processor and a remote machine consists of two parts: a data portion and a command portion. It is assumed that diagnostics will be executed as microinstruction sequences in the faulty processor. Consequently, the data portion of an interprocessor message may be (1) an address in main storage to be used as a memory reference in the next main storage operation, (2) a data word to be directed to any of the faulty processor's internal registers, or (3) a microinstruction to be loaded in the MIR.

The command portion of the interprocessor message is decoded by the faulty processor to provide the necessary control signals needed to imple-

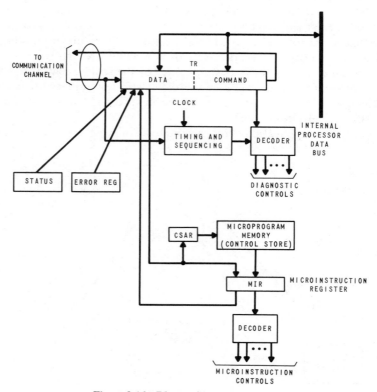

Figure 8-16   Diagnostics Access Control

ment the operation implied by the interprocessor message. For example, the microinstruction in the data portion of the message can be loaded into the MIR *and* the microinstruction then decoded and executed by the faulty processor. Under the direct control of the command portion of the interprocessor message such registers as the system status register, the error register, and the program counter may be read by the centralized maintenance processor to determine the possible reasons for the difficulties experienced by the failing processor. Typically, private gating paths are connected directly to the *transmit-receive* (TR) register. These private gating paths allow the maintenance processor to access the system status register and the error register completely independently of the faulty processor's internal bus structure and associated bus structure.

The primary function of the diagnostic access ports, as shown in Figure 8-16, is the ability the port offers the centralized maintenance processor to control the faulty machine at its most basic operational level (i.e., the microoperational level). The maintenance processor performs these fundamental control functions by sending a microinstruction as the data portion of the interprocessor message. The microinstruction is loaded directly into the MIR and then executed using the faulty processor's microcontrol logic. A sequence of microinstructions which forms a microdiagnostic can be processed by the faulty processor at the message rate of the serial communication link. The bit rate of the data link is the limiting factor in terms of how rapidly a microdiagnostic may be run on the faulty machine. The results of each microinstruction can be read out by the maintenance processor and analyzed to determine the reason(s) for any improper behavior. In this mode, the maintenance processor will do the following:

1. Transmit a microinstruction to the diagnostic access port; the microinstruction will be treated as the data portion of an interprocessor message. The microinstruction will be loaded in the MIR.
2. The command portion of the next interprocessor message will cause the microinstruction in the MIR to be executed.
3. The microcontrol logic of the faulty processor will *halt* after it is finished executing the current microinstruction in the MIR.
4. The remote maintenance processor can then read out internal registers in the faulty machine such as the system status register and the error register by transmitting another sequence of microinstructions to the faulty processor.
5. On the basis of the information transmitted back from the faulty processor, the maintenance processor can then determine the next sequence of microinstructions to be sent to the remote machine.
6. This procedure is continued until the faulty processor has been remotely diagnosed and the necessary repair procedures identified by the centralized maintenance staff.

The capability of the maintenance processor to *remotely* obtain the contents of any internal register in the faulty processor also permits another important diagnostic function to be achieved: the *verification* of the contents of the microprogram memory or control store. The *maintenance processor* accomplishes this procedure in the following manner:

1. It halts the faulty processor.
2. It transmits an address in control store as data to be loaded in the CSAR.
3. It initiates a READ operation of control store at the location specified by the CSAR.
4. It transmits the contents of the MIR which has been loaded with the referenced control store word back to the maintenance processor.
5. The transmitted word is then compared by the maintenance processor with an expected value to determine if the control store location in the faulty processor contains the correct information.

In this manner, the control memory contents of the faulty processor can be read one word at a time by the maintenance processor until the entire contents of the microprogram memory are verified.

In a similar fashion, the contents and operation of main storage can be extensively tested by the centralized maintenance processor using a diagnostic access port and performing READ or WRITE operations of main storage using microinstructions to initiate the operations. In addition, other basic circuits in the remote processor can be controlled and accessed by the maintenance processor using a diagnostic access port. For example, the clock circuit can be checked logically on a *static basis.* This can be accomplished by having the maintenance processor stop the clock of the remote processor and then use the diagnostic access port to step the clock along one clock phase at a time. In between each control step, the state of the clock circuitry is transmitted to the maintenance processor for analysis and evaluation. Other timing circuitry may be similarly checked in this manner.

8.8   SUMMARY

The techniques to diagnose a fault in a digital system have been discussed in this chapter. In particular, the reason for isolating a fault to a replaceable unit (i.e., ease of repair) was developed starting with the concept of validating the hardcore portion of a processor. The processor hardcore is the fundamental portion of the machine that *must* be operating correctly before any useful fault diagnosis may be performed. The validation of the hardcore may either be done manually or via a special test set built to verify the integrity of the hardcore's logic. In either case, manual intervention by a maintenance person is required to initiate the hardcore validation process.

A diagnostic test program, in many cases, is much more effective written as a microcode module in which the individual control primitives may be manipulated. A diagnostic program written in assembly language (macroinstructions) does not provide the capability to exercise the individual microcontrol points. Such diagnostic programs written in microcode are also called *microdiagnostics*. A microdiagnostic may be stored as resident code in control memory; this procedure wastes on-line control storage since a microdiagnostic is normally run *only* after a fault is detected or on an infrequently scheduled basis to perform routine processor maintenance. A microdiagnostic can be stored in an off-line ROM module; in this case, the maintenance person must manually *swap* the off-line ROM module with a designated on-line ROM module used in control store. The on-line ROM module is regarded as a replaceable unit when fault diagnosis is to be performed. Manual intervention is cumbersome and can lead to errors introduced by the maintenance person performing the manual service. A third alternative is to store the microdiagnostics on a bulk storage device such as a magnetic cassette unit or a floppy disk. A portion of control store would be made from READ/WRITE RAM modules to form a WCS. The microdiagnostics would be requested by the fault detection logic only when a hard fault had occurred. The microdiagnostics would be rolled into the WCS paging buffer and executed from WCS. In this way, the microdiagnostics would be resident in control store *only* when they were needed. Otherwise, they would be stored off-line on the system bulk storage device.

It is quite attractive to have the hardware logic designer and the maintenance software developer work closely together to provide access points *in the hardware* that may be used by the diagnostic test programs. These access points may function as private control ports into the hardware for the diagnostic to both control and examine the internal state(s) of the hardware. Procedures of this kind permit diagnostic programs to be written that can exhaustively test the hardware and validate that the hardware is operating properly.

In many instances, it is attractive to execute a microdiagnostic from main storage. Effectively, main storage is used as a WCS. However, this approach requires a careful examination of the word lengths associated with control store and main storage; in general, the control of this mode, also called a *microinterpret* (MI) *mode*, can be fairly complex. The control logic should have some form of self-checking associated with it.

Finally, fault diagnosis may be performed remotely using a centralized maintenance processor. This allows an organization to concentrate its skilled maintenance personnel at a single site, instead of dispersing them, individually, over a wide geographic area. It can represent a substantial financial saving for the organization as well as a means of *concentrating* expertise on a specific fault condition so that it can be quickly resolved.

8.9 REFERENCES

1. R. P. ALMQUIST, J. R. HAGERMAN, R. J. HASS, R. W. PETERSON, and S. L. STOENS, "Software Protection in No. 1 ESS," in *1972 International Switching Symposium Record* (Cambridge, Mass.: 1972), pp. 565–569.

2. A. AVIZIENIS, "Digital Fault Diagnosis by Low-Cost Arithmetical Coding Techniques," *Proc. Purdue Centennial Year Symp. Inf. Process., 1* (1969), 81–91.

3. T. R. BASHKOW, J. FRIETS, and A. KARSON, "A Programming System for Detection and Diagnosis of Machine Malfunctions," *IEEE Trans. Comput., 12* (Feb. 1963), 10–17.

4. H. J. BEUSCHER, G. E. FESSLER, D. W. HUFFMAN, P. J. KENNEDY, and E. NUSSBAUM, "Administration and Maintenance Plan," *Bell Syst. Tech. J., 48,* No. 8 (Oct. 1969), 2765–2815.

5. M. A. BREUER and A. D. FRIEDMAN, *Diagnosis and Reliable Design of Digital Systems* (Woodland Hills, Calif.: Computer Science Press, 1976).

6. T. E. BROWNE, T. M. QUINN, W. N. TOY, and J. E. YATES, "No. 2 ESS Control Unit System," *Bell Syst. Tech. J., 48* (Oct. 1969), 2619–2668.

7. W. C. CARTER, H. C. MONTGOMERY, R. J. PREISS, and H. J. REINHEIMER, "Design of Serviceability Features for the IBM System/360," *IBM J. Res. Dev., 8,* No. 2 (April 1964), 115–126.

8. W. C. CARTER and P. R. SCHNEIDER, "Design of Dynamically Checked Computers," *IFIP Conf. Proc., 2* (1968), 878–883.

9. H. Y. CHANG, "Algorithm for Selecting an Optimum Set of Diagnostic Tests," *IEEE Trans. Comput., 14* (Oct. 1965), 706–711.

10. H. Y. CHANG and G. W. HEIMBIGNER, "Controllability, Observability and Maintenance Engineering Technique (COMET)," *Bell Syst. Tech. J., 53* (Oct. 1974), 1504–1534.

11. H. Y. CHANG, G. W. HEIMBIGNER, D. J. SENESE, and T. L. SMITH, "Maintenance Techniques of a Microprogrammed Self-Checking Control Complex of an Electronic Switching System," *IEEE Trans. Comput., L-22,* No. 5 (May 1973), 501–512.

12. H. Y. CHANG, E. G. MANNING, and G. METZE, *Fault Diagnosis of Digital Systems* (New York: Wiley-Interscience, 1970).

13. H. Y. CHANG and J. M. SCANLON, "Design Principles for Processor Maintainability in Real-Time Systems," *AFIPS Conf. Proc., 35* (1969), 319–328.

14. R. W. COOK, "Microprogram Controlled Data Processor for Executing Microprogram Instructions from Microprogram Memory or Main Memory," U.S. Patent No. 3,859,636, issued Jan. 7, 1975.

15. R. W. COOK, W. H. SISSON, T. F. STOREY, and W. N. TOY, "Design of a Microprogrammed Control for Self-Checking," in *Digest of 1972 Fault-Tolerant Computing* (Newton, Mass.: June 1972), pp. 160–164.

16. R. W. COOK, W. H. SISSON, T. F. STOREY, and W. N. TOY, "Maintenance Design of a Control Processor for Electronic Switching Systems," in *Proceedings of the Third Texas Conference on Computing Systems* (Austin, Texas: Nov. 1974), pp. 9–1–1 to 9–1–6.

17. R. W. DOWNING, J. S. NOWAK, and L. S. TUOMENOKSA, "No. 1 ESS Maintenance Plan," *Bell Syst. Tech. J., 43,* No. 5 (Sept. 1964), 1961–2019.

18. A. D. FRIEDMAN and P. R. MENON, *Fault Detection in Digital Circuits* (Englewood Cliffs, N.J.: Prentice-Hall, 1971).

19. R. M. GUFFIN, "Microdiagnostics for the Standard Computer MLP-900 Processor," *IEEE Trans. Comput., C-20* (July 1971), 803–807.

20. A. M. JOHNSON, "Microdiagnostics for IBM System 360 Model 30," *IEEE Trans. Comput., C-20* (July 1971), 798–802.

21. F. LEE, "Automatic Self-Checking and Fault-Locating Methods," *IRE Trans. Electron. Comput., 11* (Oct. 1962), 649–654.

22. E. J. McCLUSKEY, "Test and Diagnosis Procedures for Digital Networks," *Computer* (Jan.– Feb. 1971), 17–20.

23. E. G. MANNING, "On Computer Self-Diagnosis: Parts I and II," *IEEE Trans. Electron. Comput., EC-15,* No. 6 (Dec. 1966), 873–890.

24. C. V. RAMAMOORTHY and L. C. CHANG, "System Modeling and Testing Procedures for Microdiagnostics," *IEEE Trans. Comput., C-21,* No. 11 (Nov. 1972), 1169–1183.

25. C. V. RAMAMOORTHY and W. MAYEDA, "Computer Diagnosis Using the Blocking Gate Approach," *IEEE Trans. Comput., C-20* (Nov. 1971), 783–794.

26. S. SESHU and D. N. FREEMAN, "The Diagnosis of Asynchronous Sequential Switching Systems," *IRE Trans. Electron. Comput., EC-11* (Aug. 1962), 459–465.

27. R. E. STAEHLER, "1A Processor—A High Speed Processor for Switching Applications," in *International Switching Symposium Record, 1972* (Cambridge, Mass.: 1972), pp. 26–35.

28. T. F. STOREY, "Design of a Microprogram Control for a Processor in Electronic Switching System," *Bell Syst. Tech. J., 55,* No. 2 (Feb. 1976), 183–232.

29. *Tandem 16 System Description* (Cupertino, Calif.: Tandem Computers, Inc., 1976).

30. W. N. TOY, "Fault Tolerant Design of ESS Processors," *Proc. IEEE, 66,* No. 10 (Oct. 1978), 1126–1145.

31. S. H. TSIANG and W. ULRICH, "Automatic Trouble Diagnosis of Complex Logic Circuits," *Bell Syst. Tech. J., 41* (July 1962), 1177–1200.

CHAPTER 9

Fault-Tolerant

Design

of ESS Processors

9.1 INTRODUCTION

Next to computer systems used in space-borne vehicles and U.S. defense installations, no other application has a higher availability requirement than a Bell System *Electronic Switching System* (ESS). These systems have been designed to be out of service no more than a few minutes each year. Further, design objectives permit no more than 0.01 percent of the telephone calls to be processed incorrectly [1].* For example, when a fault occurs in an ESS, only a few calls in progress might be handled incorrectly during the recovery process.

At the core of every ESS is a single high-speed central processor [2–4]. To establish an ultrareliable switching environment, redundancy of system components and duplication of the processor itself have comprised the approach taken to compensate for potential machine faults. Without this redun-

---

* Bracketed numbers are references to the notes at the end of this chapter.

dancy, a single component failure in the processor might cause a complete failure of the entire system.   With duplication, a standby processor takes over control and provides continuous telephone service.

When the system fails, the fault must be quickly detected and isolated. Meanwhile, a rapid recovery of the call processing functions by the redundant component(s) and/or processor is necessary to maintain the system's high reliability.   Next, the fault must be diagnosed and the defective unit repaired or replaced.   The failure rate and repair time must be such that the probability is very small for a failure to occur in the duplicated unit before the first one is repaired.

9.2 ALLOCATION AND CAUSES OF SYSTEM DOWNTIME

The outage of a telephone (switching) office can be caused by facilities other than the processor.   While a hardware fault in one of the peripheral units generally results in only a partial loss of service, it *is* possible for a fault in this area to bring the system down.   By design, the processor has been allocated two-thirds of the system downtime.   The other one-third is allocated to the remaining equipment in the system.

Field experience indicates that system outages due to the processor may be assigned to one of four categories, shown in Figure 9-1 [5].   The percentages in this figure represent the fraction of total downtime attributable to each cause.   The four categories are the following:

1. *Hardware reliability.*   In the past, before the accumulation of large amounts of field data, total system downtime was usually assigned to hardware. We now know that the situation is more complex than this.   Processor hardware actually accounts for only 20 percent of the downtime.   With the growing use of stored program control, it has become increasingly important to make such systems

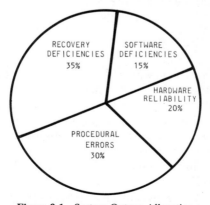

Figure 9-1   System Outage Allocation

more reliable.   Redundancy is designed into all subsystems so that the system can go down *only* when hardware failures occur simultaneously in duplicated units. However, the data now show that good diagnostic and trouble location programs are also very critical parts of the total system reliability performance.

   2.   *Software deficiencies.*   Software deficiencies include all software errors that cause memory mutilation and program loops that can only be cleared by major reinitialization.   Software faults are the result of improper translation or implementation of the original algorithm.   In some cases, the original algorithm may have been incorrectly specified.   Program changes and feature additions are continuously incorporated into working offices.   Software accounts for 15 percent of the downtime.

   3.   *Recovery deficiencies.*   Recovery is the system's most complex and difficult function.   Deficiencies may include the shortcomings of either hardware or software design to detect faults when they occur.   When faults go undetected, the system remains extensively impaired until the trouble is recognized.   Another kind of recovery problem can occur if the system is unable to properly isolate a faulty subsystem and configure a working system around it.

   The many possible system states that may arise under trouble conditions make recovery a complicated process.   Besides those already mentioned, unforeseen difficulties may be encountered in the field, leading to inadequate recovery.   Because of the large number of variables involved, and because the recovery function is so strongly related to all other components of maintenance, recovery deficiencies account for 35 percent of the downtime.

   4.   *Procedural errors.*   Human error on the part of maintenance personnel or office administrators can also cause the system to go down.   For example, someone in maintenance may mistakenly pull a circuit pack from the on-line processor while repairing a defective standby processor.   Inadequate and incorrect documentation (e.g., user's manuals) may also be classified as human error.   Obviously, the number of manual operations must be reduced if procedural errors are to be minimized. Procedural errors account for about 30 percent of the downtime.

   The shortcomings and deficiencies of current systems are continually being corrected to improve system reliability.

9.3   DUPLEX ARCHITECTURE

When a fault occurs in a nonredundant single processor, the system will remain down until the processor is repaired.   To meet the ESS reliability requirement, *redundancy* is included in the system design; continuous and correct operation is maintained by duplicating all functional units within the processor.   If one of the units fails, the duplicated unit is switched in, maintaining continuous operation.   Meanwhile the defective unit is repaired. Should a fault occur in the duplicated unit during the repair interval, the system will, of course, go down.   If the repair interval is relatively short, the probability of simultaneous faults occurring in two identical units is quite small.   This technique of redundancy has been used throughout each ESS.

   The first-generation ESS processor structure consists of two store com-

munities: *program store* (PS) and *call store* (CS). The program store is a
read-only memory (ROM), containing the call processing, maintenance, and
administration programs; it also contains long-term translation and system
parameters. The call store contains the transient data related to telephone
calls in progress. The memory is electrically alterable to allow its data to
be changed frequently. In one particular arrangement, shown in Figure 9-
2(a), the complete processor is treated as a single functional block and is
duplicated. This type of single-unit duplex system has two possible configurations: Either processor 0 or processor 1 can be assigned as the on-line working
system, while the other unit serves as standby backup (active redundancy).
The *mean time to failure* (MTTF), a measure of reliability developed in
Chapter 5, is given by the following expression [6]:

$$\text{MTTF} = \frac{\mu}{2\lambda^2}$$

where μ is the repair rate (reciprocal of the repair time) and λ is the failure
rate.

The failure rate (λ) of one unit is the summation of failure rates of

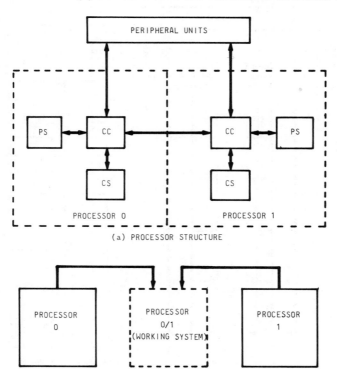

(a) PROCESSOR STRUCTURE

(b) TWO POSSIBLE CONFIGURATIONS

Figure 9-2 Single-Unit Duplex Configuration

all components within the unit.   For medium and small ESS processors, Figure 9-2(b) shows a system structure containing several functional units which are treated as a single entity, with λ still sufficiently small to meet the reliability requirement.   The single-unit duplex configuration has the merit of being very simple in terms of the number of switching blocks in the system.   This configuration simplifies not only the recovery program but also the hardware interconnection.   It does this by eliminating the additional access required to make each duplicated block capable of switching independently into the on-line system configuration.

In the large No. 1 ESS, which contains many components, the MTTF becomes too low to meet the reliability requirement.   To increase the value of the MTTF, either the number of components (failure rate) or the repair time must be reduced.   Alternatively, the single-unit duplex configuration can be partitioned into a multiunit duplex configuration, as shown in Figure 9-3.   In this arrangement, each subunit contains a smaller number of components and is able to be switched into a working system.   The system will fail only if a fault occurs in the redundant subunit while the original is

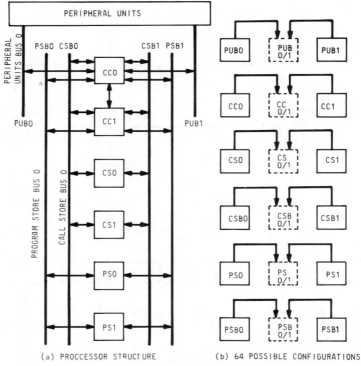

(a) PROCCESSOR STRUCTURE   (b) 64 POSSIBLE CONFIGURATIONS

Figure 9-3   Multi-Unit Duplex Configuration

being repaired. Since each subunit contains fewer components, the probability of two simultaneous faults occurring in a duplicated pair of subunits is reduced. The MTTF of the multiunit duplex configuration can be computed by taking into consideration the conditional probability of a subunit failing during the repair time of the original subunit.

An example of a multiunit duplex configuration is shown in Figure 9-3. A working system is configured with a fault-free CCx-CSx-CSBx-PSx-PSBx-PUBx arrangement, where x is either subunit 0 or subunit 1. This means there are 2^6 or 64 possible combinations of system configurations. The MTTF is given by the following expression:

$$\text{MTTF} = \frac{r\mu}{2\lambda^2} \tag{1}$$

where

$$r = \frac{1}{(\lambda_{CC}/\lambda)^2 + (\lambda_{CS}/\lambda)^2 + (\lambda_{CSB}/\lambda)^2 + (\lambda_{PS}/\lambda)^2 + (\lambda_{PSB}/\lambda)^2 + (\lambda_{PUB}/\lambda)^2} \tag{2}$$

The factor r is at a maximum when the failure rate (λ_i) for each subunit is the same. In this case,

$$\lambda_{CC} = \lambda_{CS} = \lambda_{CSB} = \lambda_{PS} = \lambda_{PSB} = \lambda_{PUB} = \lambda_i \tag{3}$$

or

$$\lambda_i = \frac{\lambda}{s} \tag{4}$$

where s = number of subunits in Eq. (2), $s = 6$, and $r = s$. At best, the MTTF is improved by a factor corresponding to the number of partitioned subunits. This improvement is not fully realized since equipment must be added to provide additional access and to select subunits. The partitioning of the subsystem into subunits as shown in Figure 9-3 results in subunits of different sizes. Again, the failure rate for each individual subunit will not be the same; hence, the r factor will be smaller than 6. Because of the relatively large number of components used in implementing the No. 1 ESS, the system is arranged in the multiunit duplex configuration in order to meet the reliability requirement.

Reliability calculation is a process of predicting, from available failure rate data, the achievable reliability of a system and the probability of meeting the reliability objectives for ESS applications. These calculations are most useful and beneficial during the early stages of design in order to assess various types of redundancy and to determine the system's organization. In the small- and medium-sized ESSs, the calculations have supported the use of single-unit duplex structures. For large ESSs, it was necessary to partition the system into a multiunit duplex configuration.

9.4 FAULT SIMULATION TECHNIQUES

One of the more difficult tasks of maintenance design is fault diagnosis. Its effectiveness in diagnostic resolution can be determined by simulation of the system's behavior in the presence of a specific fault. By means of simulation, design deficiencies can be identified and corrected prior to field use of the system. It is necessary to evaluate the system's ability to detect faults, to recover automatically back into a working system, and to provide diagnostic information (the location of the fault). Fault simulation, therefore, is an important aspect of maintenance design.

There are essentially two techniques used for simulating the faults of digital systems: *physical simulation* and *digital simulation. Physical simulation* is a process of inserting faults into a physical working model. When compared with digital simulation, this method produces more realistic behavior under fault conditions. Also, a wider class of faults can be applied to the system, such as a blown fuse or shorted backplane interconnection. However, fault simulation cannot begin until the design has been completed and the equipment is fully operational. Further, it is not possible to introduce faults to interior points of the logic (i.e., integrated circuits).

Digital fault simulation is a means of predicting the behavior, under failure, of a processor modeled in a computer program. The computer used to execute the program, called the *host,* is generally different from the processor being simulated, called the *object.* Digital fault simulation provides a high degree of automation and excellent access to interior points of logic, which permits designers to monitor the signal flow. Another advantage of this method is that it allows diagnostic test development and evaluation to proceed well in advance of unit fabrication. The cost of computer simulation can be quite high for a large, complex system.

Physical simulation was first employed by the Bell System to generate diagnostic data for the ESS field test described in Section 9.5 [7]. Over 50,000 known faults were purposely introduced into the *central control* (CC) to be diagnosed by its diagnostic program. Test results associated with each fault were recorded, sorted, and then printed in dictionary format to formulate a *trouble-locating manual* (TLM). Under trouble conditions, it was possible for maintenance personnel to determine which circuit packs *might* contain the defective component by consulting the TLM. Using this dictionary technique, the average repair time was kept low, and maintenance was made much easier.

The experience gained by using physical fault simulation in this field test was applied and extended in the development of the No. 1 ESS [1]. Each plug-in circuit pack was replaced one at a time by a fault simulator which introduced every possible type of single fault. The system's reaction was then recorded on magnetic tape. This was done for all circuit packs in the system. In addition to diagnostic data for TLMs, additional data was collected to determine the adequacy of hardware and software in fault detection and system recovery. Deficiencies were corrected to improve the overall maintenance of the system.

A digital logic simulator called *LAMP (Logic Analyzer for Maintenance Planning)* [8] was designed for the No. 1A ESS development. It played an important role in the development of the 1A Processor's hardware and diagnostics. The simulator is capable of simulating a subsystem with as many as 65,000 logic gates. All classical faults for standard logic gates are simulatable with logic nodes stuck at 0 or stuck at 1. Before physical units are available, digital simulation can be extremely effective in verifying the design, evaluating diagnostic access, and developing diagnostic tests. Both fault simulation techniques were integrated for the development of the 1A Processor to take advantage of each method's strengths simultaneously. The use of *complementary simulation* allows faults to be simulated physically (in the system laboratory) and logically (on a computer). Most of the deficiencies of each simulation technique are compensated for by the other technique. They *complement* one another—hence the term *complementary simulation.* The complementary method provided both a convenient method for validating the results and more extensive fault simulation data than would have been available if either process was used individually. Figure 9-4 shows the com-

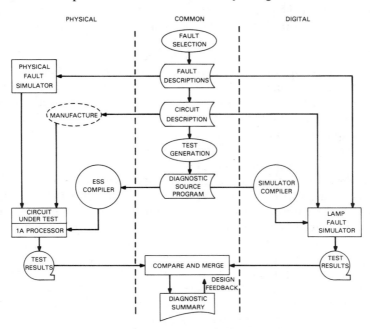

Figure 9-4 Complementary Fault Simulation System

plementary process of fault simulation used in the development of the 1A Processor [9,10].

9.5   FIRST GENERATION OF ESS PROCESSORS

The world's first ESS provided commercial telephone service at Morris, Illinois in 1959 for about a year on a field trial basis [11]. The system demonstrated the use of stored program control and the basic maintenance philosophy of providing continuous and reliable telephone service. The trial established valuable guides for designing a successor, the No. 1 ESS.

9.5.1   No. 1 ESS Processor

The No. 1 ESS was designed to serve large metropolitan telephone offices, ranging from several thousand to 65,000 lines [12]. As in most large switching systems, the processor represents only a small percentage of the total system cost. Therefore, performance and reliability were of primary importance in the design of the No. 1 Processor; cost was secondary. To meet the reliability standards established by electromechanical systems, all units essential to proper operation of the office are duplicated (see Figure 9-3). The multiunit duplex configuration was necessary to increase the MTTF of the processor because of the large number of components in each of the functional blocks.

Even with duplication, troubles must be found and corrected quickly to minimize exposure to system failure due to multiple troubles. All units are monitored continually so that troubles in the standby units are found just as quickly as those in the on-line units. This is accomplished by running the on-line and standby units in the synchronous match mode of operation [1]. Synchronization requires that clock timing signals be in close tolerance so that every operation in both halves is performed in step and key outputs are compared for error detection. The synchronization of duplicated units is accomplished by having the on-line oscillator output drive both clock circuits. There are two match circuits in each CC. Each matcher compares 24 bits within one machine cycle of 5.5 μs (microsecond). Figure 9-5 shows that each matcher has access to six sets of internal nodes (24 bits per node). In the routine match mode, the points matched in each cycle are dependent on the instruction being executed. The selected match points are those most pertinent to the data processing steps occurring during a given machine cycle. The two matchers in each CC compare the same sets of selected test points. The capability of each CC to compare a number of internal nodes provides a highly effective means of detecting hardware errors.

If a mismatch occurs, an interrupt is generated, which causes the fault

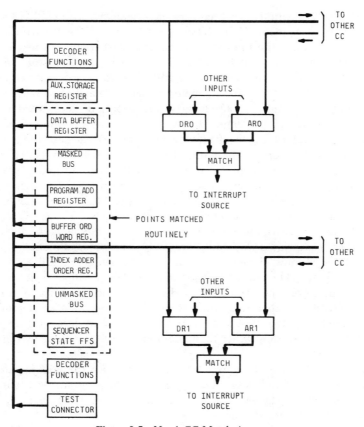

Figure 9-5   No. 1 CC Match Access

recognition program to run. The basic function of this program is to determine which half of the system is faulty. The suspected unit is removed from service, and the appropriate diagnostic program is run to pinpoint the defective circuit pack.

The No. 1 ESS was designed during the discrete component era (early 1960s) using individual components to implement logic gates [13]. The CC contains approximately 12,000 logic gates. Although this number appears small when compared to *large-scale integration* (LSI) *technology,* the No. 1 processor was a physically large machine for its time.

The match circuits capable of comparing internal nodes are the primary tools incorporated into the CC for diagnosing as well as detecting troubles. Specified information can be sampled by the matchers and retained in the match registers for examination. This mode of operation obtains critical data during the execution of diagnostic programs.

The early program store used *permanent magnet twister* (PMT) *modules* as basic storage elements [14]. They are a form of ROM in which system failures cannot alter the information content. Experience gained from the Morris field test system, which used the less reliable flying spot store, indicated that Hamming correction code was highly effective in providing continuous operation. At the time of development, it was felt that PMT modules might not be reliable enough. Consequently, the program store word included additional check bits for single-bit error correction (Hamming code). In addition, an overall parity-check bit which covers both the data and its address is included in the word. The word size consists of 37 bits of information and 7 check bits. When an error is corrected during normal operation, it is logged in an error counter. The maintenance program has access to this counter. Also, detection of a single error in the address or a double error in the word will cause an automatic retry.

The call store is the temporary read and write memory for storing transient data associated with call processing. Ferrite sheet memory modules are the basic storage elements used in implementing the call store in the No. 1 ESS [15]. The call store used in most No. 1 offices is smaller than the program store. (At the time of design, the cost per bit of call store was considerably higher than that of program store.) Also, ferrite sheet memory modules were considered to be very reliable devices. Consequently, single-bit error detection rather than Hamming correction code was provided in the call store.

There are two parity-check bits: one over both the address and data and the other over the address only. Again, as in the program store, automatic retry is performed whenever an error is detected, and the event is logged in an error counter for diagnostic use.

Troubles are normally detected by fault detection circuits, and error-free system operation is recovered by fault recognition programs [1]. This requires the on-line processor to be capable of making a proper decision. If this is not possible, an emergency action timer will "time out" and activate special circuits to establish various combinations of subsystems into a system configuration. A special program which is used to determine whether or not the assembled processor is sane takes the processor through a series of tests arranged in a maze. Only one correct path through the maze exists. If the processor passes through successfully, the timer will be reset, and recovery is successful. If recovery is unsuccessful, the timer will time out again, and the rearrangement of subsystems will be tried one at a time (e.g., combinations of CC, program store, and program store bus systems). For each selected combination, the special sanity program is started, and the sanity timer is activated. This procedure is repeated until a working configuration is found. The sanity program and sanity timer determine if the on-line CC is functioning properly. The active CC includes the program store and the program store bus.

9.5.2   No. 2 ESS Processor

The No. 2 ESS was developed during the mid-1960s [16]. This system was designed for medium-sized offices ranging from 1000 to 10,000 lines. The processor's design was derived from experience with the common stored program control of a *private branch exchange* (PBX), the No. 101 ESS [17]. Since the capacity requirement of the No. 2 ESS was to be less than that of the No. 1 ESS, cost became one of the more important design considerations. (Reliability is equally important in all systems.) The No. 2 ESS contains much less hardware than the No. 1 ESS. Understandably, its component failure rate is also substantially less. Its CC contains approximately 5000 gates (discrete components). To reduce cost and increase reliability, *resistor-transistor logic* (RTL) *gates* were chosen for the No. 2's processor since resistors are less expensive and more reliable than diodes (the No. 1 processor used *diode-transistor logic* [DTL]).

Because the No. 2's CC, program store, and call store are smaller, they are grouped together as a single switchable block in the single-unit duplex configuration shown in Figure 9-2. Calculations indicate that its MTTF is approximately the same as the No. 1 multiunit duplex structure, with each of the functional blocks and associated store buses grouped together as a switchable block. The use of only two system configurations reduces considerably the amount of hardware needed to provide gating paths and control for each functional unit. Moreover, the recovery program is simplified, and the reliability of the system is improved.

The No. 2 Processor runs in the synchronous match mode of operation [18]. The on-line oscillator output drives both clock circuits in order to keep the timing synchronized. The match operation is not as extensive as it is in the No. 1 ESS. For simplicity, there is only one matcher in the No. 2 ESS; it is located in the nonduplicated maintenance center (see Figure 9-6). The matcher always compares the call store input registers in the two CCs when call store operations are performed synchronously. A fault in almost any part of either CC quickly results in a call store input register mismatch. This occurs because almost all data manipulation performed in both the program control and the input/output control involves processed data returning to the call store. The call store input is the central point whereby data eventually funnels through to the call store. By matching the call store inputs, an effective check of the system equipment is provided. Compared to the more complex matching of the No. 1 Processor, error detection in the No. 2 Processor may not be as instantaneous since only

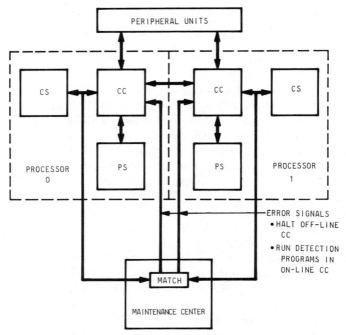

Figure 9-6   No. 2 CC Match Access

one crucial node in the processor is matched.   Certain faults in the No. 2 Processor will go undetected until the errors propagate into the call store. This interval is probably no more than tens or hundreds of microseconds. During such a short interval, the fault would affect only a single call.

The No. 2 ESS matcher is not used as a diagnostic tool as is the matcher in the No. 1 Processor.   Therefore, additional detection hardware is designed into the No. 2 Processor to help diagnose as well as detect faults.

When a mismatch occurs, the detection program is run in the on-line CC to determine if it contains the fault.   This is done while the standby processor is disabled.   If a solid fault in the on-line processor is detected by the mismatch detection program, the control is automatically passed to the standby processor, causing it to become the on-line processor.   The faulty processor is disabled, and diagnostic tests are called in to pinpoint the defective circuit pack.

The program store also uses PMT modules as basic storage elements, with a word size of 22 bits, half the width of the No. 1's word size.   Experience gained in the design and operation of the No. 101 ESS (PBX) showed that PMT stores were very reliable.   The additional protection provided in the No. 1 Processor against memory faults by error correction was not considered to be as essential in the No. 2 Processor.   This and the need to keep the cost down led to the choice of error detection *only* instead of the more sophisticated Hamming correction code.

Error detection works as follows: One of the 22 bits in a word is allocated as a parity-check bit. The program store contains both program and translation data. Additional protection is provided by using odd parity for program words and even parity for translation data. This detects the possibility of accessing the translation data area of memory as instruction words. For example, a software error may cause the program to branch into the data section of the memory and execute the data words as instruction words. The parity check would detect this problem immediately. The program store includes checking circuits to detect multiple-word access. Under program control, the sense amplifier threshold voltage can be varied in two discrete amounts from its nominal value to obtain a measure of the operating margin. The use of parity check was the proper choice for the No. 2 ESS in view of the high reliability of these memory devices.

The No. 2 Processor call store uses the same ferrite sheet memory modules as the No. 1 Processor. However, the No. 2's data word is 16 bits wide instead of 24. Fault detection depends heavily on the matching of the call store inputs when the duplex processors run in the synchronous mode. Within the call store circuit, the access circuitry is checked to see that access currents flow in the right direction at the correct time and that only two access switches are selected in any store operation. This ensures that only one word is accessed in the memory operation. Similarly, threshold voltages of the sense amplifiers may be varied under program control to evaluate the operating margins of the store. No parity-check bit is provided in the call store.

Each processor contains a program timer which is designed to back up other detection methods. Normally, the on-line processor clears the timer in both processors at prescribed intervals if the basic call processing program cycles correctly. If, however, a hardware or software trouble condition exists (e.g., a program may go astray, or a long program loop may prevent the timer from being cleared), the timer will time out and automatically produce a switch. The new on-line processor is automatically forced to run an initialization restart program that attempts to establish a working system. System recovery is simplified by using two possible system configurations rather than the multiunit duplex system.

9.6   SECOND GENERATION OF ESS PROCESSORS

The advent of silicon integrated circuits in the mid-1960s provided the technological climate for dramatic miniaturization, improved performance, and cost-reduced hardware. *1A technology* refers to the standard set of *integrated circuit* (IC) devices, apparatus, and design tools that were used to design the 1A Processor and the 3A Processor [19]. The choice of technology and the scale of integration level were dictated by the technological advances made between 1968 and 1970. *Small-scale integration* (SSI), made possible by bipolar technology, was capable of high-yield production. Because of the processor cycle time, high-speed logic gates with propagation delays from 5 to 10 ns (nanoseconds) were designed and developed concurrently with the 1A Processor.

9.6.1   1A Processor

The 1A Processor, successor to the No. 1 Processor, was designed primarily for the control of large local and toll electronic switching systems with high processing capabilities (the No. 1A ESS and No. 4 ESS, respectively) [20,21]. An important objective in developing the No. 1A ESS was to maintain commonality with the No. 1 ESS. High capacity was achieved by implementing the new 1A integrated technology and a newly designed system structure. These changes made possible an instruction execution rate that is four to eight times faster than the No. 1 Processor. Compatibility with the No. 1 ESS also allows the 1A Processor to be retrofitted into an in-service No. 1 ESS, replacing the No. 1 Processor when additional capacity is needed. The first 1A Processor was put into service in January 1976 as control for a No. 4 ESS in Chicago. Less than 1 year later, the first No. 1A ESS was put into commercial operation.

The 1A Processor architecture is similar to its predecessor in that all its subsystems have redundant units and are connected to the basic CC via redundant bus systems [9]. One of the 1A Processor's major architectural differences is its program store [22]. It has a writable *random-access memory* (RAM) instead of PMT ROM. By combining disk memory and RAM, the system has the same amount of memory as a system with PMT but at a lower cost. Backup copy of program and translation data is kept on disk. Other programs (e.g., diagnostics) are brought to RAM as needed; the same RAM spare is shared among different programs. More important is the system's ability to change the content of the store quickly and automatically. This simplifies considerably the administration and updating of program translation information in working offices.

The additional disk (file store) subsystem adds flexibility to the 1A Processor [22], but it also increases the complexity of system recovery. Figure 9-7 shows the multiunit duplex 1A Processor. This configuration is similar to the No. 1 Processor arrangement (see Figure 9-3) with a duplicated file store included. The file store communicates with the program store or call store via the CC and the auxiliary unit bus. This allows direct

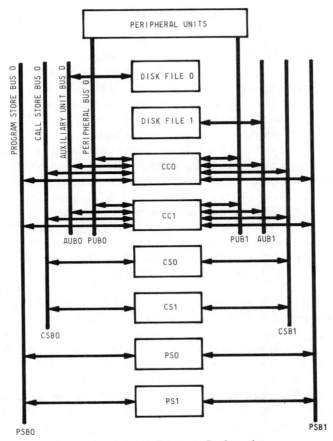

Figure 9-7   1A Processor Configuration

memory access between the file store and the program store or the call store. The disk file and the auxiliary unit bus are grouped together as a switchable entity.

Error detection is achieved by the duplicated and matched synchronous mode of operation, as in the No. 1 Processor. Both CCs operate in step and perform identical operations. The matching is done more extensively in the 1A to obtain as complete a check as possible. There are two match circuits in each processor. Each matcher has the ability to compare 24 internal bits to 24 bits in its mate once every machine cycle. (A machine cycle is 700 ns.) Any one of 16 different 24-bit internal nodes can be selected for comparison. The choice is determined by the type of instruction being executed. Rather than compare the same nodes in both CCs, the on-line and the standby CCs are arranged to match different sets of data. Four distinct internal groups are matched in the same machine cycle. This ensures the correct execution of any instruction.

The 1A Processor design is an improvement of the No. 1 Processor design. The 1A Processor incorporates much more checking hardware throughout various functional units in addition to matching hardware. Checking hardware speeds up fault detection and also aids the fault recovery process by providing indications that help isolate the faulty unit. The matching is used in various modes for maintenance purposes. This capability provides powerful diagnostic tools in isolating faults.

The program store and call store use the same hardware technology. The CC contains approximately 50,000 logic gates. While the initial design of the stores called for core memories, they have been replaced with semiconductor dynamic Metal Oxide Semiconductor (MOS) memories. The word size is 26 bits: 24 data bits and two parity-check bits. In the No. 1 Processor, the program store and the call store are fully duplicated. Because of their size, duplication requires a considerable amount of hardware, resulting in higher cost and increased component failures. To reduce the amount of hardware in the 1A Processor's store community, the memory is partitioned into blocks of 64K words, as shown in Figure 9-8. Two additional store blocks are provided as *roving spares*. If one of the program stores fails, a roving program store spare is substituted, and a copy of the program in the file store is transferred to the program store replacement. This type of redundancy has been made possible by the ability to regenerate data stored in a file store unit. Since a program store can be reloaded from the file store in less than a second, a roving spare redundancy plan is sufficient to meet the reliability requirement. As a result, Hamming correction code was not adopted in the 1A program store. However, it is essential that an error be detected quickly. Two parity check bits are generated over a partially overlapped, interleaved set of data bits and address. This overlapping is arranged to cope with particular memory circuit failures that may affect more than one bit of a word.

The 1A call stores contain both translation data backed up on the

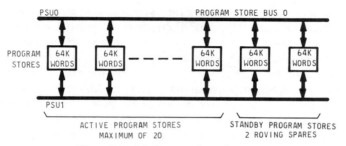

Figure 9-8 1A Program Store Structure

file stores and call-related transient data which are difficult to regenerate. The roving spare concept is expanded for the call stores to include sufficient spares to provide full duplication of transient data. If a fault occurs in a store that contains translation data, one of the duplicated stores containing transient call data is preempted and loaded with the necessary translation data from the duplicated copy in the file store. A parity check is done in the same manner as in the program store, using two check bits.

The combination of writable program store and file store provides a very effective and flexible system architecture for administrating and implementing a wide variety of features that are difficult to obtain in the No. 1 ESS. However, this architecture also complicates the process of fault recognition and recovery. Reconfiguration into a working system under trouble conditions is an extensive task, depending on the severity of the fault. (For example, it is possible for the processor to lose its sanity or ability to make proper decisions.) An autonomous hardware *processor configuration circuit* is provided in each CC to assist in assembling a working system. The processor configuration circuit consists of various timers which ensure that the operational, fault recovery, and configuration programs are successfully executed. If these programs *are not* executed, the process configuration circuit controls the CC-to-program-memory configuration, reloading program memory from file store when required and isolating various subsystems from the CC until a working system is obtained.

9.6.2 3A Processor

The No. 3A Processor was designed to control the small No. 3 ESS [23], which can handle from 500 to 5000 lines. One of the major concerns in the design of this ESS was the cost of its processor. The low cost and high speed of integrated logic circuitry made it possible to design a cost-effective processor that performed better than its discrete component predecessor, the No. 2 Processor. The 3A project was started in early 1971. The first system cut into commercial service in late 1975.

Because the number of components in the 3A Processor is considerably less than in the 1A Processor, all subsystems are fully duplicated, including the main store. The CC, the store bus, and the store are treated as a single switchable entity rather than as individual switchable units as in the 1A Processor. The system structure is similar to the No. 2 ESS. Experience gained in the design and operation of the No. 2 provided valuable input for the No. 3 Processor design.

The 3A's design makes one major departure from previous ESS processor designs: It operates in the nonmatched mode of duplex operation. The primary purpose of matching is to detect errors. A mismatch, however, does not indicate *where* (which one of the processors) the fault has occurred.

A diagnostic fault location program must be run to localize the trouble so that the defective unit can be taken off-line. For this reason, the 3A Processor was designed to be self-checking, with detection circuitry incorporated as an integral part of the processor. Faults occurring during normal operation are discovered quickly by detecting hardware. This eliminates the need to run the standby system in the synchronous and match mode of operation or the need to run the fault recognition program to identify the defective unit when a mismatch occurs.

The synchronous and match mode arrangement of the No. 1 Processor and the No. 2 ESS provides excellent detection and coverage of faults. However, there are many instances (e.g., periodic diagnostics, administration changes, recent change updates, etc.) when the system is not run in the normal match mode. Consequently, during these periods, the system is vulnerable to faults which may go undetected. The rapid advances in integrated circuit technology make possible the implementation of self-checking circuits in a cost-effective manner. This eliminates the need for the synchronous match mode of operation. Self-checking design is covered in more detail in the next section.

Another new feature in ESS processor design is the application of microprogram techniques in the No. 3A [24]. These techniques provide a regular procedure for implementing the control logic. Standard error detection is made part of the hardware to achieve a high degree of checkability. Sequential logic, which is difficult to check, is easily implemented as a sequence of microprogram steps. Microprogramming offers many attractive features: It is simple, flexible, easy to maintain, and easy to expand.

The 3A Processor paralleled the design of the 1A Processor in its use of an electrically alterable (writable) memory. However, great strides in semiconductor memory technology after the 1A became operational permitted the use of semiconductor memory in the 3A rather than core memory.

The 3A's call store and program store are consolidated into a single-store system. This reduces cost by eliminating buses, drivers, registers, and controls. A single-store system no longer allows concurrent access of call store and program store. However, this disadvantage is more than compensated for by the much faster semiconductor memory. Its access time is 1 μs (the earlier PMT stores had an access time of 6 μs).

Normal operation requires the on-line processor to run and process calls, while the standby processor is in the halt state, with its memory updated for each write operation. For the read operation, only the on-line memory is read, *except* when a parity error occurs during a memory read. This results in a microprogram interrupt, which reads the word from the standby store in an attempt to bypass the error.

As discussed previously, the No. 2 processor (first generation) is used in the No. 2 ESS for medium-sized offices. It covers approximately 4000 to 12,000 lines, with a call handling capability of 19,000 busy-hour calls. (The number of calls is related to the calling rate of lines during the busy hour.) The microprogram techniques used in the 3A Processor design allow the No. 2 Processor's instruction set to be emulated. This enables programs written in the No. 2 assembly language to be directly portable to the 3A Processor. The ability to preserve the call processing programs permits the No. 2 ESS to be updated by the 3A Processor without having to undergo a complete, new program development.

The combination of the 3A Processor and the peripheral equipment of the No. 2 ESS is designated the No. 2B ESS. It is capable of handling 38,000 busy-hour calls, twice the capability of the No. 2 ESS [25]. The No. 2B ESS can be expanded to cover about 20,000 lines. Furthermore, when an existing No. 2 ESS system in the field exceeds its real-time capacity, the No. 2 Processor can be taken out and replaced with the 3A Processor. The retrofit operation has been carried out successfully in working offices without disturbing telephone service.

9.7 MAINTENANCE DESIGN OF THE 3A PROCESSOR

The 3A Processor was put into service in late 1975. Self-checking hardware has been integrated into the design to detect faults during normal system operation. This simplified fault recognition technique is required to identify a subsystem unit when it becomes defective. Reconfiguration into a working system is immediate, without extensive diagnostic programs to determine which subsystem unit contains the fault. The problem of synchronization, in a much shorter machine cycle (150 ns), is eliminated by not having to run both processors in step. The No. 3A Processor uses low-cost integrated circuits to realize its highly reliable and flexible design.

9.7.1 General System Description

The general system block diagram of the 3A Processor is shown in Figure 9-9. The CC, the main store, and the cartridge tape unit are duplicated for reliability. These units are grouped as a single switchable entity rather than as individual switchable units. The quantity of equipment within the switchable block is small enough to meet the reliability requirement; therefore, the expense and complexity of providing communication paths and control for switchable units within the system are avoided. Each functional unit was designed to be as autonomous as possible, with a minimum number of output signal leads. This provides the flexibility necessary to expand the system and make changes easily.

As shown in Figure 9-9, the standard program store and call store are combined as a single storage unit to reduce cost. Although the processors

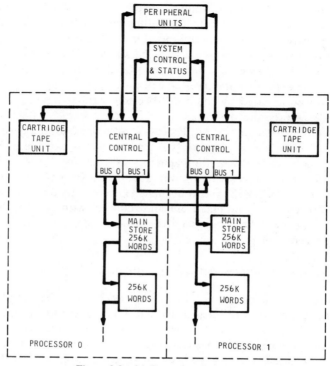

Figure 9-9 3A Processor Organization

are not run in the synchronous match mode of operation, both stores (on-line and standby) are kept up-to-date. This is achieved by having the on-line processor write into both stores simultaneously when call store data is written or changed.

Because of the volatile nature of a writable memory, low-cost bulk storage backup (cartridge tape) is required to reload the program and translation data when the latter is lost due to a store failure. The pump-up mechanism or store loader uses the microprogram control in conjunction with an *input/output* (I/O) serial channel to transfer data between the cartridge tape unit and the main store. Other deferrable, infrequently used programs (i.e., diagnostics or growth programs) are stored on tape and paged in as needed.

The system control and status panel, a nonduplicated block, provide a common point for the display of overall system status and alarms. Included in this unit is the emergency action circuitry that allows the maintenance personnel to initialize the system or force and lock the system into a fixed configuration. Communication with the processor takes place via the I/O serial channel.

9.7.2 General Processor Description

Figure 9-10 shows a detailed block diagram of the CC. It is organized to process input data and handle call processing functions efficiently. The processor's design is based upon the register type of architecture. Fast-access storage in the form of flip-flop registers provides short-term storage for information being used in current data processing operations. Sixteen *general-purpose registers* (GPRs) are provided as integral parts of the structure.

Microprogram control is the heart of the 3A Processor. It provides nearly all the complex control and sequencing operations required for implementing the instruction set. Other complicated sequencing functions are also stored in the microprogram memory, for example:

1. The bootstrap operation of reloading the program from the backup tape unit
2. The initializing sequence to restart the system under trouble conditions
3. The interrupt priority control and saving of essential registers
4. The emergency action timer and processor switching operation
5. The craft-to-machine functions

The regular structure of the microprogram memory makes error detection

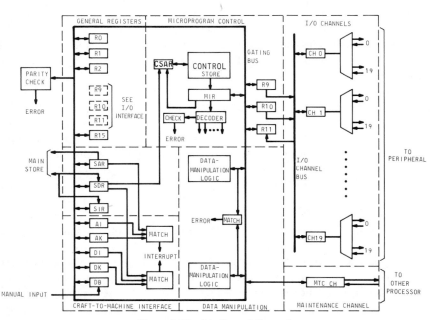

Figure 9-10 3A Central Control

easier. The microprogram method of implementation also offers flexibility in changing control functions.

The data manipulation instructions are designed specifically for implementing the call processing programs. These instructions are concerned with logical and bit manipulation rather than with arithmetical operations. However, a binary ADD is included in the instruction repertoire for adding two binary numbers and for indexing. This allows other arithmetical operations to be implemented conveniently by the software combination of addition and logical operations or by a microprogram sequence if higher speed is essential. The data manipulation logic contains rotation, Boolean function of two variables, first-zero detection, and fast binary ADD.

The remaining functional blocks in Figure 9-10 deal with external interfaces. The 20 main I/O channels, each with 20 subchannels, allow the processor to control and access up to 400 peripheral units by means of 21-bit (16 data, 2 parity, and 3 start code bits) serial 6.67-MHz (megahertz) messages. The system is expandable in modules of one main channel (20 subchannels). The I/O structure allows up to 20 subchannels (one from each main channel) to be active simultaneously. In addition, the *craft-to-machine interface,* with displays and manual inputs, is integrated into the processor. This interface contains many of the *manual functions* that will assist in hardware and software debugging. The control logic associated with this part of the processor is incorporated as part of the microprogram control. Last, the maintenance channel enables the on-line processor to control and diagnose the standby processor. The use of a serial channel reduces the number of leads interconnecting the two processors and causes them to be "loosely coupled." This facilitates the split mode or stand-alone configuration for factory test or system test.

9.7.3 Control Circuitry

The major feature of the 3A Processor's control logic is that it is microprogrammed. Microprogramming provides a more regular approach than the conventional technique to the design of control logic. It also permits checking techniques to be applied more readily. The simplified microprogrammed structure of the system is shown in Figure 9-11. Each microprogram store word contains the address of the next microinstruction and a FROM and TO control field that specifies the source and destination for a data transfer operation. The store word may also specify some other types of operation. The *control store address register* (CSAR) receives its contents from either the opcode of the main machine macroinstruction to be executed (this forms the initial address of the microprogram which interprets the macroinstruction) or the last microprogram store word. One macroinstruction fetched from the main store results in the execution of a sequence of microinstructions.

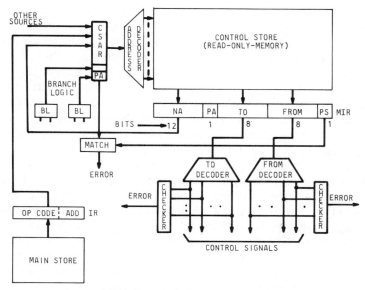

Figure 9-11 Microprogram Control

System operation consists of continually reading macroinstructions from the main store and executing the specified sequences of microinstructions.

In designing the hardware check for the microprogram control, it is essential to recognize the types of failures that are most probable. Matching the checking techniques with the types of faults that actually occur yields the best results with the least amount of hardware. The microprogram control is constructed from integrated circuits: LSI for the memory and SSI for the associated control logic. Because of the method of isolating components and because of the physical proximity of devices on an integrated circuit chip, multiple faults within a chip have been analyzed and found to be of the type that would tend to affect the bits in a unidirectional manner: these faults affect adjacent bits rather than nonadjacent bits in the word [26]. Unidirectional error refers to a fault that causes one or more data bits to assume a wrong value of one type: 0 or 1 but not both simultaneously (for example, 01100 to 01111, not to 01010).

The checking technique used in the implementation of the microprogram control takes advantage of the error characteristics mentioned above. The microprogram store contains two types of data: control and address information. The control fields are immediately decoded and checked to provide control signals. A more efficient nonsystematic check code, such as the m-out-of-$2m$ code, would give the maximum detectability at the least possible cost in hardware. This code can detect all multiple unidirectional errors.

However, for the address field, it is desirable to maintain the data in binary form for addressing and to provide immediate binary data to several sources. Consequently, the choice of a systematic check code for the address field is essential to give this flexibility.   By recognizing that the multiple-bit faults tend to affect adjacent bits rather than randomly disperse them throughout the word, the binary field is interleaved with the *m*-out-of-2*m* code, as shown in Figure 9-12.   Any multiple adjacent-bit fault would then affect both the binary and the *m*-out-of-2*m* codes.   Consequently, a single parity-check bit is adequate to detect single-bit faults in the binary field, and multiple adjacent-bit faults would be detected by the *m*-out-of-2*m* check.

In checking the binary address field, parity is maintained on the address in the CSAR and checked by (1) storing the correct parity (see Figure 9-11) in the word addressed in memory and (2) comparing the two after the word is read out.   The next address field in the *control store data register* (CSDR) or *microinstruction register* (MIR) also has a parity bit that becomes the parity bit of the CSAR when it is gated into the CSAR.   The conditional branch logic is checked by duplication.   A match is not necessary to check the duplicated logic since its output must change both the low-order bit and the parity bit of the CSAR.   One of the branch logic circuits feeds the low-order bit, and the other feeds the *parity bit (P_A)* (see Figure 9-11) so that a branch logic failure is detected because of the resultant bad parity of the CSAR.

The checking techniques (such as *m*-out-of-2*m*, interleaved parity, and duplication) are integrated into the 3A's design to detect failures that may occur in the microprogram control.   These types of checks are provided to detect multiple unidirectional types of faults that are possible with the use of integrated circuit technology.

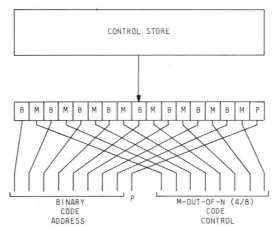

Figure 9-12   Control Store Coding Techniques

9.7.4 4-out-of-8 Decoder and Checker

Each TO and FROM control field is 8 bits wide and encoded as a 4-out-of-8 code. There are 70 valid combinations in an 8-bit field; each combination has four 1s and four 0s. The fields, which are decoded to drive the control points of the processor, are checked by a self-checking checker that detects faults in the decoder and the input codes [27].

Because of the large number of output leads in a fully decoded 4-out-of-8 code to 70 outputs, the decoder circuitry is divided into two groups. A control function is represented by two outputs, one from each group. Figure 9-13 shows the decoding arrangement whereby each group is sorted into five logic subgroups with 4, 3, 2, 1, and 0 inputs and designated as 4(1), 3(1), 2(1), 1(1), and 0(1), respectively. The numbers of gates belonging to the respective subgroups are 1, 4, 6, 4, and 1, as shown in the figure. Similarly, the second 4 bits in the 4-out-of-8 code are decoded and divided into the same subgrouping. The A subgroups are paired with the B subgroups to obtain the 70 possible 4-out-of-8 code combinations. The $4_a(1)$ group pairs with the $0_b(1)$ group to give one combination; the $3_a(1)$ group pairs

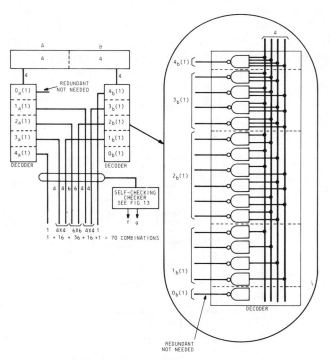

Figure 9-13 4-out-of-8 Decoding Arrangement

with the $1_b(1)$ group to give 16 combinations; and so on, as indicated in Figure 9-13. The $0(1)$ subgroup is redundant, and therefore it is not used.

The total number of decoder outputs from each group is 15 instead of 16. Within a decoder group, more than one output may be active simultaneously. For example, the 1111 input code can cause all gates to be active. This is entirely satisfactory since only the gate in the corresponding subgroup of the second decoder [in this case the $0(1)$ subgroup] would be active; gates in the other subgroups would *not* be active. Hence, one and only one pair of decoder outputs is active. This condition uniquely defines one of the possible 70 combinations in the 4-out-of-8 codes.

The decoder design provides the proper outputs that facilitate the implementation of the self-checking 4-out-of-8 checker. The self-checking circuit is realized by subdividing the checker into two separate independent subcircuits. Each subcircuit generates a single output whose values are arranged to be complementary for normal 4-out-of-8 input codes. For any errors in the input code, decoder, or check logic, the two outputs are alike (00 or 11).

A totally self-checking checker has the advantage of not requiring periodic tests in order to ensure that any faults occurring in the functional circuits will be detected immediately. The check scheme involves pairing the subgroups, corresponding to exactly four 1s, as follows: $0_a(1)$-$4_b(1)$, $1_a(1)$-$3_b(1)$, $2_a(1)$-$2_b(1)$, $3_a(1)$-$1_b(1)$, $4_a(1)$-$0_b(1)$. An output is generated for each pairing. The alternating pairs are divided into separate groups, f and g, as indicated in Figure 9-14. Since only one pair will be active for a correct 4-out-of-8

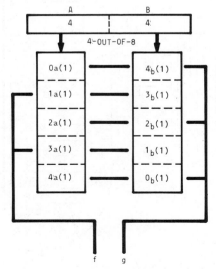

Figure 9-14 General Diagram of 4-out-of-8 Checker

input, the response from f and g will be 10 or 01 for the normal operating condition. If the input is other than a 4-out-of-8 code, the f and g outputs will be 11 or 00. For example, if the input is 11100011, the $3_a(1)$, $2_a(1)$, $1_a(1)$, and $0_a(1)$ from the A group and the $2_b(1)$, $1_b(1)$, and $0_b(1)$ from the B group will be active. This means two pairs of subgroups will be active: $3_a(1)$-$1_b(1)$ in the f group and $2_a(1)$-$2_b(1)$ in the g group. The alternating pairs are chosen to be in separate groups to ensure that when there is more than one pair active, the resultant fg output is 11, representing an input with more than four 1s. If the input contains less than four 1s, none of the four pairs will be active. For example, if the input is 01110000, the $3_a(1)$, $2_a(1)$, $1_a(1)$, and $0_a(1)$ of the A group and the $0_b(1)$ of the B group will be active. These are outputs from each group, but none of them belong to a pair; hence, the fg output is 00, corresponding to an input combination with less than four 1s. The logic implementation of the 4-out-of-8 checker is shown in Figure 9-15.

The $0(1)$ subgroup represents the condition of no 1 or any number of 1s in the 4-bit input. This means the $0(1)$ gate is always active and redundant. The pairing of $4_a(1)$-$0_b(1)$ does not need to include the $0_b(1)$ subgroup at all. Its gate and output are ignored in the implementation.

The FROM and TO decoder outputs fan out to various functional

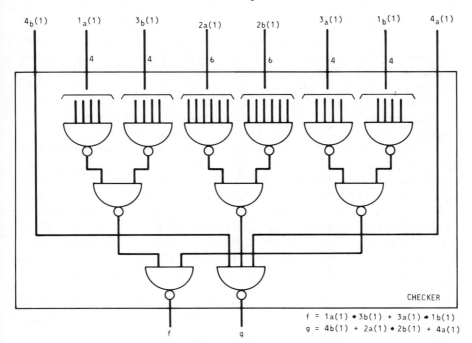

$$f = 1a(1) \bullet 3b(1) + 3a(1) \bullet 1b(1)$$
$$g = 4b(1) + 2a(1) \bullet 2b(1) + 4a(1)$$

Figure 9-15 4-out-of-8 Checker Logic

units for controlling logical operations or data transfers within the CC. Those that go to the data transfer logic control the gating of data from one register to another via the data bus. The circuitry of this functional block is partitioned on a 2-bit slice; all logic gates associated with the 2 bits are contained on a single circuit board. Since the decoder outputs fan out to 2 bits, any malfunction of the control within a circuit board would affect only those 2 bits of data. When the word is used at a later time, the error will be detected by the parity check on the data. Consequently, it is sufficient to check the control signals prior to entering the data transfer block. This is also true for the data manipulation block since the circuitry is duplicated.

A number of microoperations consist of setting or clearing individual flip-flops or enabling dedicated paths where the use of a single TO or FROM field crosspoint would be inefficient. A miscellaneous decoder is provided; it takes inputs from both the TO and FROM fields. In this way, a 10 × 10 matrix (100 crosspoints) is generated by assigning only 10 of the 70 combinations from each of the TO and FROM fields. Most of these types of crosspoints control duplicated circuitry; hence, the decoding gate itself is duplicated. A fault in this area will result in an error in the data path and will be detected by a parity check.

9.7.5   Data Registers

There are two types of internal data registers: general-purpose and special-purpose. The latter type is dedicated to specific functions. Examples are the *interrupt status* (IS) *register* and the *error register* (ER). The general-purpose registers are involved with the handling of data associated directly with the instructions. The checking of the data transfer logic is done by partitioning two bits of the register on a single circuit board and then carrying two parity bits. This partitioning and the definition of the parity bits are illustrated in Figure 9-16, with the first circuit board containing two bits of every general-purpose register. Partitioning the registers in this way ensures that any fault on a circuit board will not affect more than two bits of any register. This also ensures that the fault will be detected by the two parity bits. If all of one register's bits were grouped on a single board, a catastrophic failure of that board could affect all the bits, and the failure would not necessarily be detectable by the two parity bits. The main memory is also organized as a 2-bit slice per circuit pack plus two parity-check bits. A consistent parity check is done throughout the entire system; I/O is included.

For any data transfer, the information from the source register is checked by the parity checker at a common point: the data bus. In a register-to-register transfer, the data in the destination register is not checked. This is satisfactory since it will be checked when the data is used either to address the store or to be operated on by the data manipulation logic.

CIRCUIT BOARDS

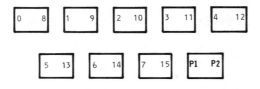

P1 = PARITY   OVER BITS 0,1,2,3,4,5,6,7
P2 = PARITY   OVER BITS 8,9,10,11,12,13,14,15

Figure 9-16   Layout of General-Purpose Registers on Circuit Boards

9.7.6   Data Manipulation Logic

The *data manipulation logic* (DML) contains rotation, Boolean function of two variables, first-zero detection, and fast binary ADD.   The DML is duplicated and matched to allow full checking in this area.   Other coding techniques, such as parity prediction and residue coding, are available for arithmetical functions.   However, for all logical functions of two variables, duplication is the simplest method of checking.   Duplication eliminates the need for checking if the data arrived at the modification logic correctly.

As shown in Figure 9-17, a match circuit detects faults, and a parity

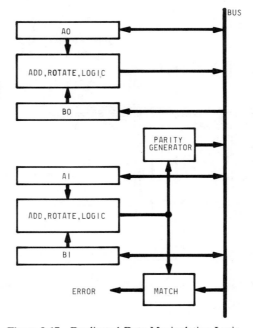

Figure 9-17   Duplicated Data Manipulation Logic

generation circuit supplies parity on the DML output to interface with the rest of the system.

9.7.7   I/O Channels

The 20 I/O channels are 6.67 MHz serial channels.   Each channel has 20 subchannels.   Figure 9-18 shows the data flow from the processor to the I/O buffers.   Three of the general-purpose registers, R9 through R11, are used: R9 loads the control buffer (IOS), R10 loads the data buffer (IOD), and R11 receives data from the I/O channel.   All command and selection signals are encoded in 3-out-of-6 codes and decoded to 1-out-of-20 codes. The channel address stored in R9 is used to direct the data and microinstructions to one of the 20 specified main channels.   The decoding of the enable address is done individually in each main channel, with the output returning to a common point for checking.   This is done to ensure that only the right channel is enabled.   The command decoding and subchannel selector within each channel are similarly checked for proper decoding of 3-out-of-6 codes.

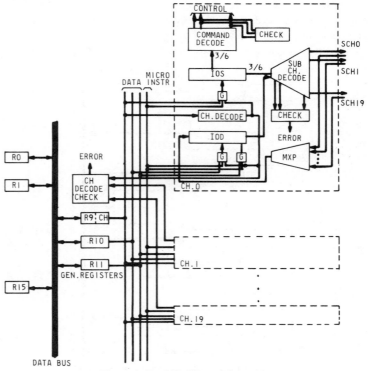

Figure 9-18   I/O Channel Structure

The data message containing two parity-check bits from R10 is transmitted by the channel and checked by the peripheral unit. In addition, prior to transmission of the message, the data is brought back by the microprogram sequence to the data manipulation logic and compared with the content of R10 to ensure that the data has been loaded properly. Messages received from the peripheral unit also have two parity bits, which are checked when they are placed on the bus.

9.7.8 Maintenance Channel

The *maintenance channel* (MCH) is used for interprocessor communication as well as for the diagnosis of one processor by the other processor. The MCH's structure is similar to the I/O channel, and therefore the checking technique is the same. The data field used the standard 2-bit parity in order to remain consistent with the rest of the processor. The command field is encoded in 3-out-of-6 codes.

9.7.9 Method of Checking Error Detection Circuits

Any circuitry used for checking purposes is incorporated as part of the system. Such circuitry should be as fail-safe as possible so that a failure in the system will cause a failure alarm. It has been shown that such a check circuit can be realized if the output is in the form of a 1-out-of-2 code, with 01 or 10 for the normal operation and 00 or 11 for the error condition [28]. Ultimately, these two outputs must be monitored to generate a single-error output.

The final gate is not completely fail-safe. A failure in this gate will prevent the circuitry from giving any error indication, and faults normally detected will be ignored. A good design allows only a small portion of the detection hardware to be non-fail-safe. The checking of the non-fail-safe portion of the check logic is essential to guarantee reliable operation of these circuits. This is accomplished by a combination of hardware and software. This approach has been proved to be very effective in checking the check circuits, with both hardware and software costs kept to a minimum. The hardware provides the means of simulating test conditions or circuit faults which are extremely difficult or awkward to set up normally in the system. A flip-flop register, called the *maintenance state* (MS) *register,* is used for this purpose. Each bit represents an error or test condition. By appropriately setting up the MS register and applying a well-designed test sequence, the detection circuitry can be checked on a periodic basis to ensure its proper application.

9.7.10 Method of Detecting Hardcore Circuit Faults

Although the system is designed to be nearly self-checking, it contains a small hardcore portion that must be operating properly prior to running a program sequence. The circuitry usually includes the sequencing logic of the microprogram control and the addressing and fetching of instructions from the main store. For example, if the control to advance the *program counter* (PC) cannot be activated, the PC remains in one particular state. The same address is used at each reading, resulting in the same outputs from the store. The program, therefore, is stuck at one location, executing the same instruction repetitively, with no means of advancing through the program sequence to produce any useful work. The amount of hardcore circuitry is strongly dependent on the system design and is difficult to eliminate. In a duplicated and matched system, when both processors are running in a synchronous mode with important outputs being matched continuously, any error in the hardcore circuitry will be detected instantaneously.

In the nearly self-checking design, the system does not run in a synchronous match mode. This is done to reduce the complexity of software, thereby increasing reliability. A hardware timer is used to detect faults in the hardcore circuitry and also as backup to protect the system from control by an insane CC due to either hardware or software troubles. The use of a timer depends on the program meeting an obstacle or a series of tests arranged in a maze. If the program is successfully completed through the maze, the timer is reset by the maintenance control program. On the other hand, if the program strays off course, the timer will time out, and the emergency action circuit will select a new configuration. The sanity test is repeated to verify a fault-free system.

The telephone processing program is cyclic in nature. It returns to the starting point at each scan upon completion of a series of tasks required by the call processing [29]. Although the scan time may vary from scan to scan, depending on the amount of work required of the program, the maximum time can be easily determined.

The use of a hardware timer is closely tied with the system program. It is arranged so that a reset is generated for the timer only if the program proceeds through the scan correctly within the prescribed period. If the program deviates from the normal course, no reset will occur. In this case, the timer automatically times out, stops processing, and switches to the standby system.

There are two timers, one located in each processor; both are active at all times. Duplication is necessary in order to guarantee that the system will be capable of recovery. It is possible that a single fault can disable one processor and its timer, thus necessitating the standby to perform the function. The timers are periodically reset by the on-line program. If they are not reset, the on-line timers will time out first. If the on-line timer does not work, the off-line timer will perform the task at a later time.

9.8 RECOVERY TECHNIQUES

Fault detection is the first and most important step in realizing a highly reliable system. Two other functions of equal importance are (1) rapid recovery of the system to process calls and (2) the protection of calls in progress in the face of either hardware or software difficulties. This means the mechanism for switching controls must be highly reliable. Proper steps have been taken to give a smooth transition in the transfer of controls. In the design of the system, the combination of hardware and software is so intertwined as to provide the utmost protection against an insane CC taking control of the system. A rapid and successful recovery is achieved by a combination of hardware and software so that continuity is maintained [30].

9.8.1 Automatic Recovery

When an error is recognized in the on-line processor, several things may happen depending on the type of error. Error signals are buffered in the ER for diagnostic purposes. In addition, the error signals are sorted out and divided into three groups, with each group causing a different set of system actions. The least severe of the three are the errors associated with the I/O or MCH. These errors will cause an interrupt in which the processor has complete control in determining the exact cause of the trouble. If the error is a transient fault, it will be recorded and compiled for later analysis. If the error is determined to be a hardware fault within the switchable block of the processor, the interrupt program will initiate a reconfiguration of the standby machine by means of the MCH. This would be an orderly switch to the other processor; there would be no detrimental effect on the system.

The second type of error involves faults occurring in the standby portion of the system. These faults directly influence the on-line operation. For example, the system is organized to operate both stores asynchronously. Whenever data is written into the on-line store, it is written into the off-line store simultaneously. The processor waits for a store completion signal from both stores before proceeding with the next operation. If a response signal originates only from the on-line store, there is a 32-μs pause, and then a special timer times out and generates an error signal, indicating trouble in the off-line store. Under this condition, the processor is interrupted at the microinstruction level, and appropriate action is taken to continue call processing with the standby store isolated.

The third type of error involves hardware faults within the on-line processor. An extension of the previous discussion will serve as a good example: If the store completion signal is received from the standby store and *not* from the on-line store, this error signal causes the system to switch to the standby configuration. In this situation, the system momentarily "hangs up." A restart in the standby machine would then initialize the processor and continue with call processing, affecting, perhaps, only one call in the transient state.

Numerous check circuits are designed and integrated into the system. As soon as an error is detected, immediate action takes place to reconfigure the system into an error-free working system. In addition, duplicated hardware timers are provided to back up undetected hardware faults or software bugs which cause the program to go astray. The recovery process involves the following two steps:

1. *Reconfiguration*
2. *Restart or initialization:* to enable the new processor configuration a smooth transition into full control of the system

When a switch to the standby processor occurs, it must be initialized to a known state in order to start smoothly. This operation is divided into three stages or levels. The first stage involves the elementary control of the microprogram store, ensuring that it can start and execute a sequence of microinstructions properly at a predetermined store location. This is done by hardware before the first microcycle. The operation consists of the following steps:

1. Setting the MAR to a predetermined address
2. Setting clock circuitry to a well-defined state
3. Setting the *block hardward check* (BHC) *flip-flop* to inhibit detection hardware from possibly generating an error signal, thus initiating a switch operation
4. Resetting various control flip-flops (e.g., STOP, FREEZE) that would directly affect the running of the microprogram control

The second stage of initialization is done by microprogram. The primary function of the microprogram initialization is to set the various control bits or registers that have direct influence on running the main program sequence, for example:

1. Set the *block interrupt* (BIN) *flip-flop* to inhibit the external interrupt from interfering with the initializing program
2. Reset the *update* (UPD) *flip-flop* to inhibit the standby store from being updated

3. Set the *isolate* (ISO) *flip-flop* to prevent the off-line store operation from interfering with the on-line operation
4. Reset the hardware timer to prevent it from timing out

In addition, the microprogram decides whether or not the main store contains valid program data. If it does not, the alternative would be to switch the processor and try the other configuration since the program data is duplicated, with a copy in each store. The objective is to try to use each of the two copies before resorting to the use of a tape unit as a final backup. The sanity of the machine depends very heavily on the memory content. As a result, an arrangement (shown in Figure 9-19) has been implemented to allow a systematic way of recovering from system errors. The scheme uses two initialization sanity check bits (ISC1 and ISC2) as markers. They are part of the *system status* (SS) *register*. Normally, these two bits are in the 00 state. During the first time through the microprogram level of initialization (ISC1 = 0), this ISC1 bit is set to the 1 condition as a marker for subsequent initialization. The system then proceeds to the main program

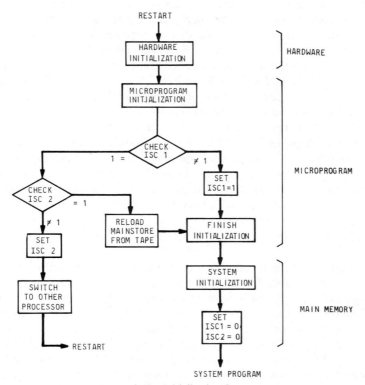

Figure 9-19 Initialization Sequence

initialization.   If the store contains correct program data and if the system is fully recovered from the initialization, this marker bit will be reset.   However, if the program data has been badly mutilated, the main program may wander aimlessly, executing bad programs.

When a second initialization occurs within the same CC and the first marker bit is set to the 1 state, the initialization at the microprogram level will set the second marker bit to 1.   It then directs the control to be passed on to the other processor with the expectation that its main memory and the rest of the hardware are in good working condition.   Otherwise, it will switch back to the original processor and try to initialize for the third time. Now, with both marker bits set to 11, the microprogram initialization sequence will recognize this condition and take the drastic step of reloading the main memory from the backup tape unit.   These operational steps are depicted in Figure 9-19.

The third and final stage of initialization is done by the main program. This stage covers both the internal status of the processor and the main store data pertaining to the peripheral equipment status, transient data, and various data associated with maintenance of the system.   The internal state of the processor is saved in the main memory for subsequent analysis by the diagnostic program.   Next, the various registers are set to a prescribed initial state.   All control flip-flops, which were set up by the first two levels of initialization to inhibit various functions (such as BLOCK HARDWARE CHECK, BLOCK INTERRUPT, and INHIBIT STORE UPDATE, etc.), are now restored to normal operation.   This handling of the memory data, which has a direct effect on the operation of the system, depends on the ability of the main program to run successfully and the frequency of initialization.   Audit programs are called in to validate and check for consistent data in the memory and peripheral equipment status.   The initialization and recovery programs clear selective portions of memory data and take increasingly severe actions on the memory, depending on the rate of system reconfiguration.   A high rate indicates the system's inability to maintain its sanity.

9.8.2 Manual Recovery

Although the system is designed to recover automatically under trouble conditions, it is conceivable for the system to be unable to reconfigure into a working mode.   This can be caused by software bugs, hardware faults, or a combination of both.   The processor may be switching continuously, spending all its available time repeating initialization work.   In other words, the control unit has gone insane and is incapable of making any rational decisions. In this case, the ultimate control of the system must be left to the judgment of qualified maintenance personnel.   Hardware has been provided to give maintenance personnel the capability of forcing the system into a fixed configuration and locking it into the mode. Under this condition, the switching operation would be made inoperative, and any system initialization would be directed to the locked processor. If both processors are defective but to different degrees, manual control makes it possible to lock out the most defective one and hope that the system will limp along.

In addition to the manual force and lock functions of the emergency action panel, provision has been made to manually generate initialization and modify different categories of data in the area of the store which is not write-protected. These categories include (1) transient data that are associated with calls in a stable talking state and (2) recent change data that are associated with the changing of customer telephone lines. The automatic recovery program is only allowed to clear the transient data that affect telephone calls in the nontalking state. If an incomplete call is interrupted, the caller must try again. On the other hand, if the stabler data are cleared, calls in the talking state are interrupted, and the talking state is taken down. Hence, maintenance personnel are given the *final control* over recovery by taking the additional action of clearing the more important stable and recent change data portions of the store.

Due to the importance of these controls, safeguards have been designed into the manual switches and circuitry to protect against an accidental switch operation. This is necessary to prevent any inadvertent actions that may have severe effects on the system. Emergency controls are grouped together with system alarms and status indicators at the common system control panel, which is readily available to maintenance personnel. Additional redundancy has been designed into the system so that if both processors are down, a positive indication must be given to maintenance personnel before the appropriate action can be taken. This is done by another hardware timer in the common system control panel. While the on-line program is progressing through the programs correctly, it must periodically reset this timer. If the on-line processor does not reset the timer, it will "time out" and set the alarm circuit, immediately bringing the stiuation to the attention of the craftsperson.

9.9   DIAGNOSTIC HARDWARE

Fault detection determines whether or not a circuit is operating correctly, whereas fault diagnosis localizes the failure to a few replaceable circuit packs. Hardware has been integrated into the design of this system to allow a systematic approach for identifying failures via software. The most commonly used procedure in fault diagnosis [31,32] is based upon the bootstrap technique. The hardcore portion of the machine can apply test sequences to itself. With a duplicated processor, the fault-free machine is used to check or diagnose the hardcore portion of the defective machine. Once the hardcore portion has been checked and found to be fault-free, it is used to start the diagnostic test of another portion of the processor.   Therefore, subunits are tested before being used to check other subunits.   This procedure continues until the fault is pinpointed.

To facilitate this diagnostic procedure, several important designs have been incorporated into the system.   One is the MCH and its associated circuitry.   Its primary function is the diagnosis of one processor by the other. The MCH is an autonomous portion of the processor which, under control of the other processor, can provide information about the state of the machine and exercise the machine at its most basic level by direct access to the microprogram control.   Another hardware feature is the maintenance instruction, which provides complete access to the system at the most elementary level of hardware.

9.9.1   Maintenance Channel Facilities

The MCH interconnects and provides the main source of communication between the two processors.   As shown in Figure 9-20, the MCH is a high-speed (6.67 MHz), serial, full duplex channel.   This method of communication reduces the number of leads at the expense of additional hardware, making the interface easier to maintain.   Since there are so few leads, the processors can be said to be "loosely interconnected"; they are isolated from each other in terms of hardware faults.   That is, a fault in one processor will not affect the operation of the other processor.

The basic structure of the MCH shown in Figure 9-20 consists of a *transmit-receive register* (MCHTR), a *command register* (MCHC), and a *buffer*

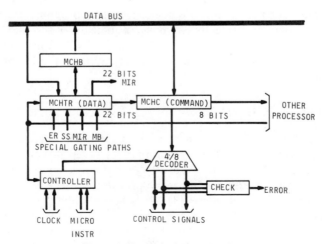

Figure 9-20   Maintenance Channel

register (MCHB). The format of an MCH message is 20 bits of data, 2 parity-check bits, and 8 bits of command. Although the processor is essentially a 16-bit machine, there are several 20-bit registers for store addressing. Consequently, the MCH message is dictated by the widest data word. For 16-bit data fields, the high 4 bits are not used. The commands are coded in 4-out-of-8 codes for ease in decoding and checking. The decoded outputs are used to control the primitive functions of the processor so that elementary operations can be observed by the on-line machine. For example, under MCH control, the clock can be stopped and stepped along one clock phase at a time. Between steps, the state of each phase is transmitted back to the other processor for analysis. In this way, the fundamental hardcore logic is exercised to permit a systematic check of the clock circuitry.

Another basic operation involves transmitting microinstructions over the maintenance channel and executing them one at a time. This is done by gating the received data in the MCHTR directly into the MIR. The command part of the message provides control for gating and executing the microinstruction. This operation allows the on-line processor to step the off-line machine along one microinstruction at a time, thereby gaining access to the entire machine at the most elementary level for fault diagnosis.

The MCHB is used to temporarily store the data transmitted over the MCH. This data source can be used for a variety of operations. For example, in a read-store operation, assume a 20-bit address has been received and buffered in the MCHB at the receiving end. When executed, the maintenance messages that follow (containing microinstructions) will gate the content of MCHB to the main *store address register* (SAR) and read main store at that address. To bring the main store output back into the on-line processor, two more maintenance messages must be sent. The first message gates the main store output to the MCHB, and the second message gates the content of the MCHB to the MCHTR and is then transmitted back to the on-line processor. Similarly, the data stored in the MCHB can also be used to write into the main store. These operations allow the on-line processor to check the off-line main store control circuitry. The MCHB, in addition to buffering the incoming data that are to be directed to any internal register within the processor, may also be used to buffer data that are to be returned to the transmitting processor (on-line processor).

The MCH registers are connected to the common data bus to permit data transfer to any of the internal registers. Also, there are dedicated gating paths, as shown in Figure 9-20, to allow specials (such as the error register, system status register, etc.) to be fetched directly without the aid of microinstructions. Some of these registers, particularly in the error register and the system status register, contain information that may be helpful to the diagnostic program and hence must be saved prior to any diagnostic procedure.

Finally, the controller block, as shown in Figure 9-20, provides all the necessary timing and sequencing operations that the MCH needs to transmit and receive messages. The off-line processor must be able to derive timing signals directly from the incoming serial data stream since the processor's clock may be stopped. Therefore, the MCH circuitry, which is closely integrated into the processor, is really an extension of the other processor since the two are connected by means of an "umbilical cord."

9.9.2   Microdiagnostic Techniques

After the circuits associated with the microprogram control and the main store operation have been checked and verified to be operational, the off-line processor can execute instructions and initiate diagnostic procedures by itself. The microinstruction, being the most elementary operation, provides the best possible access to pinpoint faults within the machine. Therefore, if the diagnosis is performed at the microprogram level, isolating faults to a few replaceable circuit packs becomes a more efficient and effective process. The ideal situation would be to store the diagnostic routines on low-cost tape units and then page them into a writable microprogram store as needed [33]. However, in this system, the microprogram store is entirely ROM. This is necessary for reasons of cost and reliability. Therefore, it is not practical to store the diagnostic in the ROM because of the increase in the size and cost of the microprogram store.

To achieve equivalent microdiagnostic capability, a special *micro-interrupt* (MI) *instruction* has been incorporated into the design to allow the machine to be exercised at the microprogram level. This is done by allowing the microsequences to be stored in the main memory. The MI instruction simply puts the processor in the interpret mode. While in this mode, the processor stops using the outputs from the microprogram memory and fetches microinstructions from successive main memory words. Any number of microinstructions may now be executed from main memory until the microinstruction which turns off the interpret mode is given.

There are several advantages to the microinterpret technique. First, it will allow maintenance routines to be stored in low-cost tape units and paged into main memory as needed at a considerable cost reduction. Since the microprogram memory is a ROM, the microprograms stored in main memory can be changed much more easily than if they were stored in microprogram memory. Second, the microinterpret mode will allow microprogram sequences to be checked out before they are encoded in ROM. Last, and most importantly, the maintenance programmer has complete access to every control signal that exists within the machine.

Microprogram sequences in the microinterpret mode do run slower than the native mode since the main memory is slower than the microprogram memory. This is not an important disadvantage since diagnostic programs are normally run in the standby machine. However, the microinstructions are executed at the same speed.

9.10 REPAIR

When the fault has been diagnosed and located to within a few circuit packs, maintenance personnel must replace the packs one at a time until the defective one has been found. In pack replacement, the power must be turned off to avoid the harmful effects of breaking current on the connector. Since there are a number of leads from the processor to various functional units, power must be turned off "gracefully" so as not to cause any disturbance to the working system. Consequently, the operation is arranged in a sequence to ensure that no harmful transient signals are generated in the process. Similarly, the same protection is given in turning power on.

During the repair process, the working system is manually locked into a selected configuration. This is done to avoid any error conditions that may cause the system to switch control to the machine under repair. Since it is under repair, the machine is without power. Therefore, if an error occurs in the working system, it would be better to restart and attempt to run again with the same configuration. The hardware required to prevent any interaction from the machine under repair is minimal, but it must be integrated into the design at the beginning.

9.11 HARDWARE IMPLEMENTATION

Maintenance has been made an integral part of the 3A CC design. It uses the standard 1A ESS logic family with its associated packaging technology [19]. Up to 52 *silicon integrated circuit chips* (SICs), each containing from 4 to 10 logic gates, can be packed on a 3.25- by 4.00-inch 1A ceramic substrate. The substrate is mounted on a 3.67- by 7.00-inch circuit board with an 82-pin connector for backplane interconnections. In the 3A CC, the 53 1A logic circuit packs average about 44 SICs, resulting in an average of 308 gates per circuit pack, or a total of 16,482 gates. Figure 9-21 shows a detailed functional diagram of the 3A CC and the percentage of logic gates used in each functional unit.

Another insight into how the gates are used in the 3A is shown in Figure 9-22. The figure shows the relationship among working gates, maintenance access gates, and self-checking logic. The working gates are the portion that contributes to the data processing functions, while the maintenance access gates provide the necessary access to make the CC maintainable (i.e., maintenance channel and control panel). The self-checking gates are required to

TOTAL GATES = 16,482

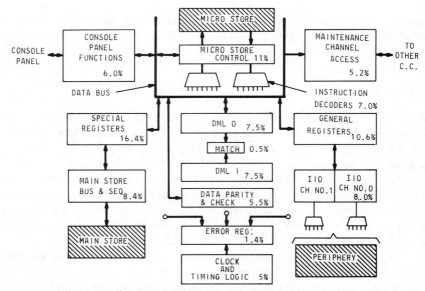

Figure 9-21 Detailed Functional Diagram of 3A CC with Percentage of Logic Gates Used by Each Functional Unit

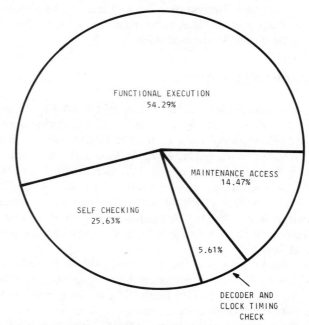

Figure 9-22 Relationship Between Working Gates, Maintenance Access Gates, and Self-Checking Logic

implement the parity bits, the check circuits, and the duplicate circuits that make the CC self-checking. As indicated, about 30 percent of the logic is used for checking. The design covers a high degree of component failures. It is estimated that about 90 to 95 percent of the faults would be detected by hardware error detection logic. Certain portions of the checkers, timers, and interrupt logic are not checked. These circuits are periodically exercised under program control to ensure that they are fault-free.

9.12   OPERATIONAL RESULTS OF THE NO. 1 ESS

The No. 1 ESS has been in commercial operation since 1965. Approximately 1000 ESS systems are providing telephone service to millions of subscribers. The performance of the No. 1 ESS continually improved over a decade of continued effort to improve all phases of software and hardware.

Figure 9-23 shows the result of field data accumulated over many machine operating hours. This curve was derived from data in a paper [34] presented at the 1974 International Switching Symposium in Munich, Germany and data supplied by W. C. Jones of Bell Labs.

When the No. 1 systems were first cut into commercial service, many outages occurred because of software and hardware inadequacies that could only be weeded out with field experience. The inexperience of maintenance personnel also contributed heavily toward system outages. Most hardware

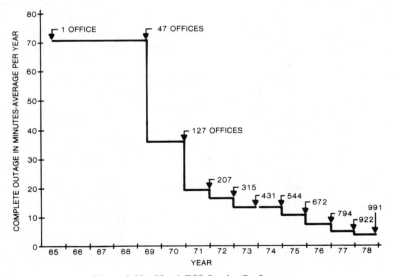

Figure 9-23   No. 1 ESS Service Performance

and software bugs were corrected during the early years of operation. However, working systems are continually upgraded. Continual improvements include better diagnostic access, more complete fault recognition and isolation programs, and more effective system recovery.

Improved diagnostic capability reduces repair time and human errors by decreasing the amount of human interaction required by the machine. Better maintenance procedures and more experienced craft personnel also contribute to improved system performance. Figure 9-23 shows that the outage rate improved as machine design and operating personnel matured.

The No. 2 ESS has followed a similar trend in decreased downtime. The experience gained in working with first-generation systems provided a steeper "learning curve" in the design and operation of the second-generation electronic switching systems.

9.13 SUMMARY

To achieve their reliability requirements, all ESS subsystem units are duplicated. When a hardware failure occurs in any of the subunits, the processor is reconfigured into a working system around the defective unit. The partitioning of subsystem units into switching blocks varies with the size of the ESS processor. For the small- or medium-sized processors such as the No. 2 or the No. 3, the central control, the main memory, the bulk memory, and the store bus are grouped as a single switchable entity. A failure in one of the subunits is considered a failure in the switchable block. Since the number of components within a switchable block is sufficiently small, this type of single-unit duplex configuration meets the reliability requirement. For larger processors such as the No. 1 or the No. 1A, the central control, the program store, the call store, the store buses, and the bulk file store are treated individually as switchable blocks. This multiunit duplex configuration allows a considerable number of combinations in which a working system can be assembled. The system is down only when two simultaneous failures occur, one in the subunit and the other in the duplicated subunit. A greater fault tolerance is possible with this configuration. This type of configuration is necessary for the large processor because each subunit contains a larger number of components.

The first generation of ESS processors, which includes the No. 1 and the No. 2, has provided commercial service since 1965 and 1969, respectively. The No. 1 ESS serves large telephone offices (metropolitan); the No. 2 is used in medium-sized offices (suburban). Their reliability requirements are the same. Both processors depend on integrated maintenance software, with hardware that must (1) quickly detect a system failure condition, (2) isolate and configure a working system around the faulty subunit, (3) diagnose the faulty unit, and (4) assist the maintenance personnel in repairing the unit. The primary detection technique is the synchronous match mode of operation of both central controls. Matching is done more extensively in the No. 1 than in the No. 2 since cost is one of the major considerations in the design of the No. 2 Processor. In addition to matching, coding techniques, diagnostic access, and other check logic have been incorporated into the basic design of these processors to realize the reliability objectives.

The widespread acceptance of the No. 1 ESS and the No. 2 ESS has created the need for a second generation of ESS processors: the No. 1A and the No. 3A. They offer greater capability and are also more cost-effective. Both processors use the same integrated technology. The 1A Processor extended its performance range by a factor of four to eight times over the No. 1 Processor by using faster logic and faster memory. The 1A design takes advantage of the experience gained in the design and operation of the No. 1 ESS. The 1A Processor provides considerably more hardware for error detection and more extensive matching of a large number of internal nodes within the central control. The design of the 3A Processor benefited by the experience gained from the No. 2 ESS. A major departure in the design of the 3A processor from the design of other ESS processors is the nonsynchronous and the nonmatch mode of operation. The 3A Processor uses self-checking as the primary means of error detection. Another departure is in the design of the 3A Processor's control section; it is microprogrammed. The 3A Processor's flexibility permits emulation of the No. 2 Processor quite easily.

9.14 NOTES

1. R. W. DOWNING, J. S. NOWAK, and L. S. TUOMENOKSA, "No. 1 ESS Maintenance Plan," *Bell Syst. Tech. J., 43* (Sept. 1964), 1961–2020.

2. J. A. HARR, F. F. TAYLOR, and W. ULRICH, "Organization of the No. 1 ESS Central Processor," *Bell Syst. Tech. J., 43* (Sept. 1969), 1845–1922.

3. T. E. BROWNE, T. M. QUINN, W. N. TOY, and J. E. YATES, "No. 2 ESS Control Unit System," *Bell Syst. Tech. J., 48* (Oct. 1969), 2619–2668.

4. R. E. STAEHLER, "1A Processor—Organizations and Objectives," *Bell Syst. Tech. J., 56* (Feb. 1977), 119–134.

5. R. E. STAEHLER and R. J. WATTERS, "1A Processor—An Ultra-Dependable Common Control," in *International Switching Symposium Record* (Japan, 1976).

6. D. J. SMITH, *Reliability Engineering* (New York: Barnes & Noble, 1972).

7. S. H. TSIANG and W. ULRICH, "Automatic Trouble Diagnosis of Complex Logic Circuits," *Bell Syst. Tech. J., 41* (July 1962), 1177–1200.

8. H. Y. CHANG, G. W. SMITH, and R. B. WALFORD, "LAMP: System Description," *Bell Syst. Tech. J., 53* (Oct. 1974), 1431–1450.

9. P. W. Bowman, M. R. Dubman, F. M. Goetz, R. F. Kranzmann, E. H. Stredde, and R. J. Watters, "1A Processor–Maintenance Software," *Bell Syst. Tech. J., 56* (Feb. 1977), 255–288.

10. F. M. Goetz, "Complementary Fault Simulation," in *Proceedings of the 3rd Annual Texas Conference on Computing Systems,* (Austin, Texas: University of Texas, Nov. 1974), pp. 9–4–1 to 9–4–5.

11. A. E. Joel, Jr., "An Experimental Switching System Using New Electronic Techniques," *Bell Syst. Tech. J., 37* (Sept. 1958), 1091–1124.

12. W. Keister, R. W. Ketchledge, and H. E. Vaughan, "No. 1 ESS: System Organization and Objectives," *Bell Syst. Tech. J., 43* (Sept. 1964), 1831–1844.

13. W. B. Cagle, R. S. Menne, R. S. Skinner, R. E. Staehler, and M. D. Underwood, "No. 1 ESS Logic Circuits and Their Application to the Design of the Central Control," *Bell Syst. Tech. J., 43* (Sept. 1964), 2055–2096.

14. C. F. Ault, L. E. Gallaher, T. S. Greenwood, and D. C. Koehler, "No. 1 ESS Program Store," *Bell Syst. Tech. J., 43* (Sept. 1964), 2097–2146.

15. R. M. Genke, P. A. Harding, and R. E. Staehler, "No. 1 ESS Call Store - A 20 - Megabit Ferrite Sheet Memory," *Bell Syst. Tech. J., 43* (Sept. 1964), 2147–2191.

16. A. E. Spencer and F. S. Vigilante, "No. 2 ESS—System Organization and Objectives," *Bell Syst. Tech. J., 48* (Oct. 1969), 2607–2618.

17. E. G. Hughes and R. G. Taylor, "The No. 101 ESS Control Unit," *Bell Laboratories' Record, 42* (Feb. 1964), 61–66.

18. H. J. Beuscher, G. E. Fessler, D. W. Huffman, P. J. Kennedy, and E. Nussbaum, "Administration and Maintenance Plan," *Bell Syst. Tech. J., 48* (Oct. 1969), 2765–2864.

19. J. O. Becker, J. G. Chevalier, R. K. Eisenhart, J. H. Forster, A. W. Fulton, and W. L. Harrod, "1A Processor—Technology and Physical Design," *Bell Syst. Tech. J., 56* (Feb. 1977), 207–236.

20. A. H. Budlong, B. G. DeLugish, S. M. Neville, J. S. Nowak, J. L. Quinn, and F. W. Wendland, "1A Processor—Control System," *Bell Syst. Tech. J., 56* (Feb. 1977), 135–180.

21. J. S. Nowak, "No. 1A ESS—A New High Capacity Switching System," in *International Switching Symposium Record* (Japan, 1976).

22. C. F. Ault, J. H. Brewster, T. S. Greenwood, R. E. Haglund, W. A. Read, and M. W. Roland, "1A Processor—Memory Systems," *Bell Syst. Tech. J., 56* (Feb. 1977), 181–206.

23. E. A. Irland and U. K. Stagg, "New Developments in Suburban and Rural ESS (No. 2 and No. 3 ESS)," in *International Switching Symposium 1974 Record* (Munich, Germany, Sept. 1974), 512/1–512/7.

24. T. F. Storey, "Design of a Microprogram Control for a Processor in an Electronic Switching System," *Bell Syst. Tech. J., 55* (Feb. 1976), 183–232.

25. P. D. Mandigo, "No. 2B ESS: New Features for a More Efficient Processor," *Bell Lab. Rec., 54* (Dec. 1976), 304–309.

26. R. W. Cook, W. H. Sisson, T. F. Storey, and W. N. Toy, "Design of a Self-Checking Microprogram Control," *IEEE Trans. Comput., C-22* (March 1973), 255–262.

27. D. A. Anderson, "Design of Self-Checking Digital Networks Using Code Techniques," *CSL Report R527,* Ph.D. thesis. Urbana, Ill.: University of Illinois, Oct. 1971.

28. W. C. CARTER, K. A. DUKE, and D. C. JESSEP, "A Simple Self-Testing Decoder Checking Circuit," *IEEE Trans. Comput., C-20* (Nov. 1971), 1413–1414.

29. R. J. ANDREWS, J. J. DRISCOLL, J. A. HERNDON, P. C. RICHARDS, and L. R. ROBERTS, "Service Features and Call Processing Plan," *Bell Syst. Tech. J., 48* (Oct. 1969), 2713–2764.

30. P. J. KENNEDY, and T. M. QUINN, "Recovery Strategies in the No. 2 ESS," in *Digest of 1972 Fault-Tolerant Computing,* June 1972, 165–169.

31. P. W. AGNEW, R. E. FORBES, and C. B. STIEGLITZ, "An Approach to Self-Repairing Computers," in *Digest of the First Annual IEEE Computer Conference,* (Chicago, Ill., Sept. 1967), pp. 60–63.

32. T. R. BASHKOW, J. FRIETS, and A. KARSON, "A Programming System for Detection and Diagnosis of Machine Malfunctions," *IEEE Trans. Electron. Comput., 12* (Feb. 1963), 10–17.

33. N. BARTOW and R. McGUIRE, "System/360 Model 85 Microdiagnostics," in *1970 Spring Joint Computer Conference, AFIPS Conference,* (Atlantic City, N.J., 1970), pp. 191–196.

34. W. O. FLECKENSTEIN, "Bell System ESS Family—Present and Future," in *International Switching Symposium 1974 Record,* (Munich, Germany, Sept. 1974), pp. 511/1–511/7.

APPENDIX

MTTF Calculation

of Systems

with Repair

A.1 ACTIVE REDUNDANCY

In a duplicated active redundancy system, when the main unit has a failure, the spare unit automatically takes over and provides continuous operation. If the defective unit is repaired and put back into operation, the system can then be restored to its original state, with both units fully operational. The system is completely down (inoperative) only if both units are faulty. The probability of a complete system failure will be decreased as the repair time decreases.

Consider a duplicated parallel system as shown in Figure A-1. Each unit has a failure rate λ and repair rate μ. There are three possible states, as indicated in Figure A-1. Let $P_0(t)$, $P_1(t)$, and $P_2(t)$ be the probabilities of the system being in states 0, 1, or 2, respectively, at time t. The system will be in state 0 at time $t + \Delta t$ if (1) the system was in state 0 *and* no failure occurred in either unit during Δt, or (2) the system was in state 1

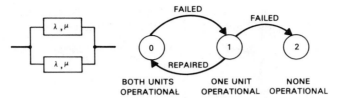

Figure A-1 Duplicated Parallel System

and no failure occurred in the working unit during Δt, *and* the failed unit was repaired during Δt.

The probability of a failure occurring in one unit within the interval Δt is $\lambda\,\Delta t$. Hence, the probability of no failure occurring in one unit during the same interval would be $1 - \lambda\,\Delta t$ and in two units would be $(1 - \lambda\,\Delta t)(1 - \lambda\,\Delta t) \approx 1 - 2\lambda\Delta t$. Therefore, to satisfy the first condition, the probability for the system in state 0 to stay in state 0 during the interval Δt is $P_0\,(t)(1 - 2\lambda\Delta t)$.

The probability that the failed unit will be repaired within Δt is given by $\mu\,\Delta t$, and the probability that the working unit continues to be good during Δt is given by $1 - \lambda\,\Delta t$. The second condition of repairing the failed unit with no further failure in the working unit is therefore given by $P_1(t)(\mu\,\Delta t)(1 - \lambda\,\Delta t)$.

The probability of the system being in state 0 at time $t + \Delta t$ is expressed by

$$P_0(t + \Delta t) = P_0(t)(1 - 2\lambda\,\Delta t) + P_1(t)(\mu\,\Delta t)(1 - \lambda\,\Delta t) \tag{1}$$

Similarly, the probability of the system being in state 1 or in state 2 at time $t + \Delta t$ is expressed by

$$P_1(t + \Delta t) = P_0(t)(2\lambda\,\Delta t) + P_1(t)(1 - \mu\,\Delta t)(1 - \lambda\,\Delta t) \tag{2}$$

$$P_2(t + \Delta t) = P_1(t)\lambda\,\Delta t + P_2(t) \tag{3}$$

In Eq. (1), (2), and (3), it is assumed that Δt is sufficiently small so that the probability of the occurrence of more than a single event within this interval is negligible.

As indicated in Figure A-1(b), when the system goes to state 2, it will remain there since no provision is made within this model to return the system to operational service when *both* units have failed [i.e., no mechanism for repair is indicated within the mode of Figure A-1(b)]. This is strictly a mathematical model to simplify the calculation of the MTTF from state 0 to state 2. Once the system reaches state 2, subsequent events are no longer of interest. Consequently, Eq. (2) does not contain the term $P_2(t)\mu\,\Delta t$, which represents the transition from state 2 to state 1 during Δt. Also, the term $P_2(t)$ in Eq. (3) is not modified by the factor $1 - \mu\,\Delta t$, which corresponds to the event that the failed unit will not be repaired within the interval Δt. Using the limit process of the differential calculus,

$$\lim_{\Delta t \to 0} \left[\frac{P_1(t + \Delta t) - P_1(t)}{\Delta t} \right] = \frac{dP(t)}{dt} = \dot{P}(t) \tag{4}$$

and

$$\mu \lambda \, \Delta t \ll 1 \tag{5}$$

Equations (1), (2), and (3) reduce to

$$\dot{P}_0(t) = -2\lambda \, P_0(t) + \mu \, P_1(t) \tag{6}$$

$$\dot{P}_1(t) = 2\lambda P_0(t) - (\lambda + \mu) P_1(t) \tag{7}$$

$$\dot{P}_2(t) = \lambda P_1(t) \tag{8}$$

It was established in Sec. 5.3 that the general expression for the MTTF is given by

$$\text{MTTF} = \int_0^\infty R(t) \, dt = \int_0^\infty [P_0(t) + P_1(t)] \, dt \tag{9}$$

$$= \int_0^\infty P_0(t) \, dt + \int_0^\infty P_1(t) \, dt \tag{10}$$

$$= T_0 + T_1 \tag{11}$$

where the reliability of the duplicated system is given by the sum of the probabilities that (1) both units are operational (state 0) and (2) one unit is in operation (state 1). The values of T_0 and T_1 can be found by solving the following integral equations:

$$\int_0^\infty \dot{P}_0(t) \, dt = -2\lambda \int_0^\infty P_0(t) \, dt + \mu \int_0^\infty P_1(t) \, dt \tag{12}$$

$$\int_0^\infty \dot{P}_1(t) \, dt = 2\lambda \int_0^\infty P_0(t) \, dt - (\lambda + \mu) \int_0^\infty P_1(t) dt \tag{13}$$

$$\int_0^\infty \dot{P}_2(t) \, dt = \lambda \int_0^\infty P_1(t) \, dt \tag{14}$$

Substituting $T_0 = \int_0^\infty P_0(t) \, dt$ and $T_1 = \int_0^\infty P_1(t) \, dt$ into the above integral equations, one obtains the following linear equations:

$$P_0(\infty) - P_0(0) = -2\lambda T_0 + \mu T_1 \tag{15}$$

$$P_1(\infty) - P_1(0) = 2\lambda T_0 - (\lambda + \mu) T_1 \tag{16}$$

$$P_2(\infty) - P_2(0) = \lambda T_1 \tag{17}$$

The initial conditions for the probabilities $P_0(t)$ and $P_1(t)$ are

$$P_0(0) = 1 \quad \text{and} \quad P_1(0) = P_2(0) = 0$$

Similarly, the final conditions for the probabilities $P_0(t)$ and $P_1(t)$ are given by

$$P_0(\infty) = P_1(\infty) = 0 \quad \text{and} \quad P_2(\infty) = 1$$

These boundary conditions correspond to the situation in which the system began to function with both units operational and terminated with both units not working properly. Substituting the boundary conditions into Eqs. (15), (16), and (17) yields the following results for T_0 and T_1:

$$T_0 = \frac{\lambda + \mu}{2\lambda^2} \tag{18}$$

$$T_1 = \frac{1}{\lambda} \tag{19}$$

so that

$$\text{MTTF} = T_0 + T_1 \tag{20}$$

$$= \frac{\lambda + \mu}{2\lambda^2} + \frac{1}{\lambda} \tag{21}$$

$$= \frac{3\lambda + \mu}{2\lambda^2} \tag{22}$$

Since μ (the reciprocal of the repair time) is usually much greater than λ (the failure rate), the expression for the MTTF can be rewritten as

$$\text{MTTF} \approx \frac{\mu}{2\lambda^2} \tag{23}$$

A.2 STANDBY REDUNDANCY

In the standby case, the failure rate of the spare unit is assumed to be zero. It is assumed that the probability of reaching state 1 from state 0 will be half the value of the corresponding probability for the active redundancy case. The equivalent sets of equations are

$$\dot{P}_0(t) = -\lambda P_0(t) + \mu P_1(t) \tag{24}$$

$$\dot{P}_1(t) = \lambda P_0(t) - (\lambda + \mu)P_1(t) \tag{25}$$

$$\dot{P}_2(t) = \lambda P_1(t) \tag{26}$$

Solving these equations with the same set of initial and final conditions (see the previous discussion) yields the following set of equations for T_0, and T_1:

$$-1 = -\lambda T_0 + \mu T_1 \tag{27}$$

$$0 = \lambda T_0 - (\lambda + \mu) T_1 \tag{28}$$

$$1 = \lambda T_1 \tag{29}$$

where $T_1 = \int_0^\infty P_2(t)\, dt$.

Solving these equations gives

$$T_0 = \frac{\lambda + \mu}{\lambda^2} \tag{30}$$

$$T_1 = \frac{1}{\lambda}, \qquad T_2 = \frac{1}{\lambda} \tag{31}$$

so that

$$\text{MTTF} = T_0 + T_1 \tag{32}$$

$$= \frac{\lambda + \mu}{\lambda^2} + \frac{1}{\lambda} \tag{33}$$

$$= \frac{2\lambda + \mu}{\lambda^2} \tag{34}$$

Assuming that

$$\mu \gg 2\lambda \tag{35}$$

then

$$\text{MTTF} \approx \frac{\mu}{\lambda^2} \tag{36}$$

Index